Marga  es
with   hes
Diana Spencer

God is not like that

Or

Making sense of Christianity:
A new look at an old faith

by

Diana Spencer

I welcome this opportunity to commend to the Church at large an interesting and provocative book which I believe is both timely and necessary as a contribution to the theological debate of our times.

The author is a retired Anglican priest in my Diocese, and, while the book is written from "orthodox" point of view (without, however, succumbing to the literal or "primitive" thought so condemned by some modern scholars and theologians), it also raises some challenging questions for the Church at large to think about and discuss and possibly resolve. The author believes that the work of the Reformation was never finished, because the various factions at that time split apart from each other without finding any common resolution to the problems facing the mediaeval Church, and the conclusions reached in this book have been arrived at after years of thought, to try to stimulate a new look at some of these issues: although, as she is at pains to point out, while she is an Anglican, the Anglican Church itself is not to be held responsible for the conclusions she has reached!

The author's main purpose in the beginning was to try to reach people who had become disillusioned with Christianity and explain the faith to them in a reasonable way which they could accept. As stated in the Introduction, "because people are aware of anomalies and inconsistencies in the inherited faith (for example, misunderstandings of the nature of God arising from mediaeval thinking about the Atonement, or the contradiction of teaching about the flames of hell in the same breath as teaching that God is Love), many people have come to disregard the Christian religion altogether, without realizing that what they are rejecting is not the faith itself, but distortions of it that should indeed rightly be challenged."

The book has been written in ordinary, everyday language, for the ordinary person to read easily, yet, at the same time, footnotes and references have been provided for those who want to dig more deeply into the issues raised. While this book necessarily deals with a vast range of subjects, in the hope of meeting all the questions that people ask, it follows that it has not been possible, in one book, to deal with them in depth, hence the opportunities given for follow-up, if desired.

I believe that thinking about these issues, and contributing to discussion about them, can only be of benefit to the Church as a whole, and, indeed, to the world at large, where Christianity is so often tragically misunderstood.

As the author states, "if all the mainstream religions started to give more emphasis to the idea that God is Love, and the fact that God requires loving behaviour from all who would want to call themselves His disciples, regardless of past historical grievances or injustices, perhaps some of the murderous ideologies and conflicts of the present century might be more widely seen for what they are: direct disobedience to the will of God. Whatever the problem may be, nothing can justify hatred, which is the antithesis of love."

If this book will lead anyone to a more complete understanding of the Christian faith, or help people to explain it to their loved ones who have left the Church, or help the moderates of the other great world religions to proclaim again the love and goodness of God, emphasizing the need for all of us to co-exist without intolerance or exclusiveness or bigotry, it will have been worthwhile.

James A.J. Cowan
Bishop, Diocese of British Columbia

Note for Librarians: A cataloguing record for this book is available from Library
and Archives Canada at www.collectionscanada.ca/amicus/index-e.html

Printed in Victoria, BC, Canada.

ISBN: 978-1-4269-1120-0 (sc)
ISBN: 978-1-4269-1463-8 (dj)

Our mission is to efficiently provide the world's finest, most comprehensive
book publishing service, enabling every author to experience success.
To find out how to publish your book, your way, and have it available
worldwide, visit us online at www.trafford.com

Trafford rev. 8/25/2009

 www.trafford.com

North America & international
toll-free: 1 888 232 4444 (USA & Canada)
phone: 250 383 6864 ♦ fax: 812 355 4082

In loving memory of

Francis Tracey Spencer

This book is dedicated to all those, still living or now dead,
who have believed in me and helped me.

CONTENTS

Intellectual or theological problems that face us:

Returning to the original doctrine of the Atonement

INTRODUCTION

Christianity has been so much misrepresented or mis-portrayed that the world today, in sheer reaction, has backed away from it. Many are the death notices in the newspapers which say *"no funeral service by request."* I believe that it is not Christianity *itself* that is being rejected, as much as a caricature, a travesty, of it, that has come to be mistaken in people's minds for the real thing.

The problem is that *the Christian religion does not make sense,* in the way it is too often presented. Many people have an intuitive, emotional, experience of it, in that they feel they "know the Lord" and are convinced of the truth of what they believe; but at the same time it is not clear what that faith is, everyone seems to have a different version of it, and they cannot explain it to others in a convincing way. In fact, their often simplistic, sometimes illogical, explanations can often make an unbeliever all the more sceptical, as Bishop Spong has noted.[1] Others proclaim that they believe the Christian faith while at the same time belittling the Bible that testifies to it, and do not apparently see the inherent contradiction in this. People are aware of anomalies and inconsistencies in the inherited faith (for example, misunderstandings of the nature of God arising from mediaeval thinking about the Atonement,[2] or the contradiction of teaching about the flames of hell in the same breath as teaching that God is Love), and as a result many people have come to disregard the Christian religion altogether, without realizing that what they are rejecting is not the faith itself,

---

1   See his *Twelve Theses,* quoted later

2   see Glossary for definition, and the chapter on the Atonement

but distortions of it that should indeed be rightly challenged. I hope this book will not only set out the faith in a convincing way, but also provide reasonable answers to the problems that have caused so many distortions of it.

As I see it, there are several main problems. One, and perhaps the most important one, is that many people no longer believe in "the divinity of Christ". The second is the whole question of the Atonement: [3] "why did Jesus *have to 'die for our sins,'* why did He have to be crucified, and how did this accomplish our salvation?" A third major problem is the traditional teaching on hell. Many good people, who have seen the blatant faults of many of the churches, have not been able to believe that a good and loving God, if He existed, would consign someone to everlasting damnation because of a justified criticism or an honest doubt. Then there is the misuse, or misunderstanding, of the Bible, where people go from one extreme to another: some take everything absolutely literally, regardless of common sense or logic or historical criticism, and others, probably in sheer reaction, go to the opposite extreme and deny everything, as in the examples given in Bishop Spong's *Theses*. Others express varying degrees of disbelief, from the nativity stories to the miracles, to the statements in the Bible (even in the popular Synoptic Gospels)[4] about "the divinity of Christ," to the reality and significance of the Resurrection and the *reason* for it, to the point where one wonders: *"what is left to believe in?"*

Another problem is that we tend not to define very clearly in our minds what real "love" is like. We need to *think about* the words we use, like "eternal life", which I will come to shortly, and "love". We need to think about *what real Love is like:* not just a feeling a sense of gratification for ourselves because "God loves *us*", but how do we find, and approach, and come to know, and *live in,* that Love? It is essential that we understand what "Love" really means if we are to worship a *God* of *Love* and act accordingly.[5] Some modern biologists argue that care for others has come to be built into our inherited nervous system

---

3   see Glossary for definition, and the Chapter on the Atonement

4   Matthew, Mark and Luke, currently "preferred" by modern scholars as a source of information about Jesus – see Glossary for definition

5   Some Christians seem to relish contemplating the punishment they *think* will be meted out to others.

because of the necessity of group survival, and they equate *that* with "love", denying the existence—or necessity—of "God" in the process. It is pointed out that some of the very people who *talk* about "love" in actual fact, in practice, often do not show love to others, or indeed (many of them) any kind of integrity, whatever they may *say* about believing in God and love and goodness, hence many well-publicized scandals, and it is rightly stated that atheists can be just as moral and loving and kind as those who claim to believe in God. It is also stated that "religion" is the cause of much of the trouble in the world, because of the hatred it can engender between people of different belief systems (although a major argument of this book is that, if *the Christian idea of God as Love* is taken seriously, that should preclude Christians, at least, from behaving in that way). This explains Jesus' emphasis on loving God and one's neighbour, because, if we do not learn how to love, we cannot come to be like Him, or "abide" in Him: if we do not learn how to love we cannot come to eternal life in Him, because *the eternal God is Eternal Love.*

"Eternal life" has been taken to mean "a place called heaven" as opposed to "a place called hell", but the words literally mean *"everlasting life, life that continues for ever,"* and I will try to show that there has been an unacknowledged conflict in thinking on this subject since the very early days of the Church.

I think that in every generation we need to analyse again for ourselves what is written in our inherited documents, such as the Bible, the Prayer Book and traditional liturgies, and the so-called Athanasian Creed when it is properly understood, as I set out to demonstrate (the latter being a major document of the historical western Church); and reflect again on the merits of past decisions of the Church, such as, for example, the Fifth Lateran Council of the Roman Catholic Church held in 1513, *which was only four years before Martin Luther started the Reformation,* a time when the Church of the day was already much in need of reform, and at that time hardly qualified to make major theological decisions about the traditions which it had inherited from the past.[6] People today, who would claim to be Protestant, and not

---

6   See Glossary re. *"Annihilationism"* or *"Conditional Immortality",* the idea that the human soul is only immortal under certain conditions, which has generally been disregarded, as the human soul has been thought to be immortal in its own right (the so-

bound by the decisions of the Roman Church, nevertheless take for granted assumptions generated in the past, without being aware of the historical background, or weighing the possible mistakenness, of those assumptions. When people do not really think about the implications of what is written, or understand what is being said, as in, for example, the Athanasian Creed, they often tend to dismiss it out-of-hand as being wrong or irrelevant, without ever stopping to think that the problem might lie in their own lack of understanding of it, rather than the text itself. It is a central argument of this book that the Athanasian Creed in particular has been badly misunderstood, but the Bible has been, too, as I will try to show.

For example, the traditional teaching on "hell", and the idea that the soul can survive for ever in hell, is contradicted in the Bible, in the inherited liturgy, and in the so-called Athanasian Creed if the latter is properly understood, as I set out to demonstrate: and even the Catechism refers to *"everlasting death"*. [7]

The faith is so simple, if reduced to its basic terms. People query the purpose of our existence. I reply that I believe that we were put on this earth because *the force that is the origin of Love and Goodness,* whom we call God, wanted humanity to come to be *united with Him* in that Divine Love *for ever,* which presumably is *what Love would want if* Love *is* Love, and that *the whole purpose* of Christ coming to earth and being born as a human being was *to bring us to come eventually to be united with that God of Love,* and thus be with Him for ever. This book sets out to explain *how* I believe this comes about, through Christ. I describe God the Trinity as being Three Persons *between whom love flows,* and in the chapter on the Atonement quote Jurgen Moltmann's description of how, *in Christ,* we can be *caught up into that love at the very heart of God.* A most important verse in the Bible is that God so loved the world (because God *is* Love) that Christ came to earth to bring us to God: not just for the "forgiveness of our sins" or so that

---

called "Christian Doctrine of Man"); but I believe this "doctrine" is faulty, and needs to be re-thought, because it is contradicted by Biblical passages such as 1 Corinthians 15 "this perishable nature must put on the imperishable, and this mortal nature must put on immortality" and many others which I document in this book

7   See the Biblical evidence quoted in the chapter on the Atonement: and *The [Anglican] Book of Common Prayer, 1962, Canada,* p.550.

we might "be saved" (whatever that means) and go to "a place called heaven" [8], but that we might *live for ever in a union of love with Him* (hard though this may be to imagine): "God so loved the world that *[He gave Himself]* to the end that all [who *eventually* come to believe in Him and *are reconciled with Him*—not *necessarily* in this lifetime, I argue] should not *perish*, [note the word *"perish,"* and the fact that *this is the word used in the Athanasian Creed]*, but have *eternal life"*, St. John also saying: *"God is love"* and *"God gave us eternal life, and this life is* [literally] *in His Son."* This is what our faith is all about. However, it has taken me many years to come up with such a simple definition of the faith, complicated as it has been by many layers of human speculation over the centuries which I believe have substantially departed from the original Biblical faith. The whole point of the Incarnation, God coming to earth in human form, was that, in Christ, *humanity and divinity came together*, so that humanity and divinity can similarly come together in us. So, while we cannot deny His humanity, we cannot deny His divinity either, or the extraordinary circumstances that His being with us on earth must have entailed. I think that problems have arisen because both the Bible and the Athanasian Creed have long been badly misunderstood, and this lack of comprehension has been compounded over the centuries. To summarize briefly: the teachings of St. Paul and St. John (a major part of the New Testament) have both come to be largely disregarded in modern times, with the result that the faith itself has been badly undermined, and I believe that the Athanasian Creed has been misunderstood in two major ways. One is that it has been taken to mean that the only way to "be saved" is to be a professing Christian *in this lifetime*, after death being "too late", (with the alternative to salvation being hell for ever), but I argue that that Creed was mainly intended to be a description of *the nature of God*, rather than *qualifications for salvation*. My second major point is that it is not a statement of belief in hell: the description of "eternal

---

8   Marcus J. Borg, *The God We Never Knew: Beyond Dogmatic Religion to a More Authentic Contemporary Faith* (HarperSanFrancisco, a Division of HarperCollins Publishers, New York, 1997, p.2 ("the 'popular-level Christianity' of a previous generation…defined salvation as 'afterlife'—as going to heaven")

9   John 3:16; and 1 John 4:8 and 1 John 4:*16* *"God is love, and he who abides in love abides in God,* and *God abides in Him"*

fire" *must* be metaphorical, as in the Epistle to the Hebrews, because, although this Creed has long been understood in the context of "eternal fire" literally burning sinners in hell for ever (which is why it is largely disregarded today), I argue that this cannot be its original meaning. "Perishing eternally" *cannot* mean surviving for ever in hell, because *if one perishes one ceases to exist*, and if one has ceased to exist one cannot be tormented for ever by eternal fire. It must rather mean therefore *ceasing to exist, and remaining dead for ever.* Moreover, I demonstrate that the use of the word "perishing" (as opposed to hell-fire) is true to the teaching of the Bible. However, as a result of these misunderstandings, which have led to this Creed being disregarded in modern times, we have come to disregard its basic teaching about the Trinity as well, thus undermining the faith still further.

Which brings us to the subject of "the divinity of Christ" and our abiding in Him which is the heart of the Christian faith. The problem of reconciling "the historical Jesus" with the Risen and eternal Lord is one that has vexed the Church for many centuries, problems arising when people stress only *one* of these aspects, rather than *both.* I believe that this always arises from not fully and logically understanding what the Incarnation entailed. Jesus in His manhood on earth had the limitations of His humanity (for example, He did not know when the Second Coming would be);[10] but this human condition in time and space must be allowed for, and not confused with the role of the Risen Christ, the Second Person of the Trinity, in His eternal glory. As St. Paul wrote to the Philippians, Jesus, "though in the form of God," being still of the same substance as God, in taking on humanity *"did not count equality with God a thing to be grasped"* in His life on earth, *"but emptied Himself, being born in the likeness of men,"[11]* with all our human limitations: (though I think it is reasonable to believe that if, on one occasion in human history, God took such an action, to save, or bring to Himself, all the human race for all time, there must have been some exceptional circumstances surrounding that event, even if some details, such as some of the nativity stories, may perhaps be apocryphal). I believe therefore that more credence needs to be given

---

10   Matthew 24:36 "But of that day and hour no one knows, not even the angels of heaven, nor the Son, but the Father only"

11   Philippians 2:57

to the historical fact that people (including people who knew Jesus in His earthly lifetime) have believed in the historical faith since the time of the Resurrection, and that miracles *did* happen (maybe not all of them that have come down to us, perhaps), to show us that *God* was involved. Jesus was not just purely an ordinary historical man. If He *had* been, we would not be able to come to God through Him, the whole point of the Christian faith. I believe that it is *because* humanity and divinity came together in Christ that humanity and divinity can similarly co-exist in us, if, in our human living, we consciously identify ourselves with Jesus in His humanity, so that, by His grace and in His strength, His Spirit working in us, we may come to encounter in ourselves something of His divinity, "abiding *in* Him," now, in this lifetime, and for ever. This hypothesis, if followed up, would explain how the concept of "eternal life" is made possible for those who are eventually reconciled with God through Christ:

> Becoming incarnate [Christ] *united the nature of God with the nature of man* and thus deified the latter, *giving it the quality of divinity —immortal life — in which it was lacking.*[12]

Because God is eternal, and if Jesus is One with God, we too can come to live for ever, if we forever "abide in Him", sharing in both His humanity and something of His divinity. Thus it is necessary that we take seriously both the humanity and the divinity of Christ. However, there has been a growing tendency in recent years to downplay the divinity of Christ. *More than sixty years ago* a Roman Catholic Jesuit[13] wrote that, even then, he believed that "the vast majority of liberal critics" did not think St. Paul regarded Jesus Christ as true God. I think it is clear from the evidence (which I set out) that St. Paul *did* believe it; his teaching ties in with that of St. John, and was supported from the beginning by the testimony of many people *who had known*

---

12   Arthur Cushman McGiffert. *A History of Christian Thought, Volume 1: Early and Eastern, from Jesus to John of Damascus.* New York, London: Charles Scribner's Sons, 1947, pp. 142-148, re. Irenaeus; and see 2 Peter 1:4: re. *"enabling us to share in the divine nature".*

13   Anthony Cotter in 1945: see the section on Romans 9:5 and the other New Testament passages quoted in it

Jesus in His lifetime; and *it has always been the basis of our faith.* It is fashionable among modern scholars today to put what I believe is too much emphasis on the Synoptic Gospels (Matthew, Mark and Luke) and to discount that of St. John, and, by implication, not only his teaching but that of St. Paul. Marcus Borg writes (italics mine):

> The historical Jesus was either more like the Jesus of the synoptics or more like the Jesus of John. The differences are so great that the synoptic and Johannine portraits of Jesus cannot be harmonized into a single whole. *For mainline scholars, the choice is the synoptics* [though he adds "this does not mean that John's gospel should be cast aside as worthless. Rather it is 'the spiritual gospel' "] .[14]

It will be seen that, *on the contrary,* although the whole of Scripture does need to be taken together as one whole, (and *all* the Gospels are only accounts written much later, usually at second-hand), my theological perspective has been shaped *more by the Gospel of St. John* than by the Synoptic Gospels, because I believe that St. John's theological teaching ties in with that of *St. Paul, who knew the first disciples, and was active in Christian communities, and writing to them, long before* the Synoptic Gospels ever appeared in the form in which we have them now.

A distinguished modern theologian, who belongs to the school of thought that puts more emphasis on the Synoptic Gospels than on that of St. John (an idea which, as stated, I disagree with), nevertheless agrees with my thesis that *"some of Paul's letters are earlier than any of the Gospels, and are more similar to John than the synoptics,"*[15] an argument which I develop later in this book, and which to my mind strengthens the argument for taking John's Gospel seriously. (Examples of the similarity in theology between St. Paul and the author of the Gospel of St. John are St. Paul talking about being *"in* Christ", saying that if anyone is *in Christ* that person is a new creation, reflecting the metaphor of the vine and the branches about "abiding in Christ" in

---

14   Marcus J. Borg. "The Historical Study of Jesus and Christian Origins" in *Jesus at 2000.* Boulder, Colorado: Westview Press, 1997, p. 132.

15   Keith Ward. *Re-thinking Christianity.* Oxford: Oneworld, 2007, p.24

John's Gospel which even then must have been well-known, and talking about "being rooted and grounded in love"; using John's metaphor of the paschal lamb; and teaching about eternal life being *only in God,* the alternative being *"perishing."*)[16]

This theologian wrote recently that "the person of Jesus, for his disciples...shows...[that] God, through Jesus, genuinely liberates humans from sin and *unites them to the divine"* and that "a historian who is open to seeing divine acts in history may well be persuaded that in Jesus there is a distinctive disclosure of God as forgiving, suffering love, *and the origin of a distinctive way of achieving unity with God* through the inner working of the Spirit that was in Jesus" (italics mine).*[17]* But he does not say *how* this is accomplished. In fact, it appears that he goes on to undercut what, in my view, is the only possible way of understanding *how that union with God is made possible* by admitting that he is one of the modern scholars who do not believe that Jesus actually *said* what is attributed to Him in the Gospel of St. John. He concedes that *"the beliefs may be correct, even though Jesus did not utter them,"* (although this does not seem logical to me: if these beliefs did not come to us *from Jesus Himself,* but were concocted by some purely human source later, what authority and authenticity do they have, how therefore can they be *"correct"* or true? in which case, without divine authority behind it, there would be no foundation for the Christian faith itself); and he goes on to say:

> Then John comes along and says '...we believe the following things about Jesus: he is the bread of life, the true vine, the good shepherd, and the eternal word of God.' In writing his Gospel, John puts these beliefs into the mouth of the character 'Jesus'. [18]

This may be so, though I personally doubt it. I agree that statements like "I am the light of the world" or "I am the way, the truth and the life" are not what one would normally expect to hear someone say over breakfast, and I could possibly agree that statements about Jesus being "the Good Shepherd" or "the bread of life" or the "eternal word

---

16   details of many examples are given in subsequent chapters

17   Keith Ward. *Re-thinking Christianity.* Oxford. Oneworld, 2007, p.30

18   Keith Ward. *Re-thinking Christianity.* Oxford: Oneworld, 2007, page 23.

of God" *might* have been understandings about His divinity that were attributed to Him later and then purported to have been actually said by Him, but, *because* they signify His divinity, I do not think that they could have been suddenly arrived at without Jesus Himself being aware of the situation in His lifetime: and this applies especially to the metaphor of "the true vine", which I will come to in a minute.

I think the author of this Gospel tended to write in a cryptic kind of way,[19] like headings or notes, when dealing with profound subjects to be explained in more detail later (as in "I had much to write to you, but I would rather not write…I hope to see you soon, and we will talk together face to face").[20] Although I believe the statements quoted *can* be attributed to Jesus, it is *possible* that St. John used "I AM" rather as the author of a detective story might describe a perpetrator as "X," as a way of underlining who was speaking ("I AM" being the divine Name of God),[21] in which case "I AM" would carry a whole theology of the Incarnation; and phrases like *"lamb of God,"* and I believe *"the water and the blood,"* may well be *a kind of shorthand* for theological profundities not easily expressed. In fact I think that Jesus' statement that *"I AM* the Resurrection and the Life",[22] in effect contradicting Martha's reflection of the existing, pre-Christian, beliefs on the subject of resurrection, may carry a whole theology of *eternal life being only in God* that I have tried to unwrap in this book.

Moreover, I believe that the author of St. John's Gospel tended to write as if not so much wanting to *repeat* what is in the Synoptic Gospels, ideas which were already well-known anyway, but rather as if to underline the *meaning* of what those Gospels had said. For example, the Synoptic Gospels record Jesus' saying "what does it profit a man, to gain the whole world, and *forfeit his life?"* or *"lose his own*

---

19   A modern example of such cryptic shorthand would be *"go green, burn blue"*, which is understood by its hearers to mean "be environmentally conscious and use gas instead of electricity", although that meaning is not spelled out

20   3 John 1:13-14

21   as in Exodus 3:13-15: God said to Moses, "I AM WHO I AM…say this to the people of Israel, 'I AM has sent me to you' "

22   John 11:25-26 re. the raising of Lazarus; and the Synoptic Gospels also report Jesus raising people from the dead, e.g. Jairus' daughter (Mark 5:22-43, Luke 8:41-56), and the son of the widow of Nain (Luke 7:11-17)

soul?" [23] That statement is not repeated in John's Gospel: like many others in the Synoptics it would presumably already have been known to his readers; but the First Epistle reminds them that: "He who does not love *abides in death.* Anyone who hates his brother is a murderer, and *you know* that no murderer *has eternal life abiding in him."*[24] I make a similar argument about "the water and the blood", where it is assumed that Christian congregations already knew the story of the Crucifixion.[25] I think, too, that St. John's Gospel, appearing *after* the Synoptic Gospels appeared in the form in which we have them now, was setting out to correct and clarify misapprehensions about other subjects as well, such as Good Friday coinciding with the time of the killing of the lambs for Passover (supporting the belief that Jesus Himself was the ultimate paschal lamb), [26] and the fact that the popular belief in hell, which appeared to be supported by documents such as the Synoptic Gospels, was not the original understanding of the first disciples and St. Paul;[27] this would explain the references to *"perishing"* in St. John's Gospel and the insistence that eternal life is (only) *"in His Son."*[28]

I believe that the writings attributed to St. John, appearing at the end of the first century, were intended to support what St. Paul had taught decades before, ideas now in danger of being lost with (for example) the belief in "eternal punishment" derived from the Synoptic Gospels, and that they were never intended to be just another account of what Jesus said and did, which was basically the purpose of the Synoptics. That does not mean, however, that Jesus did not say what John attributed to Him, or that "a later church" produced a document recognizably different from the much earlier teaching of St. Paul. However, I gather that one is supposed to infer from the above quotations that it was "the later church" that attributed divinity to Christ, that in reality "the historical Jesus" portrayed in the Synoptic Gospels was "not like

---

23   Mark 8:36, quoting also the King James version; see, too, Mattthew 16:26 and Luke 9:24-25

24   1 John 3:14-15

25   see the chapter on the divinity of Christ.

26   See John 13:1, John 19:14; compare with Matthew 26:17, Mark 14:12, Luke 22:7

27   See the chapter on hell

28   e.g., John 3:16, John 10:27-28, 1 John 5:11 — and see the chapter on the Atonement

that"; and so the Synoptic Gospels are the ones to be believed, and one can therefore disregard the teaching of St. John and St. Paul (and the evidence of the many eye-witnesses from the actual time of the Resurrection whose testimony agreed with theirs).

The Synoptic Gospels, put together much later from earlier oral and written sources, were written more as accounts of what Jesus *said and did* than theological treatises about *how* our salvation is accomplished through Him. However, if they are indeed seen as being no more than the record of a historical figure who had no idea of His divine identity (as would seem to be implied by these quotations), it would seem to me that some selective "picking and choosing" must have been going on in scholarly circles. I cannot agree with Marcus Borg that there are differences between the Synoptic and Johannine portraits of Jesus "so great that they cannot be harmonized into a single whole". How can this statement be allowed to stand when *all* the Synoptic Gospels include such major events as the Transfiguration, the Last Supper and the Resurrection, and Jesus talking to His disciples after the Resurrection,[29] (and Luke and the end of Mark specifically refer to the Ascension)?[30] In fact, even one of the Synoptic Gospels that people like Marcus Borg so rely on states that St. Peter acknowledged to Jesus his belief that "you are the Christ, *the Son of the living God,*"[31] which is echoed in the other two. One cannot put *all* the blame on the Gospel of St. John! And as I show in the chapter on the divinity of Christ, the Synoptic Gospels which many regard as the more authentic testimony about "the real, historical, Jesus", because they tend to discount the teaching of St. Paul and St. John—the Synoptic Gospels *themselves* testify to the ultimate divinity of Christ (in addition to His humanity), although in a less obvious way. In particular, I quote three examples of this: Jesus forgiving the sick man let down on a pallet through the roof, in spite of the fact that the question had been asked: "who can forgive

---

29 People who do not believe in a physical Resurrection (see over) need to explain passages in the *Synoptic Gospels* about Jesus talking to His disciples after the Resurrection, e.g., Matthew 28:9-10, Matthew 28:16-20, Mark 16:9-20, Luke 24:13-53, especially Luke 24:27: Jesus *"interpreted to them in all the scriptures the things concerning himself"* and Luke 24:45: *"then he opened their minds to understand* the scriptures"

30 Matthew 17:1-8, Mark 9:2-8, Luke 9:28-36; Matthew 26:26-28, Mark 14:12-16, Luke 22:19-20; (Matthew 28), Mark 16, Luke 24.

31 Matthew 16:16, with equivalent statements in Mark 8:29 and Luke 9:20.

sins, *but God alone?"*[32] and the disciples, knowing the Old Testament teaching about only *God* being able to control the elements, saying *"Who then is this, that even wind and sea obey Him?"*[33] and last, but not least, Jesus saying "whoever receives…one child in my name receives me; and *whoever receives me, receives not me but him who sent me"*[34] which would not be possible if God were not Trinity—a truly Trinitarian statement in a Synoptic Gospel! People like to disbelieve accounts of miracles, but the feeding of the Five Thousand is recorded in all four Gospels[35]—including the Synoptic Gospels—because it was understood from the earliest time that, in this, *God* was present and again feeding His people.

In the account in St. John's Gospel [36] of Jesus turning water into wine we are told that his mother confirmed to Him (I believe through the guidance of the Holy Spirit) that it was time for Him to embark on His ministry; but it was in one of the *Synoptic Gospels* that we are told that another woman then confirmed to Him that His ministry was to the whole world, not just the Jews.[37] He could not have considered Himself to be just an ordinary man, nor was he regarded as such by

---

32   Mark 2:1-12

33   Mark 4:41; and Matthew's Gospel goes even further, in the account of Jesus walking on the sea (Mark 6-47-52) saying (Matthew 14:33), *'those in the boat worshipped him, saying 'Truly you are the Son of* God' "

34   Mark 9:37

35   Matthew 14:13-21; Mark 6:32-44; Luke 9:10-17; John 6:1-15; see the chapter on the Trinity and the metaphor of "the Bread of Life" which links the Old Testament to the New, and to our experience of God in the Eucharist today

36   John 2:1-11

37   Matthew 15:22- 28 (verse 24: Jesus said "I was sent only to the lost sheep of the house of Israel" but His encounter with the woman changed His mind); Mark 7:24-30; and the Great Commission was to "make disciples of all nations" (Matthew 28:19). I think that proponents of "the historical Jesus movement" were mistaken in putting undue emphasis on verses such as Matthew 10:5 "go nowhere among the Gentiles..but go rather to the lost sheep of the house of Israel" and Matthew 10:23 "you will not have gone through all the towns of Israel before the Son of Man comes," assuming that Jesus was thinking in purely human terms about the end of time, and, being mistaken, could not therefore be divine. This could have been merely a purely temporary injunction and we are not to rely on isolated verses but to take the total evidence of the Bible as a whole, which is that that the Gospel was eventually intended for the whole world; and the "coming of the Son of Man," initially at least, was indeed revealed in the Resurrection

those around Him, and the Synoptics would appear to agree with the Gospel of St. John in this regard, though perhaps not so obviously. *I think we have to face the reality* of what the early Christians believed, *as shown throughout the New Testament,* and *even in the Synoptic Gospels themselves,* because it was the underlying core of their faith that *God was in Christ,* [38] and that, *through abiding in Christ, they could come to be united with God,* even if at the same time the Synoptic Gospels concentrated more on what Jesus *said and did* than on *Who He was* and *Why.*

With regard to St. John's phrases about the divinity of Christ, I think there is a problem with including the metaphor of "the true vine" in the list of "I AM" statements quoted above as allegedly being not actually said by Jesus to His disciples. If it is *not* a claim to divinity like the others, it is meaningless; and, if it *does* signify divinity, it can only be in the greater context of our *abiding in Christ:* because the implication of the metaphor of "the vine" is that it has *branches,* and *sap* that circulates in both the vine and the branches to keep the whole alive, and so it can only refer to Christ and His people, with the Holy Spirit mutually flowing between them, *so that they become one.*

That means accepting the teaching about our *"abiding in Christ,"*[39] and thus, necessarily, His divinity, without which this would not be possible, and the fact that *this metaphor describes the whole method of our salvation, the means by which we can come to God through Christ;* and if it is valid at all, it *had* to have come to us *from Jesus Himself,* not "the later Church". Jesus' teaching about "the vine and the branches" is *fundamental* to any understanding of *how we can come to God through Him,* and I cannot believe that He did not at some time expound this to His disciples *(even if only after the Resurrection),* [40] even

---

38 2 Corinthians 5:19: "in Christ God was reconciling the world to himself"

39 John 15:1-10 (vv.5-10): "I am the vine, you are the branches. *He who abides in me, and I in him,* he it is that bears much fruit, for apart from me you can do nothing…*abide in my love.* If you keep my commandments, *you will abide in my love* [the Divine Love], just as I have kept my Father's commandments and abide in his love."

40 See earlier footnote re. Jesus talking to His disciples after the Resurrection, e.g. Matthew 28:9-10 and 16-20; Mark 16:9-20, Luke 24:13-53; also John 20:15-17; and John 20:21-29; note especially Luke 24:27: Jesus *"interpreted to them in all the Scriptures the things concerning himself"* and Luke 24::45: "then *he opened their minds to understand the scriptures;"* and John 12:16: after Jesus had quoted Zechariah 9:9, "His disciples did

if not precisely in the "I AM" format, in which case the account in St. John's Gospel would be consistent with what *Jesus Himself* taught them. As well, St. Paul, who knew the first disciples and lived among the earliest Christians, must have been familiar with this concept in order to talk about "being *in* Christ," and write to the Ephesians about being "rooted and grounded *in* love."

Jesus' claim to be one with the "I AM" who was the Old Testament understanding of God makes sense of His claim to be the Good Shepherd (who in Old Testament teaching was God Himself); and is important because if, in fact, Jesus was *not* God Incarnate we could not come to God through Him, because it is through our identifying ourselves with His humanity that we can come to encounter His divinity and thus move further into union with God. We could not otherwise in all our human fallibility come lumbering into the presence of the eternal God. Another problem in discounting the Gospel of John is that it states categorically that Jesus said "Before Abraham was, I AM" [41] ("I AM" being the Divine Name), and He was consequently pursued by people who tried to stone Him for blasphemy until He made a precipitous escape. Is that incident a total fabrication, a falsehood? And, if so, people alive at the time when the Gospel first appeared would have known that (because, as I argue later, when that Gospel first appeared, it was within the living memory of people still alive at the time, or their direct descendants and close associates), and therefore any such fabrication would have served to cast doubt on that Gospel when it first appeared, and then it would not have been accepted as the revered Gospel that it became.

St. John's Gospel goes on to recount the story of Doubting Thomas

---

not understand this at first, *but when Jesus was glorified then they remembered* that this had been written of him and had been done to him." I think the latter is probably true of many things that Jesus said, that they were unsure of at the time but understood more fully later, and "I AM" may have been a convenient way of encapsulating these truths in written form. But I also think that concentrating on "the historical Jesus" and not believing in the Resurrection or *the effect that the appearance of the Risen Christ must have had on His disciples*, causes people to miss the fact that *much of Jesus' most profound teaching* may well have been done *after the Resurrection when the disciples could see Him as He really was and more easily understand the significance of it,* and see how humanity can come to God *in Him*

41   John 8:58

finally saying to Jesus "My Lord and *My God.*"[42] To me, this has in it the ring of truth, and, if these ideas were known at the time of St. Paul, and, as I believe, St. Paul endorsed them,[43] surely the contents of St. John's Gospel can be taken to be truth of the Gospel *as it was understood at the time of the Resurrection,* and not as something philosophically "added to" or edited or corrected later. I think that it is because of this kind of misunderstanding of the Biblical texts that the faith has become so distorted over the years that people like Bishop Spong can now suggest that *"the Christology of the ages is bankrupt"* (see his *Twelve Theses* in Chapter 3).

A major problem today is that many people concentrate on "the historical Jesus", thinking only of His humanity, and seeing nothing of the divinity that connects Him to the eternal God. Many people, clergy included, are questioning whether the Resurrection ever happened, or is necessary to the faith. This is to treat Jesus of Nazareth as just another prophet, no more, perhaps on a par with Mohammed: or perhaps less. The divinity of Christ—and the idea of "abiding in Him"—tend to be down played in some of the new liturgies today.[44] Marcus Borg seems to sum up this kind of attitude to the historical fact of the Resurrection, and its meaning and significance, when he says (italics mine):

> In my judgment *Easter need not involve an empty tomb or anything happening to the physical body of Jesus.* Some scholars disagree. For example, N. Thomas Wright, a scholar poised on the edge of becoming the most important British New Testament scholar of his generation, and also a good friend, argues that *the truth of Christianity depends on whether the tomb was really empty.* Wright is not a fundamentalist but a mainline scholar with conservative-evangelical leanings. So I want

---

42 John 20:28. Note that there are also accounts of the Resurrection in *all* the Synoptic Gospels

43 see the section on Romans 9:5 in the chapter on the Divinity of Christ, and the other New Testament passages quoted in it, especially the discussion of Colossians 1:15-20; and see also the section on St. Paul on *"flesh and spirit"* in the chapter on misunderstandings of the Bible, and the chapter on "abiding in Christ".

44 See the discussion in Chapter 1 of the treatment of Colossians 1:15-20 in the Canadian *Book of Alternative Services*

to recognize disagreement among scholars even as I say, 'I don't think that's what Easter, or the Resurrection, is about'. [45]

I would have put it this way, saying "the truth of Christianity depends on *whether the disciples saw God in human form* in the Risen Lord, and realized that *the union of humanity and divinity in Christ was not only a reality, but one in which we can share* (as we abide in Him)". The empty tomb was only a corroborating detail. It is not just that Jesus, the man, came out of the grave, and goes on living, but that the hesitant disciples saw *God in human form* in the Risen Lord, and this was for them a life-changing experience, which gave them a new understanding of things they had not really understood before, especially when the Risen Christ "opened their minds to understand the Scriptures" in the light of this new reality.[46] People who concentrate unduly on Jesus' humanity seem to have forgotten St. Paul's teaching about *the union of humanity with divinity in Christ,* the "first fruits" of which were seen in the appearance of the Risen Christ: it was when the disciples saw how *humanity and divinity had come together* in Him that they were convinced, beyond all possible doubt, of the reality of what St. Paul meant in calling Christ "the first-fruits" of the "new creation" of which *we can be a part* if we are *in Him:*[47] they finally understood the significance of this, that it is as we share His humanity, and "abide in Him," that we can come to experience the divine and the eternal, and, *in* Him, come to God.

Another part of St. Paul's teaching that has been widely misunderstood, because of the modern tendency to disregard him altogether, is that of *"being crucified with Christ",* which is part of "abiding in Him". St. Paul was only amplifying Jesus' own teaching

---

45   Marcus J. Borg. "From Galilean Jew to the Face of God: The Pre-Easter and Post-Easter Jesus" in *Jesus at 2000,* Boulder, Colorado: Westview Press, 1997, p.16.

46   Luke 24:45; and see John 12:16: "when Jesus was glorified, *then they remembered…*"; and John 2:22: "when… he was raised from the dead, *his disciples remembered* that he had said this; *and they believed* the scripture and the word which Jesus had spoken"

47   2 Corinthians 5:17: "if any one is *in Christ,* he [that person] is *a new creation",* and 1 Corinthians 15:20-23 re. Christ being *"the first fruits"* of that new creation (see also Ephesians 2:14-16, to the effect that Christ has made both Jew and Gentile *one, creating in Himself one new man in place of the two).*

about *"taking up one's cross,"* which is contained in *all* the Synoptic Gospels. [48] I believe that this expression has sometimes come to be understood to mean that we should be prepared to suffer for political ends, but I think it is about something much more profound and fundamental than that: *it is how we share the life and death of Christ* as we abide in Him. I believe we have to learn to overcome (as it were, *to crucify in ourselves)* the natural tendencies and instincts which were built into the whole of creation for its preservation, whatever biologists such as those quoted above may say about group survival, basic instincts like struggling for food, for territory, for life, and striving to procreate, which in the course of nature would lead us to put our own interests ahead of everything else.

Jesus made this explicit in equating carrying the cross with denying in ourselves all the temptations to sin inherent in human nature ("if any man [anyone] would come after me, *let him deny himself* and take up his cross and follow me"). We have to learn to love and be unselfish and sacrifice and care for others: in effect, as St. Paul would say, to live *"in the Spirit" and not "in the flesh"*, which we *have to do if* we are going to *abide in Christ* through the Spirit of God within us; but I think this most significant part of New Testament teaching, taught by Jesus and expounded by St. Paul, (and contained in *all* the Synoptic Gospels!) has long been disregarded, because it has not been understood, just as much of the rest of St. Paul's teaching and, indeed, much of the teaching of the New Testament, and, thus, in many cases, the Christian faith itself, has not been properly understood, otherwise we would hardly be having the current debates over the divinity of Christ and the doctrine of the Trinity—see the section on St. Paul on "flesh and spirit".

I believe that coming to God through abiding in Christ is the true explanation of the Atonement, a problem that has vexed the Church for many years:*" why* did Jesus have to 'die for our sins' and *how* did this accomplish our salvation?" Most people do not think of it in theological terms, some may not know or care what the word "atonement" means, but the basic question is there for almost anyone

---

48   The Synoptic Gospels *all* refer to Jesus' teaching that His disciples must carry their cross in order to follow Him, thus corroborating that of St. Paul and St. John, as explained later, (e.g., Matt.16:24, Mark 8:34, Luke 9:23)

who thinks at all about the Christian faith: why did Jesus *have to be crucified?* How does His death two thousand years ago bring about "the forgiveness of our sins" today? With the concomitant question: if that was something God *required* for us to be "forgiven", *what kind of God does that make God?*

The Church has never come up with one official definition of the Atonement, preferring to let the many New Testament images speak together to show us a greater truth than any one simplistic definition alone could provide. Truth can be as fragile as a butterfly's wings. If one were to load a heavy lead weight onto them, the butterfly's wings would be crushed, and the butterfly would no longer be able to fly. This metaphor could be used to illustrate what happens when Biblical fundamentalists try to saddle onto Truth the weight of *one verse* of the Bible out of many, or even only one part of one sentence (see example in the footnote below)[49] instead of comprehending the greater truth found in taking Biblical verses together.

As I describe in the Chapter on the Atonement, the theory of "penal substitution" was developed in the Middle Ages, to the effect that Christ took our place and bore in Himself on the Cross the *punishment* for our sins, which is in itself an over-simplification, indeed a dangerous perversion, of a greater truth, and one which has caused a great deal of trouble in the history of the Church. As I quote more fully in that Chapter, one writer has said, of the various "vicarious suffering" theories, ("vicarious meaning "instead of", "in place of"), that:

> Many popular objections to the Atonement are due to this fatal separation between the deed [Christ's death] and our response [in the present time],…so that it is viewed as the work of a substitute [for us] and as a 'transaction' accomplished on man's behalf. *So powerful in their effect are these objections that,* although the theories of the Atonement on which they rest belong

---

49   1 Corinthians 15:34: "Christ died for our sins…" but this was written in a much larger context: first to say that it was *"in accordance with the Scriptures"*, emphasizing its relation to Old Testament prophecy, then to say that "he was buried", i.e., that He was truly dead, and then to say that He rose again and appeared to many people, i.e. the *Resurrection* is of equal significance, it all goes together.

to the past, *theological reconstruction is impeded by them to this day.* [50]

Another has come up with what I believe to be the best description of the Atonement that I have ever seen:

> We cannot be saved without full repentance [but] we cannot perform this full repentance nor the penance which should go with it. Yet, on the other hand…no one, not even Christ, can do these things for us, if by 'for' is meant 'instead' of us. To this problem there is only one solution. Since we cannot do it alone and He cannot do it instead of us, *it must be both together who do it, He in us and we in Him.* And in saying this we have stepped out of that whole region of substitutions, contracts and external relationships [and] come back at last to that which was missing…*we find our salvation after all in our mystical union with Christ*

and he goes on to say

> *to be in Christ is to be a new creature… 'Not I, but Christ in me'. 'Not in myself, but in Christ'.* This is the true substitution, which the theories mishandle and misconceive, but which the Bible and the Church proclaim and on which Christian devotion continually dwells.[51]

This explains why *"abiding in Christ"*, and how it accomplishes our salvation, is the main theme of this book. It also makes sense of Jesus' teaching about *"taking up one's Cross* to follow Him" (which, as noted, is recorded in *all* the Synoptic Gospels), and why St. Paul's teaching about crucifying in ourselves the sinful lusts of the flesh that impede our union with God's Spirit is so important: it explains that we do metaphorically share in Christ's crucifixion[52] and the death of the flesh

---

50   Vincent Taylor. *The Atonement in New Testament Teaching.* London: The Epworth Press, 1940, p.179.

51   H.A. Hodges. *The Pattern of Atonement.* London: SC.M. Press Ltd., 1955, p.55

52   I think we sometimes make *assumptions* about the meaning of a passage: e.g., 1 Corinthians 1:18 "the word of the cross is folly to those who are perishing, but to us who

in its selfish sense in order to attain "new life" and eternity in Him: we live out His life again in our own, as we become united with Him in the Spirit, in this life and the next.

The legacy of the Reformation is not only the split in Christendom between Roman Catholics and Protestants, and the proliferation of differing groups and sects among the latter, but the recent sharp dissension between fundamentalists and so-called "liberals" in the mainline Anglican and Episcopalian churches on the question of the authority of the Bible and what it is to be "a Biblical Christian". On the surface the homosexual question has appeared to be the main issue (whether certain verses of the Bible still apply), but the problem goes much deeper. Examples such as Bishop Spong's *Twelve Theses,* and the references given above about some scholars not understanding the significance of the Resurrection and therefore not believing in it, would appear to demonstrate that *the Christian faith itself* is under attack *from within* as never before.

Unfortunately, those Christians who do maintain the traditional faith of the Creeds, and believe in the divinity of Christ and the doctrine of the Trinity and the authority of the Bible as God's way of conveying to His people "the things concerning Himself," [53] and want to stand up for those beliefs, now find themselves allied with a fundamentalist section of the church which has pronounced and judgmental views about "only Christians being saved" and everyone else "going to hell", and that extreme position is not a palatable choice for many people either.

A problem that needs to be re-thought in this context is the traditional doctrine of "hell": if some are "saved" and many are not, *what happens to the latter:* the whole problem of the traditional teaching on hell, and why resolving it *matters* to the integrity of the Christian faith. (Integral to this is defining what "eternal life" actually *is.)* One

---

are being saved it is the power of God"; this *could* mean *"the Gospel of Salvation* is not understood by those who reject God" but I think it means, literally, that the teaching of *the way of the Cross,* the self-discipline involved in *"being crucified with Christ,"* as, "abiding in Him", we crucify in ourselves all that is not of God, is something the world does not understand, but in it we experience *the power of God*

53   Luke 24:27 Jesus "interpreted to them in all the scriptures the things concerning him-self"; and Luke 24:45 "Then he opened their minds to understand the Scriptures"

of the problems arising from the Synoptic Gospels, I believe, is the fact that "hell" is mentioned in some of the parable stories, and in particular there is a reference in St. Matthew's Gospel to "everlasting *punishment*", [54] (although I believe that that might be even less of an accurate transcription of what Jesus actually *said* than is alleged about the Gospel of St. John, because, logically speaking, everlasting *punishment* is not the opposite of everlasting *life)*, but this led the Church in its earliest days to develop a theology about eternal punishment for sinners in hell (adopting the pre-Christian belief in hell and the popular belief in the culture of the time that everyone lived for ever anyway), even though such an inference from the Synoptic Gospels is contradicted not only by the apostolic teaching of St. Paul and St. John and others, (including the Biblical statement that *God alone* is immortal)[55], but *in the Synoptic Gospels themselves,* as I show in the chapter in question: and also the Athanasian Creed, which specifically refers to the possibility of *"perishing".*

"The waters have been muddied" when it comes to defining what "eternal life" actually is. There are theories that have existed since pre-Christian times that the human soul exists for ever anyway,[56] in hell, if necessary, so that it is not seen as being necessary to be *"in"* God in order to survive for ever, thus making a mockery of the term "eternal life" as it is used in Christian practice, but I show in detail that such theories are not only pre-Christian but they are not consistent with the overall apostolic teaching of the Bible. However, the Synoptic Gospels appeared to tie in with the idea, popular in the culture of the time, that everyone automatically lived for ever, but that some went on to eternal damnation in hell, and this made the necessity of "abiding in Christ" less crucial, *because the significance of the "victory over death," in which we share if we are "IN Him,"* became obscured, as no one was thought to die for ever anyway. I have tried to show how the traditional teaching on hell conflicts with the original apostolic teaching of St. Paul and St. John (and others), as stated earlier.

---

54   Matthew 25:46, which I discuss in detail later; see the chapter on hell. I believe that references to "eternal fire" in passages such as Matthew 25:41 are really metaphorical in nature, and *on that level* true

55   1 Timothy 6:13-16 "[God the Trinity] *alone has immortality"*

56   The so-called *"Christian doctrine of man",* which, incidentally, is not listed as such in *The Oxford Dictionary of the Christian Church* — see Glossary re. *"Annihilationism"*

People who accuse some in the liberal wing of the Anglican and Episcopal Churches of departing from the traditional faith have used the terms *"unitarian and universalist"* to describe them.

The term "unitarian" implies denial of the divinity of Christ and the doctrine of the Trinity, and, insofar as I have encountered that tendency in my church, I have tried to fight it, for nearly thirty years, hence this book.

However, I think the term "universalist" has sometimes been used erroneously. If it is taken to mean that the divinity of Christ need not be an objective fact for the salvation of the world, because people of any religion can "get to God" in the end regardless, *because the existence and divinity of Christ do not matter, and can still be denied at the end of time,* then of course I would say that such a view must be challenged at all costs. However, I do not think that we can presume to make the judgment that God the Trinity (which includes Christ), the God who is Love, may not one day, *if He so wishes,* reconcile to Himself those who know what it is to love, and *who then accept Him as He is* (not concentrating on "the historical Jesus" per se, [57] but understanding "God" in this context as *the Trinitarian God within whom love flows).* [58] We need to re-think what we mean by "universalism", and not be so simplistic in our definitions. The idea of God the Trinity *reaching out with love to all those who know what it is to love,* to bring them to Himself at the end of time, need not, *in itself,* imply or entail denial of "the divinity of Christ". For example, I cannot see a loving God rejecting a small Jewish girl who died in a concentration camp in World War II just because she was not "a Christian", or that child rejecting Him either.

A problem arises when very enthusiastic, but naïve, Christians assume that "preaching the Gospel" means threatening non-Christians with "eternal punishment" in hell if they do not convert to Christianity *in*

---

57   after all, Jesus did say that anyone "who speaks a word against *the Son of Man will* be forgiven": what will *not* be forgiven is blasphemy against *the Holy Spirit, the Truth and Essence of the Living God* (the Trinity) (Luke 12:10)

58   even if *good people who have walked with Love all their lives* without understanding the Christian Gospel *in this lifetime are* eventually reconciled with God, when they see Him as He is at the end of time, and *if He so wishes,* I believe that what St. Peter said will still apply, that "there is no other name under heaven…by which we must be saved" (Acts 4:12), *because Jesus is still the gateway, as it were, by which we come to the Trinitarian God.*

this lifetime, ("some...were teaching...that *'unless* you are circumcised... *you cannot be saved'"),[59] a condemnation and a threat that has caused much grief in the world, and which I do not believe was Our Lord's intention when He told His disciples "to make disciples of all nations... *teaching them to observe all that I have commanded you"*—which is to *love.*[60] I think St. Paul's way should be commended, which was to assert *first of all the nature of God,* a God of Love who wanted to be reconciled with the human race:

> What...you worship as unknown...I proclaim to you.
> The God who made the world and everything in it...
> made from one every nation of men to live on all the
> face of the earth... *that they should seek God,* in the hope
> that they might feel after him *and find him...*in Him
> we live and move and have our being

only *then* going on to describe how God purposed our reconciliation with Him through Christ.

I think that an analysis of the true meaning of the Athanasian Creed would bring clarity to all sides in this situation, because I think that misunderstandings of it have influenced all traditions of Christianity, not only on the subject of hell, but the idea that "the decision for Christ" must be made *in this lifetime* or else it would be "too late" for anyone ever to come to God. Over earlier centuries, the Church desperately tried to enforce orthodoxy, sincerely believing that one *had to* hold the Christian faith in this lifetime "or else," and the wording of that Creed seemed to fit that way of thinking, *but I do not think that that was necessarily intended to be the case.* As I see it, that Creed was intended primarily to set out the Christian belief in *the nature of God,* rather than qualifications for salvation. It stated as a fact, what I believe to be true, that the Christian faith is that God is a Trinity of Persons to whom we can come through Christ; and if that belief is correct, it will be to that Trinitarian God that all nations will one day come, whether they know it during this lifetime or not. That does not mean, however, that God may not receive them with love, if they are already acquainted with Love. That is a decision for God, and not for us to decide.

59   Matthew 28:19-20
60   Acts 15:1

But the traditional belief, that one had to be *a baptized Christian in this lifetime* if one was ever "to be saved" and come to God, led the Roman Catholic Church in earlier centuries to promulgate the belief that babies who died unbaptized would never know the presence of God, but would remain for ever in a state of Limbo, in neither heaven or hell. This doctrine has now been rescinded by the current Pope. I think that, if the earlier thinking that lay behind it was wrong, and rescinding this doctrine was the right decision to make (and I believe it was), all denominations should now think about the possible consequences of this new understanding, in considering the relationship of Christianity with people of other faiths, because the same thinking behind the belief in "Limbo", that one had to be baptized during this lifetime, that after death would be too late to come to God, led Protestants at the time of the Reformation to continue to believe that only those who were Christians *in this lifetime* would *"be saved"*, often quoting Jesus' saying that *"no one comes to the Father but by me"*[61] as if it only applied in the present tense, and could not be equally true in the eternal future. Not only do I think that that is an unwarranted assumption from the actual grammar, and not only do I think that the Athanasian Creed was also wrongly assumed to support this conclusion, but I think there has been a misunderstanding of "Judgment Day" itself. Of course the end of our earthly life is significant, in that we have grown into, and finally become, the people we are, and there is no going back from that fact. We have lived our lives, and, for better or worse, our characters are formed: our sins confirm "who we are" and what we are like. It is on that basis that we come to be judged by God; but I argue that it does *not necessarily* follow that intellectual belief in the truth of Christianity *in this lifetime* will be "the main deciding factor" at that point. What *will* matter is whether people are good and kind and loving, and compatible with the nature of God, already familiar with Love, if not with Christian terminology, who, when they finally see God, recognize Him, and accept that realization with joy; and, most important of all, whether *God wishes* to forgive and accept them into His Kingdom.

The reason why I am so concerned to make this point, that the Gospel is about *coming to God through Christ* (the alternative being

---

61   John 14:6

perishing, not hell, if a person uses his or her last act of free-will to refuse to accept the Trinitarian God of Love when meeting Him at the end of time), is that many reasonable people—especially those who believe that God, if He existed at all, would have to be a God of Love to be worth worshipping—no longer subscribe to the idea of "only Christians being saved", all others being consigned to hell regardless, and as a result of modern thinking about "heaven" and "hell", the Christian faith is under adverse scrutiny as never before.

A special part of my ministry has been to those ordinary people (and they are many) who have fallen away from Christianity, usually because of some problem of doctrine that has never been explained to them in a way that they can accept. Often it is a caricature or a mistaken understanding of the faith that they quite rightly reject, and yet they do not know what to put in its place. They have a deep need, and yet have not found it to be met in the Church. Often such people, even many churchgoers, are afraid of the unknown when they come to die, and it has been my task and privilege to talk to them of a God of love, and encourage them to be reconciled with God and not be afraid, to assure them that "it will be all right", and to help them to die in peace.

I believe that people can indeed be reassured that they can trust in God's mercy and His love *if they are willing eventually to be reconciled with Him,* (remembering that God is love, and requires love in us), and so they need not be afraid of death, but can be glad to go to Him.

I used to visit a very old lady in a nursing home, who told her nurse in a lucid moment, (and the nurse told me), that she was worried about what was going to happen to her when she died. She said she did not feel *"good enough for heaven,"* but she did not really think she was *"bad enough for hell".* What had years of churchgoing taught her about the faith? (The kind of thinking that Marcus Borg has described, as mentioned earlier, that defined salvation *as going to heaven; "salvation meant going to heaven").* It is for this kind of person that I have written my book, wishing it could have been available for them before it was too late.

I knew a middle-aged man, a distinguished medical specialist, who, as a youngster, had been a Roman Catholic, and at the time when the Roman Catholic Church decided to relax the rules on eating meat on a Friday, he asked his parish priest, perfectly innocently, not meaning to be cheeky, but seeking to understand, *"what, then, happened to all those people who had already gone to hell for eating meat on a Friday,"* if this was no longer a "hell" offence. He was rebuffed because his question was taken to be insolent, the taunting of a cheeky boy, but it was a serious question in his mind, and the refusal to answer it led to his not only leaving his church but his never going to any other. As a patient of his at the time, it was difficult for me to take the time to persuade him otherwise: but the question has haunted me. What was the Church saying to its people about the infallibility of its doctrines if they could be changed *without explanation?* How could people then be certain about its future pronouncements? What *did* happen to those people who had allegedly "gone to hell"? And how could the offence of eating meat on a Friday possibly, in the eyes of a *Just* God, receive the same punishment as that given to the perpetrators of some of the monstrous cruelties and wickedness that have been experienced in this world? How many people are there out there who have been turned away from "the Church" (I speak in the generic sense) for lack of answers that would have satisfied them that they were at least being listened to?

The book's central theme is "abiding in Christ", which is not as esoteric a concept as it sounds: it is like "practising the presence of God", only in an interior, as well as an exterior, way, identifying ourselves with Jesus in the present time as we consciously share in His humanity and live as He did ("not I, but Christ in me"). It describes how the concept of living IN the eternal God, with the Spirit of God dwelling in, and with, His people, runs through the whole Bible, as does the theme of divine Love. But this necessarily entails the idea of the divinity of Christ and the doctrine of the Trinity, without which "abiding in Christ" would not be possible, and there would be no way for us ever to be eternally united with God (and we need to think again about what "Love" really means), and, in the climate of today's liberal theology, I believe these concepts need to be set out again, and reasonably explained.

"Abiding in Christ" is not only a fundamental part of our faith, but it is also a major part of the doctrine of the Atonement, only it has not usually been understood that way. The main emphasis has historically been just on the forgiveness of sins. "Abiding in Christ" explains the concept of *immortality*, people *living and abiding for ever IN the eternal God,* only this understanding became blurred very early on in Church history.

Trying to spend one's life "abiding in Christ" raises another issue: if Christ is part of God, *what is the nature of that God whom we aspire to abide in,* the God "in whom we live and move and have our being?"[62] It is not really profitable, except for purposes of Biblical meditation, to reflect only on the historical Jesus, because we cannot "live in" an ordinary man who lived in history and died like the rest of us. To practise the concept of "abiding in Christ" in our own lives we have to see Jesus in the complete sense of His being *the Risen Lord in whom divinity and humanity meet,* and accept Him as a bridge to coming to abide in the eternal God: which brings us back to the question: *what is the nature of that eternal God?*

St. John emphasizes that *God is love,* and *specifically links "abiding in Christ" with keeping the commandments to love.* Many people, of all religions, even Christians who are supposed to know better, often talk about "God" without, apparently, having any idea of what that God must be like, if He is to be worthy of respect and homage and love: and, if so, how can they love Him? I believe that God *must* be Love to be worth worshipping in the first place, and that it is *love that brings us to Him* (the metaphor of the vine and the branches shows that it is *Love, the Spirit and Essence of God,* within us that is the sap, as it were, that makes us one with God through Christ: abiding in Christ and abiding in Love were firmly linked in Jesus' use of this metaphor). Some people today are very keen on *"justice",* as if it were a political objective, separate from the concept of *loving people in God's Name, for His sake,* which is why I believe we are called again to think about *loving God through our neighbour,* rather than just pursuing political causes for their own sake (particularly if those "causes" end up in our minds as a kind of idolatry). And, although love and care for others are mandated in the holy books of many religions, people often speak of God without, apparently, any awareness of the divine mandate to love. They try to make God in their own image, not the other way around. This book is predicated on the

---

62   Acts 17:28

fact that God is "love" and that people of all religions are supposed to "abide" in that love which will one day transcend all our human differences; and calls the world to reflect on the nature of the God whose Name we misuse so casually.

I wanted to respond to the many questions that both churchgoers and non-churchgoers have asked me over the years, and also to challenge people *of all faiths* to return to the truth of their own historic teachings in the light of the understanding that God is the essence of peace and mercy, love and truth: not hatred, cruelty, and exclusivity. What cannot expect to exist in God's eternal Kingdom, and *this needs to be understood by everyone,* is selfishness, evil, and continuing hate.[63]

I am convinced that the earliest understanding of the Christian Gospel was *not only* that *"we are saved"* in the sense of our sins being forgiven, but that we can *come to God* through *"abiding in Christ,"* (being "saved" from *"perishing"*[64] rather than hell, see later discussion), so we need to go back to what I believe to be the original understanding of the Atonement for a clearer understanding of the traditional faith, and *reaffirm belief in the divinity of Christ, His being both God and Man,* because that is the necessary component and essential prerequisite on which the Christian faith depends. However, *at the same time,* I think it needs to be emphasized that, *if God is love,* it must therefore follow that His love extends and reaches out to all those people who have lived their lives in sincerity and love and goodness, even though they may not have subscribed to the Christian faith *in this lifetime:* in which case I believe that whether or not they are eventually accepted into His Kingdom depends on whether, when they see Him, they accept Him as He is, (God the Trinity), and He accepts them. I explain later that my belief is based on Biblical teaching,[65] (Biblical teaching that has long been misunderstood and ignored), and is not the same thing as "universalism".

---

63   eg. Isaiah 60:18: "Violence shall no more be heard in your land, devastation or destruction within your borders..."

64   e.g., 1 Corinthians 1:18: "For the word of the cross is folly to *those who are perishing,* but *to us who are being saved* it is the power of God."

65   e.g., 1 John 4:7: *"love is of God, and he who loves* is born of God and *knows God.* He who does not love does not know God; *for God is love"* and many other examples given, from Old Testament prophecy to Jesus Himself.

I believe that it is partly because of historical misunderstandings of the Athanasian Creed, which I will try to explain, (and Biblical texts such as John 14:6 and Acts 4:12 referred to earlier), that believers in the divinity of Christ *assume* that it would be too late for a non-Christian to be reconciled with God the Trinity when meeting Him after death. Christians—and others—must remember that it is not up to *any* of *us* to judge what God will "do with His own", [66] and remember that Jesus judged harshly those who *"trusted in themselves that they were righteous and despised others."*[67]

We have to draw a fine line between, on the one hand, *the certainty of our own faith for ourselves, and our preaching of it because we sincerely believe it to be true,* and, on the other hand, the idea that all those who do not subscribe to our understanding of salvation *in this lifetime* must *automatically* be alienated from God for ever (and non-Christians who condemn others as "infidels" need to think this way too), *leaving the final judgment to God.*

If this was really understood, and accepted, too, by the other major faiths, surely some of the terrible distortions of faith in the world today might be overcome: and the concept of *God being love,* without insisting, *in the present time,* on God's *also* being Trinity, might bring God-fearing people together in His Name.

If all the mainstream religions started to give more emphasis to the idea that God is love, and the fact that God requires loving behaviour from all who would want to call themselves His disciples, regardless of past historical grievances or injustices, perhaps some of the murderous ideologies and conflicts of the present century might be more widely seen for what they are: direct disobedience to the will of God. Whatever the problem may be, nothing can justify hatred, which is the antithesis of love.

---

66 Matthew 20:15: (the parable of the labourers in the vineyard): "I choose to give to this last as I give to you. *Am I not allowed to do what I choose with what belongs to me? Or do you begrudge my generosity?"*

67 Luke 18:9-14, the parable of the two men who went down to the Temple to pray: and Luke 15:11-32, the parable of the prodigal son: though it is one thing to be confident in one's faith, it is also important to balance this confidence by remembering what Jesus was trying to teach us about the sinfulness of supposing oneself to be "better" or more deserving than others, as if God's grace was not God's to bestow on someone else as well *if He wished to do so.*

Because the world is in such religious turmoil at this time, and clarification of people's conflicting beliefs is needed on all sides, (for them, and for others), I believe it is crucially important that these ideas be thought about and discussed before old liturgies are discarded and their traditional teaching lost.

And because *God is love,* I want to reassure people that one should not be afraid to die, because *eternal life in God* is the goal of our earthly journey.

CHAPTER 1

Who Am I, And What Was My Own Journey In The Faith

I am an Anglican, baptized in the Church of England many years ago, and I am now a member of the Anglican Church of Canada—but the views I express in this book are my own: they have been arrived at through a long process of engaging with the experiences of my life, and I think they may well mirror the experiences of other people, who, over the years, have asked the same questions; but the Anglican Church is not to be held responsible for the conclusions I have reached!

When I was a small child, and was afraid of the dark, as children so often are, I remember a phosphorescent cross that hung on the wall by my bed and literally comforted my darkness. This was in the days when grown-ups did not "pander" to children by giving them night-lights, or the benefit of a dim light from another room, to alleviate their fears. I remember my disappointment when that cross was taken away, on the grounds that someone said it was dangerous to one's health because it was radioactive, and I was back in the darkness again! So somehow I was unintentionally introduced to the Christian faith in a subtle way that had nothing to do with church-going or Sunday School. I just associated the presence of the Cross with light and comfort in the darkness: and somehow, without realizing it, I came to experience the presence of God.

I was fortunate in this, because, when confronted, later on, with some of the difficult questions that we have inherited because of the misunderstandings and confused philosophical speculations about the faith that have occurred over the centuries, which have largely continued to be misunderstood in our generation, I did not, as so many have done, throw up my hands, as it were, and say "this does not make sense, and I can't believe it": I *knew* that it *must* make sense, if only I could sort it out and find the answers, because I *knew* that *"God is not like that"*.

Ever since I can remember, I have been asking questions, as I know that other people have, too. Many have left the Church, as a result of feeling that their questions were not answered. I have been fortunate in that I feel that God has rooted me in the Christian faith from the beginning, and protected me from unbelief even at the bleakest times, but even so I have been on a life-long quest to reconcile faith with understanding, and want now to share my discoveries with others to help them, too.

Perhaps I should elaborate, if it helps people to understand "where I am coming from". I felt the call to the priesthood as early as the age of eight, when I was told that that would never be possible for me, because at that time it was unthinkable that women would ever be ordained. (So I decided to marry a clergyman and write his sermons for him, not realizing that one can't just go out and pick a certain brand of husband, and not realizing that, if I did marry a clergyman, if he was any good, he would not let me write his sermons for him! That just shows you how young I was. But it means, also, that I was already critiquing some of the sermons that I heard at the age of eight!)

But I was fortunate, in the long term, in that I came to believe in God, and be firmly convinced of His existence, and His presence with me, and His love, when I was still very young, because that has protected me in the subsequent griefs and sorrows that one encounters in life. This has enabled me to minister to people who have faced abuse and tragedy, as one who has experienced both, and can understand and identify with them, while also reassuring them that it was not *God* who was to blame, and that one can still with integrity turn to Him. So many people have had to face tragedy before they had the strength of the faith behind them, and as a result they are angry with God, and they need special pastoral care to bring them to a position where they can accept the truths of the faith. I believe that I have had a special ministry to try to help such people from the benefit of my own experience; but love and sympathy and self-identification with them are not enough: one has to be prepared to answer hard questions as well: hence my long search for understanding on an intellectual level as well as a spiritual one.

During my early teens, I think I was provoked into doubting the faith by an over-enthusiastic parish priest who was strong on the "penal substitution" theory of the Atonement.[68] My grandmother had left the Church years before, after my grandfather committed suicide; there were no suicide-survivor support-groups in those days, or modern counselling techniques, and she encountered unhelpful clergy at that time. She always said that the Church made her feel "guilty", and the burden of even an ordinary bereavement, let alone a spouse's suicide, can be enough to make *anyone* feel guilty at the best of times, and this convinced me at a very early age that the Church needed to be more pastoral and sensitive in its dealings with people who are suffering.

I have felt ever since a call to minister to such people and bring them back to God (including women and girls who have suffered sexual abuse, and have trouble thinking of God as "Father"), because I would want to assure them that God loves them and *understands,* that sin is caused by humans, and that, whatever mistakes the Church may make, *"God is not like that".*

I assumed originally that what upset my grandmother was the phrase in the General Confession, which has now been dropped from our current Anglican Prayer Book, about "the remembrance [of our sins being] grievous to us, the burden of them intolerable". But I began to feel guilty myself[69] when a one-sided presentation of the doctrine of the Atonement (a gory and indeed sadistic presentation of the "penal substitution" theory) made me feel that it was *"all my fault* that Jesus was crucified," that He suffered all that excruciating pain for *me* because *I was* "so bad," without any hope ever seeming to be offered to me of *love and life:* which has led me to a life-long search for a more acceptable understanding of the Atonement.

So without agreeing with Bishop Spong, I understand the kind of thinking that has led him to set out the objection felt by many that

---

68   see Glossary for definition of the Atonement, and the Chapter on the Atonement

69   "guilty" *not* in the sense of the repentance rightly due for sin, but in the sense of the simplistic implication that my sins were so grievous that *I deserved* to be *crucified* and that Jesus was kind enough *"to take my place"*

"the view of the cross as the sacrifice for the sins of the world is a barbarian idea [sic] and must be dismissed".[70]

And this was at the time of the Nuremberg War Crimes Tribunal after the Second World War, when of course one was well aware that Jesus of Nazareth was not the only person in the world to suffer horrible atrocities, and I was not, in my teenage self, the most criminal person in the world, so I was asking both the old question of "how could a God of love allow terrible things, such as the Holocaust, to happen", and how could one rationally understand the Atonement, because the answers I received did not satisfy me. These are both old questions which have vexed humanity for centuries, but to me at the time they were new, and the answers were not easy to find.

When I came to be confirmed, in 1948, the girls in my class at school were each given a few minutes alone with the old clergyman who was preparing us, and I took advantage of this opportunity by asking him for an explanation of the Atonement. I do not remember any clear explanation being forthcoming: I imagine the emphasis was still on *"Jesus died for our sins"*, which is true, but the questions remained for me: *how,* (in the sense of "how was this accomplished by the Crucifixion?) and *why?* (in the sense of *why was this necessary?).* I do, however, remember that I got into trouble with my teachers for taking too long and "holding up the line", and I have always felt that the Church should not expect people to make a life-long declaration of allegiance to the faith based merely on blind obedience without understanding. So I made a special point of studying the subject of the Atonement when I was in seminary, studying for the priesthood, because I was still interested in it forty years later.

What sustained me during the two years of doubt that I experienced in my teenage years was the fact that I continued to take Holy Communion, in spite of not knowing what to believe. I know the Church has rules about receiving it with faith, but I believed that, if God was real and the faith was true, He would forgive me, as long as I came to it with the prayer that He would see me through this time of crisis, and *show* me, and teach me to understand. I am living proof that there is something very powerful in the Eucharist, if one can just *hold on* in spite of doubts and desolation, because in it God is *there.*

---

70   see Bishop Spong's *Twelve Theses,* quoted later

I grew up in a very "low-church," Protestant, kind of Church of England country parish, but when I emigrated to Canada when I was twenty-one I encountered a more "High Church" environment. The priest who married my husband and me offered us Holy Communion at our wedding, and, although this shocked the more traditional family friend who had introduced us, my husband and I accepted it gratefully, although we would never then have thought of it for ourselves. My son's baptism and his recent wedding were also in the context of the Eucharist. Similarly, my husband's funeral was also a Communion service, as I hope my own will be. I even ended up with a Roman Catholic nun as my spiritual director when I was in a time of crisis in a difficult parish, and she is still my valued friend.

But of course being ordained as a priest would put me at odds with the Roman Catholic hierarchy which does not believe in the ordination of women, though I would like to put it on record that I received nothing but help and kindness from the Roman Catholics and their priest in the town where I served as the incumbent of the local Anglican Church. So I am sort of a hybrid: with the mystical mind of a traditional Catholic, and the questioning one of a Protestant Reformer!

I have felt all my life the call to search for Truth, and from the time of encountering my grandmother's reaction to the Church I have seen it as my mission to find answers if I could and share them with others, and bring the doubters back to God. Even this book, though the result of many years of personal wrestling with the faith, is still basically intended to reach such people now, and restore their faith in God.

The Epistle reading at my son's baptism, forty years ago, was the difficult passage from the First Epistle of St. John about "the Spirit and the water and the blood" being "equal witnesses" (to the truth of the Gospel),[71] another hard question, and one on which there is no agreement among Biblical commentators; and no explanation was given to us young parents either! But I now think it is significant that, in the old Anglican *Book of Common Prayer,* that reading has always been set for the Sunday after Easter, and so, presumably, it must have been seen, in early days, as being of special significance in the

---

71   1 John 5:8

Easter story, but, if so, that understanding has been lost to the modern generation, the generation that is no longer sure about the divinity of Christ. However, not only does my explanation make sense, in and of itself, but it is consistent with the theme of Easter, because it is not about crucifixion (which would have come *before* Easter), it is about *the eternal life which stems from the Easter event.*

I believe, too, that the interpretation that I have come up with is particularly important because it covers a point of contention between Roman Catholics and Protestants at the time of the Reformation, when some Protestant theologians tended to ascribe our salvation solely to the one historical fact of Christ's death on the Cross in the past, and the Roman Catholics also saw ongoing sanctification by the Holy Spirit in the present time. I think this one text covers both the *Protestant* emphasis on the one act of the past, and the *Catholic* emphasis on ongoing grace in the present as well, and, *if I am right,* the writers of the Bible commentaries (who admit in the first place that they are not sure what this text means), would have to think again about its meaning, and thus resolve the outstanding larger issue.

So years of thinking about unanswered questions like this have led me to come up with answers that do make sense, as I will go on to show. I have always believed that the Christian religion *does make sense,* if only one could understand it, and not just have to hang on by blind faith — or, as so many have done, just give up!

The problem was that, with an older husband in ill-health, and a family to support, it did not appear to be possible for me ever to be ordained, even when the Anglican Church of Canada did finally agree to the ordination of women; but in the end it all came together, I went back to university in my fifties, and was ordained, and appointed as the incumbent of a parish.

While I was still a layman, I was a delegate at an Anglican Provincial Synod, a gathering of several different dioceses [72] in the Canadian Church's Province of British Columbia and Yukon, which was asked to approve a fore-runner to its current *Book of Alternative Services* in 1979. I felt then that there was a lack of emphasis in it on the divinity of Christ, *"abiding in Christ"* (as was covered in the old Anglican *Book of Common Prayer* by the request that we might so receive the

---

72   see Glossary

sacrament of the Eucharist *that we might evermore dwell in Him and He in us)* not being mentioned at all! [73] and when I pointed this out, the Synod was sufficiently concerned not to approve the liturgy, which led me into correspondence with the national Canadian Church, there being no Bishop in my Diocese at the time. The *Book of Alternative Services* which the Anglican Church of Canada then produced has, to my mind, followed the same trend. I describe in the next chapter how, for example, the lectionary printed in it omitted from Bible readings at Sunday church services the passage about Christ being *"the image of the invisible God"*, presumably on the grounds that some scholars have believed it to be a later interpolation ("because St. Paul would not have said that about Jesus"), but then part of that passage was used out of context in its Eucharistic Prayers to describe Christ's humanity but not His divinity, presumably using the excuse that, out of context or not, *"it is in the Bible."* Because my experience at the 1979 Provincial Synod had alerted me to the tendency to unitarianism (whether deliberate or unintended) of proponents of the modern Anglican liturgies, I was aware of the pitfalls that it can pose to the unwary, and was able to avoid them by using the Book judiciously—which *can* be done. However, many clergy do not seem to be aware of the theological ramifications of some of its contents, and, accepting the duly authorized "printed book" without question, do not seem to realize, for example, that in the case cited above, by using those particular prayers, they are, in effect, denying the divinity of Christ on a regular basis, as they happily

---

73   even though St. John's Gospel, now so popularly disregarded, links *the Eucharist with both eternal life* and *abiding in Christ:* John 6:51-56: "I am the living bread which came down from heaven; *if any one eats of this bread, he will live for ever;* and the bread which I shall give for the life of the world is my flesh...he who eats my flesh and drinks my blood *has eternal life,* and *I will raise him up at the last day...*He who eats my flesh and drinks my blood *abides in me, and I in Him."* See the Chapter on *Misunderstandings regarding the Eucharist,* about how some people have confused the symbolism of what Jesus was saying with literal *"cannibalism"*. One of my reasons for writing this book is to explain what is behind passages such as this, in a world where the Church has, as in this instance, preferred to ignore the subject of linking "abiding in Christ" to the Eucharist, partly, I think, for fear of getting involved in difficult explanations, but mainly, I think, because too many of our teachers, scholars and liturgists do not understand it themselves. Indeed, how can they, if they do not really even accept the divinity of Christ in the first place?

describe Him as being *(only)* "the firstborn of…*creation."* If today's clergy can be so uncritical, I fear for the theological understanding of future generations as they become further and further removed from the original truth. I hope that this book will make both clergy and lay people *think,* and be more articulate about what it is that they really do believe and why, as opposed to being muddled and easily confused about it, so that we may be able to *"transmit the [faith] unimpaired to our posterity."*[74]

Later, in 1997, after I had spent seven years as the incumbent of a parish, and then retired from active ministry, I and another woman were asked to lead a Quiet Day at Christ Church Cathedral, in Victoria, B.C., and the subject of the Quiet Day, suggested by the Dean, not me, was *"Abiding in Christ".* This led me to think even more deeply about this aspect of our faith and its importance. This phrase is sometimes used merely as a cliché for a Christian life, "being a good Christian", but in preparing my talk for the Quiet Day I began to see more deeply how it was something that St. Paul and St. John took very seriously, how it ties in with the doctrine of the Atonement, and how it should infuse all of Christian life: how it *makes sense* of our religion!

I also encountered, both before and after ordination, the effects of the "charismatic renewal" of the last thirty to forty years, and, seeing both some of the benefits, and some of the abuses, arising from it, I have come to see much more clearly that to be "Spirit-filled", as some people so glibly claim to be, means being filled literally with the *Spirit of God,* the Spirit of Christ, as in "abiding in Christ", which is why it is so important to remember that God is Trinity, and the Holy Spirit is not to be thought of as somehow different or separate from Christ; which is why the long-forgotten concept of "abiding *in Christ"* needs so desperately to be restated today. Hence this book.

---

74   *Solemn Declaration of 1893* to be found on page viii of the Canadian *Book of Common Prayer*

CHAPTER 2

Modern objections to the Christian faith

People have complained to me that "in the old days" the Church (speaking generically) expected people to accept the faith without question: but this does not work today. People today expect answers or reasonable explanations: and, if they cannot get them in the organized churches, they either join sects based on emotional assurances of salvation, without necessarily any rational thought, or leave the Church altogether. "Blind obedience" no longer works in today's world.

Which brings me to my main reasons for writing this book: first, to try to reach those who have unanswered questions and become estranged from the Church, and bring them back to the communion of the faithful, and, secondly, to bring to the forefront of theological discussion the difficulties that have caused so many problems, so that maybe the churches can start to work together to resolve them.

A well-known journalist wrote of the Founding Fathers of America, that:

> for them, the old-time Christianity *which worshipped a fiercely jealous and basically humanoid God who took a close interest in human sexual practices* was a political danger, open to manipulation by cynical demagogues... a suitable religion for women, children and slaves... [75] (italics mine).

---

75   Gwynne Dyer, ("a London-based independent journalist whose articles are published in 45 countries"). *"The nation chosen by God."* *The Times Columnist,* Victoria, B.C., September 3, 2000

This concept is at such variance with the New Testament teaching of the concept of a *God who is Love* that one has to ask how subsequent Christian teaching could have deteriorated to the point where God could ever be thought of in such a way. I think that, in such circumstances, the world needs to be reminded again of the Christian understanding of God *as being Love Itself.* This is not a sentimental statement but is one that raises questions about much of human thinking where this fundamental attribute of God sometimes seems to have been glossed over or forgotten: by Christianity, those who have lapsed from the faith, and by the world at large.

I think it is *because* "the Church" (in its generic sense) has for centuries strayed from what I believe *should always have been* its basic teaching (union with God through Christ), thinking more of "rewards and punishments" [76] and being "saved" from "hell", thinking of God more as a vengeful Judge than as a Loving Father, and completely misunderstanding that the Atonement is about our being brought to *union with God through Christ,* that some modern scholars are now questioning the whole basis of Christianity; but what I see them as doing, in actual fact, is "shooting down" *a mere caricature,* a mistaken understanding, of it, that some people have mistakenly come to regard as *being* the traditional faith, when it should never have been taken to be the fullness of the faith in the first place, so that what is being attacked or questioned is not really true Christianity at all. [77]

The result of all this is a situation where many people are questioning *"the divinity of Christ"* without really appearing to understand the ramifications of their position. This is not an abstract question, but one that goes to the heart of the faith, which is *union with God through Christ.*

And if God is love, and Trinity, *it means being caught up into the love that is at the heart of God.* [78]

Who would not want that, if we only understood that that

---

76   e.g., *"The Faith of Damasus"* (see Glossary)

77   e.g., *the Jesus Seminar* (see *Jesus at 2000,* edited by Marcus J. Borg.   Boulder, Colo-
      rado: Westview Press, 1997).   See also my response to Bishop Spong's "theses".

78   See the chapter on the Atonement, particularly the quotations from Moltmann, Kasper
      and Rahner,

is what is being offered to us, that *that* is what "salvation" really means?

However, the trouble is that ordinary people, looking for answers to their questions, read some of these modern books questioning the faith, and, not being able to distinguish reasonable criticism of historical situations and arguments, on the one hand, from apparent denial of the faith itself, on the other, are still left with lack of understanding of what the Christian faith is really all about.

Bishop John Spong has gone as far as to say (italics mine):

> Theism, as a way of defining God, is dead...A new way to speak of God must be found. Since God can no longer be conceived in theistic terms, it becomes *nonsensical* to seek to understand Jesus *as the incarnation of the theistic deity. So the Christology of the ages is bankrupt.* [79]

My response to this is contained in this whole book!

I have mentioned my concern about our new liturgies downplaying the idea of the divinity of Christ, which I believe is absolutely crucial for any understanding of our faith. For example, the lectionary used in the Canadian Anglican *Book of Alternative Services* omitted from the lectionary of Bible readings at Sunday church services the passage about Christ being "the image of the invisible God", presumably on the grounds that some scholars have believed it to be a later interpolation ("because St. Paul would not have said that about Jesus"). [80]

I have been at pains to point out that *such an argument is not consistent with the rest of his writings or the theme of the New Testament itself.*

While lectionaries have always had their strong points and their weak points, I am only raising this particular issue here because it gives me an example of how easy it is for assumptions to be made that ought to be challenged, but are sometimes in danger of *not* always

---

79   John Shelby Spong: see Internet at http://www.dioceseofnewark.org.jsspong/reform. html (see appendix II)

80   see the section on Romans 9:5 in the chapter on the Divinity of Christ regarding the authorship of Colossians 1:15-20, and the discussion in the previous chapter as well of its treatment in the *Book of Alternative Services*

being challenged as they should be (although this particular incident has now been rectified in the "the Revised Common Lectionary", the Lectionary now used by all the churches), and of how necessary it is for the Church at large properly to understand the faith, and so be able to pass it on to future generations. It is important that *people be aware of this kind of thing,* if and when it happens, and understand *what* is being changed *and why.*

In addition, at the same time as that passage was omitted from the lectionary readings, a verse from it was put into one of the Eucharistic Prayers in the Canadian (Anglican) *Book of Alternative Services*[81] to the effect that Christ is "the *firstborn* of all *creation*".[82] This is not only *out of context,* in the sense of its being only *half* of an equation of which the other, equally important, half is omitted, (Christ being *both* human *and divine, both* the *image of the invisible God and, at the same time,* the first-born of all creation), but I believe it is also dangerous, in that it distorts and mis-portrays Biblical teaching, (literally here, since it is a case of material being taken out of context), again without ordinary people being aware of what is happening.

Instead of dealing openly with apparent anomalies and inconsistencies in inherited documents, such as, for example, the Creed commonly known as "The Creed of Saint Athanasius," or writing about them as I am doing, to provoke thought and discussion about them, there has been a tendency just to give them less exposure, so that future generations for the most part will never be led to think about the truths which they might have been found to contain. I have found this Creed, though often misunderstood, and needing clarification, to have much truth in it with regard to the Trinity, and I try to show that it *does* make sense, if properly understood.

So, to portray both the faith and the historical distortions of it, in order to put matters right, so that people may be able to accept their faith again, is part of the purpose of this book. I have set out, in the section on the Good Shepherd, the belief that *God Himself* wants

---

81   *The* [Anglican] *Book of Alternative Services,* Eucharistic Prayer #3, p.200; also used in Funeral Service, p. 583

82   an example of words being used *"just because they are in the Bible" without regard for context;* and it is also illogical: without a connotation of divinity, why would Jesus of Nazareth be the senior member of the created order?

His lost sheep found and "fed": so I believe, on that score alone, this book is needed. I have been to too many homes where the big family Bible was proudly displayed on the coffee table but had obviously never been read.

I felt it necessary in this book to address the full gamut of issues that people raise, from the basic questions of "is there a God, and what is He like, and why do bad things happen if God is both loving and all-powerful", "why doesn't He always answer prayer the way we want Him to", to the divinity of Christ and the doctrine of the Trinity, and problems arising from questions of doctrine that have had a major effect on such people's attitude to the divine, culminating in questions about the Atonement, such as why did Jesus *have to die* to reconcile us to God? *What does that say about the nature of God?*

I believe that if I had been where I am now, when my grandmother died, I could have helped to rescue her from her estrangement from the Church. I have watched friends with baptized children, where both children and grandchildren have now strayed from their Christian heritage to the point of now knowing nothing about the faith, and I have been unable to help them. I have wanted to produce a book which they might find easy to read, in order to make them think, and start them on the journey back to God: a book that we could discuss, and, in doing so, in response to the reactions it aroused, uncover what each person's problems really were and try to deal with them as I believe God would wish us to do.

I am suggesting that Christian Education would be more effective if *children* were taught to *worship,* instead of being sent to Sunday School, and if *adults* were given more advanced teaching at an age when they were able to comprehend the depth of it. There are good Bible studies and books available for adults, but Christian Education for adults necessarily targets those who are already interested in learning more, and who already have a basic understanding of the faith. Theological books at any depth are almost always written, in scholarly, often technical language, with an assumption that their readers already have some understanding of the issues being discussed. It is hoped that this book will reach those who, somewhere along the line, have found themselves *not* in the Church, not involved in adult Bible

Study, and who have somehow found themselves left without answers or the incentive for further study.

It is written, too, for those who *are* in the Church but who are at a loss to come up with valid arguments about the reasonableness of the faith to convince loved ones who have unanswered questions. It is my hope, also, that people from other religions will be reminded that God is love, and will reflect *not only* on the fact that Christianity's belief in the God of Love means that it should be treated with respect for the great religion it is, but that *any other understanding of God has to be unworthy of His greatness.*

Although my main purpose was to present Christianity to them as a living and reasonable faith, I have had to touch on briefly what I see as distortions of it that sometimes occur in both the "liberal" and "fundamentalist" camps, of Christianity: because one cannot "explain" Christianity without differentiating between these widely varying points of view.

I should perhaps make it clear that I am not setting out to oppose any one group of theologians, either "liberal" or "fundamentalist". Perhaps it might be said that I have been setting out to find a middle way between two extremes of thought, to find a compromise that satisfies *me,* and, where I disagree with either of them, to explain *why.*

Basically, I could sum up my theology as being traditional and orthodox, particularly in the fact that, in spite of modern trends of scholarship, I do believe in the divinity of Christ, and the truth of most of the Gospel! Yet I also recognize that Christians themselves have sometimes trampled over and disfigured the Truth by well-meaning simplicities, or even downright perversions of it which should have been corrected long ago, and enthusiasm for such views has done so much more harm than good that these obstacles to the faith need to be recognized and dealt with.

Bishop Spong has set out in *Twelve Theses* what he sees as the main popular misconceptions of the Christian faith, which I think have arisen because of the problems mentioned above, and because over-simplistic literal fundamentalism can sometimes arouse extreme scepticism in the outside world, and make matters worse, as he clearly illustrates. These *Twelve Theses,* and my responses, which in fact the rest of this book addresses as well, are set out in the next chapter.

Bishop Spong demonstrates the reality of some of the dissatisfaction and frustration existing in the world today with regard to the Christian faith, which I think have, in the main, been caused by two facts: one is the tendency of human beings, especially some fundamentalists but also others, to over-simplify complex questions, to the point of making them all the more incomprehensible, if not nonsensical, so that rational explanations are now urgently needed; and the other is that, during the course of history, mistakes have sometimes gone uncorrected, and Christians have tended not to scrutinize very carefully some of the ideas that they have inherited, taking given propositions "as a matter of faith" without critical thought. Those who do criticize, often quite rightly, can, however, also end up by "throwing the baby out with the bath water".

I believe that, early in its history, the Church moved away from the understanding of "perishing" contained in much of the New Testament, as it began to concentrate more on what could be called the "negative" side of the Atonement—*rescue from sin and resulting punishment* [83]— rather than *love and life in God*, which could be called the "positive" side, e.g.,

> He died to bring us to God (1 Peter iii 18). The determinative conception is the intention that *we should know God and enjoy Him for ever* [84]

This perhaps unconscious emphasis on sin and punishment, rather than *love and life*, has permeated Church history for centuries, as I describe in the Chapter on the Atonement. I believe that Christ's death and Resurrection was not *just* about the forgiveness of our sins; it was enable us to come to God, to live in *the Divine Life and Love*, by abiding in Christ: that that is really what the Atonement is all

---

83   In a book which I would otherwise thoroughly agree with, Claude Beaufort Moss writes, in *The Christian Faith: An Introduction to Dogmatic Theology* (London: S.P.C.K., 1954), p.120: "For man as he is, *death is a punishment*". I believe that the explanation I give of this is equally true and means the same thing (although it may perhaps be more of a *"consequence"* of man's fallen nature than actual *punishment* for it), but I have tried to explain it in a rational way that does not arouse questions from the unchurched, especially when dealing with the death of the innocent, and the isssue of "original sin".

84   Vincent Taylor. *The Atonement in New Testament Teaching*. London: The Epworth Press, 1940, p.179

about. We need to think *more* about union with God, in this life and in the next, because this is what our faith is all about, and for this we need to understand that *love is crucial, because God is Love.* But this understanding of the Atonement, and thus of the faith itself, became distorted by the popular belief, current at the time, that everyone would live for ever anyway, so that the significance of Christ's *"victory"* over *"death"* (in which *we share, if* we are *"in Him"*) became blurred from very early on; and then in the Middle Ages the other component of the Atonement equation, Christ's victory over *"sin and evil"* became equally blurred, because of obsessions with punishment and retribution, and dealings with the Devil, that the modern world has now rejected or discarded, without, however, putting what I believe to be the original understanding of the Atonement back in its place.

I think that it is largely because of mediaeval misunderstandings of the Atonement that Jesus has come to be seen as some sort of third party, apart from God, detracting from the idea of God as Trinity; and, when the modern world rejected the idea of God requiring some sort of a mediaeval "whipping boy", it rejected at the same time what it *thought* Christianity represented, not realizing that this was a distortion of it: that, in effect, *God Himself, in the person of Jesus,* was somehow involved in bringing the world to Himself,[85] the original understanding of the Atonement: which is, as well, the original understanding of the faith itself, which we need to recover in this modern world.

A major problem for the Christian Church today is the fact that the Bible has been so misused and misunderstood over the years that many people have understandably lost confidence in it—not to mention the problems that have arisen in the course of history from misperceptions of what the Christian faith really is. People have gone from one extreme to another: some taking everything in the Bible so literally, without regard to common sense or historical accuracy, that others, in reaction to this, go to the opposite extreme, and think that, if they can prove some error in this so-called infallible authority, then Christianity cannot exist at all. It is not only a matter of the written record of what Jesus did or did not say: Jesus has been *experienced* by countless millions over the centuries, and the faith thus handed down does not depend for its authenticity *only* on words on paper.

---

85   2 Corinthians 5:19 : "In Christ, God was reconciling the world to Himself"

I think we need to re-state the underlying themes in the Bible about *the nature of God being love;* and the fact that the Bible, taken as a whole, does attest to God as Trinity, and can still be a vehicle through which God can speak to His people about *"the things concerning Himself.*[86]*"* Of course modern Biblical scholarship must be taken seriously, and the human element in the Scripture recognized, but my understanding of the underlying themes of the Bible does not conflict with that. If one draws from the spirit of the Bible as a whole, without being too literal or legalistic, or put off by what, in many cases, is just an ancient record of a primitive people struggling to learn more about God, one can still be nourished by it spiritually.

And, because God is love, we need to restate the fact that *the nature of God* is love; and I would comment here that, when I set out my belief that good and loving people from other great world religions may well come to God at the end of time, in spite of traditional Christian teaching to the contrary, I think the "test", if one can call it that, will be not so much what our "religion" is, but *do we know how to love* (something which all religions have often failed in). *Will we recognize the God of love when we see Him?* Will there be love in our hearts to connect with the love in His?

This is the message that Christians are supposed to proclaim to the world, and show in their living, about the salvation offered to us by the God of Love: that "eternal life," free from this world's pain, is God's greatest gift to us, but it is only when wickedness and hate have been purged from our existence that we find our home for ever with the God who is Love. That is what I understand is meant by the idea of our *sharing in* Christ's death and Resurrection.

---

86   Luke 24:27: [Jesus, on the road to Emmaus after the Resurrection] *"beginning with Moses and all the prophets…interpreted to them in all the scriptures the things concerning himself."* This has always been the basic Christian understanding of the role of the Scriptures in illuminating the Christian faith.

CHAPTER 3

Bishop Spong's Twelve Theses,
and my response

Theism, as a way of defining God, is dead. So most theological God-talk is today meaningless. A new way to speak of God must be found.

Inasmuch as I have defined God as Love, this may be the new way to speak of God that Dr. Spong is thinking of. If not, I can only refer him to my book, in particular the chapter on "If there is a God, what is He like?" and my whole theory of the Atonement which does, to me at least, make sense of the old-fashioned theories.

2. Since God can no longer be conceived in theistic terms, it becomes nonsensical to seek to understand Jesus as the incarnation of the theistic deity. So the Christology of the ages is bankrupt.

I have defined Christ as Divine Love revealed on earth, and explained my belief that, as St. Paul said, "in Christ [Divine Love revealed on earth]—God was reconciling the world to Himself". I do not think the Christology of the ages is bankrupt if thought of in this way.

3. The Biblical story of the perfect and finished creation from which human beings fell into sin is pre-Darwinian mythology and post-Darwinian nonsense.

I think that, as the Epistle of Peter states, the early Church sometimes misunderstood what St. Paul meant, and that a particular example may be 1 Corinthians 15:21-22 (in addition to Paul's arguments about faith and works); and that physical death is not, in itself, *a punishment* ("for the sin of *Adam*"), but something built into the creation of the world for the reasons I give, which seem to me to make sense: "in [the flesh] all *die* [it is an inevitable result of being human], but *in Christ* [in the resurrection *in Him* which brings us into *union with the eternal God,* after physical death] shall all be made alive".

It is the eternal death of those who refuse ever to be reconciled with God that is, I think, what St. Paul is talking about when he says, for example, that "the wages of sin are *death";* but the Church developed theories about *"original sin"* derived from the story of Adam and Eve which is probably what Bishop Spong is reacting to—see Glossary: and my explanation of human nature and sin in this book.

4. The virgin birth, understood as literal biology, makes Christ's divinity, as traditionally understood, impossible.

I believe in the virgin birth myself, but I have not interested myself in St. Mary's "literal biology". I do not think that Christ's divinity, His being the Second Person of the Trinity, depends on how He was conceived as a human being.

5. The miracle stories of the New Testament can no longer be interpreted in a post-Newtonian world as supernatural events performed by an incarnate deity.

You would be surprised at what God can do when He wants to! But I have dealt with the possibility that some minor miracles may have been later exaggerations by the faithful, for example, the money in the mouth of the fish; but I have stated adamantly my belief that the main miracles, for example, the many miracles of healing, the turning of water into wine, and the Feeding of the Five Thousand, which were all symbolic of the fact of the actual presence of God, and the Resurrection itself, were miracles attested to by countless people, which I believe did in fact take place.

6. The view of the cross as the sacrifice for the sins of the world is a barbarian idea [sic] based on primitive concepts of God and must be dismissed.

I think Bishop Spong may be reacting to a distortion of Christian teaching, which sometimes arises when people over-emphasize Christ's *physical* suffering, as if no one else on earth had ever suffered similarly, as if this somehow "proved" God's love for us, as if this somehow *"proved"* that we are forgiven.

(Such people, in their emphasis on Christ's *physical* suffering, though it needs to be appreciated, appear to overlook the fact that it was the *spiritual* aspect of the Crucifixion that was unique. The *physical* suffering involved in a crucifixion was known to, and had been endured by, many, but *the spiritual battle which Jesus fought on the Cross* was unique in the history of the world— see the Chapter on the Atonement.)

I sometimes think that people with psychological problems arising from their own sense of guilt equate Christ's *physical* suffering with their own forgiveness, as if the more brutally He suffered the more we can feel forgiven. The result is that they dwell the more on the physical pain and suffering of what He endured (forgetting altogether the spiritual side of it), equating that, too, with God's love, in that He "didn't have to" die for us, He didn't have to suffer like that, so that is a measure of God's love for us and of the retribution paid in full for all our guilt.

Other people react by saying they do not believe in capital punishment in the first place even for the worst criminals, let alone the innocent, they do not believe that crucifixion is justified in any situation (and *is God different,* that it takes a *crucifixion* to "satisfy" Him?), and what is the "sin" of six-year old girls that demands crucifixion as "atonement"? As a result, they dismiss the distorted "view of the cross" described above, and, often the Christian faith itself as well.

I have dealt with this in detail in the Chapter on the Atonement, when I describe the problems that have arisen from some of the earlier theories about the Atonement (of which this caricature is one), and give my understanding of what it was all really about. I emphasize that the nature of God is Love, and that Love gave Himself (e.g., Ephesians 5:12, John 10:17-18), so that, as He conquered sin and temptation in His own body, "in the flesh", humanity can now identify itself with Him, to do the same in His strength, and come to God.

If God, in the person of Jesus, could so demonstrate that, in spite of the handicap of a human body, vulnerable to all the temptations with which we are faced, and tortured to death, *He could still love and forgive and remain Himself,* there is now no situation in which we can be overcome by evil if we are *in Christ.* There is also now no situation in which God cannot ask of us that we similarly love and forgive, in His strength, in Him.

And, inasmuch as the Cross is symbolic of ultimate love and self-sacrifice, we can identify ourselves with Christ in His ultimate offering of Himself to God (see the chapter on the Atonement.)

7. Resurrection is an action of God. Jesus was raised into the meaning of God. It therefore cannot be a physical resuscitation occurring inside human history.

I have set out my belief that the whole point of the Resurrection was that when the disciples saw the Risen Lord they saw how humanity and divinity had come together in Him (before that, they had only really seen His humanity), and they realized that this was what St. Paul called "the new creation" in which we can share if we learn to "abide in Him".

8. The story of the Ascension assumed a three-tiered universe and is therefore not capable of being translated into the concepts of a post-Copernican space age.

I think we are guilty of literal thinking here. I do not think of a physical corpse being propelled through space, nor do I believe in a three-tiered universe.

However, I do believe that someone can fade away from our view: film and television producers can produce this effect all the time. I think the Biblical description of "a cloud taking Him up" was just the best description that human beings could come up with in telling how Jesus disappeared from their view, as if He just melted away into the mist, as it were.

9. There is no external, objective, revealed standard writ in scripture or on tablets of stone that will govern our ethical behaviour for all time.

Again, I think the problem is literal thinking, and not just on the fundamentalist side. "Life in the Spirit", "abiding in Christ", identification of ourselves with God through Him, has to entail love, truth, goodness, selflessness, self-sacrifice, and all the spiritual virtues.

I am not getting into the issue of homosexuality. However, I do think we should be concentrating more in terms of the spiritual virtues rather than the desires of the flesh, and the section in the book on St. Paul's teaching about "life in the Spirit" as opposed to "life in the flesh", describes, I believe, a principle that should govern our ethical behaviour always, if we are ever to attain union with God.

10. Prayer cannot be a request made to a theistic deity to act in human history in a particular way.

I think Dr. Spong is reacting to the primitive idea that one can ask God for whatever one wants, and then, if one does not get it, one can be accused by others of "not having enough faith" to accomplish the "miracle" that is prayed for, as if God were a sort of "juke box" that automatically delivered what we ordered: or, if the desired result is not achieved, one may then say that "God does not answer prayers anyway," or even that "there is no God".

Dr. Spong is right, in that God does not work that way. Such a situation is untenable, both for God and for us.

I think he is also right in believing that something is wrong with the mindset that thinks that a whole lot of people praying for an important person will "produce results" because of the volume of prayers being offered up, whereas a poor person with no such connections, having no such benefit, suffers accordingly, in comparison. If this were true, it would mean that God has a less developed sense than we have of what is "fair" and reasonable; that God was guilty of favouritism, or being swayed by pressure. Again, I do not think God works that way. God is quite capable of having pity on someone without our "pulling on His sleeve": He is as kind and intelligent and compassionate as we are, and more so! And we do not, or ought not, to "believe in God" just for what "we can get out of Him"!

It is true that the united will of the whole Church praying for a specific cause in the furtherance of God's will (which does not often happen with the kind of intensity that got the apostle out of prison in the Book of Acts) can have great effect: but to ask for a benefit for a single person because that person is well known and sympathised with does not fall into that category. In fact, the opposite is true: if the well-known person cannot take a negative answer to his prayer without railing against God, something more is necessary for his spiritual well-being than the immediate miracle asked for.

It should be noted that, even though St. Peter was released from prison on that occasion, in order to carry on the work of shepherding the very young Church at the crucial time of its early formation, he still suffered eventually the fate of being crucified for his faith; his rescue from prison on that early occasion was not a case of "God doing a favour for a friend" simply because "someone prayed hard or well enough" —although it did serve to give the young Church a salutary shock by such a demonstration of God's power.

St. Peter was not delivered from his eventual cruel death by crucifixion: a death which was a lasting witness to others of the strength and power of his faith. Similarly, although the disciples who were in the boat with Jesus at the time when He stilled the storm were indeed saved from drowning on that occasion, most of them died martyrs' deaths in the end.

This is not to deny the very real efficacy of prayer, or to say that one should not pray for help and deliverance, or rely ceaselessly on God at all times: but it is to say that one's so-called "faith" cannot be judged, by oneself or others, in such a facile way that it can be measured by "whether or not one always gets one's prayers answered".

The same applies, in reverse, to miraculous preservation when it does occur: one may indeed thank God for one's own deliverance, if and when appropriate, but not in such a way as to imply, hurtfully and offensively, that the unfortunate ones who were not similarly blessed were less righteous or had obviously found less favour in God's sight. It is this kind of simplistic, and, indeed, selfish and objectionable, enthusiasm, which I think has contributed to Bishop Spong's pessimism on the subject of prayer.

In addition, as I tried to explain in my book, in both the chapter on healing, and the section on prayer in the chapter on Love, and, in particular, writing of Christ's prayer in the Garden of Gethsemane, where His human prayer was that He might be spared the agony of the Crucifixion, (but God's overall agenda was the redemption of the world, which Christ realized took precedence over His own human wish to be spared the ordeal ahead)—God sometimes has other priorities than our own.

On the other hand, I do believe that God works in human history, but that He does this within the limitations which He has imposed on the creation. I mentioned, for example, in connection with the Holocaust, that, although God allowed for the working-out of human free-will in the immediate present (instead of suspending everything and thus immediately bringing the world to an end for ever as the consequence of such a decision), even so, the fact remains that Hitler's regime *was* defeated in the end.

I believe that God works under the constrictions imposed by His long-term will as opposed to our short-term desires, as I describe in the book. But I do believe that He has our ultimate well-being at heart, in the long term, and that we must continue to trust Him.

Whereas for Christ the issue was being saved from crucifixion versus the redemption of the world, for us it can sometimes be the long-term benefit that our faith shines more strongly if we can still believe and trust in God even if disaster happens to us, which, in turn, enables us to help others and do God's will in working with them (see the chapter on Death and Dying, about my husband's death, when I told that young couple that "if my world fell apart tomorrow, I hoped I would still have faith in God," and my husband had his fatal stroke the next day and my world *did* fall apart—and I still have faith).

And I also write of how we can find union with Christ even in suffering: a much deeper aspect of the faith than just getting "our prayers answered" in the way we want them to be at the time. It is a juvenile idea of prayer that is being criticized: really attaining union with Christ through "abiding in Him" is much more profound, if we can achieve it.

11. The hope for life after death must be separated forever from the behaviour control mentality of reward and punishment. The Church must abandon, therefore, its reliance on guilt as a motivator of behaviour.

It will be seen that my whole book is about *life in God*, as opposed to eternal punishment, the former being "eternal life", and the latter being *not* an eternity of *being punished* but "perishing", "eternal death", a destiny that is final and for ever; and that I am criticising the rewards-

and-punishment mentality summarized in "the Faith of Damasus," [87] saying that for more than a millennium and a half Christianity has put its emphasis in the wrong place, and the idea of abiding in Christ, with the concomitant need to live a life of love, has faded with time.

On the other hand, while I agree that the Church cannot rely on "guilt as a motivator of behaviour", (a primitive idea reflected in the Faith of Damasus but not consonant with a life motivated by love of God and neighbour—my whole book is about Love, not selfish thought for ensuring one's own wellbeing), I think that the call to live in the Spirit and not in the flesh, if one wants to abide in Christ and thus come to God (see the section on St. Paul and "flesh" and "spirit") is a warning that must be heeded.

It is not simply a question of sin and guilt and punishment and forgiveness, or, for that matter, heaven as a reward or hell as a punishment: it is a question of union with Christ, now and into eternity—or, if it must be, in the end, perishing altogether.

12. All human beings bear God's image and must be respected for what each person is. Therefore, no external description of one's being, whether based on race, ethnicity, gender or sexual orientation, can properly be used as the basis for either rejection or discrimination.

The immediate question here is what does Bishop Spong mean by "bearing God's image", ("being made in the image of God") ? Because, if, in his first Thesis he rejects the traditional thinking about God, such a statement is an illogical premise to start with.

With regard to the thesis itself, I do not think anyone could rightly disagree with this statement. Yet there is a difference between not discriminating between people, *as people,* on the one hand, and, on the other, positively and actively advocating and encouraging patterns of behaviour that one disagrees with.

And, if he is talking about homosexuality, I would say that the dangers posed by the temptations of "life in the flesh" and giving in to "the lust of the world" apply to heterosexual and homosexual alike.

---

87   See Glossary

CHAPTER 4

Belief in the existence of God: if there is a God, what is He like?

I believe that Christianity—the real thing—is not what some of its adherents have led the world to believe it is, but is the most reasonable and probable of all religions.

What other religion not only worships the Power that created us, but believes that that Power knows, from firsthand experience, what it is to live, and suffer, and die, and still to forgive and go on loving? As I see it, "God" would not be completely "God" if the human dimension was missing from His experience and understanding. The origin of our being might be a creative force, a divine intelligence, a glorious being, a judgmental power, a source of rewards and punishments, perhaps, but what could be greater than Love that forgives and goes on loving and *understands,* a Love that can identify with us in suffering and in love, and with whom we can find the beginnings of union while still on this earth?

People have asked how God could possibly "have time to spare" in His great universe to think about us and our comparatively small concerns, let alone really care about us each one of us individually. If He really is *Love,* how is it that there is so much suffering in the world? How can He be both Almighty and just? And it has not helped that the history of the Christian church has so often seemed to be the opposite of love: the world has not seen the love of God in it, as Jesus prayed it would, on the night before He died.[88] But I believe that, whatever the shortcomings and failures of human institutions may be, God is still

---

88   John 17:20-23

there for us, and still loves us. The faith, if properly conveyed, is still believable: but it needs the language and ideas of the Bible as a means of explaining it.

If there is a God....

How would you envisage God?

I do believe that there is an intelligence behind the universe whose existence we can deduce by looking at some of the wonders of nature, from the wings of a butterfly to the peaks of the mountains, from the stars in the sky to the roar of the sea, by listening to music, by admiring love and courage and goodness, by seeing how scientific and mathematical principles hold the world together, and so on. I was looking at bluebells the other day, and the different shades of blue caused by sunlight dancing through the shadows cast by overhead leaves, and thinking of the intelligence that had even imagined those colours in the first place, and brought such beauty into being. Not only is there physical beauty, in the colour and smell of a red rose, or the wings of a butterfly, or the fur of a small animal, or the eyes of a child, but there are the virtues of love and courage and truth and integrity, which we cannot see, but, if we admit their existence, we have to ask where they come from. We did not invent them for ourselves, although some of us may exemplify them in our living.

It has been claimed that there are patterns and rhythms in mathematics that could not be the result of pure chance: any more than the putting together of certain notes of music in a symphony could just "happen" to result in beautiful music quite by chance. When one looks at all the evidence put together, on a cumulative basis, this universe could not just have "arrived" all on its own by blind chance. When I drive in my car on the highway, I take it for granted that it is not just coincidence that I can fit into a car, and cars are available for me to buy and drive at my convenience; that my car "works", and that there is a highway to drive on, to take me where I want to go. I do not indulge in endless speculation as to how it might all have come together out of nowhere, and think "isn't it convenient that I can travel this way?" I know that human minds designed and made the car for driving, just as human engineering and experience designed and made the roads: the drivers and the cars and the highways were all meant to be used together for a joint purpose. Can we think differently about such a vast and complex universe as we find ourselves inhabiting?

I believe that there is a God who created the universe. The Christians inherited from the Jews the tradition of "the One Great God who had created the universe" who was yet knowable in some way by His people: and, indeed, they had improved on it, by claiming that, through Christ, it was possible to know this Great God in a new, and more intimate way, in this present life—something that was, and still is, completely unique in the history of the world.

This Christian offspring of the Jewish faith originated at a time when people as civilized as the Greeks and Romans were still "worshipping" a variety of gods and goddesses whose morals were not much more than their worshippers'—religions that no one takes seriously any more. Most other religions today accept that "God" must be the one creator of the universe, however they define that "God". This does not alter the fact that *none of them* have the Christian understanding of a God who knows, *from personal experience,* what it is like to live as a human being, to know the human emotions of pain and temptation, as well as love and happiness, and to suffer and to die.

Could we really worship, in the truest sense, a God "up there", or wherever God is, if we human beings knew more about living and dying than He did? Could we truly worship a God who knows less about "life" than we do? To my mind "the Great God of the Universe" would be incomplete in some way without the experience of the Incarnation (God being part of the human scene at some time and place). If, by the very definition of "God" it is not possible for us to be superior to Him in anything; if God, by definition, is greater than we are; then it must follow that God has shared our human life, in some way, at some time, and knows as much about it as we do. (And no other candidate has ever had a claim equal to that of Jesus of Nazareth—who, incidentally, could not be called "a good man" or "a great prophet" if he was not who He said He was.)

It seems to me that, quite apart from the Christian experience of knowing the Risen Christ for oneself, which has been vouched for, again and again, by many people, over many generations, and in many lands, for many centuries, it surely must be *an intellectual "given"* that somehow, at some time, God must have entered, encountered, and experienced, human history to be God. Would any other kind of "God" be worth worshipping?

In addition, would such a God have the moral right to ask me to forgive an injury done to me, if He had never been injured Himself? He might have the right of force, of "being God", to make us obey Him, but *ethically* would He have the right to tell us to do something which He had never done Himself at the personal, human, level? No other religion that the world has ever known has had the compelling power of a Crucified God,[89] telling us to love one another, and forgive our enemies, just as He Himself has loved and forgiven, and, moreover offering to help us to do this, through union with Him, through the power of His Spirit.

One of my parishioners once asked me: "If the Trinity came to dinner, how many place settings would you lay at the table?" I replied "one—for Jesus". I said that the whole of the Godhead was too great to be known to us, which was a reason for the Incarnation: but, although Jesus appears to us in a form which we can recognize, *in Him the whole of the Trinity is represented, and, where He is, God is also.* [90]

I believe that the Incarnation (God coming into the world in human flesh) is reasonable from the point of view of *what kind of a God do we believe in.* I believe in a God who knows all that there is to know about human life and suffering, and can still rise above it: and, Who, moreover, has made it possible for us to do likewise, in Christ. But the Incarnation was logical and reasonable from the human point of view, too. If God is so great, that He could create the universe and all that is in it, and beyond it, and all that flows in it and through it, and is the ultimate to be worshipped, as I think all the major religions would agree, then, without some revelation of Himself, He would be too great to come within our human knowing. While we might worship Him, we could hardly relate to Him as a person and *love* Him.

If God is love, and loves us and wants that love to be reciprocated—

---

89   The expression *"The Crucified God"* is also the title of a book by Jurgen Moltmann: *The Crucified God,* Munich: Christian Kaiser Verlag, 2nd edition 1973; translated from the German by R.A. Wilson and John Bowden; c. SCM Press Ltd., London, 1974.

90   John 14:7-10: [Jesus said] "If you had known me, you would have known my Father also; henceforth you know him *and have seen him...He who has seen me has seen the Father...I am in the Father and the Father in me"*

which presumably would be the case, if He were the source of all love and goodness—then He would have to make Himself known to us in some way which we could comprehend and relate to. The Christian belief that He came into the world in a given time and place in history, to show us what God is like, and to enable us to go on to relating to Him, through His Holy Spirit, and live in love with Him and with each other, is the only one that satisfies this argument also. Does not "Love" in itself necessitate some way of showing itself and conveying that love? (Another argument for the Incarnation! I *said* that the Christian faith, to my mind, is the most logical of any that the world has ever known.)

In trying to understand the Trinity, as best we can, we need to differentiate in our minds between the great and glorious Godhead which is beyond our reach or understanding, on the one hand, and the three Persons of that Trinity, on the other. The Almighty and Everlasting God, Who in His glory is almost unknowable, has become revealed to us through the three Persons of the Trinity, (the Father, Son, and Holy Spirit), Who God in His love has enabled us to come to know through His revelation to us in Christ. [91] I will describe in more detail as I go on my understanding of God as Trinity (an understanding implicit in the fact that part of God took on human form on earth). However, we must also hold onto the fact that the *nature* of God is One. We have to avoid the trap of dividing "God", in our minds, into three different people, in the sense that we see *one as having a different nature from the others,* as if "Jesus" talked about "love" and "God" created the AIDS virus. It is all too easy to imagine three "gods" in images of our own making. In that sense we do have to believe that "the Lord our God is One Lord". [92] We are dealing, after all, with a great paradox—at one and the same time both approaching the edge of Mystery and being welcomed into the heart of God.

So how do we come to find and know Him? One can begin by deducing that "spirit" and "intelligence" created beauty, music and logic, designed mathematical principles, and "generated" love and

---

91   Colossians 1:15: "He is the image [i.e., the manifestation] of the invisible God", i.e., *the invisible God made visible in Him;* and 1 John 1:1-2: "the word of life…was made manifest, and we saw it"

92   Deuteronomy 6:4

truth and goodness, but then we need to move on to draw closer to Him than that.

......What is He like?

I believe that God is love [93], and that evil, while it may grow like a cancer, once it gets started, was not caused or created in any way by God, and is not a "rival power", in the sense of the dualistic tradition of "God versus the devil". I believe that evil is very real, and can try to destroy us spiritually, as it tried to destroy God, by trying to undermine and break Love's power to love, when Jesus was on the Cross, which I will talk about more in the chapter on the Atonement; but, although evil exists and is very real and terrible, it could not break God, and Christ is our protection from its power, and so it cannot really be visualized in the old mediaeval way of "the Devil" bargaining with God almost as if it were an equal power. I think that evil in itself stems from the absence of goodness and love, and grows and flourishes where God is not. That is why I believe that, if we and the rest of creation were always fulfilling God's plans, and functioning as He intended us to do, there would be no evil: and that that will be the situation at the end of time when His Kingdom finally comes in power. In the meantime, trouble comes to us in this life when we move away from "how things were meant to be", (although sometimes people suffer for what is not their fault, but what is caused by the situation in which they find themselves—I will talk about that a little later); but, by and large, with some exceptions, that is the price we human beings have to pay for our God-given freedom of choice, until the time comes when either we willingly align ourselves with the will of God, or He "takes over" at the end of time, and brings to an end all suffering and evil, and all that is not holy, good and true.

We may pay a price for our freedom to choose, but I believe that God also pays another price Himself at the same time, in His own suffering: not only once, historically, on the Cross, but all the time, in the suffering of every creature as He shares its pain and grief. I think I can fairly make that claim, otherwise He would not be Love.

And if God is not love, where did goodness and kindness and other such virtues come from in the first place? Evil can be seen as

---

93   1 John 4:16

coming from the absence of goodness and love, but love in its strength is more than the mere absence of evil: so one has to deduce that love comes from God, the ultimate Creator.

Furthermore, if the price of our free-will, the freedom to choose and decide for ourselves, and fail sometimes, and grow, is that "man is born to trouble as the sparks fly upwards" [94], to the point where many people say "how can God allow it?", I would respond that God, through the Incarnation, through His revelation of Himself and His love, has "met us half-way", as it were. Having given us the priceless gift of free-will and the opportunity to grow through the experience of living, He is still ready to be with us, and go "through the valley of the shadow" with us, if necessary: we have that assurance that He loves us and we are not alone. [95]

"Is God a Person or pure spirit?"

One of the questions that I have been asked is: "Is God pure invisible spirit, or can He be recognized as a Person, i.e., *does He have some kind of a body?*"

We have inherited traditions of thought that have been influenced by the tradition of Greek philosophy, which tended to move people's thinking away from the Jewish idea of "God with His people" to an idea of God as being remote and changeless, and in His absolute purity far removed from human contact. [96] Traces of this philosophy are to be found in *Article I* of the *Thirty-nine Articles* of the Church of England, which states that

> There is but one living and true God, everlasting, *without body, parts, or passions;* of infinite power, wisdom, and goodness; the Maker, and Preserver of

---

94 Job 5:7

95 Psalm 23:4: "Even though I walk through the valley of the shadow of death...thou art with me"; and Matthew 28:20: "[Jesus said] 'I am with you always, to the close of the age'. "

96 Though E.J. Bicknell states rightly that *"behind it all lies the one immutable purpose and character of God, giving consistency and unity to all that He does."* A *Theological Introduction to the Thirty-nine Articles of the Church of England* by E. J. Bicknell, D.D. with additional references by the Rev. Canon H.J. Carpenter, M.A. London. Longmans, Green and Co., 1919, 1929, 1939,1946, page 37.

all things both visible and invisible. And *in unity of this Godhead there be three Persons, of one substance, power, and eternity;* the Father, the Son, and the Holy Ghost. [97] (italics mine)

The definition is correct, in itself, as far as it goes, in saying that the Godhead is too great to be pinned down, as it were, in any form of understanding that we can put our minds around, but that, *within this Godhead,* there are three Persons, whom we can know as "Father, Son and Holy Spirit". (It might be worth noting that, in the wording of the above paragraph, the part about *"body, parts or passions"* refers to *the Godhead Itself,* rather than specifically to the Persons within that Godhead.)

I believe that the wording of the *Article of Religion* set out above, to the effect that God has *"no body, parts or passions",* has had an unfortunate effect on people's understanding of the nature of God. While correct in one sense, I think it has proved to be very limiting in another. This is an example of how words which may be correct in themselves, in the sense in which they were intended, can impose their own limits on our understanding. I do not think this definition goes far enough in attempting to outline for us something of the nature of God. This may have been done deliberately, because sometimes too fine a definition can be counter-productive and dangerous. However, this precaution, if it was indeed that, may have misfired, because, even though I believe the wording is correct, as far as it goes, I do not think that it addresses some of the problems arising from the tradition from which that *Article* came.

— *".....without body...."*

St. Augustine argued that the Trinity itself was a vehicle for loving and being loved, each Person of the Trinity being the Lover, the Beloved and *Love Itself.* He believed that it makes sense for *Love* to need someone to love, even in the heart of God. And, quite apart from love flowing in the Godhead, surely if that love was to extend to us, it must take on personhood in some way: how can you love something that is completely and eternally formless, invisible and silent?

---

97   *The [Anglican] Book of Common Prayer, 1962, Canada.* p. 699.

I believe that God must be a *Person* (or Persons), as opposed to being just invisible spirit, and *have some form that we can recognize and relate to:* and that there is truth in the Biblical affirmation that in some way we are made in His image.[98] Presumably "in His image" would mean that in body, mind and spirit we have something of affinity with God which we can relate to, as being kindred.[99]

I think it is important that Jesus taught us to think of God as *Father,*[100] and in that He was drawing on Old Testament Scriptures as well—forget the controversies about "Mother" for a moment, I am talking about *parenthood.* This has connotations of being of the same family, as opposed to a being a mere created object. The apostolic teaching is that we are "children of God".[101] We are, as it were, more than a sculpture which a sculptor has chiselled into being; we can relate to God *as His children.*

How do we one day come to see God Our Father, if we can never see invisible spirit? There must surely be some way of knowing Him as a Person, and seeing Him some day, if He is to *be* a Father to us. If we have eyes with which to express love, and arms to hold, and hands to minister to people with, it was God's idea in the first place, and surely He must have comparable ways of showing love and comfort to His people. Can He be less than we are?

We do believe that "God", the Creator of both male and female,

---

98 Genesis 1:27

99 *A Theological Introduction to the Thirty-nine Articles of the Church of England.* E.J. Bicknell, D.D., with additional references by the Rev. Canon H.J. Carpenter, M.A. London. Longmans, Green and Co., 1919,1929, 1939,1946, pages 33-34: "human personality is the highest form of existence within our own experience, and we are obliged to think of God in terms of the highest that we know. However far God's life may excel our own, it cannot fall below it. *The God who created human personality cannot Himself be less than personal... We cannot love or pray to an 'unknowable'....* to a Christian the Incarnation has proved that *human personality is in its measure a mirror of the Divine Personality....If man is made 'in the image of God', the original cannot be wholly unlike the image.* So, then, we speak of God as 'personal ' because that is the loftiest conception of Him that we are able to form. We believe that, though it is inadequate, yet it is not in its measure untrue."

100 Matthew 6:9: Jesus said "Pray then like this: *"Our Father....."*

101 e.g., St. Paul (Romans 8:16-17): "we are children of God", and St. John (1 John 3:1-2): "we are God's children".

from whom both male and female attributes flow, is not in Himself either a male or a female being, but a God who transcends both, and is above and beyond His creation, and that He has the best characteristics of both parents in His dealings with His children, (after all, these characteristics, found in good men and women, come from, and were created by, Him). The Bible supports this understanding in many places. Jesus, however, very definitely had a human body: that was implicit in the Incarnation; and Jesus, both God and Man, is one of the Persons of the Trinity. He took on humanity in His human incarnation, so is it unreasonable to believe that, in some way, if we are to be as *children* to God, we *are* indeed made in His image? [102] The Holy Spirit *is* Spirit, of course, in the sense that God can come to us now in a spiritual form, in many times and places, for us unseen and intangible, but nonetheless He is still very real. I believe that God the Holy Spirit is an equally real participant in the Trinity, one could say *"the very essence of God"*.

But even if God on His throne is spirit, in the sense that He is so far beyond us that we can barely discern Him in all the light and majesty and glory, *if He is also Love,* and a Father to us (in the best sense of the meaning of the word 'father'), presumably one day we *will* see Him as such. In fact, the Biblical teaching of St. John is that we will in fact, one day, *"see Him as He is" and we shall be like Him.* [103] Jesus Himself taught us that we can approach God, in prayer, in the love and intimacy that children ought to be able to expect from their parents, and expect a Father's love and care and protection in return. Surely this would be very difficult if we were just dealing with disembodied spirit! Surely we should be able to seek comfort in the arms of God, if God is love? ("Underneath are the everlasting arms.") [104]

---

102   Genesis 1:27

103   1 John 3:1-2: "See what love the Father has given us, that we should be called children of God; and so we are... Beloved, we are God's children now; it does not yet appear what we shall be, but we know that when he appears we shall be like him, for *we shall see him as he is.*"

104   Deuteronomy 33:27: "The eternal God is your dwelling place, and underneath are the everlasting arms." This could be seen as metaphorical language for something we could not otherwise attempt to describe; but it would seem that, for it to be true in any real sense, to have some real meaning, there must be more to God than just invisible, intangible, spirit.

We do have the assurance that we can relate to Jesus, who shared our human nature and had a human body, the whole point of the Incarnation. He had hands and feet that could be seen and touched [105]—and pierced by nails. It is significant that Isaiah spoke of *God* as "carving us on the palms of his hands." [106]

Although we cannot see Jesus in the physical sense, now, I believe that He does have a spiritual body—with the marks of the nails still in His hands—which we will some day come to see. (That was part of St. Paul's great teaching on the resurrection of the dead: "if there is a physical body, there is also a spiritual body" [107]).

The whole point of the Christian faith is that Christians believe that, though Jesus, we have a unique pathway to God, through the operation of the Holy Spirit in our lives.

I am convinced that many of our problems have arisen because of the difficulty which we human beings can so easily have in distinguishing in our minds between the idea of the Godhead, the great and glorious Trinity, which may indeed be just blazing light, on the one hand, and the *Three Persons* of the Trinity, the Father, Son and Holy Spirit, on the other. Even if the Godhead itself should prove to be just pure blazing light, I think that the *Persons of that Trinity* can reveal Themselves as Persons in a way that we can, or will be able to, recognize and relate to, in some kind of bodily form, even if not in actual human flesh. To put it simplistically, that is why God is Three as well as One.

— "....without...passions": and the understanding of God as "changeless"

Of course God is without "parts and passions" in the sense that the Judeo-Christian God was, from the beginning, completely

---

105   1 John 1:1-2 "That which was from the beginning, which we have heard, which we have seen with our eyes, which we have looked upon, and touched with our hands, concerning the word of life—the life was made manifest and we saw it and testify to it, and proclaim to you the eternal life which was with the Father and was made manifest to us..."

106   Isaiah 49:16: "I have graven you on the palms of my hands"; and John 20:24-28: the disciple Thomas saying "unless I see in his hands the print of the nails..." and the Risen Lord showing His hands and side to Thomas, who then said "My Lord, *and my God*".

107   1 Corinthians 15:44

to be distinguished from the pagan gods and goddesses who were unabashedly sexual creatures. That goes without saying. He is not like the Greek and Roman gods and goddesses who were thought of as some kind of "super human" beings, with many of our human faults and follies. It was the Greek idea, in revulsion against that kind of paganism, that came to think of God as disembodied spirit, so holy and pure that it had to be far removed from humanity in order that the divine was not corrupted by any contact with humanity. It is some of that kind of thinking that I think has had an influence on the *Article* referred to above, and we have inherited many problems from it.

I can think of at least three such problems. I have already referred to the fact that we often fail to distinguish clearly in our minds between the Godhead on the one hand, and the Three Persons of the Trinity, *as Persons,* on the other, which I think has been a major problem over the centuries, and still is; and the question of whether or not God has a recognizable form or *body,* or is *just pure spirit,* which has led me to believe that our understanding of the clear statement in the *Article of Religion* quoted above, that God is "without body, parts or passions," needs to be understood in context.

Another problem arising from the idea, expressed in the *Article of Religion* quoted above, about God having no body, parts or passions, is the implicit issue of *"changelessness"* in the belief that He could never be stirred by any *passion,* or emotion, or feeling, as that would mean that some event in time had an impact on Him, and "changed" Him from what He was before. This too is drawn from the Greek idea of God having to be so far removed from anything of this earth that nothing temporal could ever sully that divine purity, the idea that God was so great that nothing could ever have the power to *"change"* Him.

While it is true that *the eternal nature of God* does not change, this idea that God, changeless in eternity, could not be affected by anything temporal that happened on earth, because that would "change" Him from "what He was before it happened," is, to my mind, a complete denial of the concept of God being Love, and Incarnate in human history, and involved in the lives of His people through the working of the Holy Spirit.[108] It is almost as if what we have derived from this is a non-Trinitarian understanding of God. The words in the *Article* are correct in themselves, but I think that the implications that have been unwittingly derived from them are actually Unitarian or Deist, and this has not helped people to understand the Christian faith. In other words, the implication of that *Article* is that it was not seen to be thinkable that God could have a "history" with us in time. He had to stay unsullied by this world, untouched by anything that might happen in it, unmoved by the sorrows of His people. (That would mean the whole of the Christian idea of *"union with God through Christ"* would be impossible—no wonder people get muddled!) If the "changeless", "without passions", statement stood without any qualification in our thinking, it would mean that our love or joy or grief could never reach Him and we could never share in His.

Such an understanding of God would imply that, if He is stiff, remote, unchanging, unmoved by what happens to His people, and the world He has created, He would not make decisions, or take actions, in the course of history, as that would "change" Him from what He was before. An ultimate extension of this argument is the position taken by people known as Deists. As *The Oxford Dictionary of the Church* puts it, "The chief mark of later Deism was belief in a Creator God whose further Divine intervention in His creation was rejected as derogatory to His omnipotence and unchangeableness." [109]

I think that this "Deist" attitude is much more prevalent than is generally recognized, even among people who sincerely see themselves as Christians. The tradition of God being "pure spirit" and "eternally unchangeable" has lingered so much in the Church that much of the anthropomorphic tradition of the Jewish people—"Emmanuel...

---

108   It is also completely illogical, because, if God never *did* anything except exist, motionless in eternity, for ever, how could He have created the world in the first place? Even if it was billions of years ago, He *did something, He made something happen.* To my mind, our very existence on this planet argues against any such theoretical speculation that God cannot "do" anything because it might "change" Him from what He was before He did it!

109   F.L. Cross, editor, and F.L. Cross and E.A. Livingstone, editors of the revised second edition, of *The Oxford Dictionary of the Christian Church.* Oxford: Oxford University Press, 1958, 1974, 1983, p.388.

means "God [is] with us" [110]— leading up to the Incarnation of God in human history and the indwelling of God's Spirit in His people, has been overshadowed by it. I know that, in my early youth, I thought of God as being far away, transcendent and glorious, even Jesus, as it were, being "on hold", waiting in heaven until the Second Coming; and about the Holy Spirit I thought not at all. How many other people are still in that position?

As I have said, the thinking that we have inherited was that, if God is changeless, outside Time, living in eternity, He could not be affected by any new developments that took place *inside time* (which I think is ridiculous, as He created "time", and could surely enter it if He wished to); but this argument of changelessness, if taken to its logical conclusion, would mean that nothing that happens in time could therefore have any effect on Him: He could not be moved by it, He wouldn't *care*. But then, could He, at the same time, be a God of *Love?* There is a basic contradiction here. And another basic contradiction lies in the fact, that, in spite of the inherited tradition that God is remote and inaccessible, and impervious to what may happen to us here on earth, many people have known from their own personal experience what it is like to feel they have a relationship with "God", and felt, in their prayer, and His response, that He is involved in their lives. This is another example of where "theology" and "practice" seem to part company, and leave many people confused, but I am convinced that this need not be so.

With regard to God having no *"passions"* (implying that He is completely immobile in His eternal changelessness), I would say that I know He loves, and *love is a passion,* in one sense at least; *righteous anger is a passion; and grief is yet another.* You could say they are not *"sinful* passions", which I think was partly what was in the minds of the writers of the Article referred to; but I believe that to love, and to suffer, and to be moved to righteous indignation in the face of acts of evil and cruelty and injustice, are inevitably tied up both with the nature of God Himself, and with God's relating to His creatures in the realm of Time, a theme running through both the Old and New Testaments of the Bible. I do not believe that He can look on this world which we have so abused, and all the creatures who suffer, and not be deeply grieved. I think this whole

---

110   Matthew 1:23, based on Isaiah 7:14

problem arises from our human difficulty in distinguishing between time and eternity, and our lack of faith that God can be, at one and the same time, both changeless in His essential nature *and* affected by what happens to His people in this world of time and space. We try to contain God within the narrow limits of our own minds.

— *"Love" as a "passion"*

God is changeless in the sense that *we can rely on Him never to change His basic nature.* "God *is* Love", [111] someone "whose property [it] is always to have mercy," [112] and so on: but that very love means that He can feel and care. This is where I believe the doctrine of the Incarnation, and the love of God in Christ, really needs to be re-emphasized, and the kind of thinking which we have inherited needs to be qualified in our minds.

I say again—because I think that it is so important—that we need to acknowledge and keep in mind the distinction between the Triune God, on the one hand, and the Three Persons of the Trinity on the other. Above all, I think we must remember that, whether we are speaking of the Godhead or the Son of God, the nature of God is still One. This fatal separation in thinking has been the cause of a great deal of trouble in the history of Christianity, from Marcion rejecting "the God of the Old Testament", in the second century, to people rejecting the "God" of some of the Atonement theories of the Middle Ages, to people having problems with the idea of the divinity of Christ at the present time.

— *Anger as a "passion": the righteous anger of God must surely be a "passion" in the sense that He is moved by it*

Just as I believe that love and grief are passions, so I believe that *anger,* the righteous anger of God, is a passion, at least in the sense that He feels it and is moved by it. How could He otherwise be a God of justice and truth? I am not talking about unrighteous anger, our purely human kind of resentment. I am talking about *the judgment of God in the face of evil.* That, too, has to be seen in the context of human time and history, because how could He "judge", if that judgment

---

111   1 John 4:8
112   *The [Anglican] Book of Common Prayer, 1962, Canada,* p. 83.

had no relation to what took place in time and history? I believe that the judgment of God is necessary if there is ever to be justice in the long term. The anger of God is surely tied to His love. Could He see children tortured, for example, and not be moved to anger? Would He be a God of love if atrocities left Him unmoved? Even we would be moved to anger, and we are not God.

And while God's anger, and God's judgment, have to be factors to be reckoned with eventually, even though, for His own reasons which we do not always understand, He may hold back action for the time being (to the point where, sometimes, we wonder why God "isn't doing anything about it"), He does do something about it eventually. (" 'Vengeance is mine, I will repay, says the Lord.' ") [113]

—Grief as a "passion": God Himself suffering in our sin and suffering

This belief, that God, in His eternal changelessness, would of necessity be indifferent to all that happens to His creation in the unfolding of time, and so could never therefore be involved in human history, has affected many people, leading them to think that *"God does not care"* about what happens to them. On the contrary, I believe that He cares more deeply than we can ever imagine, and that being aware of *the suffering of God,* in and with His creation, is a key to beginning to understand something of this mystery. People have come to think that God is so far above and beyond, and removed from, all that happens to us, that all the terrible things that can happen in this world leave Him unmoved. They think that He is too "great" to bother about their small concerns, or too uncaring to be moved by their grief, or too indifferent to do anything about dealing with injustice and cruelty. To me such thinking is a denial of the whole principle of the Incarnation. I am not surprised that so many people have lost their faith, if that is their idea of "God". How could such a God be compatible with St. John's assertion that "God is love" ? *Surely Love must care.*

People have argued that, if God really was "good" and loving, He would do something about evil situations. When apparently, no divine action has been taken, they have drawn the conclusion that either He was not powerful enough to do anything about it, and therefore that He could not be omnipotent, or that He was not loving enough to do

---

113   Romans 12:19

anything about it, and therefore He could not be a God of love: or that He was so far removed from this world that nothing of ours could touch Him. So people have more or less shrugged their shoulders and said "what is the point in believing in God?"

If only people stopped to think about it, they would realize that such a God, if this were a true portrayal of Him, would be less "loving" than we are—if we care about suffering, so much more must He—and that, therefore, such an understanding of God, in itself, not only denies the goodness of God, but implies that we are "better" than He is: a very wrong inference drawn from something of which the essence is correct, if taken in the sense in which it was intended.

It is this, to my mind, terribly mistaken, understanding of the nature of God that has led many people to reject a God they have never really known. As the whole of Scripture testifies to God's involvement with His people, this idea of God being changeless to the point of immobility has to be challenged.

It is beginning to be challenged in the more modern thinking of "the suffering of God"; [114] but a lot of people have been lost to Christianity because this point has not been explored, and explained, and understood in the complexity of the total picture, even though there is Biblical warrant for the suffering of God. Quite apart from the Suffering Servant and the sufferings of Jesus on earth, the prophet Isaiah wrote, many centuries before Christ:

> I will recount the steadfast love of the Lord ...For he said, Surely they are my people... and he became their Saviour. *In all their affliction he was afflicted,* and the angel of his presence saved them; *in his love and in his pity he redeemed them;* he lifted them up and carried them all the days of old. [115]

—*Suffering, sin and death in the present creation being the price of human free will: and God sharing in the suffering, rather than "inflicting" it*

People tend to "blame God" when misfortune strikes them, and

---

114 e.g. the book by Terence E. Fretheim *The Suffering of God: An Old Testament Perspective.* Philadelphia: Fortress Press, 1984.

115 Isaiah 63:7-9

often blame Him for the sorrows which, quite the reverse, have often have been caused by human sin or neglect or carelessness or folly or unintentional ignorance: it is often we ourselves who have brought sin and suffering into the world. There are mysteries of suffering that we do not understand, but I am certain that they do not arise from any malevolence on the part of God, even if at present we do not yet understand them.

Many people, both Jews and Christians, lost their faith as a result of the Holocaust in the Second World War. However, the question has to be asked: how *could* God could have intervened, other than through the processes of human history (which I believe He did), except by supernatural means, which would have meant over-riding our God-given free will, and bringing an end to the world as we know it, at that time?

Instead, He has allowed the world to continue a little longer, and new generations have been born since those years, which would never have existed if He had brought the world to an end at that time, new generations of people who have been given a chance to live out their lives, a chance to learn to know and love God, and to take their places in the time hereafter—although I am not sure that God is going to continue to be so patient with us indefinitely!

I think the time will come when He will call a halt to it all, and firmly establish His Kingdom where evil and suffering no longer exist.

I believe that God does love us, cares deeply what happens to us, and suffers with us. I believe that, for example, He certainly had the power to stop the Holocaust in the Second World War, and the fact that He did not does not mean either that He did not care, or that He was not powerful enough do anything about it. I believe that He could have brought the world to an end at any moment that He chose, but He "gave us another chance"—suffering in the process more than we can possibly imagine over every hapless victim.

Moreover, we have now been forced to face the fact that human beings, as a race, are not on a continual progress to perfection, as my parents' generation thought they were! A salutary reminder, and yet our churches now down-play "sin," because they are over-reacting to the over-penitential gloom of the past. We do need to keep a right balance in our thinking.

It has also been demonstrated that even the might of the regime that started the Second World War, all-powerful and unscrupulous as it was, did not, after all, prevail. Those who fought against it, in every area of the war, facing impossible odds and often dying lonely, desperate deaths, eventually succeeded in bringing about its defeat, which, by human standards, would not have seemed, at the time, to be possible.

The thinking behind the *Article* quoted above worked against people thinking in terms of the "suffering" of God, although that suffering is documented in the Old Testament as far back as Isaiah,[116] and God's love and pain and grief and anger run through many of the prophetic writings.

This issue of "changelessness" *has* to be addressed in a religion that purports to be about an Incarnation of God in history, and a God of Love who cares about His creation and what happens to it. We have to think of a living, loving, vital, God who cares so deeply about His people that He still moves among them, suffers with them, helps them when He can in compliance with the laws of the universe which He has already set; and cares deeply, deeply, about what happens to all His creation and all His creatures.

After all, *if God is love, what else could Love be like?*

The idea of "changelessness" has led some people, like the Deists, to think in terms of the "watchmaker theory": that God, having created the world as a watchmaker makes a watch, then left it on its own to carry on by itself, doing what it was supposed to be doing, as if He had no further interest in it: which, to my mind, cuts right across what we believe about God being love, about the Incarnation, and about God working in His people in history through the Holy Spirit.

I hope that my suggestion, a little later, that "God does not interfere in every duck pond" will not be taken at all as subscribing to the watchmaker theory. I will only be trying to show that God has given a certain freedom to His world, and does not subject it to constant divine interference "from the outside", as it were, which is why we cannot "hold Him accountable" for every evolution or happening in the course of nature. The world was made that way on purpose.

I think God wanted to work in partnership with His creation, continuing to create and recreate, and mend and heal, nurturing

---

116 Isaiah 63:7-9

and loving His world into, one day, a new future: but He also gave it *freedom*. I believe we were created to live and love and work in partnership with Him, and that it is when we do not do that, perhaps on a cosmic basis, that things go wrong. The problem of evil is very real. I am certain that He did not create it, but that it emerges when His will is perverted and defied.

For example, I have heard how it has happened that male ducks, in their eagerness to mate, have so overloaded the female duck in the water that she drowned, but obviously that was not the will of God. I imagine that God cared very much about that poor duck—I would, and I am not God. You could argue cynically that it was not the will of God, if only because the female duck did not live to hatch her eggs and bring up her offspring, and thus the very process of procreation that was intended was brought to nothing. So I think I can say, on two counts, that it was not the will of God that that female duck should drown; but it is also true that He does not intervene in every duck-pond, because freedom from divine interference was also His precious gift to His creation. That does not mean He does not care about a suffering duck. I am certain that He grieves very much when things go wrong and His divine plan is thwarted.

Another way in which we can see how the created order was given a certain amount of freedom from constant divine interference and control, is, for example, the way in which germs and antibiotics react with each other to create new strains of drug-resistant germs, which have "newly-arrived" on the human scene, forming in the process a new entity for which we can hardly blame God. The theory of evolution itself is comparatively new in human understanding. We have to acknowledge that there may be other things which we do not yet understand, and not automatically assume at once that God must have done something wrong.

And we need to realize, too, how much human suffering is collectively our fault, not God's. We let people starve. There have been grave injustices in history, and aggression and oppression and exploitation still continue. We took our time about discovering elementary hygiene and sanitation. We are careless and make mistakes, or suffer at the hands of others. Sometimes we can and do discover the reasons for some of the things that go wrong in the world, although too often only after the fact, as when, for example, we learn how to prevent such illnesses as polio and tuberculosis and smallpox, or come to realize the necessity for hygiene in order to save lives in childbirth.

I think that some of the natural disasters arise from the complexities of the universe in which we live. I sometimes think that God deliberately created the world in a way in which human beings do have to struggle in order to survive, so that they might learn to think, and be challenged, and grow.

I believe that the inborn need to eat and sleep, and keep warm, and procreate and bring up the next generation, common to all living creatures, "makes the world go round", otherwise we might all just still be sitting on the grass doing nothing, and creation would stagnate. As it is, the seasons come and go, the trees and plants ripen and wither, harvest follows seed-time, and one generation follows another, and so on.

However, terrible natural disasters, earthquakes, forest fires, floods and volcanoes and so on, and all the suffering that has resulted, have led many people to ask how a "loving" God could permit all this. Sometimes the way to deal with such questions is to ask what the reverse scenario would be; what would it be like if all these natural phenomena never occurred, and the weather was unchangeably predictable from day to day, and human beings were never challenged by forces greater than they were.

The only explanation that I have been able to come up with for myself is that the created universe was made vast and complicated enough to challenge human understanding, self-sufficiency and complacency. Possibly the human race needs to be reminded from time to time that we are not "lords of creation", "mini-gods"; we need to be reminded that we are fragile beings, that the world is bigger than we are, there are forces greater than we are, and the power of the universe has to be treated with respect. In some way, the immensity of it all does pave the way to our seeking to know the God behind it. Our bodies are fragile, in the sense that they can be destroyed by accidents or misadventure, or disease or old age; in our human setting we are not invincible, eternal, all-powerful, and I think God may have made the world in this way deliberately because other alternatives would have had greater disadvantages. We have been made in such a way that, needing air, we drown in water, needing food, we starve without it, needing fire, we are burned if it comes too close;

and we have been given free-will to make decisions for ourselves which sometimes carry grave consequences; so we cannot live on this earth without ever knowing what it is to suffer and die.

It seems to me (and I can only speculate) that human, physical, death had to be tied in with God's giving to humanity the gift of free-will in the first place. We think of death as a "tragedy", and wish it did not have to happen, we fight against it, we pray for it to be averted, and we are often angry with God when people die and our "prayers" do not appear to have been answered—we wish people did not have to die, and wonder why the world was made that way. (I am not talking about unexpected tragedies and the untimely death of young people whose lives have been prematurely cut short, but death in the normal course of events, which we still rebel against, because of its accompanying grief which we want to avoid at all costs, and naturally so.)

But look at the situation from the other point of view: the options facing God in the creation of our world.

Think what the world would have been like if human beings never died, and the good and the bad continued just as they were for all time. Imagine what it would be like, for example, if evil dictators lived for ever, inflicting eternal cruelty on their victims, who would never then have open to them even the prospect of the blessed relief of death. Such a scenario seems unthinkable. Human, physical, death, as closure to our sin and suffering, seems to me to be the essential remedy for continuing human sinfulness, and a compassionate blessing for those who suffer.

It is in this context that I am certain that God, knowing that our free-will would sooner or later end in sin and suffering, provided two remedies for the situation: one was to build into the creation the certainty of eventual physical death (for all creatures, not just humanity, and not as *punishment,* for human beings, per se, but as a *remedy* for the problems inevitably arising from the human situation), to provide eventual closure for every intolerable situation; and the other was to provide the possibility of ongoing life after our human, physical, death had occurred, eternal life where death no longer had power over us; but the price of *that* was that *we would then have to be changed people,* where our free-will no longer conflicted with the will of a good and loving God.

At least, we would still have free-will, but we would at some stage have chosen to bring our wills into conformity with God's, so that only goodness would prevail, and evil would have been overcome for ever.

If God is love, and God is eternal, and, through Christ, it is possible for us to "abide" in that God for ever, then for us *physical death is not the end.* We continue to *abide in Him, in His love, for ever.*

The argument I have set out above also makes sense of St. Paul's writing about death, as for example, when he wrote that

> as *by a man* came *death, by a man* has come also the resurrection of the dead. For as *in Adam* all *die,* so also *in Christ* shall all be made *alive.* [117]

People have assumed that Paul is saying that physical death was the *direct* result of human sin, ours or that of a possibly mythical ancestor, ("Adam"), as a sort of *punishment* for wrongdoing, [118] and, when we see that *everyone* dies in due course in the natural course of events, (small babies, and the innocent and kind and good, as well as those who wreak havoc on others), it does not seem to be tied in with the notion of punishment or the direct result of "sin", but rather to be a natural and universal event, and we find St. Paul's argument to be confusing.

However, if human dying had to be automatically tied in to our human condition to counterbalance our God-given freedom, this would start to make sense. *"In Adam all die"* would mean that the human race, *as* human *flesh,* must eventually come to die, as a safeguard against misuse of our free-will, so giving up this physical existence with all its limitations where we are free to cause havoc on God's earth. But *"in Christ shall all be made alive"* would mean that, through Christ, we can continue *to live in the Love that is the eternal God, to all eternity.*

It would explain St. John's insistence that God is Love, and how imperative it is that we live in love, and not in the darkness of human feuds and hatred, because, without God, who is Love, we cannot go

---

117   1 Corinthians 15:21-22

118   see earlier footnote re. the old teaching that "for man as he is, death is a *punishment*" (Claude Beaufort Moss in *The Christian Faith: An Introduction to Dogmatic Theology* London: S.P.C.K., 1954, p.120.)

beyond our human, physical death. *Eternal life is found in the eternal God who is eternal Love.*

To me this makes more sense than some concept of "rewards and punishments", [119]and ties in with Biblical concepts of spiritual, (i.e. eternal), life, and spiritual death. I think the possibility of the latter does exist, in the sense of the death of the spirit—finding, at the end of time, that there is no part of oneself left any more that can align itself on an eternal basis with the goodness and love that is God. [120] Such an understanding of God, as *creating human death for practical reasons,* but *offering us eternal life in Himself beyond that dying,* does makes the concept of God as being both reasonable *and* loving seem to be much more feasible.

Of course there are no simple answers that one can give. God is mystery. The universe is mystery. But it is quite possible that there are answers to some of the questions with which we are faced, for example, new discoveries in medicine waiting for us to find them, even if we do not yet know what they are. We often find that God has provided in nature substances that are beneficial for certain conditions of the human body, and it is often our fault and our loss that we have not had the wisdom to discover and make use of them. I do not know, I can only guess: but if one trusts God, one has to believe that He knew what He was doing in the creation of the world, and the way things are, and that He is still there for us, if we will only turn to Him and trust Him.

And He *has* given us some revelation of Himself, so that, if only we applied it rightly, we could help, rather than destroy, the world in which we live: and bless each other, rather than damaging each other. We live in a world where we do need to ask God to help us; and perhaps His protection is given more often than we realise; and we do have an assurance, in our Christian faith, to the effect, that even if we are affected by tragedy and suffering, He can and will support us through it, and that it will not last for ever. We do have the promise of it "being all right" in the end, without which it might be possible to claim that

---

119   see Glossary re. The Faith of Damasus and my response to Bishop Spong on the subject of reward and punishment

120   see later discussion of "perishing", "eternal death", rather than survival for ever without God in hell

"it was not fair" for God to put us in this world.[121]   But, with the challenges, we have also been given, if we will take it, the assurance of His love, the gift of faith, and the strength of hope.[122]

But while human sorrows continue, can we see a God of love not grieving terribly in this whole situation? To people who have taken the position that "the fact that it happened means either that there is no God, or that He does not care", I would respond that I think it would be closer to the truth to say "God does exist, and He does care, and He grieves most terribly for all His people." This is all part of the price which I believe God pays, as much as we do, for our having the great gift of free will. And He has provided love, and mercy, and redemption and forgiveness, for those who sincerely ask for it, and we have to believe that, even if it takes death to end suffering, eventually relief is provided, and God is there to take the suffering ones into His arms in love, and wipe away every tear from their eyes.[123]

The sense that He is among His people, and does care what happens to them, has seemed to become all but lost to much of the present generation.

We must have the strength to believe that there may sometimes be good reasons for His non-intervention in our tragedies, even though we may not understand them at the time. We need to have the faith to believe that He does care, and stands beside us with a breaking heart, even though we cannot see Him or feel His presence; and that He will bring us to Himself in the end.

We have to look at the argument not from our immediate point of view, but from the other end, as it were: not at what is worrying us, in itself, but at *what kind of a God do we believe in?* If He is a good God,

121   Romans 8:18-19: "I consider that the sufferings of this present time are not worth comparing with the glory that is to be revealed to us. For the creation waits with eager longing for the revealing of the sons of God.."; verses 22-23: "We know that the whole creation has been groaning in travail together until now; and not only the creation, but we ourselves ... as we wait for...the redemption of our bodies." verse 21: "The creation itself will be set free from its bondage to decay and obtain the glorious liberty of the children of God", in other words, will one day be transformed. What is now is not forever.

122   1 Corinthians 13:13: "So faith, hope, love, abide [or continue to exist], these three; but the greatest of these is love."

123   Revelation 7:17 "God will wipe away every tear from their eyes"

surely we have to see Him as suffering too. He could not rejoice in, or be indifferent to, our calamities and remain a "good" God. We need to think of Him as being with us, and weep *with* Him, not *apart from Him:* we are "in it together".

And this is where the Christian understanding of God does makes sense: that God took on human suffering, to share it with us, in order to give us the strength to go through it, the courage to bear it, and the ability to redeem it.

In fact, the suffering of God, to my mind, is a key point to understanding more of the nature of the God, revealed in Christ, whom Christians worship.

However, as I have said, the idea that God can "suffer" is a fairly modern one, given the old idea expressed in the *Thirty-Nine Articles* of the Church of England described above, that God has no "body, parts or passions". Terence Fretheim's book on *"The Suffering of God"* [124] was only written in the nineteen-eighties. I am certain that God does, *must,* suffer, if He is who we think He is. He gave us free-will, that we might have freedom to choose, and love of our own volition, and grow in partnership with Him; but I see more and more how that free-will which He gave us, which we so casually accept, must over and over again, break the heart of God.

In fact, if we are to talk about time as against eternity, it could be that the Crucifixion, a physical act which took place at a given place and time in history, stands for ever, outside time, as an eternal symbol of the love and heart-break of a compassionate and loving God.

As I said to a young couple when I was talking to them on the evening before my husband's fatal stroke, we need to decide on what it is that we believe, once and for all, regardless of what may or may not happen to us later: we cannot say we believe in God at one minute, and deny Him the next: He either exists or He does not. He either is love or He is not. If "believing in God" were to give us automatic protection from all the things that go wrong in this world, then *everyone* would strive "to believe" as a sort of insurance policy, and that is not what God wants. He wants us to love Him *for Himself,* because we care about the Love and Goodness that He is, not just, selfishly, because we

---

124 Terence E. Fretheim. *The Suffering of God: An Old Testament Perspective,* Philadelphia:Fortress Press, 1984.

want to be "safe". He wants us to believe in Him from a genuine sense of love, on a voluntary basis.

And it is important to remember that, in actual fact, our faith and our love shine out most strongly when we still believe in Him, and want to go on serving Him, in spite of misfortunes that may have befallen us. No other religion can offer us such a way of "being in God" and "He in us". [125]

No other religion can offer us a way of being united to God in being united with Christ in His suffering. [126]

While God does not want us to suffer, and it was a bad mistake for Christians to say in the past that it was "God's will" that people should become ill, or suffer, or die prematurely, because, on the contrary, He loves us and wants our well-being, and the Church is now rediscovering its ancient ministry of healing, nevertheless, there is a sense in which it is inevitable that a good and kind and loving person will sooner or later meet grief, in encountering all the trouble that is on this earth.

And there is a sense in which suffering, while not good in itself, can have the result of producing in us sterling character which we might not otherwise have attained to *(in the part of us that is eternal, and, in that sense, matters most).* Tad Guzie has said that the "appropriation" of suffering and conflict, as opposed to merely "tolerating" it, is "a necessary part of the 'personal process', the process of human and religious growth." [127]

And St. Paul said, in his Epistle to the Romans, there is a sense in which we can rejoice in our sufferings because

> suffering produces endurance, and endurance produces character, and character produces hope, and hope does not disappoint us, because God's love has been poured into our hearts through the Holy Spirit which has been given to us. [128]

---

125   see chapter on "Abiding in Christ"

126   Romans 8:17 "...if children, then heirs, heirs of God and fellow heirs with Christ, *provided we suffer with him* in order that we may also be glorified with him." 2 Corinthians 1:5: *"as we share abundantly in Christ's sufferings, so through Christ we share abundantly in comfort too";* Philippians 3:10: "that I may know him...*and may share in his sufferings, becoming like him...*" 1 Peter 4:13: "Rejoice *in so far as you share Christ's sufferings...*"

127   Tad Guzie. *Jesus and the Eucharist.* Ramsey, New Jersey: Paulist Press, 1974, p.148.

128   Romans 5:3-5.

If, instead of blaming God, we can realize that God grieves too, and that we can share in His grief, *we can experience God even in that suffering.*

While not making exclusive claims that "only Christians" will be "saved", we do have, in Christ, a special way of access to the God of the universe while still on this earth, *a means of union with God in this life* that can be found in no other way, in no other religion that the world has ever known.

Again, to me, Christianity makes more sense than all the other religions, as *in Jesus* the focus is on an actual Person, whom we have some chance of being able to relate to and understand, even though *the Great Godhead Itself* may remain beyond the range of our vision and understanding.

I believe that it is *because* the Godhead, ("Almighty and Everlasting God"), is beyond the reach of our imagination that Christ came into human history, in human form, in order to give us a way to reach that great God during our human lifetimes: it is *as we learn to identify ourselves with Him in His humanity that we can come to know something of His divinity.* [129]

The Incarnation of God makes sense, if one believes that God is love, and that Divine Love, loving His creation, wanted to bring it to Himself, now and for eternity.

The basic Biblical understanding of the Atonement, union with God through Christ ("abiding in Christ") clarifies this in a way so simple that one wonders why the Church seems to have been "off course" in this regard for nearly eighteen hundred years, by concentrating almost entirely on the "sin and forgiveness" *("being spared from punishment")* aspect of the Atonement. The Atonement is not just about sin being forgiven: it is also about *"life"* being *(only) in God.* [130] But the idea of "abiding in Christ" of necessity involves belief in the divinity of Christ and the concept of God as Trinity and Love.

I believe that, since early in the second century, as set out in the

---

129   John 14:6-7: "I am *the way,* and the truth and the life; no one comes to the Father, but by me [which, as I will try to show later, I believe applies to our *present human living* rather than defining future salvation]. *If you had known me, you would have known my Father also".*

130   see the Chapters on the Atonement and "Abiding in Christ"

Chapter on the Atonement, the main emphasis in the Church has been on the *forgiveness of sins* (and whether or not one will be punished for one's transgressions), rather than on the equally important concept of *"abiding in Christ," the gift of eternal life, the at-one-ment with the God of Love through Christ* that I have referred to as "the second arm of the Atonement."

This one-sided emphasis can be seen throughout Church history, in spite of the fact that the Bible readings and the traditional liturgies over the centuries have continued to speak of both of these aspects of the Atonement, especially the "at-one-ment" that was supposed to follow our forgiveness, attesting to the fact that "eternal life" is *only* to be found through being reconciled in some way with the God of Love: *which has to mean learning what it is to love.*

The corollory of this—I believe—is that those who are not capable of reconciling themselves, sooner or later, with the Divine Love, will eventually cease to exist, so that, in the end, there will be destruction of all wickedness and an end to all evil.

In re-emphasising that God is love, we have to deal with the old question, asked over many centuries, of "how can God permit sin and suffering and evil to exist in the world if He is both loving and all-powerful?" It is often deduced, from the undoubted existence of evil and suffering in this world, that, either God is not loving, or He is not all-powerful — another criticism from the atheist.

I think it helps sometimes to turn questions the other way around. I think we need to ask instead "what other alternatives were available to Him, in the creation of the world?" I believe that God gave us free-will, in order that we might choose for ourselves what we want to become, and learn to grow in maturity and love; and, indeed, work in partnership with Him; but that entails the opposite possibility, that human beings *can* be cruel and wicked if they so choose: otherwise we would all be like mere puppets, or robots, and what then would be the point of our existence? I think the whole point of our creation was that we were to learn to *love*, to be one with each other and with the God of love who created us. If we were mere puppets or robots, could our "love" be real?

I think, too, that it is necessary for some basic problems to be addressed that are causing people anguish, such as, for example, "how can I say in the Creeds and believe in my heart, that God is good and loving and created all things, if He also created the 'AIDS' virus?" — a misunderstanding, as I see it, of *the very nature of God.*

God *is* Mystery, even if Mystery that is knowable to a certain extent. We cannot expect to understand all the details of the creation of the universe, or the reasons for them, but, if love and goodness came from God (and where else could they have come from?) it would surely follow that there was reason and order and goodness behind all that He made: and that we will understand one day. In fact, it seems that discoveries are being made all the time that shed light on problems that seemed unsolvable only a generation or two ago. We must remember, too, that the world is obviously no longer the place that I believe a good God would have wanted it to be, and surely, if He is a God of love, it must break His heart again and again to see our misuse of His creation: but His willingness to pay that price must have been a necessary cost entailed in the freedom which He has given us—and not only freedom to the human race, but also to the microcosms of nature itself, which develop and evolve and mutate, in their own way, over time.

If God is indeed a loving and good creator, I am sure He grieves greatly when His people suffer, and in fact suffers with them, even when, in our suffering, we sometimes find that hard to believe. We need to be reminded of the question: *"What kind of a God do we* believe in?" and, instead of being tempted to blame *Him* for our misfortunes, we should ask ourselves "what do we think is *His* reaction to the way this world is turning out?"

This is where St. Augustine's theory about the Trinity being *Persons between whom love flows* is so helpful, when looking beyond religious denominations to the nature of the God whom we all worship: Augustine taught that each member of that Trinity is in turn *the Lover, the Beloved, and Love Itself,* and Jesus can be seen as *Divine Love revealed on earth.*

We can put more emphasis on Love than on Trinity, when dealing with our non-Christian brethren, but I find God's being understood as Trinity as helpful to understanding that God is Love, and I think that what matters is whether in the final analysis one can relate to and abide in Divine Love—which "abiding in Christ" can help us to do while still on this earth. In the chapter on "Abiding in Christ" I give powerful quotations illustrating *how we can be caught up into the love and life of the Trinity* through *our being in Christ—truly at-one-ment with God:* but the common denominator necessary for this *has to be Love.*

The Biblical—and Christian—understanding of God as Trinity

The idea of God as "Father" is present in the Old Testament, but was not much used by the Jews, possibly for fear of undue familiarity, but it is there, as I will show in the Chapter on "God as *Father*". So when Jesus taught his disciples "when you pray, say '[Our] Father' " [131] He was not teaching them something new, but reinstating a long-standing idea of God which was already in the Old Testament Scriptures that they regarded as sacred.

There are many references in the Old Testament to the Spirit of God. [132] I have not given New Testament references to the Holy Spirit, because, if one accepts that Jesus is the Christ, they speak for themselves—and, if one doesn't, there is no point.

The Old Testament sees God as the One Almighty and Eternal God who created the universe; and yet also speaks of a God who is able to be known to human beings as Father, as well as the Holy Spirit of God, who is equally real. Two-thirds of the Trinity being thus accounted for, even in the Jewish Scriptures themselves, it only remains to be seen whether the long-awaited Messiah, the Son of Man seen in the prophecy in the Book of Daniel, has yet materialized on the human scene:

> I saw in the night visions, and behold, with the clouds of heaven there came one like a son of man, and he came to the Ancient of Days and was presented before him. And to him was given dominion and glory and kingdom, that all peoples, nations, and languages should serve him; his dominion is an everlasting dominion which shall not pass away, and his kingdom one that shall not be destroyed. [133]

---

131 Luke 11:2. Matthew 6:9 "Pray then like this: Our Father who art in heaven, hallowed be thy name..."

132 For example, Genesis 1:2; Isaiah 57:16; Isaiah 63:10-14; Ezekiel 36:26; Joel 2:28-29 (the passage quoted in Acts 2:16-18)

133 Daniel 7:13-14

In the chapter on "the divinity of Christ", the Incarnation of God in human history, I will set out the Old Testament prophecies about the Messiah, and argue that no other person who has ever lived has ever fulfilled them in the way that Jesus of Nazareth did. There has not been a comparable candidate for that role in the whole history of the human race so far; and many, many people have not only accepted this on the word of others, but have discovered the truth of this for themselves in their own hearts and minds and living.

The doctrine of the Trinity must necessarily imply the "divinity" of "Christ", as a Person of that Trinity. The only question remaining might be: *was Jesus of Nazareth* the Messiah, the Christ? And as the human race has progressed to the point where we can land on the moon and send rockets to the planets, and blow up the earth if we choose, and clone life, it does not seem to me that we are at the "beginning" of time, and one would deduce, therefore, that surely the Messiah would have come by now, if He was going to come—and Christians believe He has.

The Biblical—and Christian—understanding of God as Love.

I believe that, although we give lip-service to the idea of God as "love", in fact we have not really appropriated it into our lives and living. The history of the Christian churches alone will attest to that.

The writings of St. John, in which this teaching on love is most emphasized—as is the union with God through *abiding in Christ*, living in and sharing the divine love, which *is intended to flow throughout the membership of the Body of Christ on earth* as it flows *between the members of the Trinity in the Godhead*—are the very ones which tend to be the most disregarded today.

I believe that many misunderstandings of the Christian faith might well have been avoided if "Christians" had been seen, by the world at large, over the centuries, as taking more seriously the basic apostolic teaching of the Bible about the nature of the faith and the nature of God, which this book is aiming to restate; and if the world had seen in us the love of God, which, so often, it has not.

CHAPTER 5

God as "Father"

Jesus, in teaching His disciples to pray to God as their Father, was drawing on teaching that was already in the Hebrew Scriptures, but giving it new emphasis.

Because of problems involved in centuries of subordination of women and abuse of children, there is now a tendency to avoid the word "Father" when speaking of God, because it implies that God is purely male—whereas He is greater than either male or female and the characteristics of both men and women come from Him—and because the word conjures up an unnecessarily unpleasant and frightening image of God in the minds of women and children who have been abused by their fathers.

However, we should concentrate on the image of *parenthood*—the fact that we are God's children—and remember that God is Love: so that we can think of the word "Father" as conveying to us an image of the love and protection that we *should* be getting from our earthly fathers.

For example:

Psalm 68, verse 5: "*Father of the fatherless,* and protector of widows, is God in his holy habitation"

Psalm 89, verse 26: [David] shall cry to me '*Thou art my Father,* my God, and the Rock of my salvation.' "

Psalm 103, verse 13: "*As a father pities his children,* so the Lord pities those who fear him."

Isaiah 63, verse 16: *"For thou art our Father,* though Abraham does not know us, and Israel does not acknowledge us; *thou, O Lord, art our Father, our Redeemer from of old* is thy name."

Isaiah 64, verse 8: *"Yet, O Lord, thou art our Father,* we are the clay and thou art our potter; we are all the work of thy hand"

and there is the lament in Jeremiah 3:19 where God is portrayed as saying "I thought you would call me *My Father,* and would not turn from following me."

We should, however, remember, too, that there are also references in the Bible to what might be called "the feminine side" of God. Some examples are the passage in Isaiah "shall I bring to the birth and not deliver?", [134]the fact that Wisdom, which has been equated with the Spirit of God, is written of as being feminine, [135]and Jesus Himself lamented that He would have taken His people under His wing as a mother hen shelters her chicks.[136]

It is desperately important that we do not "get hung up on" mere words and images, but look for the truth behind them which they are trying to express. We can take the Bible seriously without substituting our own material images for metaphors which were meant to describe a much greater, spiritual, reality.

Another example of this is the way in which we have sometimes confused the Godhead itself with the Person of God the Father. It is true that Jesus told us that we could pray to the Great God of the universe as children approaching a loving Father (although what He actually *said* was "Our Father *Who art in heaven"* rather than "Almighty

---

134   Isaiah 66:9: "Shall I bring to the birth and not cause to bring forth? says the Lord; shall I, who cause to bring forth, shut up the womb? says your God

135   Proverbs 8:27-30: "When I established the heavens, I [Wisdom] was there...when he marked out the foundations of the earth, then I was beside him, like a master workman, and I was daily his delight" (although this passage has at times also been equated with Jesus, the Divine Word, the Logos); Proverbs 8:35: "For he who finds me finds *life* and obtains favour from the Lord" (the Nicene Creed refers to the Holy Spirit as the *"giver of life")* and Proverbs 9:1: "Wisdom has built *her* house, she has set up *her* seven pillars"

136   Matthew 23:37 "O Jerusalem, Jerusalem, killing the prophets and stoning those who are sent to you! How often would I have gathered your children together as a hen gathers her brood under her wings, and you would not!"

God Our Heavenly Father" which we have become accustomed to after centuries of use). *However,* He also said that "I and the Father are one," [137] and "He who has seen me has seen the Father…Do you not believe that I am in the Father and the Father in me?" [138]

I think Jesus' prime concern, when He taught His disciples "The Lord's Prayer" was on *relationship:* to teach them that God could be approached as a Father—an ideal Father—in confidence and love. I do not think that we can go from that to denying that God is Trinity on the basis of a translation of St. Basil's liturgy which states that "the Father alone is God".[139]

I will try to show that God is Trinity, both in the relationship of love that flows between the Persons of the Godhead, and in the way that those Persons can relate to human beings during their life on earth, and also to show how confusing and dangerous it can be when we start getting confused between the Three Persons of the Trinity, on the one hand, and the Godhead itself, on the other. If *we* are confused, no wonder the rest of the world has so badly misunderstood the Christian faith!

Worshipping God as "Father" should not preclude belief in God as Trinity, of which "the divinity of Christ" is a key component.

But that belongs more appropriately in the Chapter on the Trinity.

---

137 John 10:30
138 John 14:9-10
139 see the chapter on God as Trinity

CHAPTER 6:

The Incarnation of God in human history: the divinity of Christ: if Jesus of Nazareth were not God Incarnate, there would be no Atonement, no "abiding in Christ"

Why do we believe that Jesus of Nazareth is the Christ, the "Son of God"? If one accepts that a God who had taken on human form and experience at some time would be a God greater and more worthy of worship than one who had not, who, then, in all of human history, could be more likely than Jesus of Nazareth to have fulfilled that role? In fact there has never been another "candidate" of His stature, as all history will attest: nor ever another faith in a Triune God such a Christianity has posited. Christianity, whether one accepts it or not, has left an indelible mark on the world, and is unique in its claims. So let us look at Jesus of Nazareth.

I think a problem has been that, in recent years, focus has tended to be on the "historical" man, and debate has been about the likelihood, or unlikelihood, of His being also "divine". Many people have dismissed stories of miracles and so on as being "unlikely" and "probably concocted", and so on: and some of them may have been well-meaning, but credulous and superstitious, exaggerations, repeated uncritically by the faithful, as happened in the Church in Europe in the Middle Ages—but that should not detract from the truth at the heart of the Gospel, which was not affected by any subsequent embroidery of the story around the edges.

I believe that enough in the way of thundering miracles did take place, culminating in the Resurrection, that convinced people that Jesus of Nazareth was indeed the promised Messiah, come from God, in fulfillment of the prophecies in the Hebrew Scriptures, with power that no human being ever had before, and this changed many people's lives for ever. The actual details of what happened are of lesser importance.

However, while I think it might be legitimate to speculate on which story might be a re-run of another story, for example, I think the current trend to try to dismiss *everything* is both unreasonable and dangerous. It still brings us back to the question of the divinity of Christ.

If Jesus was indeed God in human form on earth, some kind of upheaval could be expected, regardless of what "the norm" might be. God coming into human history is not "the norm". Some manifestation of His power was needed to support His claim of being Who He was, as in the story of the healing of the paralytic let down through the roof by his friends for Jesus to heal him: "...that you may know that the Son of man has authority on earth to forgive sins..." [140] (this was in the context of the scribes and Pharisees having just said: "Who can forgive sins but God only?")

This, to me, has much more of a ring of authenticity about it than the story of St. Peter and the fish, for example. [141] The latter may well be true, because God can, and does, do miracles in the experience of His people; but if it were *not* true, it would not matter. Our faith does not hinge on it.

All the testimony of all the early Christians, and all the New Testament writings, cannot be discounted just because something (may have) crept into one of the accounts which was not as widely attested to as, for example, the Last Supper, the Crucifixion, and the Resurrection. The Church may have its faults, there may even be inconsistencies and faults in the very Scriptures themselves, if the human element has crept in, at times; but the God to which the Church and the Scriptures point is above and beyond them, and cannot be destroyed, even if human evidence were found to be frail in places: what else would you expect of human evidence? Just because a human being (may have) got a fairly minor detail wrong, it does not mean that the Trinity does not exist.

---

140   Luke 5:18-26
141   Matthew 17:24-27

In·a court of law one is asked whether a case is proved "beyond a reasonable doubt". Arguing about which miracle might or might not have happened, when or where, does not, to my mind, prove, beyond a reasonable doubt, that *all* that I have spoken of, touching the logic and reasonableness of the Incarnation, is therefore invalid.

I discovered at seminary that a Roman Catholic theologian, writing more than sixty years ago, said, even then, that he believed that "the vast majority of liberal critics today deny that Paul regarded Jesus Christ as true God" [142] — St. Paul who was writing within only a few years after the Crucifixion, and whose own words, I believe, show that he *did* believe it. Not only that, but his major theological arguments only make sense in that context. [143]

However, if one takes it from the opposite end of the argument, as it were, accepting the likelihood, as I have suggested, that *the very nature of God* would seem to call for someone to fulfil this role, to be the incarnation of God in human history, as all the Hebrew Scriptures would seem to attest, then the question becomes one of *whether or not that great event has happened yet,* and, if it has, *who was that person.* The argument, taken from this angle, would point to Jesus of Nazareth as being the only serious candidate.

People have "muddied the waters" by saying that He was a good man, a great prophet, and so on, without realizing that that is to talk nonsense. Great men, good men, prophets of God, do not claim to *be God.* He said "before Abraham was, I AM" (the divine name), [144] so either He was who He said He was, or he was not a good man, he was a blasphemer (a view that led to his crucifixion), or a fraud, or someone with severe mental problems. One cannot "escape" the problem by just calling Him "a good man, a great prophet". If He was a great man, He was God, as He said He was. If He was a liar and a fraud, he was *not*

142   Anthony C. Cotter, "The Divinity of Jesus Christ in Saint Paul" in *The Catholic Biblical Quarterly,* Volume VII Number 3, July 1945, pp. 260-263. (See the section on Romans 9:5 following)

143   e.g., "being *in Christ";* the "new creation"; life in the flesh versus life in the Spirit; and how the new creation in Christ was no longer "under the law".

144   John 8:58 (it could be argued that this was in St. John's Gospel, "the later church", but I am arguing (a) that St. John's writings stem from a time when eye-witnesses were still around, and (b) that it ties in with the rest of the Bible, and thus it is not an isolated claim to divinity, but consistent with the rest of Scripture, as I will try to show)

someone to be looked up to and respected, and patronized by remarks about his greatness.

I have heard it said that *"Jesus"* means different things to different people. I can understand people feeling their relationship with Him is uniquely their own, but there comes a point where one has to say that the nature and existence of the *real Jesus* —whatever they may be—are not affected by our varying opinions.

If He exists eternally at all, *He is who He is,* (as in "I AM Who I AM"[145]), "the same yesterday and today and forever".[146] He is not a creation of our own devising.

This is where we need to come back to the Bible and see what He was believed to be by the people who actually knew Him in His life on earth, people who passed on to their successors their first-hand testimony to that knowledge—the "apostolic" witness, in fact: that is, if we accept that He was of God at all, in which case the apostolic witness recorded in the Scriptures is valid and should be taken seriously. We can't have it both ways: if Jesus is divine, we have to accept the integrity of the Bible as a whole and its testimony to that fact. If we do not accept the Biblical testimony, we cannot "play games" with who or what we think "Jesus" is.

I would just like to refute a few of the arguments that I have found to be unconvincing, to help other people to feel that there is enough "reasonable doubt" on the subject that they might equally well accept the Christian faith.

One of our senior modern churchmen (I won't say of what denomination), said recently that he did not believe in the Resurrection or the divinity of Christ, but he said that "Jesus does live on in people's hearts". With all due respect, I believe that such a statement is absolute nonsense, because it essentially contradicts itself. As I see it, Jesus can only "live in our hearts" through the Holy Spirit *because He is divine,* because He is *part of the Trinity.* If Jesus is not of God, if you deny that divinity, the truth of that Gospel, then a purely human historical figure of the past *cannot* "live" in our hearts today. Either He lives

---

145 Exodus 3:14: "I AM WHO I AM.....say.....'I AM has sent me to you.' " and Jesus in John 8:58 said "before Abraham was, I am" (and the crowd tried to stone Him for blasphemy)
146 Hebrews 13:8.

in our hearts because He is divine, or, if He is not divine, He does not "live in our hearts". Such people do not seem to be able to hear what they are saying! And they cause a lot of grief to many of God's people.

People at funerals talk about the memory of loved ones being always with them, and that is valid, in the sense that the *memory* of the person they loved is always with them, in their lifetimes; but that does not apply to us with regard to Jesus. If we have never known Jesus in the flesh in the past, and so cannot have a human memory of Him, and if He is not divine, so that we cannot know Him in the Spirit in the present time either, we cannot say that we know Him or "love" Him, or that He "lives in our hearts".

Jesus said to His disciple, Thomas, "blessed are those who have not seen and yet believe",[147] but that was predicated on His *divinity*, on our believing that He is who He said He is—Thomas had just said "My Lord and my God!"[148]

Christians have a personal relationship with Jesus in this life through the power of the Holy Spirit, and know Him and believe in Him and love Him, and *this is only possible* because *Christ is of God.* If Jesus was only a mortal man, and so there was no access to Him through the Holy Spirit in the present time, how could we possibly "love" what we would have had no means of ever knowing? And without our ever having known and loved Him, how could He possibly "live in our hearts" today? And even if we contorted ourselves into believing that we do "love" "Jesus", and that He does "live" in our hearts, what are we talking about? The memory of a "good man" who lived in the past, who we have heard about, (although we do not accept the Scriptures that tell us about Him)? Or is it just an idea that we have in our minds, an ideal that we hold, of a great moral teacher inspiring us? As I have said, good men and great moral teachers are not habitual liars. We can't have it both ways.

Christianity is a relationship with a Person, who we know, and love, and have experienced in our lives, which is at the heart of Christianity, and that is what this book is all about. Mere *words*, like "divinity", and sentimental phrases about "loving Jesus" and "Jesus in our hearts",

147 John 20:29
148 John 20:28

seem to be so easily thrown around without ever appearing to have been thought about and analyzed—or at least this is the impression that one is given. This is why I think it is so important that we stop to think for a moment about what we do believe, and why.

If Jesus was divine, in the sense of being one of the Persons of the Trinity, the incarnation of God on earth, then, to me, it follows that the Bible, as the testimony to that truth, has to be taken seriously and believed: if not in every detail, at least in its main themes about the nature of God, of which the divinity of Christ is one, and the doctrine of the Trinity is another. Otherwise there is no point in talking about "Jesus in our hearts".

The chapter on the Atonement deals with the whole subject of "abiding in Christ", and His living in us, the analogy from St. John's Gospel of the vine and the branches, the union with God through Christ, which I believe is at the heart of the Christian Gospel, and an aspect of the faith that I believe has long been neglected in the teaching of the Church.

Often it seems that mere words have become a substitute for *meaning,* as, for example, in our use of the expression "in Christ", *which only makes sense* in the context of "abiding in Christ" and the apostolic understanding of the Atonement set out in this book, but the latter is never explicitly acknowledged.

Indeed, some people question whether the Resurrection literally happened or had to be fundamental to the faith, presumably not understanding that the Risen Christ was *a sign* that demonstrated to His disciples the *reality* of that new creation of which He was the first-fruits, as it were, [149] the new creation where humanity and divinity come together, *in Him:* [150] *the union of God with humankind which was the whole point of the Incarnation and Atonement, and the focus of God's love.* It must surely follow that much of the most profound teaching of

149   2 Corinthians 5:17: "if any one is *in Christ,* he is *a new creation*" and 1 Corinthians 15:20-23 re. Christ being *"the the first-fruits"* of that new creation

150   Ephesians 2:14-16: "For [Christ] is our peace, who has made us both [Jew and Gentile] *one,* and has broken down the dividing wall of hostility, by abolishing in His flesh the law of commandments...that He might create *in Himself* one new man *in place of the two,* so making peace"; Ephesians 3:12 (NIV): *"In him* and through faith in him we may approach God with freedom and confidence."

the New Testament has not been fully explored in recent years: and to set that right is really the heart and purpose of this book.

The theory that there was a conspiracy to perpetrate a hoax—then or later

I cannot believe that there was any conspiracy on the part of Jesus' disciples to pervert the truth and foist a false religion on the world. I do not think that His friends and followers somehow conspired to steal His body after the crucifixion and hide it so that they could then claim that He had risen from the dead. For one thing, you have to look at the character of the people involved; for another, you have to consider the time-frame that would have been involved. His little band of followers was scattered and demoralized after Jesus' arrest; no one dared to come to His defence to prevent the crucifixion at the time (there is no record of a riot); and yet the radiance and bravery of those men immediately after Easter Sunday was in stark contrast with their earlier cowardice. They no longer feared the authorities, they were no longer afraid to die. Even torture was not able to break many of the martyrs, to the extent that it came to be said that "the blood of the martyrs is the seed of the Church".[151]

That contrast in their behaviour, almost overnight, cannot be ignored: nor can their powerful and immediate conviction that the Resurrection somehow betokened the fact that, through union with the Risen Christ, mankind could come to God.

The time factor is important, too. Whatever may or may not have been added on as "frills", in the way of detail in the oral or written traditions, later on, the fact remains that Jesus was believed to have risen from the dead on the Sunday after the crucifixion, *within forty-eight hours after His death.* If there *was* a conspiracy, its essential details had to be in place within hours of the crucifixion. If He *did* rise from the dead on that day, it can be taken that He was no ordinary mortal man, and "the Church" was indeed justified in exploring in more detail over time exactly what all this meant. If Jesus did not rise from the dead on that Sunday, or been alleged to have done so *at the time,* there would never have been a "Church" to speculate about His divinity in the first place.

---

151 Tertullian (c.160—220 AD) *Apologeticus.* J.M. and M.J. Cohen. *The Penguin Dictionary of Quotations.* Harmondsworth, England: Penguin Books, c. 1960.

In addition to the fact that there was hardly time for a "conspiracy" to be arranged within such a short time-frame, surely, if it *had* been, it would have been done more tidily and efficiently. The conspirators (if there had been a conspiracy) would surely have "got their act together" and come up with one coherent story, that agreed in all its details, just as criminals fix their alibis. What we actually have is several different accounts, which sometimes differ from each other, just as honest witnesses to an accident, for example, may sometimes sincerely differ from each other in their subsequent reports, or mistakes are made in reporting what has been heard from others. The fact that the accounts do differ, to my mind, is evidence of their authenticity and compatibility with human experience.

None of the "conspiracy" or "later church" theories have convinced me. On the contrary, if I can rebut them easily, it only points up to me their greater futility! For example, it has been suggested that the soldiers on guard at Jesus' tomb would never have confessed to falling asleep on duty, because that was a capital offence, and such an admission would have resulted in their being put to death. On this hypothesis, I gather, we are being asked to deduce that the Biblical account has to be false and is not to be trusted. People who come up with such arguments can have no imagination! It does not seem to occur to them that worse threats than normal execution might well have been made in order to stop the soldiers from talking about what might really have happened.

Nor does it seem to occur to them that the tomb obviously *was* empty or *the authorities would have put the corpse on display to refute rumours about a resurrection.* I am sure they would not have wanted the populace to hear—from the soldiers yet—about Jesus' rising from the dead, if that is what did happen. It would be much more convenient for them to allege that the body was stolen by the disciples, even if the soldiers did have to "lose face" over it. I imagine that "an order was an order" in the Roman army!

I am not saying that this *did* happen. I am merely pointing out the futility of the suggestion that the Biblical account *must* be false, simply because no soldier would normally want to admit that he fell asleep on duty. As I said earlier, if Jesus was divine, these were not normal times!

And, *of course* a soldier would not normally want to say he had fallen asleep on duty, that goes without saying: but if the soldiers were *ordered* to make that statement under threat of worse punishment if they refused, I think it is quite possible that they would have complied and the Biblical account could well be true. The authorities had a lot at stake: the stability of the city, for one thing. I think this hypothesis is at least as reasonable as the other; in fact I think it is more reasonable!

The passage from St. Matthew's Gospel says:

> ...the chief priests and the Pharisees gathered before Pilate and said, 'Sir, we remember how that impostor said, while he was still alive, "After three days I will rise again." Therefore order the sepulchre to be made secure until the third day, lest his disciples go and steal him away, and tell the people, "He has risen from the dead," and the last fraud will be worse than the first.' Pilate said to them, 'You have a guard of soldiers; go, make it as secure as you can.' So they went and made the sepulchre secure by sealing the stone and setting a guard. [152]

The reference to telling the people obviously implies fear of some kind of a riot or public unrest; certainly we can infer from it concern on the part of the authorities that the people not be encouraged to think that Jesus had risen from the dead (even if it did mean Roman soldiers having to say that they all fell asleep on duty). Then the account goes on a little later:

> some of the guard went into the city and told the chief priests all that had taken place. And when they had assembled with the elders and taken counsel, they gave a sum of money to the soldiers and said 'Tell people, "His disciples came by night and stole him away *while we were asleep*." [italics mine]. And if this comes to the governor's ears, we will satisfy him and keep you out of trouble.' So they took the money and did as they were directed;   and this story has been spread among the Jews to this day. [153]

---

152   Matthew 27:62-66
153   Matthew 28:11-15

The suggestion by some modern theologians that this account is most unlikely, because no soldier would want to admit to falling asleep at his post because that was a capital offence, is the kind of apparently plausible argument, used to discredit the authority of the Bible, which I think can equally well be shown to be discredited itself. Someone who had been in the forces said to me that, in his experience, the best troops available were always put into any crucially key assignment: the kind of troops who *wouldn't* fall asleep on duty. Guarding Jesus' tomb in the expectation that something might be attempted would have qualified for the assignment of good and trustworthy soldiers; and it would be highly unlikely for them (and *all of them* at that!) just to fall asleep while the disciples rolled away the stone and came in and stole Jesus' body. It is not likely, either, that they would have refused to give an explanation which satisfied their employers, who would have preferred the story of human dereliction of duty and a hoax to that of a supernatural action of God, even at the risk of the soldiers appearing to incriminate themselves in a way that they would not normally want to do. This was the Roman era, remember, when the authorities had ways of ensuring that their wishes were obeyed. Nothing about the events of those days could be seen as at all "likely!" But to my mind it strains the imagination *more* to come up with reasons for not believing the apostolic witness to the faith than it does to accept that the coming of God into human history would necessarily have been a momentous occasion.

The theory that "the later Church" created the idea of the divinity of Christ

I strongly disagree with arguments that attempt to attribute belief in the Resurrection or the divinity of Christ to the Church of later years. Too many people were involved and knew about it from the earliest days. Embellishments to the story may have been added later, but that would not affect the main core of Christian belief, *that Jesus was the Son of God, who was crucified, and then rose from the dead:* and whose miracles were not "magic" or legend, but a *sign,* a demonstration, of *Who He was.* [154] Some of our problems today have arisen because too many people seem to have lost understanding of this significant fact.

---

154   e.g.: Jesus' response to John the Baptist was that *the Old Testament prophecies about the Messiah were being fulfilled.* The Feeding of the Five Thousand (echoes of the Old

It is *possible* that stories of shepherds and angels, and Wise Men, at Jesus' birth, might have been inserted into the tradition later on, without anyone being any the wiser, but I believe that details of what happened in Jerusalem, that momentous weekend of the Crucifixion, were too well known and talked about to have been "made up" in a subsequent account written at anywhere near the time that these events occurred. Parts of the Gospels in oral form, or accounts from which they were drawn, were circulating almost from the beginning, and the early epistles were being copied and handed around only a few years later. St. Paul would only have written one letter to Philemon, but it must have been treasured, and copied, and circulated to many people, for it to have become well enough known to be accepted later into the Canon of the New Testament.

The historical fact of the Crucifixion, and the resulting activities of the early Christians that occurred *within days, weeks and months* (not centuries or millennia) thereafter, documented within two or three decades, surely prove that the Christian faith could not have been "invented" *years later.* Belief in the Risen Lord dates from as early as the first Easter Sunday, and was sustained and continued without a break thereafter. We need to remember the historical continuity of witness to that fact, which is not affected by what may, or may not, have happened later.

Whatever "the Church" may have "come up with" later, even if there were little "embroideries" on the main theme, the basic idea of Jesus' resurrection had to date basically from the weekend of the Crucifixion and Resurrection. "The Church" *has* subsequently added many things to the basic faith. That was one of the root causes of the Reformation in the sixteenth and seventeenth centuries, a fact of history. However, we are talking about, basically, one facet of the faith,

Testament: "you shall *know* that I am the Lord your God"), with Peter saying to Jesus "we have believed, and *have come to know,* that you are the holy One of God," and Jesus Walking on the Water ("the disciples worshipped Him, saying 'Truly, you *are* the Son of God' ") convinced the disciples that *the power of God* was involved, as with the man let down through the roof on a stretcher for Jesus to heal (when the scribes said "Who can forgive sins *but God alone?*" Jesus *then* healed the man, saying *"that you may know* that the Son of Man *has authority* on earth to forgive sins"). The fact that Jesus *healed* people was also consistent with the Biblical understanding of *the nature of God* (see the Chapter on Healing).

because everything else depends on that: *did Jesus rise from the dead? Was He, is He, the Son of the Living God?*

And as the Christian faith "took off" rapidly, after Easter Sunday, after Pentecost, I cannot see that it *matters* —in the sense of *cancelling out the basic faith—what* the Church may or may not have dreamed up, centuries later, in the way of additions to that faith, or even variations or serious misunderstandings of it. Mistakes made centuries later, while they may put people off what they wrongly suppose to be "Christianity", something I am trying to address, still do not affect the basic facts of the faith itself, known, believed and attested to, from earliest times. Some deviations were challenged at the time of the Reformation; some, I think, have still not been put right, leaving people confused, hence this book; but I believe that, *even if* "the Church" *has* made mistakes in the past (and it is obvious that it has), the true Church, what St. Augustine called "the invisible Church," *will* survive.

I am talking about the basic, apostolic, faith, which is based on *what happened within the space of a few days and weeks after the Crucifixion,* reported in writing, and discussed and remembered in the lifetimes of many survivors, with documentary evidence from those years still in existence.

It is true that the early Christians were so staggered by what had happened, and by their own experience of their risen Lord, that it was only later that the more profound theological implications were worked through in any detail, particularly in the Gospel of St. John.[155]

It has been popular to date this Gospel as being written at a much later time (part of the theory that "the divinity of Christ" was an idea produced by a later generation, not based on historical fact); but modern scholarship is now attributing to it a date much closer to the events which it describes. The Introduction to "the Gospel according to John" in *The New Oxford Annotated Bible* says:

the historic basis of the Gospel has become increasingly recognized. When it appeared, whether around

155 e.g., John 12:16 (after Jesus quoted Zechariah 9:9): *"His disciples did not understand this at first;* but *when Jesus was glorified, then they remembered* that this had been written of him and had been done to him". Similarly they came to have a new understanding of many other Old Testament passages, and of what this must entail.

> A.D.90-100 *or much earlier as some now hold, it was*
> *accepted as an authentic and apostolic testimony to Jesus.*

Even 100 A.D., the *latest* of the dates referred to above, is less than seventy years after the crucifixion. Even if the author had not been alive sixty-odd years before (and can we be sure that the author was not indeed an old man in his eighties?) that author—and his contemporaries—must have known people who *were* alive at the time of the Crucifixion, and who had, in their own lifetimes, also known many *other* people who had been involved in, or aware of, all those momentous events. The distilled teaching from all these sources that is in the Gospel could, and would, have been contradicted by many people who were still alive at the time that it appeared, if it was erroneous, instead of which it was accepted by them as being true, and later incorporated into the Canon of Scripture.

Many of us have known our grandparents, who, late in life, may have been able to tell us what happened fifty or sixty, or even seventy, years before, so that we would have had that information from them at first hand, and accepted it as an eye-witness report. Multiply that by many, many people having heard the same story from people they knew and loved and trusted, and you have something of an idea of the weight of corroborative evidence that existed from the beginning of the Christian era. Most of us have known veterans from World War II. Although many of them are now old and frail, and many have died, enough of the rest of us have heard their testimony to believe, for example, that the Second World War did happen. Many of us have lived through it. Later historians could not possibly claim that somebody "made it up" in the year 2000.

St. Paul was writing major Epistles, such as the Epistle to the Romans and the First Epistle to the Corinthians, and congregations were reading them, within twenty or twenty-five years after the Crucifixion, in *the middle of* the first century, when actual survivors of that era would certainly still have been around. Not only that, he was writing to Christian communities which had *already been established before that.*

Even if one makes an issue of the fact that the Gospel of St. John *may* not have been circulated much before A.D. 90-100 — although some people maintain that it was earlier than that (and I maintain that, even if it was   as late as that, there would still have been people alive *at that time* who would have known for themselves, at first-hand, other people who *had* been alive then) — *it did not conflict with the teaching propagated by St. Paul within twenty-five years or so after the Resurrection.* In particular, St. Paul and St. John *both* taught that "eternal life" was given by God *in Christ.* [156]

The teaching described by St. John about *"abiding in Christ"* [157] must have been known to St. Paul. It was implicit in all his teaching, before St. John's Gospel ever appeared: statements like, for example, *"in Christ* shall all be made alive", [158] "there is...now no condemnation for those who are *in Christ Jesus";* [159] "if Christ is *in you",* [160] "this mystery, which is *Christ in you,"* [161] and "your life is hid *with Christ in God,"* [162] — the whole theme of being *in and with God through Christ,* which is the theme of this book: the mutual indwelling which could not be possible if Christ were not seen as being somehow *"of God".* *"Rooted and grounded in love"* [163] not only picks up the idea of the vine and the branches from John's Gospel, [164] but also St. John's emphasis on *love,* (which is what "abiding in Christ" — the vine and the branches) is all about, and "being one". [165] *And all the teaching about "the new creation" is based on this.*

There is a further link between St. John and St. Paul, in that the latter said "there are varieties of gifts, but the same Spirit; and ...varieties of service...but it is the same God *who inspires them* all in every one. To each is given the manifestation of the Spirit for the common good...*All these are inspired by one and the same Spirit* who apportions to each one individually as he wills," and *"the mystery of Christ...now...revealed* to

---

156   e.g., 1 John 5:11 ("God gave us *eternal life, and this life is in his Son"),* and Romans 6.23 ("The free gift of God is *eternal life in Christ Jesus our Lord").*

157   John 15:1-10

158   1 Corinthians 15:22

159   Romans 8:1

160   Romans 8:10

161   Colossians 1:27

162   Colossians 3:3

163   Ephesians 3:17

164   John 15:1-10 (which specifically links the metaphor of the vine and the branches with the commandment to love)

165   John 17:20-26

his holy apostles and prophets *by the Spirit"*, while St. John records Jesus' saying *that "the Holy Spirit...will teach you all things, and bring to your remembrance all that I have said to you."* [166]

St. Paul must also have known the teaching later expounded in the Gospel of St. John about "the Lamb of God," [167] because he wrote:

> For *Christ, our paschal lamb, has been sacrificed...*Let us, therefore, celebrate the festival...with...sincerity and truth. [168]

I am convinced that St. Paul believed in the divinity of Christ so passionately affirmed by St. John. Because St. Paul was writing these same things in the early fifties, I do not see how anyone can maintain that St. John was coming up with "new ideas" at the end of that century.

The canonization of certain documents into the canon of the New Testament—accepted as Scripture—was based on the fact that those documents had been *in constant and uninterrupted use from the earliest days of the Church,* even though the *formal* acceptance of them came later. That final decision, as to which documents should be considered as Scripture, only occurred when dispute arose as to which of many documents should be so accepted, (or whether, as proposed by Marcion—who died about 160 A.D.—most of them should be disregarded, including the whole of the Old Testament), and was based not on the fact that "the winning party" in an argument about heresy decided that certain documents "supported their case" but on the fact that the documents finally selected *had been used and agreed upon in all the churches in living memory,* in the true spirit of the original meaning of the word "catholic".

Too many people would have known key details of what happened for someone suddenly to come up with "a brand-new story", at least until many generations later, by which time the Canon of Scripture—

---

166   1 Corinthians 12:4-13, Ephesians 3:4-6, and John 14:26

167   John 1:29 "Behold the Lamb of God!" John 19:14 "Now it was the day of Preparation of the Passover..." and John 19:36 "that the scripture might be fulfilled, *'Not a bone of him shall be broken'* " referring to the passover lamb of the Exodus, (Exodus 12:46: "In one house shall it be eaten... and *you shall not break a bone of it.'*)

168   1 Corinthians 5:7-8

writings in existence almost from the beginning and long held to be authoritative—was already fixed. Not only would the current generation have known what happened, but the story would have been passed on for at least two or three generations, as, in most families, we pass on to our children information about momentous events that have taken place in our own lives. No one has produced evidence that has convinced me that events unfolded in any other way than that described in the New Testament, which I find much more believable than any other theory.

Moreover, if, having accepted the faith intellectually, one seeks to know Christ for oneself, the confirmation will then come abundantly into one's very living, in a relationship with the Living God. Of course, human beings do make mistakes, and not everything that gets reported may be exactly what happened, not everything that is said may be entirely accurate, and one has to make allowances for that fact, but it should not destroy one's faith in God if minor details of the tradition can be proved to be not so, if one holds onto the basic, essential, aspects of the faith.

The New Testament was put together drawing on only some of many documents. St. Luke said at the beginning of his Gospel that

> Inasmuch as many have undertaken to compile a
> narrative of the things [which happened] among us,
> it seemed good to me also, having followed all things
> closely for some time past, to write an orderly account
> for you.....that you may know the truth concerning
> the things of which you have been informed. [169]

It was the strong belief of the early Christians that Jesus was the fulfillment of the Hebrew Scriptures, now our "Old Testament". Right from the very beginning, Christians have found authentication for their faith in the words of the Old Testament, as well as in their personal experiences of the Risen Lord. The phrase *"according to the Scriptures"* was considered to be so important that it was incorporated into the Nicene Creed. St. Paul wrote as early as his First Epistle to the Corinthians: "I delivered to you as of first importance what I also received, that Christ died for our sins *in accordance with the scriptures,*

---

169   Luke 1:1-4

that he was buried, that he was raised on the third day *in accordance with the scriptures".* [170]

Biblical "proofs" in themselves will not convince anyone who is not open to discovering more about how Christians understand their faith. However, they can be a vehicle through which we can draw closer to the God whom those Scriptures describe, and I set some of them before you now. Sometimes people can get discouraged when they get "bogged down" in some of the more difficult passages of the Bible, but I am hoping to show you that there really are jewels of spiritual understanding in the Bible, if you prayerfully seek them, because they can confirm our faith, strengthen our will, and nourish our souls in prayer.

Many people, from Marcion onwards, have not been able to relate the Old Testament to the New, or the God of the Old Testament to the Christian understanding of God in the New Testament. I hope to show that in all the diversity of the Bible there is a basic unity, and it is the nature of the One God that holds the whole Bible together.

St. Luke's account of the journey to Emmaus shows that the disciples' belief in *Jesus as Lord* was corroborated by their new understanding of the existing Hebrew Scriptures, and that this understanding was acquired on the *actual day of the Resurrection.* They immediately began to remember what Jesus had told them during His earthly ministry, which often, at the time, they had not really understood, and, although this new understanding may have been refined by people like St. John and his disciples in later years, the apostles were publicly referring to the prophecies of the Hebrew Scriptures right from the beginning, as the Book of the Acts of the Apostles clearly shows. A key example is St. Peter saying of Jesus *"he is the one ordained by God to be judge of the living and the dead. To him all the prophets bear witness* that every one who believes in him receives forgiveness of sins through his name". [171] That is a clear statement both about the divinity of Christ—*"judge of the living and the dead"* — and the fact that *"to him all the prophets bear witness".*

St. Luke's account of the journey to Emmaus on the first Easter Sunday is as follows (the emphases are mine):

---

170   1 Corinthians 15:3-4
171   Acts 10:42-43

one of them, named Cleopas, [said] 'Are you the only visitor to Jerusalem who does not know the things that have happened there in these days?...Concerning Jesus of Nazareth, who was a prophet mighty in word and deed...and...our chief priests and rulers delivered him up to be condemned to death, and crucified him... we had hoped ...he was the one to redeem Israel....it is now the third day since this happened [and] some women of our company....were at the tomb early in the morning and did not find his body; and....came back saying that they had...seen a vision of angels, who said that he was alive. Some of those who were with us went to the tomb, and found it just as the women had said; but him they did not see.' And he said to them 'O foolish men, and slow of heart to believe all that the prophets have spoken! Was it not necessary that the Christ should suffer these things...?' And *beginning with Moses and all the prophets, he interpreted to them in all the scriptures the things concerning himself.* [172]

They invited him to stay the night with them, and

when he was at table with them, he took the bread and blessed, and broke it, and gave it to them. And their eyes were opened and they recognized him; and he vanished out of their sight. They said to each other, *'Did not our hearts burn within us while he talked to us on the road, while he opened to us the scriptures?'* And they rose that same hour and returned to Jerusalem; and they found the eleven gathered together, and those who were with them, who said 'The Lord is risen indeed, and has appeared to Simon!' Then they told what had happened on the road, and how he was known to them *in the breaking of the bread.* [173]

This passage really describes the Christian experience, dating from the day of Resurrection itself: Jesus being known to His people in the

---

172   Luke 24:13-27
173   Luke 24:30-35

breaking of bread, and having their understanding illumined by the Scriptures: "the word and sacrament" of the Church ever since. The illumination of the understanding through reading of the Scriptures has been rekindled in every generation, though in some more than others: but it is in danger of becoming lost to us today, if we too readily discount the authority of the Bible, and fail to pass on to succeeding generations *"the things concerning Himself"* to be found in it.

At the time referred to above, the New Testament had not yet come into existence, so the Scriptures referred to, and used by Jesus on that occasion, had to have been the Hebrew Scriptures of the Old Testament. But the whole of the New Testament is based, *not only* on the fact that Jesus was the Son of God who was crucified and rose from the dead, but also that *He was the fulfillment of the Jewish Scriptures already in existence.* The apostles taught the faith in the context of the Hebrew tradition from which it had sprung, giving people a new insight into the Old Testament, to help them to understand more fully their new-found faith in Christ.

The second chapter of the Book of Acts records the coming of the Holy Spirit on the faithful on the day of Pentecost, fifty days after that first Easter, which has been described as the official launching of "the Church", and almost immediately St. Peter preached the first public sermon, based on the Jews' own Scriptures:

> Peter [addressed the crowd, saying] 'Men of Judea and all who dwell in Jerusalem.....these men are not drunk, as you suppose....this is what was spoken by the prophet Joel: "And in the last days it shall be, God declares, that I will pour out my Spirit upon all flesh" ' [174]

referring to a prophecy in the Book of Joel. In that same speech, St. Peter also referred to verses in Psalms 16, 110 and 132.

In a second sermon, described in the third chapter of the Book of Acts, St. Peter gave a longer account of the Christian faith, and said

> '…The God of Abraham and of Isaac and of Jacob, the God of our fathers, glorified his servant Jesus, whom you delivered up…I know that you acted in ignorance, as did also your rulers. *But what God foretold by the*

---

174   Acts 2:1-17 - quoting Joel 2:28-32

mouth of all the prophets, that his Christ should suffer, he thus fulfilled.....*And all the prophets who have spoken, from Samuel and those who came afterwards, also proclaimed these days.'* [175]

St. Stephen, before his martyrdom, gave a long speech recounting the history of the Jewish people from the time of Abraham and the patriarchs, and ended by saying, what infuriated the crowd gathered round him at the time:

'Which of the prophets did not your fathers persecute? And they killed those who announced beforehand the coming of the Righteous One, whom you have now betrayed and murdered.' [176]

When St. Philip met an Ethiopian struggling to understand a passage from Isaiah which he was reading ("As a sheep led to the slaughter, or a lamb before its shearer is dumb, so he opens not his mouth") [177], St. Philip explained it to him in a Christian context, *("beginning with this scripture* he told him the good news of Jesus"), and, as a result, the Ethiopian asked to be baptized immediately. [178]

The early Christians found in the Book of the prophet Isaiah many things which they attributed to Christ: the Suffering Servant, for one, and His self-offering, which is important for an understanding of the Atonement, and quite possibly "sheep led to the slaughter" would have resonated in their minds with teaching about Jesus as the Lamb of God, the Passover Lamb *par excellence.* In a description in St. Matthew's Gospel of how Jesus healed people, it was said: "This was to fulfil what was spoken by the prophet Isaiah, 'He took our infirmities and bore our diseases'." [179]

There is no doubt that the earliest Christians believed that Christ was the fulfillment of Old Testament prophecy, and that Jesus Himself had taught them that this was so. For example, St. Luke's Gospel records that Jesus said:

---

175 Acts 3:12-24
176 Acts 7:52
177 Isaiah 53:7
178 Acts 8:27-38
179 Matthew 8:17

'...For I tell you that *this scripture must be fulfilled in me,* "And he was reckoned with transgressors"; *for what is written about me has its fulfilment*[180]

and St. Matthew records that on the night before the Crucifixion He said: "But all this has taken place, that *the scriptures of the prophets might be fulfilled*".[181]

Right from the beginning of His ministry He made this claim.

He went to the synagogue, as his custom was, on the sabbath day. And he stood up to read; and there was given to him the book of the prophet Isaiah. He opened the book and found the place where it was written, 'The Spirit of the Lord is upon *me.....' And he began to say to them,* 'Today this scripture has been fulfilled in your hearing'.[182]

When John the Baptist was in prison, he sent word to Jesus, to ask Him if He really was the Messiah:

'Are you he who is to come, or shall we look for another?' And Jesus answered them, 'Go and tell John what you hear and see; the blind receive their sight and the lame walk, lepers are cleansed and the deaf hear, and the dead are raised up, and the poor have the good news preached to them. And blessed is he who takes no offence at me.'[183]

referring, of course, to the prophecies of Isaiah that such would be the situation when the Messiah came,[184] and saying, in effect, "go and tell

---

180   Luke 22:37

181   Matthew 26:56

182   Luke 4:22

183   Matthew 11:3-5

184   Isaiah 29:18-19: "In that day the deaf shall hear...the eyes of the blind shall see. The meek shall obtain fresh joy in the Lord, and the poor among men shall exult in the Holy One of Israel"; Isaiah 35:5-6: "Then the eyes of the blind shall be opened, and the ears of the deaf unstopped; then shall the lame man leap like a hart, and the tongue of the dumb sing for joy." Isaiah 61:l: (quoted) "The Spirit of the Lord God is upon me, because the Lord has anointed me to bring good tidings to the afflicted...."

John what you can see for yourselves is happening—isn't it obvious? Yes, I am He who is to come."

Luke's Gospel records that just before the Ascension, when Jesus disappeared from their physical sight for the last time, He said to the disciples:

> 'These are my words which I spoke to you, while I was still with you, that *everything written about me in the law of Moses and the prophets and the psalms must be fulfilled.*' Then he opened their minds *to understand the scriptures,* and said to them, '*Thus it is written....*' [185]

The apostles continued this teaching. In addition to the passages quoting St. Peter, already referred to, it is also described in the Book of Acts how St. Paul

> *argued with them from the scriptures,* explaining and proving that it was necessary for the Christ to suffer and to rise from the dead, and saying, 'This Jesus, whom I proclaim to you, is the Christ.' [186]

I have said before that, while perhaps it is possible to discount one or another of the documents of the New Testament, for some reason, if one is so minded, it does become much more difficult credibly to discount them *all.*

I have tried to show, *not only* that, if St. John's teaching had been radically different from that of St. Paul, one or the other of them would have been challenged, and not incorporated into the Canon of Scripture on a par with the other, but *also* that there are common motifs running through the writings of both men, so that what St. John wrote later on had already been vouched for, as it were, by St. Paul (and others) much earlier.

I do not see how anyone can reasonably argue that St. John, or

---

185   Luke 24:44-46. See also John 5:39-40: "You search the scriptures, because you think that in them you have eternal life; and it is *they that bear witness to me;* yet you refuse to come to me that you may have *life*"; and John 1:45: "Philip...said...'We have found *him of whom Moses in the law and also the prophets wrote,* Jesus of Nazareth...'"

186   Acts 17:2-3. Similarly Acts 28:23: [Paul was] "trying to convince them about Jesus *both from the law of Moses and from the prophets.*"

his followers, or anyone else, came up with "something new" "much later".

Lee Strobel has written *"The Case for Christ: A Journalist's Personal Investigation of the Evidence for Jesus"* which documents his conviction that the historical evidence supports the claims of the Bible.[187] (I am dealing more with the spiritual side of the argument that the traditional faith is early and authentic.)

But, even if you felt like discounting the whole of the New Testament, how would you explain away the many references in the Old Testament which the Christian church has traditionally accepted as referring to Christ which still remain in the Hebrew Scriptures, *and for which there is no satisfactory understanding apart from Him?*

It could be said that those Old Testament Scriptures foretold a Messiah who has not yet come: but, as I try to show, there has been no other human candidate in the history of the world so far who would "fit the bill" in the way that Jesus of Nazareth did. And, as it would appear that we are today burning up the resources of the earth at a tremendous rate, and, indeed, could destroy this planet at any moment, and are starting to clone creatures and "create life", it could be thought that the world as we know it will soon have run its course. I would have thought, therefore, that the Messiah would have had to have come by now, in the middle of history, for the Incarnation of God in human history to make sense in the way that I have described. And, as Jesus can be known to anyone who really seeks to know the truth "concerning Himself", and has been known to many millions of people who have truly sought to find Him, I do not think that anyone who claims not to believe in His "divinity" can seriously have tried to find Him.

The Jews were expecting that the coming Messiah, the great Prophet foretold by Moses,[188] would be a great and mighty king and leader, who would confirm the greatness of the Jewish people; a great and glorious King; which, I personally believe has come true in the person of Jesus, although not in the way the Jews expected. The Book of Revelation refers to him as "King of Kings and Lord of Lords".[189]

---

187   Lee Strobel: *The Case for Christ: A Journalist's Personal Investigation of the Evidence for Jesus.* Grand Rapids, Michigan: Zondervan, 1998.

188   Deuteronomy 18:15, 18

189   Revelation 19:16

Yet Isaiah spoke of Him as "a man of sorrows, and acquainted with grief": [190]

> He was despised and rejected by men [191] —He had no form or comeliness that we should look at him, and no beauty that we should desire him [192] —he was despised and we esteemed him not. [193]

These two aspects—of kingship and glory, combined with servanthood and suffering—are held in unique tension in the Christian understanding of Christ.

But the passages that are really hard to understand, except in the context of the crucified Messiah, are the ones that speak of our redemption through His suffering:

> Surely he has borne our griefs and carried our sorrows; yet we esteemed him stricken, smitten by God, and afflicted. But he was wounded for our transgressions, he was bruised for our iniquities; upon him was the chastisement that made us whole, and with his stripes we are healed. All we like sheep have gone astray; we have turned every one to his own way; and the Lord has laid on him the iniquity of us all. [194]

In the chapter on the Atonement I will explain my belief that, although it was physically the body of Jesus that was on the Cross, the whole of the Godhead was involved in the events of the Crucifixion and Resurrection. It was not, as the old-fashioned belief had it, that a vindictive God who had to be appeased laid on "poor Jesus" "the iniquity of us all". The passage goes on immediately to say:

> *when he makes himself* an offering for sin.....*he shall see the fruit of the travail of his soul and be satisfied* [195] and *He poured out his soul to death,* and was numbered with

---

190   Isaiah 53:3
191   Isaiah 53:3
192   Isaiah 53:2
193   Isaiah 53:3
194   Isaiah 53:4-6
195   Isaiah 53:10-11

the transgressors; *yet he bore the sin of many, and made intercession for the transgressors.* [196]

Jesus was not just a passive victim: the context of the whole passage indicates that *"He [made] himself an offering for sin".* [197] The next chapter goes on to say: ".....with everlasting love I will have compassion on you, says the Lord, *your Redeemer....."* [198]

Other passages that would seem to be inexplicable without reference to Jesus are the verses in Psalm 22:

> they have pierced my hands and feet—I can count all
> my bones....they divide my garments among them, and
> for my raiment they cast lots

and the passage in Zechariah: "they shall look upon him whom they pierced". [199]

I do not see how these passages can be interpreted and understood, except in the context of their referring to Jesus of Nazareth being the crucified Christ.

I can see a possible argument, if one even considers the conspiracy, "hoax" theory, that Jesus and His disciples might have deliberately acted out what was in some of the prophecies: for example, they might have "staged" the procession into Jerusalem, to be seen to be fulfilling the prophecy:

> *Lo, your king comes to you; triumphant and victorious is*
> *he, humble and riding on an ass, on a colt the foal of an*
> *ass* [200]

but even then I would have a counter-argument. That verse is still inexplicable unless it is understood from the Christian perspective, because of the unlikelihood of someone fulfilling the unexpected

196   Isaiah 53:12

197   Isaiah 53:10: see the footnote in the chapter on the Atonement re. this being the RSV and Vulgate version though not the actual Hebrew

198   Isaiah 54:8-10

199   Psalm 22:16-18; Zechariah 12:10: "And I will pour out on the house of David and the inhabitants of Jerusalem a spirit of compassion and supplication, so that, when they look on him whom they have pierced, they shall mourn for him"

200   Zechariah 9:9

qualification of being *both* a *triumphant king,* and, at the same time, *someone humble, and riding on an ass* rather than on a greater and more dignified and expensive animal.

The words themselves, in the original Old Testament, *pose this problem of inconsistency* which cannot be explained other than by being taken in the context of the Crucified King,[201] and the Suffering Servant of Isaiah who was also the King of Kings and Lord of Lords of the Book of Revelation.[202]

Even if Jesus had deliberately sought crucifixion in order to fulfill Psalm 22—highly unlikely! —there is no way that the disciples could possibly have known that Roman soldiers, dividing His garments among them, would throw lots for His seamless robe,[203] nor would they have been able to cause them to do so. I would imagine that there would have been no way in which ordinary Galileans would have been able to influence Roman soldiers to be party to any "plot" of their making.

Even if one argues that some subsequent "reading back" went on, there still remains the massive weight of prophetic evidence in support of the legitimacy of the Christian claim, much more than a small group of humble Galileans could possibly have accounted for. I think it is more difficult to believe in a "hoax" theory than it is to accept the Christian faith.

The verse in Isaiah 49 "I have graven you on the palms of my hands" might well be understood to be only a poetic way of saying that God not only has His people as close to Him as His people were supposed to be to Him when they carried His Law on their hands and foreheads,[204] but in the case of God He was closer, because God has the remembrance of us engraved deep into Himself: not superficially

---

201 Matthew 27:37: "over his head they put the charge against him, which read [mockingly] 'This is Jesus, *the King of the Jews* ' "

202 Isaiah 53 and Revelation 19:16

203 Psalm 22:16-18: "They divide my garments among them, and for my raiment they cast lots".

204 Isaiah 49:16; and Deuteronomy 6:4- 8: "Hear, O Israel, the Lord our God is one Lord, and you shall love the Lord your God with all your heart....And these words which I command you this day shall be on your heart; and you shall teach them diligently to your children....And you shall bind them as a sign upon your hand, and they shall be as frontlets between your eyes."

on the surface only, as was mandated to God's people in the Law, but permanently imprinted in Himself — *engraved* on the palms of His hands.

In itself, alone, that is all that this verse might be seen to convey; but if one starts to see a Christian significance in the other verses I have quoted, one can't help seeing a possible connection between this verse and the marks of the nails in the hands of the crucified and eternal Christ: it all seems to go together. Similarly, it is recorded in all four Gospels that Jesus was given vinegar, or wine mixed with gall, to drink, when He was on the Cross, and part of Psalm 69 comes to mind.[205] There are too many such examples for them *all* to be "just coincidence".

There are references in the Old Testament to God being the one who could still the sea, and in the New Testament to Jesus being the One who did.

> Psalm 107 says: 'They cried to the Lord in their trouble, and he delivered them from their distress; *he made the storm be still, and the waves of the sea were hushed.*'[206]

> Psalm 65 refers to God as being the one '*who dost still the roaring of the seas.*'[207]

> Job described God as the one '*who alone stretched out the heavens, and trampled [walked on] the waves of the sea*', and said of Him '*By his power He stilled the sea*'[208], i.e., as its Creator, He has power over the sea.

It is in the context of the Jews knowing these passages, referring to the power of God to control the elements, that Jesus' stilling of the storm made such an impact. This account is from St. Mark's Gospel:

> [Jesus] "awoke and rebuked the wind, and said to the

---

205 Matthew 27:34, Mark 15:36, Luke 23:36, John 19:29: Psalm 69:21 "for my thirst they gave me vinegar to drink"

206 Psalm 107:29

207 Psalm 65:5-7: "O God of our salvation, who art the hope of all the ends of the earth, and of the farthest seas; who by thy strength has established the mountains, being girded with might; who dost still the roaring of the seas"

208 Job 9:8 and Job 26:12

sea, 'Peace, be still!' And the wind ceased, and there
was a great calm..." [His disciples] were "filled with
awe, and said to one another *'Who then is this, that even
wind and sea obey him?'"* [209]—knowing, of course, that
such attributes were applicable to descriptions of God
in the writings of the Hebrew Scriptures.

Even if some modern theologians do not think that St. Paul believed
in the divinity of Christ, [210] I am *convinced* that Paul believed that
Jesus of Nazareth was the Incarnation of God on earth: that, though
in human form, *He was of the same substance as God Himself* (see the
following discussion of Romans 9:5). The words of Paul's writings in
many places speak for themselves, even his statement at one point that
he was resolved to preach only "Jesus Christ and *him crucified*". [211] In
the latter case, St. Paul was not referring to Jesus of Nazareth, the man,
who was crucified, to which one might reply, "so what?" Many people
were crucified in those days. The very words he used imply that he
was preaching about the "Christ", the Messiah—otherwise what was
the point of preaching about Him?—and *the Messiah being crucified*,
something quite different from the crucifixion of an ordinary man:
and the implication, arising from that fact, of *the Messiah* being risen
from the dead, otherwise there would have been no point in preaching
about His death in the first place.

People might argue about "the Messiah" being a great *man*,
"anointed by God to fulfill that role", but one immediately has to ask:
what role, if the Messiah were not essentially from and of God, to
bring the human race to God in the way that I am trying to describe?

I believe that the Atonement is not just about "somebody doing
something so that we are forgiven our sins": it is about *our coming to
union with God through abiding in Christ,* and for *that* Christ has to
be a part of God.

And arguments that question St. Paul's belief in the divinity of
Christ contradict, or do not explain, passages such as his Trinitarian
reference in the Epistle to the Ephesians [212]

---

209   Mark 4:41

210   see the section following on Romans 9:5 , re. Anthony Cotter, writing in 1945

211   1 Corinthians 2:2

212   Ephesians 3:4-19

> I bow my knees before *the Father*...that...he may...
> grant you to be strengthened with might through
> *his Spirit*...and that *Christ* may dwell in your hearts
> through faith; that you, being rooted and grounded in
> love...may be filled with *all the fulness of God*

and his statement in the Epistle to the Colossians,[213] (which was,
of course, written *after* the Resurrection) saying of Christ that "in
[Him] *the whole fullness of deity dwells bodily*"; nor his equating
"The Lord" (God) with Christ in the First Epistle to the Corinthians,
in referring to the verse in the Book of the prophet Isaiah where it is
written:

> Who has measured the waters in the hollow of his
> hand and marked off the heavens with a span..... .and
> weighed the mountains in scales and the hills in a
> balance? Who has directed the Spirit of the Lord, or
> as his counselor has instructed him? Whom did he
> consult for his enlightenment, and who taught him the
> path of justice, and taught him knowledge, and showed
> him the way of understanding? [214]

St. Paul, who would have known the writings in Isaiah well, wrote
to the Corinthians, in the context of Christ: "The spiritual man judges
all things, but is himself to be judged by no one. 'For who has known
the mind of the Lord so as to instruct him?' But we have the mind of
Christ." [215] A footnote in *The New Oxford Annotated Version* of the
Bible states: "The man with the Spirit has *the mind of Christ,* and no
one is in a position to instruct *Christ. The Lord* (Isaiah 40.13, referring
to God) is here applied to Christ."

With these examples alone, how can one allege that the early
Christians, as exemplified by St. Paul for instance, did not see Jesus
of Nazareth as being somehow of the very substance of God? Words
such as "Messiah" and "Christ" used in any sense other than this make
nonsense of the whole. And then there is the following, in the Epistle
to the Philippians which is even more dramatic:

---

213 Colossians 2:9

214 Isaiah 40:12-14

215 1 Corinthians 2:15-16

Christ Jesus who, *though he was in the form of God,*
did not count *equality with God* a thing to be grasped,
but emptied himself, taking the form of a servant,
being born in the likeness of men. And being found
in human form *he humbled himself and became obedient
unto death, even death on a cross.* Therefore God has
highly exalted him and bestowed on him the name
which is above every name, *that, at the name of Jesus,
every knee should bow....and every tongue confess that
Jesus Christ is Lord, to the glory of God the Father.* [216]

St. Paul, well versed in the Scriptures, must have known that when
he said *"every knee shall bow,"* he was using for Jesus the same words of
Isaiah *that applied to Almighty God.* And every Jew would have known
the *Shema: "the Lord* your God is *One Lord".* [217] St. Paul—trained
by Gamaliel [218] —must have known the implications of what he was
saying, and done it deliberately.

The passage in Isaiah runs:

*I am the Lord, and there is no other....there is no other
god beside me, a righteous God and a Savior; there is
none besides me.* Turn to me and be saved, all the
ends of the earth! *For I am God, and there is no other.*
By myself I have sworn, from my mouth has gone forth
in righteousness, a word that shall not return: *'To me
every knee shall bow, every tongue shall swear.'* [219]

St. Paul was making quite a statement, and must have known what
he was doing, and done it on purpose.

The Book of Revelation carries a similar message: " *'I am the Alpha
and the Omega', says the Lord God,* who is and who was and who is to
come, the Almighty, [220] [which is fair enough, talking about Almighty

---

216   Philippians 2:6-11

217   Deuteronomy 6:4

218   Acts 22:3: Paul said: "I am a Jew...brought up...*at the feet of Gamaliel, educated according to the strict manner of the law of our fathers";*   Acts 5:34: "... a Pharisee in the
council named Gamaliel,   a teacher of the law, *held in honor by all the people..."*

219   Isaiah 45 v. 18, and vv. 21-23

220   Revelation 1:8

God; but the passage then goes on to say:] I [the writer] turned to see the voice that was speaking..., and...saw...one *like a son of man* ..[who said] 'Fear not, *I am the first and the last* and the living one; *I died* and behold *I am alive for evermore,* and I have the keys of Death and Hades.' " [221] "Alpha" and "Omega" are the *first and last* letters of the Greek alphabet (the original writings of the New Testament were in Greek). The One who is "the first and the last and the living one" must be *Christ,* because it says that He *"died".* The expression *"the first and the last"* is, however, used *of God* in the Old Testament, [222] and the expression *"Alpha and Omega",* with a similar meaning *("the beginning and the end")* is used of God in the Book of Revelation. The latter passage also goes on to talk about "the water of life" which comes from God, and runs as follows:

> *I am the Alpha and the Omega,* the beginning and the end. *To the thirsty* I will give from *the fountain of the water of life* without payment. He who conquers shall have this heritage, and *I will be his God and he shall be my son.* [223]

It would appear, therefore, that *the water of life* that comes from God was seen as coming from Christ also, and that therefore Christ must be part of God the Trinity for this to be so.

This would make sense of a lot of things, from the passage in Isaiah ("every one who thirsts, come to the waters"), [224] to Jesus saying:

> *'whoever drinks of the water that I shall give him will never thirst; the water that I shall give him will become in him a spring of water welling up to eternal life'* [225]

to the passage in the Book of Revelation about "the Lamb in the midst of the throne will be their shepherd, *and he will guide them to springs of living water".* [226]

I will put at the end of this chapter a tentative explanation of St.

---

221   Revelation 1:12-18
222   Isaiah 44:6-8
223   Revelation 21:6-7
224   Isaiah 55:1
225   John 4:14
226   Revelation 7:17

John's emphasis on the water that flowed from the side of the crucified Christ on the Cross, and his enigmatic statement in his first Epistle about "the Spirit, the water, and the blood", and St. Paul's statement that the "Rock" which was the source of supernaturally-supplied water in the Old Testament "was Christ". [227] This was in his first Epistle to the Corinthians, which was one of the earliest of his letters. I believe that the fact that that Epistle was widely accepted and later put into the Canon of New Testament Scripture means that St. Paul was not saying anything that the earliest Christians would have taken exception to.

There are quite a few references to God as being "the Rock" in the Hebrew Scriptures which are our Old Testament (they are listed in the Appendix) but I would remind you specifically of the following one, because it draws together the theme of *"the first and the last"*, referred to above, with "the Rock":

> Thus says the LORD, the King of Israel and his Redeemer, the LORD of hosts: *'I am the first and I am the last; besides me there is no god.* Who is like me? Let him proclaim it.... *Is there a God besides me? There is no Rock; I know not any.'* [228]

These passages, taken together, not only show an identification of Christ with "God", in Biblical understanding, in other words, His membership, if you can call it that, in the Trinity, so demonstrating His "divinity", but also support a major argument of this book: that the "living water" that transforms the spiritual deserts of this life comes to us *from God through Christ* — which would not be possible if Christ were not somehow part of God. (And how could St. Paul, who would have known the above quotation and agreed with it, equate Christ with *"the Rock"* unless he did believe that He was *part of* that One God?)

We have come a long way, on the subject of Biblical references implying the divinity of Christ, without relying heavily on the teaching of St. John. I believe that teaching about the Trinity runs through the Bible, and is not dependent upon what we may or may not like about the writing of St. John. However, if one accepts the Christian faith at all, even if only based on the evidence produced so far, I see no

---

227   1 Corinthians 10:1-4

228   Isaiah 44:6-8

reason to discredit the teaching of St. John simply because it is a more explicit exposition of its theology.

When, according to the Gospel of St. John, Jesus used the words "I AM" on many occasions, *He was using the divine Name.*[229] On one occasion He said "before Abraham was I AM" [230] which did several things at once, including thoroughly, infuriating His listeners: He was using the divine Name of Himself and claiming to have been in existence before Abraham was ever born, in other words, He was claiming to be God, the eternal "I AM". His audience, seeing this as blasphemy, tried to stone Him, but He escaped.

There were several instances of the similar use of "I AM": "I AM the way and the truth and the life",[231] and "I AM the resurrection and the life"; [232] "I AM the light of the world;" [233] and, in particular, "I AM the vine and you are the branches",[234] *which I believe only makes sense in the context of "abiding in Christ," and His being of and from God.*

Even if, as some modern scholars allege, the phrase "I AM" was only attributed to Jesus *later,* which I dispute, *it still means* that the earliest Christians who accepted that Gospel *believed* that Jesus *really was* I AM: and if one is to believe accounts in the Synoptic Gospels as well as St. John, Jesus Himself *must* have been aware in His lifetime of the reality of Who He was.

The passage about Jesus' claiming to be the Good Shepherd is of particular significance, because again He used the "I AM", and claimed to be the Shepherd of God's people, (the "Good" Shepherd, as opposed to the human and sinful ones that God rejected), *which was a role reserved for God Himself,* according to the prophet Ezekiel:

As I live, says the Lord God [strong language!]...because

---

229 Exodus 3:13-14: "Moses said to God 'If I come to the people of Israel and say to them, "the God of your fathers has sent me to you," and they ask me "What is his name?" what shall I say to them?' God said to Moses 'I AM WHO I AM.' And he said 'say this to the people of Israel, I AM has sent me to you...' "

230 John 8:58

231 John 14:6

232 John 11:25-26

233 John 9:5

234 John 15:5

my shepherds have not searched for my sheep....and have not fed my sheep...Thus says the Lord God...*I will require my sheep at their hand....I will rescue my sheep.*. For thus says the Lord God: Behold, *I, I myself will search for my sheep, and will seek them out*...I will feed them with good pasture....*I myself will be the shepherd of my sheep....says the Lord God*...*they shall know that I, the Lord their God, am with them....you are my sheep, the sheep of my pasture, and I am your God,* says the Lord God. [235]

In addition, Psalm 23 says: *"The Lord is my shepherd,* I shall not want, He makes me to lie down" [in other words, be free to relax and rest because all dangers have been taken care of] "in green pastures" [i.e. with all needs supplied]. So when Jesus said "I AM the Good Shepherd" [236] *He was claiming affinity with the God of the Hebrew Scriptures, and His hearers knew it.*

His statement that "I AM the Bread of Life" [237] is harder to understand, but it does make sense when looked at in the context of the Bible as a whole. I believe this is so important to understanding the faith that I have elaborated on it in the chapter on the Trinity.

Similarly, in the chapter on the Atonement, I have shown how *"abiding in Christ"* not only ties in with the Old Testament concept of living *in God,* but necessarily entails the divinity of Christ.

Although scholars can dispute, and weigh, the different books of the Bible, and different passages in them, and possibly attribute less weight to some than to others, I think that the sheer weight of evidence, over all, speaks for itself, as being powerfully the message of the Bible as a whole. We do not need to depend for our faith on a verse here or there, but on the Bible in its totality, as the Word of God comes to us through it, as a common theme, the many parts of it making up together a consistent whole; and I hope that I have shown that it does "all hang together" as a piece.

---

235   Ezekiel 34:1-15 & 31; see also Psalm 80:1-4: "Give ear, *O Shepherd of Israel,* thou who leadest Joseph like a flock! Thou *who art enthroned upon the cherubim,* shine forth.... Stir up thy might, and come to save us! Restore us, *O God,* let thy face shine, that we may be saved! *O Lord God of Hosts,* how long wilt thou be angry..."

236   John 10:11

237   John 6:35

Even if one or two parts of it could be argued over, or even dispensed with, to my mind *the message of the whole cannot.* Even if, perhaps, superstitious and credulous beliefs did creep into some of the stories around Jesus' birth, for example, that, to me, is not as important, in itself, as the fact that *I still believe in the Incarnation:* that God did somehow come into the world, at a certain time and place in history, to be born as the son of a woman called Mary, *somehow,* in a way beyond our understanding, being *in Himself both God and Man.*

I now come to two passages in the New Testament that I believe to be of particular significance but which are also ambiguous or hard to understand. I think that they should be seen, not as standing on their own, in which case I think it would be quite legitimate to question them, but in the context of all that has gone before. If what has gone before is convincing testimony to the faith, why should one then assume that the divinity of Christ, which can be inferred from these last two, cannot be the intended meaning?

These two particular instances are, first, the question of what St. Paul meant to say in *Romans 9:5,* because the lack of punctuation in the original Greek makes the verse capable of two different translations; and, secondly, a possible explanation of a very difficult verse in the *First Epistle of St. John,* which I believe is related to the peculiar emphasis given in the *Gospel* of St. John to the piercing of Jesus' side at the Crucifixion. There is no unanimous agreement among scholars with regard to these passages: in fact, I believe that the Johannine ones have been much misunderstood.

Romans 9:5

With regard to St. Paul's understanding of the divinity of Christ, Romans 9:5 is, I believe, a passage of great importance in this regard. It is one which, because it is possible to interpret it in two different ways because of its lack of punctuation, has often been understood in what I consider to be "the wrong way," *a view shared by one of the two editors of The Oxford Annotated Version* of the *Revised Standard Version* of the Bible, [238] as I will go on to show.

This whole book is based on the premise that the Bible, when

---

238   Bruce Metzger

interpreted and understood in the way in which it was meant to be, is to be taken seriously in describing for us *what God is like.*

I believe that the Bible testifies to the Trinitarian God of the Christian faith, *the God of Love,* and that, indeed, *it is the only definition of "God" the world has ever known that really makes sense:* one that answers questions that the other religions do not even address.

I believe that this book will show that there are so many passages in the Bible that carry the same message about the nature of God that their teaching should guide us when dealing with texts that are capable of more than one interpretation.

I have problems with people who take a text, (e.g. Romans 9:5 or Colossians 1:15-20), and say "Oh, St. Paul would never have said that", when it is (to me anyway) *quite obvious from his other writings* exactly what St. Paul said and believed.

St. Paul wrote in his Epistle to the Romans, speaking of the Jews:

> They are Israelites, and to them belong the sonship, the
> glory, the covenants...to them belong the patriarchs, and
> of their race, according to the flesh, is the Christ....

— so far there is no problem. Then the original Greek continues:

> *"......God over all blessed for ever   Amen."* [239]

Because there is no punctuation in the original Greek, there are several equally legitimate ways in which this could be translated into English, but with different meanings.

One, for example, is to put a full-stop after the word "Christ", and then make a new sentence, a doxology, as if the writer was suddenly saying, in effect, "Praise God!" In that case the translation would read:

> of their race, according to the flesh, [is] the Christ.
> God over all [be] blessed for ever, Amen. (There is no
> "be" in the Greek.)

This is the translation—or the rendition—used in *The Revised Standard Version* of the Bible. [240]

---

239   Romans 9:4-5

240   The New Testament section, copyright 1946: Cotter (referred to herein) was writing in
    1945.

However, there is another equally valid way of rendering this passage, which is to assume that *"God over all, blessed for ever"* refers *to Christ,* and that it is all one sentence, in which case it would read: "of their race, according to the flesh, *[is] the Christ, God over all, blessed for ever"* —in other words "of their race, according to the flesh, *[is]* the Christ *[who is]* God over all, blessed for ever, Amen." This is the version used in *the New International Version* of the Bible as its primary translation, (with just a footnote about the alternative reading), and it runs as follows:

> Theirs are the patriarchs, and *from them is traced the human ancestry of Christ, who is God over all, forever praised! Amen.* [241]

This is the meaning that I believe St. Paul meant to convey, partly because I believe it to be the truth, and partly because I do not think that St. Paul was so stupid or careless as to make an unintentional "mistake" of such potential gravity. He may deliberately have camouflaged his message in ambiguity, for his own reasons, but he was a literate, scholarly man, a Roman citizen, at home in the Roman Empire, familiar with Greek, who had been trained, as has been noted, by one of the most famous Rabbis, Gamaliel: [242] and I cannot believe that he was *unaware* that what he wrote could convey more than one meaning in Greek.

I am sure that, as a devout Jew, if he had sincerely believed that Jesus was *not* "God", he would have been the first to correct something in his writing which could be interpreted as "blasphemous". Instead, he not only let it go, but the Church of his day accepted it as being in accordance with their understanding of the Gospel, that Jesus, although "the *Son* of God," was indeed *of the substance of God:* ("in the form of God, [he] did not count equality with God a thing to be grasped, but emptied himself...."). [243]

---

241 *The Holy Bible, New International Version*...Grand Rapids, Michigan: Zondervan Bible Publishers, c. 1973, 1978, 1984 by International Bible society (Romans 9:5)

242 Acts 22:3: Paul said "I am a Jew...brought up...at the feet of Gamaliel, educated according to the strict manner of the law of our fathers..." see also Acts 5:34 "...a Pharisee in the council named Gamaliel, a teacher of the law, held in honor by all the people...."

243 Philippians 2:6-7

Sanday and Headlam in their *Commentary on the Epistle to the Romans* state that: "an immense preponderance of the Christian writers of the first eight centuries refer the word 'theos' [God] to Christ" [244] ("theos" being the Greek word for "God" which was used by St. Paul in this passage).

That was basically the interpretation used in *"the King James Bible"*:

> [the Israelites]....whose *are* [insertion in italics] the fathers, and of whom as concerning the flesh Christ *came,"* [italics again, denoting an insertion in the translated text], "who is over all, God blessed for ever. Amen.

The King James Bible was based on manuscripts that were of later date than the earliest ones now known to be in existence, but in this case the oldest Greek manuscripts that modern scholarship currently agrees upon are the same, and the same problem remains: that the original Greek, with no punctuation, can be translated, equally legitimately, in these different ways.

The word "Amen" does not necessarily—in my view—mean that one has to accept the "doxology" version, simply because of thinking that the "Amen" must be the end of a thanksgiving to God, e.g., "God be praised, Amen!" It could equally well have the equivalent meaning of "yes, indeed", almost "hear, hear!" in today's language, or "so be it".

In that case the passage could be rendered:

> and of their race, according to the flesh, is *the Christ [who is] God over all, [who is] to be [praised or] blessed for ever, indeed.*

I wrote a paper on this when I was at theological college, and I found an article by a Roman Catholic Jesuit who wrote, more than sixty years ago, that, in his view:

> the vast majority of liberal critics today deny that Paul regarded Jesus Christ as true God....The current is so strong in that direction that Protestant commentaries,

---

244   William Sanday and Arthur C. Headlam, *A Critical and Exegetical Commentary on the Epistle to the Romans* (Edinburgh: T. & T. Clark, 1902), p. 233

even those supposedly orthodox, often leave the reader doubtful whether Paul's Epistles contain even one unmistakeable profession of his faith in the divinity of Christ. [245]

I was saying that the old *King James Version* of the Bible had the translation attributing divinity to Christ, an interpretation now revived in *The New International Version*. However, in the years between, *The Revised Standard Version* was published, which favoured the first of the renditions set out above, (the "doxology" one); and I think that *that* is probably "the newly proposed punctuation" referred to by Anthony Cotter in 1945 when he wrote:

> *the newly proposed punctuation* [of Romans 9:5] sins against the context, against Greek grammar, and against the invariable structure of doxologies. [246]

I agree with Anthony Cotter. Especially I believe that it sins against the context. It is not clear to me why such an extravagant doxology should be used, praising Almighty God ("God [who is] over all"), *if* Jesus were only a man descended from the Jews, and not somehow of and appertaining to God. If such great praise were to be given to God for sending Jesus, surely it *must* have been because Jesus was more than a mere man, even an anointed, gifted, one.

If St. Paul can refer, in his earlier Epistle to the Corinthians, to Christ being "the Rock" that was the God of the Old Testament, [247] or, in the Epistle to the Philippians, speak of Christ being *"in the form of God"* but not thinking that "equality with God" was a thing to be grasped, [248] or say that "at the Name of Jesus every knee shall bow," [249] when he knew that Isaiah was using that phrase for God Himself, [250] I can hardly see that he would speak differently of Him here.

---

245 Anthony C. Cotter, "The Divinity of Jesus Christ in Saint Paul" in *The Catholic Biblical Quarterly,* Volume VII, Number 3, July 1945, p. 260

246 Anthony C. Cotter, as above, p.263.

247 1 Corinthians 10:1-4

248 Philippians 2:6

249 Philippians 2:10

250 Isaiah 45:23

All his writing about being *"in Christ"*, as *a new creation,* can *only* be understood in the context of the union of humanity with God. [251]

In the Epistle to the Romans St. Paul was both reminding the Gentile converts that the Jews were God's own original people, and not to be despised, and also lamenting his own heart-break, that, *of all people,* they were the ones to reject their own long-foretold Messiah. In this context, it would have made sense for him to emphasize the paradox that it was from their own stock that the Messiah of God had come, and that they had not recognized Who He was. In such a context, referring to Christ as "theos" would be a way of emphasizing what they had rejected, and his own corresponding heart-break.

I do not see how a "doxology", praising God, fits into a scenario like this at all. It seems to me to be much more likely that it was *not* a doxology to "God over all", but a description of the divine nature of the "God over all" who had been revealed in Christ—and rejected by His people.

Although *the Revised Standard Version* of the Bible contains the *first* of the two possible renditions quoted above, the "doxology one," (the one that says Jesus was descended from the Jews according to the flesh, and then praises God for sending Him, but holds back from saying that Jesus, born of the Jews, actually is "God"), I discovered, during the course of my research, that one of the two editors of the *New Oxford Annotated version* of the *Revised Standard Version* of the Bible, [252] Bruce Metzger, *himself* believed that the *other* interpretation (the one referring to Jesus as "theos", "God") was probably the correct one. He argued in favour of ascribing the word "God" to Christ even though the version of the Bible which he helped to edit used the other interpretation.

He said that "so far as Greek grammar is concerned, the latter part of [Romans 9:5] can be punctuated in at least eight different ways", and he argued for the one that places a comma after the word "flesh" or "body", saying:

---

251   e.g. 2 Corinthians 5:16-21: *"even though we once regarded Christ from a human point of view, we regard him thus no longer ... if* anyone is *in Christ,* he is a new creation ... [Christ] who knew no sin, [took on] sin, so that *in him* we might become *the righteousness of God."*

252   copyright 1973, 1977 by Oxford University Presss, Inc.

The Textus Receptus, followed by the editions of B. Weiss, von Soden, H.J. Vogels, A. Merk, J.M. Bover, and G. Nolli, punctuates with a comma after σαρκα [the Greek word for flesh] [253]

which of course would make it read "Christ according to the flesh, [who is] God over all".

He goes on to say (the italics are mine):

Among the other ways of punctuating the sentence, all of which appear to be legitimate on the basis of the preceding discussion, *the one that seems to be most in harmony with the thought of the apostle, as well as in accord with the convention of modern editors of Greek texts,* is no.1, namely

Κάι ἐξ ὧν ὁ Χριστός τὸ κατὰ σάρκα ὁ ὢν ἐπὶ πάντων θεὸς εὐλογητὸς εἰς τοὺς αἰῶνας ἀμὴν

which, in English, is the second version of the ones I have given above, where "theos", "God", referred to Christ.

I think it would have been sensible for St. Paul not to speak of Jesus as "God" very often, (a point which has worried some people), both because of the confusion it might well have caused, in the minds of his readers, between God the Father, and Jesus, the Son of God, and because of the necessity to continue to preach and believe in "One God." He had enough problems in preaching the Gospel as it was, without adding to the confusion.

However, an early understanding of Trinitarian doctrine is apparent, underlying the writings of the Epistles; and it also appears in a verse in the (Synoptic) Gospel according to St. Mark, quoted earlier,[254] as well as, of course, in the Gospel of St. John. I will set out in the section on "abiding in Christ" in the Chapter on the Atonement some of what St. Paul wrote about *"being in Christ"* —with all that that would imply.

---

253 Bruce M. Metzger. "The Punctuation of Rom.9:5" in *Christ and Spirit in the New Testament,* edited by Barnabas Lindars and Stephen S. Smalley "in Honour of Charles Francis Digby Moule". Cambridge: Cambridge University Press, 1973, p.95.

254 Mark 9:37: "whoever receives one...child in my name receives me; and *whoever receives me, receives not me but him who sent me."*

The early Christians were aware that there were God the Father, and Jesus, the Son of God, who was equal to God, (but "did not count equality with God a thing to be grasped, but emptied himself..."[255]), and the Holy Spirit, the Spirit of God, who was known and experienced by the early Church: and yet there was only one God. This was not explicitly spelled out at this early stage of the Church's history—Paul had other things to do—but the foundations were already there.

As Bruce Metzger says (and I think this is important, although it is not written in the kind of language used by the average layman):

> The reason why there are so few statements in Paul's epistles bearing on the essential nature of Christ .... is doubtless connected with a feature often noticed by others, namely that the apostle, for purposes of instruction bearing on Christian nurture, usually prefers to speak of the functional rather than the ontological relationships of Christ. [256]

However, given the nature of Paul's distress at the beginning of chapter 9 of the Epistle to the Romans, he might very well have relaxed his caution for a moment in order to emphasize just *Who it was* that God's own people were refusing to accept.

Surely he must have believed in God as *a Trinity of which Christ was part* in order to write the following, which only makes sense in that context:

> But if *Christ* is *in you,* although your bodies are dead because of sin, your spirits are alive because of righteousness. *If the Spirit* of him who raised Jesus from the dead *[i.e., the Spirit of God] dwells in you,* he who raised Christ Jesus from the dead *[i.e. God]* will give life to your mortal bodies also through his Spirit which dwells in you. [257]

How could Christ be *in us* in the present time if He were only a

---

255   Philippians 2:6

256   Bruce M. Metzger. "The Punctuation of Rom 9:5" in *Christ and Spirit in The New Testament,* edited by Barnabas Lindars and Stephen S. Smalley in Honour of Charles Francis Digby Moule (Cambridge: Cambridge University Press, 1973), p.112.

257   Romans 8:10-11

mortal man who lived in past history? And how can *Christ and the Spirit of God* (the God who raised Jesus from the dead) *be in us at the same time,* while the God who raised Jesus from the dead gives us *life,* unless we are talking about *one God —and that God understood as Trinity?*

In fact, even the statement *"[God] will give life to your mortal bodies",* when we all know our bodies will eventually suffer physical death, only makes sense in the context of St. John saying *"God gave us eternal life"—* a life that transcends and goes beyond this one—*"and this life is in his Son";* [258] and Jesus saying: "I am the resurrection and the life; he who believes in me, *though he die,* [physically] *yet shall he live* [eternally], and whoever...believes in me *shall never die* [in the eternal sense]". [259]

To me, none of this makes sense if one does not accept that Jesus is the Second Person of the Trinity. God-given, eternal, life does not come to us from anything less than God Himself. Only the concept of God *understood as Trinity* makes sense of this.

It is worth noting that the passage just quoted (about Christ being *in us),* appears in the *eighth* chapter of the Epistle to the Romans, *immediately before* the ambiguous sentence in the *ninth* chapter which we have been thinking about. Surely, it would be hard to argue that St. Paul would never have referred to Jesus Christ as "theos", after he had just written a passage with undeniable Trinitarian implications a few paragraphs earlier. [260]

I believe that it is important that Christians think about this, because arguments that "St. Paul would never have [attributed divinity to Christ]" undermine our historic faith.

Similarly, St. Paul's Epistle to the Ephesians refers to Christ in the context of the Trinity (that *the Father...*may grant you to be strengthened...*through his Spirit...* and that *Christ may dwell in your hearts* through faith; that *you, being rooted and grounded in love,*

---

258   1 John 5:11

259   John 11:25-26

260   Similarly, 2 Corinthians 1:18-22: "all the promises of God find their Yes in *[the Son of God, Jesus Christ]* ... That is why we utter the Amen through him, to the glory of God. But it is *God* who establishes us with you *in Christ,* and has commissioned us; he has put his seal upon us and given us *his Spirit in our hearts as a guarantee."* St. John, too, spoke of the *Holy Spirit testifying in the human heart* as to the truth of the Gospel — 1 John 5:7-11

may…be filled with all the fulness of God) in a way that surely could only be understood as showing that he *did* believe in both *the divinity of Christ and the understanding of God as Trinity.* [261]

Just as the passage in Romans discussed above has been thought by some to be more legitimately translated as a doxology rather than as attributing divinity to Christ, it has been suggested that the passage in Colossians about Christ being *"the image of the invisible God…. [in whom] all the fullness of God was pleased to dwell"* [262] must have been a later interpolation on the grounds that "St. Paul would never have attributed divinity to Christ", an idea which Anthony Cotter was complaining about as long ago as 1945.

Peake's Commentary states that:

> The Pauline authorship of Col. has often been questioned. But its obviously close connection with Phm. (see below), whose genuineness there is no cause to question, makes it difficult to believe that it is not at least substantially Pauline. The theory that, though mainly Pauline, Col. has suffered interpolation, depends largely upon the fact that the description of Christ (especially in 1:15ff.) is in part unparalleled in the acknowledged Paulines. *But there is nothing there, either in vocabulary or in ideas, which it seems impossible to attribute to the Paul who is known from other epistles, or even unlikely for him to have written, given the circumstances implied by the epistle.* The relation of Col. to Eph. is indeed problematic; but if suspicion is cast by the comparison, it falls more naturally on Eph. than on Col. … [263] (italics mine).

If St. Paul did indeed, as discussed earlier, attribute divinity to

---

261 Ephesians 3:14-19: "…I bow my knees before *the Father….*that…he may grant you to be strengthened with might *through His Spirit…* and that *Christ may dwell in your hearts* through faith; that you, being rooted and grounded in *love,* may have power to comprehend…and to know *the love of Christ which surpasses knowledge* [and be] *filled with all the fullness of God"*

262 Colossians 1:15-20

263 *Peakes' Commentary on the Bible,* p.990, re. the Epistle to the Colossians, especially Colossians 1:15-20.

Christ in the Epistle to the Romans, which is acknowledged to be one of his most important and influential writings, then any arguments that the Colossian passage *must* be a later interpolation "because St. Paul would never have said that" would no longer be valid. In fact, it should be noted that, in very close proximity to that passage, the Epistle speaks both of Christians dwelling *in Christ* and *Christ dwelling in them,* [264] the mutual indwelling through the Holy Spirit which I elaborate on later, which could only be *possible* if Christ were indeed "theos", God.

I would ask anyone who questions "whether St. Paul would have attributed divinity to Christ", how they can possibly explain these passages in any other context.

It may well be fashionable to question "the divinity of Christ", but, as St. Paul himself said, in effect, "if this isn't true, you are wasting your time, and it is all for nothing anyway—what's the point?" [265] The history of the Christian faith, and the persecution of the early Christians, all attest to the fact that Jesus Christ was believed by them to be the Incarnate Son of God, of the same substance and nature as God. We cannot deny that historical fact.

St. Ignatius, Bishop of Antioch, who lived in the first century, also used the word "theos" to describe Christ. Born at about the time of the Crucifixion, and dying probably *after* the Gospel of St. John had appeared, (the dates of his life are approximately AD 35-107), he would have known people who could have given first-hand testimony of what they had seen and heard, and people who had had the tradition handed down to them by their immediate predecessors who they could personally vouch for. Thus, it would seem to be likely that his use of the word "theos" would have been based on his personal knowledge of the faith of many of the early Christians, and a knowledge, too, of St. Paul's understanding of the Person of Our Lord; living as he did in St. Paul's own lifetime, and active in the Christian community, he must have been aware of the latter's views. I believe that he would also have known the Gospel of St. John, and not disagreed with it. He obviously had no problem with the use of the word "theos" for Christ.

---

264   Colossians 1:27 and Colossians 2:6-7

265   1 Corinthians 15:17: "If Christ has not been raised, your faith is futile and you are still in your sins."

I would ask those who believe that St. Paul would never have used the word "theos" of Christ, (proponents of the "newly-proposed punctuation" of Romans 9:5, as Cotter puts it), how they reconcile the combination of that verse, ambiguous in the first place, with Ignatius' clear reference to "our *God* Jesus Christ" only a few years later:

("ὁ θεὸς ἡμῶν Ἰησοῦς Χριστός.")[266]

I stand with Cotter and Metzger in believing that St. Paul meant the word "theos" to be ascribed to Christ, and thus the early Christians understood it.

In addition, the word "theos" was also used of Christ in the Second Epistle of St. Peter *("our God* and Saviour Jesus Christ"), and in the Letter to Titus *("our great God* and Saviour Jesus Christ").[267] Although these Epistles are believed to be of later authorship,[268] their acceptance into the Canon of the New Testament shows that they were *consistent with earlier Christian belief.* The preface to the Second Epistle of St. Peter, in *The New Oxford Annotated Version* of *the Revised Standard Version* of the Bible, states:

> *The authority of the New Testament books is dependent,* not upon their human authorship, *but upon their intrinsic significance, which the church, under the guidance of the Spirit, has recognized as the authentic voice of apostolic teaching* (italics mine).

It *could* be argued that this was "the later church", if one goes by the fact that the earliest surviving record of the present Canon of New Testament Scripture, with its inclusion of these particular documents,

---

266 F.L. Cross, editor, and F.L. Cross and E.A. Livingstone, editors of the revised second edition, of *The Oxford Dictionary of the Christian Church.* — "Ignatius, St.", p. 689.

267 2 Peter 1:1; Titus 2:13

268 The preface to *2 Peter* in *the New Oxford Annotated Version* of *the Revised Standard Version* of the Bible states that "most scholars ... regard [it] as the work of one who was deeply indebted to Peter and who published it under his master's name early in the second century." The *Introduction* to *1 Timothy,* in the same version of the Bible, referring to the *Epistles to Timothy and Titus,* also suggests later authorship in connection with these Epistles: "..... it is easier to assume that a loyal disciple of Paul used several previously unpublished messages of the apostle and expanded them to deal with conditions confronting the church *a generation after Paul's death".*

is 367 A.D.; [269] but the Canon as it is now must have been finalized *long before then,* if it was to be referred to definitively at that time, which means *at least* by the early part of the fourth century; and work on defining it had begun much earlier than that. Marcion, who first raised a question of urgency about the matter, with his proposal to disregard the Old Testament and much of what is now the New, which led the churches in Europe to canvass one another to see what was, and what was not, universally accepted, died in A.D.160, *i.e., in the second century.*

The main point to be considered is whether or not such use of "theos" in these later Epistles is *consistent with* the teaching of earlier, established, apostles, such as St. Paul and St. John, about whom there was not the same ambiguity in the establishment of the New Testament Canon.

St. John certainly used the word "theos" at the beginning of his Gospel;[270] and I have tried to show that an understanding of God *as Trinity,* (which, in itself, of course, *must* imply "the divinity of Christ") underlies all of St. Paul's writings.

So to my mind it is deliberately perverse to try to interpret Romans 9:5 in a way that does not apply the word "theos" to Christ", because doing so *contradicts the rest of the New Testament evidence.*

St. Paul was writing *in the first century,* within a few years of the Crucifixion, as I have tried to show; St. John's writings would have become widely known either *at the end of the first century or the beginning of the second;* and St. Ignatius, quoted above, died *early in the second century,* more than 250 years before Athanasius' record of our present Canon.

2 Peter and Titus, also believed to have been written in the second century, obviously did not clash with tradition already existing at that time. Family and community memories last longer than a hundred years, and a hundred years from the Crucifixion would take us to *the middle of the second century,* by which time all these documents would have been written, within the living memory of the authors' contemporaries

---

269 *The Oxford Dictionary of the Christian Church,* page 232, states that "St. Athanasius in his Festal Ep. for 367 is the earliest exact witness to the present NT Canon."

270 John 1:1: "In the beginning was the Word, and the Word was with God, and the Word *was God...."*

and immediate predecessors. It would seem therefore that there is a continuous link between St. Paul and his contemporaries, in the first century, St. John's writings in the late first or early second centuries, and St. Ignatius, and the authors of 2 Peter and The Letter to Titus, writing in the second century; and so the Canon which St. Athanasius inherited in the fourth century must go back to much earlier times.

I do not believe it can be plausibly argued that "the later church" suddenly invented, centuries later, the idea that Jesus could be regarded as "theos," God.

The earliest understanding of the Christian Gospel was not only that we are *forgiven,* but that *we can come to God through "abiding in Christ" (we in Him and He in us)* which is our "salvation."[271] This is consistent with St. Paul attributing divinity to Christ and the development of faith in God as Trinity. What did come later was the fixation on *punishment,* and the idea of Jesus being some sort of third-party mediaeval "whipping boy" (see the chapter on the Atonement); and when that idea in turn became discredited, what was left was a vacuum, which explains our present dilemma.

It seems to me, therefore, that we not only need to go back to the original understanding of the Atonement for a clearer understanding of the traditional faith, but also *to reaffirm belief in the divinity of Christ,* His being both God and Man, because that is the necessary component and essential prerequisite on which everything else depends: or our faith *is* futile. [272]

A possible explanation of 1 John 5:8 which says: "There are three witnesses, the Spirit , the water, and the blood"

The few verses in which this statement appears, (verses 6-8), have been described as "the most perplexing passage in the Epistle, and one of the most perplexing in the New Testament": [273]

---

271   See John 14-15: and the Prayer in the Communion Service in the [Anglican] *Book of Common Prayer, 1962, "that we may evermore dwell in him, And he in us."*

272   1 Corinthians 15:17: "If Christ has not been raised, your faith is futile and you are still in your sins."

273   William Barclay. *The Daily Study Bible: The Letters of John and Jude, Revised Edition.* (Burlington, Ontario, Canada: Welch Publishing Company Inc., 1958, 1976). Page 107 states "Plummer" (no Bibliography given) "in beginning to comment on this pas-

> This is he who came by water and blood, Jesus Christ, not with the water only but with the water and the blood. *And the Spirit is the witness, because the Spirit is the truth. There are three witnesses, the Spirit, the water, and the blood, and these three agree....this is the testimony of God that he has borne witness to his Son.* [274]

"The testimony of God" *could* refer to the historical fact of God saying "This is my beloved Son" at the time of Jesus' baptism,[275] but I believe that it must refer to a deeper and more personal testimony within each believer's heart, because St. John (or the school of thought that produced these writings) says "the Spirit is the witness" and "he who believes...has the testimony *in himself.*"[276]

I think this is very important. To have the testimony in oneself means that the Holy Spirit in the heart of a believer is reassuring that person of the truth about something in an unmistakable way. It is something one knows for oneself with conviction. It is not just something which one has *heard* from someone else about, say, the Baptism of Jesus, but it is something that person *knows for himself to be true.*

St. John then goes on to say: "And this is the testimony, that God gave us eternal life, and this life is *in his Son*". [277] Thus "the testimony of God" would be the witness of the Holy Spirit in the believer's heart. And *the testimony itself is about the truth of the Gospel,* "that God gave us eternal life, and this life is in his Son." So that accounts for the witness of the Holy Spirit, but what of "the water and the blood" that St. John equates with the witness of the Spirit? ("there are three witnesses...and these three agree...").

First of all, what are "the water and the blood" that he is referring to? Secondly, how do they suffice to convince the believer in his or

---

sage [1 John 5:6-8] says: '*This is the most perplexing passage in the Epistle, and one of the most perplexing in the New Testament*'."

274 1 John 5:6-9

275 Matthew 3:17

276 1 John 5:10 (and see also: 1 John 3:24: "All who keep his commandments abide in him, and he in them. And *by this* we *know* that he abides in us, *by the Spirit which he has given us.*")

277 1 John 5:11

her heart that God gave us eternal life in His Son? And, thirdly, how are they sufficiently important that they can be ranked alongside the Holy Spirit of God in confirming the testimony of the truth of our salvation in a believer's heart and mind?

I believe that "the water and the blood" *must* refer to the *Crucifixion:* the water and the blood that flowed from Jesus' side on the Cross and, beyond that, to the deeper realities which they symbolize. If *"water"* only signified Jesus' baptism in the River Jordan, as many commentators suggest, it would hardly result in *testimony in a believer's heart;* nor explain the emphasis in the Epistle on "testimony," "witness", and "agreement" and "truth", and so on. It must surely be that, in the context of the verse in the Epistle, "the water and the blood" are *proofs* in some way that can convince one (of the fact that "God gave us eternal life in His Son"), proofs verified by the confirmation of the Holy Spirit in a believer's heart. So far, so good.

To unravel this further, I would say that, for us to have eternal life in God's Son, Jesus must indeed *be* God's Son, and that, in some way, "the water and the blood" must be of such significance that they can convince us, basically, of the divinity of Christ, without which all this ("eternal life in His Son") would not be possible—just convincing us of His humanity, by itself, would not be enough. Would you not agree, so far?

The question then would be, of "the water and the blood", *which testified to what?* And, although most Bible commentators do not seem to take this line, it is my belief that "the blood" would convince us of His *humanity,* and His physical death, because all human beings and animals have blood, and all people who are crucified bleed; and if one bleeds enough one dies; but water flowing unexpectedly from the side of a crucified victim as described in the Gospel of St. John is not such a proof of humanness—and, even if it were, what would be the point of emphasizing it, if there was also already the blood to make that point?

And if there was only proof of His humanity, where then would be the attestation to His divinity *without which* there is not *the testimony of God* to our having *"eternal life in His Son"?*

The symbolism of "water" was often used in the Old Testament as a metaphor for the outpouring of the Holy Spirit to nourish the human soul: I show some examples at the end of the Chapter on Baptism. The Biblical understanding that the metaphor of "water" could be used in this way was made explicit by Jesus when He said:

> 'If any one thirst, let him come to me and drink. He who believes in me, as the scripture has said, "Out of his heart shall flow rivers of living water." ' *Now this he said about the Spirit...* [278]

Peake's Commentary on the Bible corroborates this close connection between *"water and Spirit"*, when it says, with regard to the passage in the First Epistle to the Corinthians [279] where St. Paul refers to the pre-existent Christ as being the supernatural Rock of the Israelites' wilderness journey: [280]

> Paul could pass from the thought of..... to that of Christ as the source of the water, *water and Spirit being closely connected in Hellenistic Judaism with the divine Wisdom."* [281]

I think that St. John, and St. Paul, and other early Christians, saw a *symbolic link with divinity* in the water that flowed from Jesus' side on the Cross, St. John emphasising so dramatically in his Gospel account that *water,* as well as blood, flowed from Jesus' side on the Cross, at the expense of details to be found in the other Gospels, and St. Paul writing only twenty years or so after the Crucifixion about Christ being the *Rock.* [282] I have tried to show, too, (in the Appendix), the metaphorical Biblical identification of *God* as being *the Rock.*

This would tie in with the fact that there were seen to be symbolic re-enactments of Old Testament events in the inauguration of the New Covenant, of which the pouring out of the water from the side of the Crucified Christ on the Cross may well have been one (as water once flowed from the rock in Biblical times); and would make sense of this

---

278 John 7:37-39

279 1 Corinthians 10:1-4

280 Exodus 17:2-6, Numbers 20:2-11, Psalm 105:41

281 *Peake's Commentary on the Bible,* edited by Matthew Black and H.H. Rowley. Van Nostrand Reinhold (UK) Co. Ltd. c. Thomas Nelson and Sons Ltd., 1962; Van Nostrand Reinhold (UK) Co. Ltd., 1982; page 960, re. 1 Corinthians 10:1-4.

282 John 19:32-37, 1 Corinthians 10:1-4

very difficult passage in the First Epistle of St. John about "the Spirit and the water and the blood" being *equal witnesses* to "the testimony of God" that "God has given us eternal life, and this life is in His Son".

Because "eternal life...in His Son" would only be possible if Jesus were somehow part of God, I believe that what St. John is talking about is *convincing us* (with the testimony of God confirmed in our hearts by the Holy Spirit) that Jesus was and is *both God and Man,* so that we can indeed be sure in our hearts that, because of this, we *do* have eternal life in Him.

I am suggesting that for "the water and the blood" to be able to convince us that Jesus of Nazareth who died on a Cross was *both God and Man,* and thus, because of this dual nature, able to give us "eternal life" in Him *("in His Son")* , presumably *one* of these two elements would have to convince us of His *humanity,* and *the other* would have to convince us of His *divinity:* or they would hardly be "proofs" to validate "the testimony of God" (that through Christ we have eternal life), on a par with the witness of the Holy Spirit.

So if blood has a connotation of humanness and physical death, would it not therefore have to follow that similarly water, in this context, must carry the connotation of divinity and (eternal) life, to complete the equation?

With regard to "water" symbolizing divinity, this is not how most commentators see it, but I think it *must* do so, or *where is the testimony of "the water"* to *"the truth of the Gospel",* assuring us that *"in Christ" we have "eternal life"?* I will share with you a little later what some of them say; but first let us look at what St. John wrote about the Crucifixion in the nineteenth chapter of his Gospel (the italics are mine):

> So the soldiers came and broke the legs [of the others who had been crucified with Jesus]; but when they came to Jesus and saw that he was already dead, they did not break his legs. But one of the soldiers pierced his side with a spear, and at once there came out blood and water.

> He who saw it has borne witness—his testimony is true, and he knows that he tells the truth—that you also may believe.

> For these things took place that the scripture might
> be fulfilled, 'Not a bone of him shall be broken.' And
> again another scripture says 'They shall look on him
> whom they have pierced.' [283]

It was not until the writing of the Gospel of St. John that the incident of the "blood and water" that flowed from the side of Christ on the Cross was really described for us. Perhaps the "synoptic" Gospel writers (Matthew, Mark and Luke) did not immediately see its significance, or perhaps they were more concerned with setting down what Jesus said and did, for the immediate record, rather than tackling deep theological problems.

St. Paul certainly had practical problems to deal with, and he was not dealing with theological problems per se, except as they impinged on his flock (such as their concern about the Resurrection of the Dead and the Second Coming Being Delayed).

It was left to St. John, or his followers, after many years of meditating about these things, to cause them to be set down in more detailed form; but, even if St. John's Gospel did not appear until the end of the first century, the ideas contained in it must have been familiar to the Christians whom St. Paul was dealing with, at Corinth, decades earlier.

We know that the various epistles and Gospels were passed around and shared among the different churches, because that subsequently became a criterion for deciding what should, or should not, be accepted as Scripture: ("what was accepted and believed by all Christians, at all times and in all places", the original meaning of the word "catholic").

This practice must have been going on from the very beginning, otherwise the documents would have been lost or destroyed. These early Christians, then, would have passed their beliefs on to their immediate descendants, and, if the Gospel according to St. John appeared even at the end of the first century, that would only have been forty-odd years after the writing of the Epistle to the Corinthians, and most of us have access to family or community memories of only forty years earlier.

I attach particular significance to this because of the fact that St. Paul was writing at a much earlier date than that of the Gospel of St. John, and writing, presumably, in accordance with tradition already

---

283   John 19:32-37

current and established in his time (or, as I say, surely it would have been challenged, either then or later); and he did not hesitate to speak of Christ as being the same Rock that gave the Israelites water in the wilderness [284]—a statement that was accepted at the time, in the context of the Epistle to the Corinthians, and later included in the Christian Canon of New Testament Scripture.

It is not therefore just a case of discounting the teaching of St. John: we have to deal with that of St. Paul as well.

When the Gospel according to St. John became known, it did not clash with an understanding of the faith outlined, years before, by St. Paul, when he wrote of Christ as being the supernatural, life-giving, Rock of the wilderness journey of many centuries earlier.

The reason for my being so sure of what I am saying is that St. John gave such extraordinary emphasis to the incident of Christ's side being pierced with a sword as He hung on the Cross, and the fact that both blood and water flowed out from that gaping wound. I will quote in a minute a commentator who remarks on the surprising fact that St. John omitted many of the well-known features of the Crucifixion while emphasizing this one. I do not suppose, for several reasons, that this is because St. John had a morbid interest in this particular fact.

If one accepts the divinity of Christ in the first place, it follows that one has to accept the testimony of St. John to that divinity, and the fact of its acceptance by the Christians who knew, or who knew people who had known, the original apostles. Therefore, instead of dismissing this evidence out of hand, perhaps we should ask *why* St. John gave such emphasis to it.

Surely he must have assumed that Christian congregations would already have known the basic facts about the Crucifixion, because the other Gospels and other documents would have been circulating for some time, as well as an oral tradition that had already been in existence since the first Easter Sunday. It is quite possible that he would therefore have been particularly concerned to elaborate on what people did *not* know so well, to record and explain its significance for future generations, which was, in fact, a hallmark of his Gospel.

(That is not *at all* the same as alleging that it was all *subsequently*

---

284 1 Corinthians 10:1-4

invented by "the later church". I have been at pains to show that his teaching is corroborated by earlier evidence.)

I have already quoted, above, the passage about the crucifixion in St. John's Gospel, but let us look again at the way in which the account unfolds:

— *first, "there came out blood and water"*

—and *immediately* St. John, or the author of that Gospel, goes on to talk about *the impeccability of the witness* to that fact (that "there came out blood and water"), and implies that it is important that his hearers be assured that they can rely both on the truth of what happened and the fact that the witness's evidence can be trusted—(why?)

because that has a bearing on their belief in the Christian faith: they are told this is true, in order that they may believe, without any doubt or hesitation, *in the divinity of Christ* (the divinity implied in the quoting of those Biblical prophecies), *and consequently be assured* ("that you also may believe") *that it is true that God has given us eternal life in Him.*

In referring to the fact that Jesus' legs were not broken, when the other two men crucified with Him had their legs broken in order to hasten death because of the impending sabbath, the writer refers to the strict scriptural requirements regarding the paschal lamb which supported his belief that Christ was the ultimate sacrifice to be offered at that festival of the Passover—not an ordinary lamb but "the Lamb of God"; [285] and also the psalm that says of "the righteous" that the Lord will keep him so that not one of his bones is broken. [286]

St. John writes:

For these things took place *that the scripture might be fulfilled,*

---

285   John 1:36

286   Psalm 34:19: "Many are the afflictions of the righteous; but the Lord delivers him out of them all. He keeps all his bones; *not one of them is broken.*"

'Not a bone of him shall be broken.' [287]

He then goes on immediately to quote the prophecy from the Book of Zechariah:

> *And again another scripture says, 'They shall look on him whom they have pierced'.* (The passage in Zechariah says: "when they look on him whom they have pierced, they shall mourn for him, as one mourns for an only child."[288])

A view often expressed is that the evangelist was concerned in his writing *to repel allegations that Jesus was some kind of spirit and not human* (i.e., a denial of the reality of the Incarnation), so John was trying to emphasize the *humanness* of the body on the Cross: that it was no ethereal spirit, but real flesh and blood, a human being who really died. Another view is that St. John was also emphasizing that Jesus was *really dead* to counter one of the "hoax" theories: that He was not just rescued by someone while still alive, He had been really and truly stabbed, until blood and water flowed out, beyond any possibility of physical healing.

However, such arguments do not explain why St. John *immediately* goes on to quote passages from the Scriptures portraying Christ's *divinity.* An ordinary crucifixion of an ordinary man would not have called forth such Biblical comparisons, or talk of water flowing from the body on the Cross, so emphatically testified to by a witness whose credentials were emphasized as being so impeccable and trustworthy. One has to ask *why* this was so emphasized, if it were a fact of no particular significance.

The above passage demonstrates clearly, to my mind, that St. John was talking *not only* about Christ's humanity and physical death but *also* about His divinity and eternal Resurrection—the reason for the Biblical quotations, that this was no ordinary man—in order to support our faith that this was both Man and God, in whom we, too, can have eternal life.

---

287   John 19:36: referring to Psalm 34:30; and, re. the paschal (or Passover) lamb, referring to Exodus 12:46: *"you shall not break a bone of it";* and Numbers 9:12: *"they shall leave none of it until the morning, nor break a bone of it."* Note that St. Paul *also* referred to Christ as the paschal Lamb (1 Corinthians 5:7-8)

288   Zechariah 12:10

St. John was not *just* talking about the fact that Jesus died, but about *Who it was* who died.

Therefore, it could surely be inferred from this that he saw some significance in the fact that *water* flowed from Jesus' side, because *blood* in such circumstances was only to be expected in any crucifixion, and would not *in itself* have any relevance to justify the divinity implied in the passages of Scripture immediately quoted. Nor was water, in itself, really necessary to prove that Jesus, the man, had really died: the pouring out of blood would have been enough to testify to that.

So it would seem that St. John was talking about *both* the real and physical death of a human being, *and,* also, the life-giving death of the divine Son of God: the inauguration, indeed, of the New Covenant, taking over from the Old. [289]

It could be argued that St. John spoke of blood and water— or "the water and the blood"— as a form of "shorthand" for this duality. *"That you also may believe"* must surely imply belief in *the total Gospel* of our salvation, that we are brought to eternal life in God through Christ.

For this to be possible *Jesus had to be both God and Man;* and surely this is what St. John was so emphatically proclaiming here.

This urgent emphasis of St. John "that we may believe," that we may *know,* occurs on more than one occasion in his writings, [290] and is implicit in the passage in the First Epistle that I have referred to, regarding "witnesses" and "testimony" and resulting belief. I do not think St. John would have put such emphasis on the water and the

---

289 Jeremiah 31:31-34 (quoted in Hebrews 8:8-12): "I will make *a new covenant* with ... Israel ... and... Judah, not like the covenant which I made with their fathers... [when I brought them out of the land of Egypt]... which they broke...But this is the covenant which I will make with...Israel...I will put my law *within them,* and I will write it *upon their hearts;* and I will be their God, and they shall be my people...And... *they shall all know me.."* Luke 22:20 (see also 1 Corinthians 11:25): " 'This cup... *is the new covenant* in my blood' "

290 e.g., 1 John 5:13: "I write this to you...that you may *know* that you have eternal life" (the context would seem to *prove* that the original apostolic understanding of "eternal life" was *not* that it was something that happened to everybody, regardless, even if it meant eternity in hell; see also John 19:35: "He who saw it has borne witness...that *you also may believe"*; John 20:31 "...these are written *that you may believe* that Jesus is the Christ, the Son of God, and that *believing* you may *have life* in his name")

blood, and the credibility of the witness to it, in his Gospel account, if he was *only* concerned to say that Jesus was human and that He really died.

Of course St. John was not only concerned to emphasize Jesus' humanity; he was preaching, too, that He was, as well, the Incarnate Word of God, *without which there would have been no point in proclaiming His humanity in the first place* — unless his aim was to disprove the Christian faith altogether, but that argument does not apply here: St. John's Gospel begins with the clear and emphatic statement that "In the beginning was the Word, and the Word was with God, and the Word *was God*." [291]

The Epistle, while emphasizing Christ's humanity ("that...which we have heard, which we have seen with our eyes, which we have looked upon and touched with our hands...") *also* states, in the same sentence, that what they had heard and seen and touched was *"[the word of life] ....made manifest"*, and "we saw it, and testify to it, and proclaim to you the eternal life which was with the Father...made manifest to us..." [292].

I believe that, by talking about Biblical prophecies, and in his concern to emphasize the absolute truth of what happened, St. John was bringing his readers back to the realm of the involvement of the divine in the physical circumstances of the crucifixion.

The Interpreter's Bible gives the following commentary:

> one of the soldiers thrust his spear (an ugly weapon, with a barbed iron head, that made a gaping wound) deep into Christ's side (20:27). And, we read, at once there came out blood and water.
>
> It may be thought surprising that the evangelist who omits much that is central—e.g., the cry of dereliction—should have granted so much space and prominence to this incident. Yet be sure he had his reasons. He wants to save us from all fear of falling into Docetism.....the real Christ of God was really dead. As to the blood and water, certain medical explanations

---

291   John 1:1
292   1 John 1:1-2

that have been ventured do not satisfy the mind and appear to be medically doubtful.

It would seem difficult to understand what happened. Nor do most of us feel much indebted to this particular scripture. Yet some turn to it and linger at it, as being very near the center. The pierced side of Our Lord has a secure place among his stigmata, and a marked prominence in Christian thought and art and hymnody. Many, e.g., Augustus M. Toplady, have found here the perfect symbolism both of what they need in One who is to save them and of what they have found in Jesus Christ: *forgiveness for the sin of the past, and power to resist it for the future* (italics mine) 'Let the water and the blood, From Thy riven side which flowed, Be of sin the double cure, Cleanse me from its guilt and power.' ['Rock of Ages, cleft for me, let me hide myself in thee...'] So true is it that all Scripture is given by inspiration of God and is profitable."[293]

I think there needs to be clarification of the statement that *"the water and the blood"* are *"of sin the double cure"*, (the old emphasis always on *sin!*), but perhaps the author of that hymn had some intuitive understanding of what I have referred to as "the two arms of the Atonement".[294]

It may well be that *"the blood"* represented *the forgiveness of the sin*

---

293 *The Interpreter's Bible: A Commentary in Twelve Volumes: Volume 8: Luke, John.* Nashville, Abingdon Press, c. 1952 by Pierce and Smith in the United States of America. Copyright renewal 1980 by Abingdon Press. 37th printing 1988. pages 786 and 787.

294 "Cleanse me from [sin's] *guilt and power*" could still reflect an intuitive understanding of the duality that underlies my understanding of the Atonement. The *Blood of Christ* was indeed shed for our *forgiveness,* our being *cleansed* from our *guilt.* I think a better word regarding *power* would be *"free"* rather than "cleanse." I believe that it is only by *abiding in Christ* that we are *freed* from the *power* that sin has over us, and, indeed, we are given the help and strength we need in our struggle against sin by the power of the Holy Spirit dwelling in us to enable us to overcome it, the Holy Spirit outpoured under the New Covenant which I believe *the Water* that flowed from Christ's side on the Cross signified. I believe that it is about *God the Holy Spirit giving us power to overcome* and be free from sin for the future, about *life, in God* — much more than

of the past, wrought by the historical death of Christ on the Cross, (the Atonement in its historical sense), and *the water* —already a Biblical symbol for the Holy Spirit—symbolised the eternal *life* in God that was now being poured out for us *for the future* (the Nicene Creed refers to the Holy Spirit as "the Lord and giver of *life*"). The fact that St. John's otherwise-hard-to-understand emphasis on *"the water and the blood"* and St. Paul's statement that "that Rock was Christ" were both accepted into the Canon of Scripture, has to mean that the early Church understood the underlying implications and agreed with them.

I think that the *water* that poured from Christ's side on the Cross was indeed seen by the apostolic generation as having great symbolic significance, because it appears, at one and the same time, *to make sense of three difficult questions:* St. John's emphatic emphasis on it, in the first place; St. Paul's reference to Christ as "the Rock"; and the enigmatic statement in St. John's Epistle about *the Spirit and the water and the blood* bearing *equal witness* to the fact that it is the testimony of God that we have been given eternal life, and that this life is in *God's Son* (as we "abide in Christ", in this life and for ever).

We are brought back again and again, I believe, to the fact that God is experienced by us *as Trinity.* We have eternal life in God through Christ, [295] and the Holy Spirit sustains us, for ever, as water nourishes the earth, *the Holy Spirit outpoured in the inauguration of the New Covenant,* and often symbolised as *"living water"* from *"the fountain of the water of life."* [296] If this was so, symbolism became literal in a moment of history, in the fact that *the water of life* from all eternity could now be seen to be, both literally and symbolically, *flowing from the heart of God.* If that is what St. John was trying to convey, his extraordinary emphasis on the truth of what was being said

---

just the *forgiveness* of sin; so the much-maligned author of that hymn may have been closer to the truth than is generally realized.

295 1 John 5:11: "God gave us eternal life, and this life is in his Son."

296 Joel 2:28-29: *"I will pour out my spirit* on all flesh", quoted by St. Peter in Acts 2:14-18: "this is what was spoken by the prophet Joel...." and Ezekiel 37:14-27: "I will put my Spirit within you....I will make a covenant of peace with them...*an everlasting covenant;"* John 7:38-39; Revelation 21:6 (Jeremiah 2:13, 17:13).

about the water that flowed from Christ's side in the Gospel is the more understandable.

I do not think that the average congregation now understands for a moment the passage in the Epistle ("There are three witnesses, the Spirit, the water, and the blood; and these three agree"),[297] and there has never, apparently, been any clear consensus on this even among theological commentators, who generally use such words as "possibly" or "probably". They *do* seem to agree that, in the passage in the Epistle, the mention of *"the water and the blood"* was part of St. John's argument that Jesus was *both human and divine:* that this somehow testifies to *who Jesus is.* Some stress more the aspect that the man was also divine, some stress more that the divine being was also human, but all agree that somehow St. John was trying to describe the Incarnate God.

I am suggesting that *the water* poured out on the Cross *may be the testimony to the eternal life* that we have *through the divine nature of the Incarnate Christ.*

Peake's Commentary says that:

> *Water and blood refer primarily to the baptism and death of Jesus, demonstrating that it was no phantom that went down into the Jordan and ascended to the Cross.* They may also allude to the sacraments of Baptism and the Lord's Supper; only it is most unusual for 'blood' to represent the Eucharist (but cf. John 6:54) [the passage where Jesus says "he who eats my flesh and drinks my blood has eternal life, and I will raise him up at the last day"]. [298]

In *The New Oxford Annotated Bible,* based on *the Revised Standard Version* of the Bible, it is stated, in the footnote to the passage in the Epistle that says "there are three witnesses, the Spirit, the water, and the blood; and these three agree,"[299] that "the Spirit's witness is to *the water* (Jesus' baptism) and to *the blood* (the Cross)" (italics *theirs*). *However,*

---

297 1 John 5:8

298 *Peake's Commentary on the Bible,* edited by Matthew Black and H.H. Rowley, c. Thomas Nelson and Sons Ltd. Van Nostrand Reinhold (U.K.) Co. Ltd. 1982., page 1038.

299 1 John 5:6-8

the same *New Oxford Annotated Bible,* in its footnote to the passage in St. John's Gospel about the blood and water coming out of Christ's side on the Cross,[300] states that: "Blood and water indicate the reality of Jesus' humanity, and *perhaps also the new covenant and baptism"* (italics mine).

This comes the closest to my argument, except that I would put it another way, and say, more specifically, that *"blood"* indicates the reality of Jesus' humanity and death (and our redemption through His giving up His life for us, which this signifies); the pouring out of *"water,"* with its Biblical connotations of divinity, can be seen as *symbolizing the pouring out of the Holy Spirit,* the Holy Spirit which works for our continuing sanctification through the life of God nourishing our souls with "the water of life": and that *"the blood and the water", together,* can both be taken *as symbols of the inauguration of the New Covenant into which we are baptized.* The covenant in the Old Testament was sealed in blood,[301] as was the New Covenant;[302] but in the Old Testament the New Covenant was *also* described in terms of *the outpouring of the Holy Spirit,*[303] something for which the

---

300   John 19:34

301   Exodus 24:4-9

302   Luke 22:20, " 'This cup... is *the new covenant* in my blood' "; 1 Corinthians 11:25: " 'This cup is *the new covenant* in my blood' "; Hebrews 13:20: "the blood of the eternal covenant"; Hebrews 12:24: "[But you have come...] to Jesus, *the mediator of a new covenant,* and to the sprinkled blood that speaks more graciously than the blood of Abel"; and for a combination of "the blood of the covenant" and "the Spirit" see Hebrews 10:29: "punishment... deserved by the man who has....profaned the blood of the covenant by which he was sanctified, and outraged the Spirit of grace" and Hebrews 9:14-15: "Christ...through the eternal Spirit offered himself without blemish to God... [and is] the mediator of a new covenant"

303   Isaiah 61:8: "I *will* [note the future tense] make an everlasting covenant with them"; Jeremiah 31:31-34 (quoted in Hebrews 8:8-12): "I will make *a new covenant* with the house of Israel..."; Isaiah 44:3: "I will pour my Spirit upon your descendants"; Isaiah 55:1-3: "Ho, everyone who thirsts, come to the waters... and I will make with you an everlasting covenant"; Ezekiel 36:27: "I will put my spirit within you"; Ezekiel 37:14: "I will put my Spirit within you, and you shall live", and, *in the same chapter,* Ezekiel 37:26-27: "I will make a covenant of peace with them...an everlasting covenant"; Joel 2:28-29, quoted by St. Peter in Acts 2:16-21: "In the last days...I will pour out my Spirit upon all flesh..."

metaphors of "water" and "life" were also widely used.[304] It does not seem unreasonable to assume, therefore, that *"water,"* in the context of the Crucifixion, *also* symbolized the inauguration of the New Covenant at that time.

The early Christians were steeped in the Hebrew Scriptures, and particularly the story of *the manna in the wilderness,* in which the Feeding of the Five Thousand and the inauguration of the Eucharist had their roots, and the quail for meat, and *water from the rock,* which were all given by God. As Ezra said: "Thou didst give them *bread from heaven* for their hunger and bring forth *water* for them *from the rock* for their thirst."[305] If this was to meet physical needs in the past, and the New Covenant is to meet spiritual needs in the present and future, and, as we know, Jesus identified *Himself* as being the *"bread from heaven"* ("I am the bread of life") and, as well, the source of the water of life, saying *"if anyone thirst, let him come to me and drink,"*[306] the author of St. John's Gospel adding *"now this He said about the Spirit,"*[307] it can be inferred that *the New Covenant equivalent* of what Ezra said would be that God was still giving His people, in Christ, bread from heaven *and* water from the rock, and, if so, that would explain the emphasis on the *water* in the Gospel of St. John, and St. Paul's reference to Christ as "the Rock" of the wilderness experience.[308] They would have known Psalm 105:

> He...gave them bread from heaven in abundance. He opened the rock, and water gushed forth: it flowed through the desert like a river. For He remembered his holy promise, and Abraham his servant.[309]

In other words, if, in Christian understanding, the manna in the wilderness was succeeded by Christ as being for us now the *true*[310]

---

304   see the Chapter on Baptism.

305   Nehemiah 9:15

306   John 6:32-35,48,51, John 7:37-39; (and see John 4:14: "whoever drinks of the water that I shall give him will never thirst; the water that I shall give him will become in him *a spring of water welling up to eternal life")*

307   John 7:37-39

308   John 19:32-37; 1 Corinthians 10:4

309   Psalm 105:40-42

310   John 6:32

Bread from heaven, if the wine in the Eucharist constituted His Blood shed in the inauguration of the New Covenant,[311] it is reasonable to assume that *the second part* of the historic wilderness experience *(the water,* like a river flowing through the desert) *also* came into the picture, in the inauguration of the New Covenant.

Psalm 105 *links it specifically with the covenant with Abraham—* and *Christ Himself* identified *the "living water" from God* as being the outpouring of the Holy Spirit,[312] in the giving of which He identified Himself with the God of the Old Testament;[313] and his hearers would have known the passage from Isaiah: "Ho, every one who thirsts... come to the water...come to me, hear, that your soul may live; *and I will make with you an everlasting covenant.*"[314]

(This, incidentally, may have been another example of Old Testament writing which St. Paul would have taken as justifying his claim that salvation through Christ was available, not just to the Jews, *but to the Gentiles also, through the covenant with Abraham;* a claim supported by Biblical evidence that it was clearly apparent to the early Christians that the Holy Spirit had descended upon Gentiles as well as Jews, and consequently they were accepted and baptized into the Christian faith.[315])

---

311   Matthew 26:28 *"this is my blood of the covenant,* which is poured out for many for the forgiveness of sins' "; Mark 14:24: " '*This is my blood of the covenant,* which is poured out for many' "; Luke 22:20: " '*This cup* which is poured out for you *is the new covenant in my blood'* "; 1 Cor.11:25: " '*This cup is the new covenant in my blood.* Do this, as often as you drink it, in remembrance of me.' For as often as you eat this bread and drink the cup, you proclaim the Lord's death until he comes".

312   John 7:37-39: ".....Now this he said *about the Spirit,* which those who believed in him were to receive; for as yet the Spirit had not been given, because Jesus was not yet glorified" (the New Covenant came into effect with the Crucifixion and Resurrection).

313   John 7:37-38: "If any one thirst let him come to me and drink. He who believes in me, *as the scripture has said,* 'Out of his heart shall flow rivers of living water' ". See earlier examples given, but, in particular, Isaiah 55:1-3: "Ho, everyone who thirsts, come to the waters ... come to me; hear, that your soul may live; and I will make with you an everlasting covenant." See also John 4:14: " I shall give ... a spring of water welling up to eternal life"

314   Isaiah 55:1-3

315   e.g. Acts 10 (St. Peter in his dealings with Cornelius and the other Gentiles, who, demonstrably filled with the Holy Spirit, were then baptized in the name of Jesus Christ,

There is thus, as I try to demonstrate in detail, a definite Biblical link between "water"—and the giving of the Holy Spirit, through Christ—and the establishment of the New Covenant.

Jesus told His disciples that the Holy Spirit would not come to them until after His death.[316] It is easy to assume that this must be because Jesus could not be with us in the Spirit while He was also on earth in the flesh, and indeed the outpouring of the Holy Spirit was not *experienced* by His followers until the Day of Pentecost,[317] but it could well be that *the Crucifixion* was *the defining moment,* in time and in eternity, *between the Old Covenant and the New.*

It makes sense to assume that "the water" and "the blood" may therefore both have significance in symbolizing, *together,* in a moment of history, the inauguration of the New Covenant. This would explain St. John's emphasis on *"the water and the blood".*

Although, as commentators have said, "water" symbolizes "baptism", and it may well do so—I would not deny that fact—I have come to believe that it must *also* have significance in the context of representing the water of life that comes from God, "water in the desert," in fact.[318] I think St. John was talking about *the water of life* that flowed from the Rock, the divine Son of God, and that that was in St. Paul's mind too; and it is metaphorically into this "water of life" (the Spirit of God, through Christ) that *we* are baptized..

So I believe that there *is* a connection between the passage in the First Epistle of St. John and the account in the Gospel of the water that flowed from Christ's side on the Cross, both because the Gospel account of the latter is stressing divinity in its Scriptural quotations, and because "water" must have some symbolic significance as to the truth of the faith, if St. John can say "there are *three witnesses, the Spirit, the water, and the blood".*

"The blood", I think is fairly obvious, the Blood of Christ shed for us on the Cross, remembered at every Eucharist, poured out for

---

in spite of the fact that they were not Jews.)

316 John 16:7: "...if I do not go away, the Counselor [the Holy Spirit] will not come to you; but if I go, I will send him to you."

317 Acts 2.

318 This is a view shared by both Tad W. Guzie, S.J., and Neville Clark, as I go on to demonstrate

the remission of our sins in the death of Jesus. "The Spirit" poses no problems for our understanding either. But how should *"water"* be a witness to the fact that *"God gave us eternal life and this life is in His Son"*—unless "water" was the other half of the equation *signifying Christ's identity* as both God and Man?

Why should it be so important for us to know that the witness who saw the water pouring from Jesus' side on the Cross was speaking the truth (again, note the same connection *"that you may believe"*). Believe what? That the body was dead? No; there is more to it, I am sure, than just disposing of a heresy alleging that Jesus did not die. St. John repeats his message more than once: *that we may believe* that *"God gave us eternal life and this life is in His Son"*. Or, to draw out this rather cryptic message, it is that we may believe the total Gospel:

> that the dead figure on the Cross *was also divine, and rose from the dead;* that the water from His side *symbolized* that *"the water of life"* was now being poured out *in the New Covenant from the same God;* and that, because the Christ who taught us about His giving us *"water springing up to eternal life,"* and about *"abiding in Him"* was, indeed, *Who He said He was, and rose from the dead, we can abide for ever (have "eternal life") in Him, nourished to all eternity by the water of life.*

I believe that the water that came from Christ's side was seen by St. John and St. Paul, and, by inference, the early Church, as symbolising the giving of the Holy Spirit under the New Covenant; and *as God's silent statement as to His divinity, even as He hung as a corpse on a human cross.*

I believe that *this* is the message which *the Spirit, the water, and the blood,* bear witness to *in the heart of the believer.* At least, it is a logical explanation of that verse in St. John's Epistle, and I have never heard one that I found more convincing.

It would appear that the Holy Spirit of God is still giving this testimony in the hearts of many believers, hence the writing of hymns such as *"Guide Me, O Thou Great Jehovah"*, [319] which is obviously

---

319 *The [Anglican] Book of Common Praise (Revised 1938)*, hymn 406, translated (1771) from the Welsh of Rev. W. Williams (1745) by Rev. P. Williams

Trinitarian in character, addressing God also as *"Bread of heaven"*, and praying to be fed with that Bread, which would be through Christ in the Eucharist, *at the present time:* "feed me till I want no more" ("want" in the sense of no longer being deprived). In this context, the writer, and hence those who sing this hymn, are not referring *only* to a past, Old Testament, event. The hymn immediately continues *in the present tense: "Open now the crystal fountain, whence the healing stream doth flow;* let the fiery cloudy pillar Lead me all my journey through. Strong Deliverer, Be thou still my strength and shield."

This linking of the person of Christ and the Eucharist, in the present time, with the Old Testament miracles of the people being fed in the wilderness, in the past, with manna from heaven, and water from the Rock, depends on a Trinitarian understanding of the nature of God.

A well-known hymn, *"Lord enthroned in heavenly splendour"* [320] addresses Christ as: *"Life-imparting heavenly Manna, Stricken rock with streaming side."* Another hymn that similarly brings the Israelites' wilderness experience into the present time is *"Glorious things of thee are spoken, Zion, city of our God,"* [321] which refers to God's people as *"daily on the manna feeding* which he gives them when they pray," and *"streams of living water springing from eternal love".*

While hymns certainly do not have the authority of Scripture, perhaps we do need to be reminded at this time that we cannot "dispense with" the "divinity of Christ" without losing the core of our faith in the Trinitarian God. I think the fact that these hymns are now becoming less popular may well be tied in with a diminished understanding of the Trinity in today's world.

So, in an area where there is no general agreement, I suggest that it may well be that St. John saw *the Holy Spirit* as testifying *within the human heart* both as to the reality of Christ's being Who He Is, *both God and Man,* so that in Him we can indeed come to God; and the fact that He died for our sins *(the symbolism of the blood),* and gives us eternal life *(the symbolism of the water).*

I wrote the above before I re-read a passage from Tad Guzie's book,

---

320 *The [Anglican] Book of Common Praise (Revised 1938),* hymn 235, by Canon G.H. Bourne, 1874.

321 *The [Anglican] Book of Common Praise (Revised 1938),* hymn 618, by Rev. John New-ton, 1779.

Jesus and the Eucharist, where he writes of Christ's giving of the Spirit as being part of the outcome of the crucifixion, and found in it support for what I had written. [322]Guzie wrote:

> *But there is much more than John's insistence on the actuality of Jesus' death,* given the symbolism developed earlier in the gospel. From the physical fact of Jesus' death, the author moves us again *to the meaning of that death.* In chapter 6, Jesus had spoken of his flesh as real food, his blood as real drink. With his account of Jesus' death, John now makes it clear how Jesus' personal sacrifice— the giving of his body and the outpouring of his blood— could be identified with the eucharistic signs. In the same way, in chapter 7, *Jesus had spoken of satisfying the thirst of all who would come to him.* John there made one of his third-person editorial *remarks, speaking of the 'fountain of living water' that was to pour from Jesus' breast,* water associated with his glorification *and the spirit that was to be given* (Jn 7:38-39). *With the cross, that water is now given, and along with it the spirit that* gives *life.* In typical johannine fashion, the words referring to the moment of Jesus' death carry a double meaning—a physical meaning and a theological one, very much like the play on words between 'running' water and 'living' water in the conversation with the samaritan woman. The greek of John 19:30 at the empirical level means simply 'he gave up the spirit', he expired, he died. *At the symbolic level, the level of human and divine meaning, the same words mean 'he gave the Spirit'* [323] (italics mine)

So it would appear that my suggestion that *"the water of life"* was seen by the early Church as flowing from the Crucified Christ, was not

---

322   A view also shared by Neville Clark in *Studies in Biblical Theology: An Approach to the Theology of the Sacraments.* London: SCM Press Ltd., 1956, page 28: *"With the blood... was poured out the water of life which is the Spirit. In the water of baptism the Spirit is given, the Spirit which issues from the crucified and glorified body of Jesus...The death of Christ marks the institution of the sacrament."*

323   Tad W. Guzie, S.J. *Jesus and the Eucharist.* Ramsey, New Jersey: Paulist Press,1974, pp.95-96.

so very far off the mark after all; in which case, what I think St. John was saying was:

> That the *testimony* of *the Holy Spirit in the heart of the believer, combined with* the *evidence* of the outpouring of *both* the blood of Christ's human life and the water representing His divine one, *together testify to the reality* of both *His human death and His divine life. Together they are witnesses* to the fact that *Jesus is both God and Man, and so we can have eternal life in Him.* It is *because* He is *God as well as Man* that we can *come to God through Him. Humanity and divinity meet, and are at-one, in Him.*

I truly believe that we need to look at it in this way in order to understand what the Epistle was trying to say, or we will continue to find that verse difficult to understand. But at the same time, Tad Guzie wisely cautions against too simplistic an understanding of "Jesus as both God *and* Man". He says:

> For anyone who believes in the cross, no distinction need be made anymore between divine and human values. *In Jesus, God's world and our own are decisively joined.* It is this junction that constitutes a new chapter in the religious experience of mankind. To speak of Jesus as the 'god-man' is a very inadequate way of putting this, because it hyphenates what someone like John presents as a union. *Much of our inherited religious language implies a kind of opposition between the human and the divine in Jesus* [again, the italics are mine]; insofar as we create such an opposition in our minds, or attempt to juggle and combine divinity and humanity as separate components, we are doing a poor job of understanding the core of our christian faith. [324]

While we do have to regard Our Lord as a divine unity rather than a split personality, the point I was making is that, in order to penetrate

---

324 Tad W. Guzie S.J. *Jesus and the Eucharist.* Ramsey, New Jersey: Paulist Press, 1974, p.94.

the meaning behind texts not generally understood, we need to see both the humanity and the divinity of Christ, and *then* in our minds put them together, in order better to understand the whole.

I believe this demonstrates the link between *the physical crucifixion of a human being and the outpouring of God's Spirit through Him into our world,* which could not have occurred had Christ not also been the Incarnate God.

If all this is added together, I think the Bible—which was accepted by the earliest Christians as portraying the truth as they understood it—does make a strong case for the divinity of Christ, even though some people today may question it; and it has been confirmed, again and again, over subsequent generations for two thousand years, in the relationship of the individual believer with his or her God ("the testimony of the Spirit in the heart of the believer", as St. John would put it).[325] It is not just a question of whether or not one believes that Jesus was "divine" in the sense of being of and from God. On that depends the greater question of whether or not one believes in God *as Trinity,* and all that follows from that faith.

I hope to show convincingly my belief that the understanding of God that makes most sense of all is that of *the One God, the Trinity—the God who is Love: to whom it has been given to us to come through Christ.*

Christ came to give us salvation, and I believe that what St. John is saying in the Epistle is that our *understanding* of Him comes through *the symbolism of "the water" and "the blood" that together testify to us,* through the Holy Spirit, as to *Who He is,* both God and Man, so that we may *know* (a favourite expression of St. John's) that, through Christ, and *in Him,* we may have eternal life.

If Jesus had not been somehow both God and Man, how could we have eternal life in Him?   It all hangs together; it does not make sense otherwise.

As Ireneus put it, our humanity is caught up into His divinity, because He *is* both God and Man.[326]

---

325   1 John 5:8 re. the testimony of the Spirit in the heart of the believer

326   Arthur Cushman McGiffert. *A History of Christian Thought, Volume 1: Early and Eastern, From Jesus to John of Damascus.* New York, London: Charles Scribner's Sons, 1947, pp. 142-148 re. Irenaeus (c.130-200 AD.): *"according to [him] Christ was true God, but he was also true man, for otherwise he could not have united God and man";* and

We have the testimony of the Holy Spirit of God within us, that, in Christ, we have redemption and eternal life. [327]

Redeemed by the blood of the Cross, we are sustained to all eternity by *"living water"* from *"the fountain of the water of life"* [328]—*"streams of living waters springing from eternal love"*[329] —flowing from the heart of God.

"Becoming incarnate [Christ] *united the nature of God with the nature of man* and thus deified the latter, giving it the quality of divinity—immortal life—in which it was lacking"; and *"It is Irenaeus' interpretation of Paul...which has been received ever since in the Catholic church...To no other Father does Catholic theology owe so much."* (italics mine).

327   see also St. Paul in Romans 5:18: [Christ's] act of righteousness leads to *acquittal* and *life...*"

328   John 7:38; Revelation 21:6, Revelation 22:1, Revelation 22:17; Jeremiah 2:13, Jeremiah 17:13

329   *The Anglican Book of Common Praise [revised 1938]*, hymn 618: "Glorious things of thee are spoken, Zion, city of our God," by the Rev. John Newton, 1779.

CHAPTER 7

God the Holy Spirit

I feel frustrated by the fact that many Christians today claim to be *"born again"* when they obviously have no idea of what that phrase means, no idea of the impact that "being born again" should have on the way they live. (St. Paul had the same problem with the early Christians at Corinth.)

Jesus said *"that which is born of the flesh is flesh, and that which is born of the Spirit is spirit"* [330] meaning that what is born as flesh in the natural course of events in nature is a *child or product of "the flesh"* and that that physical offspring of human flesh needs to be "born again" *spiritually,* "a second, [a spiritual] birth", [331] being born into the spiritual realm as well, if it is to become a *child of God, and live in a close relationship with Him,* as opposed to being merely a purely physical, created, object. For this we need to learn to "abide in Christ" and learn *to love:* remember, love is one of the gifts of the Holy Spirit, [332] and it is *love* that brings us to God.

The trouble is that human beings can take a truth and then, in their enthusiasm, unwittingly distort it; the reverse (of the truth

---

330   John 3:6

331   "Born to raise the sons of earth, *Born to give them second birth"* – the hymn *"Hark the Herald Angels Sing"*, *The Book of Common Praise (Revised 1938)*, number 77: see also Galatians 4:19 "My little children, with whom I am again in travail until Christ be formed in you!"

332   1 Corinthians 12:1 "Concerning spiritual gifts…" v.31 "earnestly desire the higher gifts. And I will show you a still more excellent way *[Love:* see 1 Corinthians 13] "; and 2 Galatians 5:22 "the fruit of the Spirit is love….."

about the need to be "born again *or else*") does not always necessarily apply. It is often assumed that "an ordinary Christian" who has not consciously been "born again" is somehow lacking, possibly deprived of any hope of salvation, (and as for non-Christians....!) and I make the major argument that it is up to *God*, not any religious denomination, to judge what exactly His relationships with His people are, and that, in the long term, the decision about who is, and who is not, "saved" is up to Him. The Roman Catholic Church has now rescinded its long-held belief that unbaptized babies will be consigned to "Limbo" and never know the presence of God. My arguments are along the same lines, that the over-arching Love of God can sometimes over-ride what might be seen as "the normal rules", and I can well see God taking into His eternal love a child who has neither intellectual understanding of who God is and therefore no actual "faith" in Him, and who has not been baptised, simply because God is Love, and we cannot set our limits on what Love may or may not do, if Love so wishes. (We love our children before they ever know or love us.)

People assume that "being born again" means having an enthusiastic conversion into the Christian faith, "finding the Lord", and so on, and possibly "speaking in tongues", and tend to look down on traditional "church-going" which may admittedly be sometimes dry and uninspired. They assume that they are the ones who really know *"what Christianity is all about,"* as opposed to the apparent unawareness of the dynamic truth of the Gospel still regrettably to be found in many mainline churches, and too often in supposedly reputable scholars, especially those who deny belief in the divinity of Christ or the truth of the Resurrection! However, the newly-inspired "born again" converts often still do not understand what it means to "live" and "walk" "in the Spirit": "abiding in Christ" is not part of the picture for them! They carry on their lives, as St. Paul would say, as if they were *"still of the flesh."* [333] That is why I have devoted a whole section to St. Paul on the subject of "flesh" and "spirit"—see the many quotations on the subject to be found there. I think his arguments on the subject have often been misunderstood, but I believe he wrote in the urgent context of trying to persuade the new converts that they

---

333   1 Corinthians 3:1-3

needed to live lives that were *truly* "Spirit-filled", that were unselfish and loving, and not motivated by the desires and temptations of the flesh that lead to sin.

"Charismatic renewals", so-called to describe the Holy Spirit of God bringing revival to the Church (I speak of the Church at large) have occurred throughout the Church's history: the idea, or the recovery of the idea, that God Himself, through His Spirit, can dwell with, and give life to, His people, in a powerful and immediate way. In the early Church the Holy Spirit was seen as a potent force experienced in the lives of the early Christians; and the various "charismatic renewals" over the centuries have sought to recover that awareness of the power, the reality, of God's Spirit working among us.

But we need to remember that God is truth, and God is love, and for something to be authentically of the Holy Spirit it must be manifested in a spirit of truth, and righteousness, and love, with all the characteristics of the holiness of God Himself; and then we are less likely to be led astray by false claims that do occur, and have done throughout the history of Christianity. When genuinely from God, new life is breathed into institutional rigidities, and new inspiration and hope transform the lives of many people. However, human beings being what they are, human greed and a sense of personal self-promotion can sometimes take over, so that the movement, such as it is, becomes human (or demonic) in origin, rather than originating from God. The true situation may not always be apparent right away. St. Paul and his group were followed by "a slave girl who had a spirit of divination and brought her owners much gain by soothsaying", and she kept "crying, 'These men are servants of the Most High God, who proclaim to you the way of salvation'" (which was true, they were); and it took some time before even someone of the stature of St. Paul realised that something was wrong. It was only after "many days" that St. Paul "was annoyed, and turned and said to the spirit 'I charge you in the name of Jesus Christ to come out of her'. And it came out that very hour. But when her owners saw that their hope of gain was gone...".[334] So even someone like St. Paul could sometimes be temporarily deceived. We need to be reminded more often that *"discernment"* is one of the gifts of the Holy

334   Acts 16:16-19

Spirit [335] — it is not one popularly referred to! We need to remember the warnings of St. John: "Beloved, *do not believe every spirit,* but *test the spirits to see whether they are of God,* for many false prophets have gone out into the world," [336] and St. Paul: "Do not quench the Spirit, do not despise prophesying, *but test everything;* hold fast *what is good.*" [337] There is a danger that we can be deceived by something that is not authentic, and then we blame the charismatic renewal (or God). As one churchman said to me: "fire in the fireplace is good, and warms the room; a fire set by children on the living room carpet can burn the place down". I believe that good leadership is essential if the renewal, good in itself, is not to get out of control and cause damage to the church—which has happened on several occasions over the centuries. An apostle of the stature of St. Paul was needed to deal with the excited new Christians at Corinth. They may have been "born again", they may have had an enthusiastic faith, but much was still wanting, as the Epistles to the Corinthians attest. We still face that problem today.

A problem inevitably arises when someone who has newly discovered the joy and power of "the renewal" becomes aware that many of the clergy in positions of authority do not seem to be aware of, or able to convey to others, the full inspiration and dynamism of the faith (to put it kindly). In making the inevitable unfavourable comparisons, they at once assume that they know more about "real Christianity" than some of their teachers and leaders, and, in many cases, this can lead to dangerous and divisive results—especially if they do *not* know more about "real Christianity" than those whose authority they (well-meaningly enough) are questioning. It is unfortunate that the authority of the Church is thus undermined at the very moment when it is most needed to guide the faithful towards the authentic, and away from the fraudulent and demonic: and I think it would not be an overstatement to say that this is a major challenge facing "the Church" today. When John Wesley "rediscovered" the fire and the power of the original faith, he found that this was seen by the-then Bishop of Bristol as "horrid enthusiasm". "Enthusiasm" was a word widely

---

335   1 Corinthians 12:10 ("the manifestation of the Spirit.. to one....to another the ability to distinguish between spirits")

336   1 John 4:1

337   1 Thessalonians 5:19

used in the eighteenth century to denote "extravagance in religious devotion",[338] and Bishop Butler's actual words, we are told, were: "Sir, the pretending to extraordinary revelations and gifts of the Holy Ghost is a horrid thing, a very horrid thing."[339]   While it is easy to think that the good Bishop was completely lacking in understanding of what John Wesley was about—which, of course, he was—there is still a warning in his words for the Church today. Of course, no revelation or gift of the Holy Spirit could possibly be "a horrid thing" in itself, if it were genuinely of and from God: but *pretending* to them, when they are *not* authentic, which unfortunately can and does happen in some cases, is indeed most dangerous, both for the individual soul and for the Church. Possibly *that* is the long-undefined *"sin against the Holy Spirit":*[340] see footnote below regarding my suggestion as to what this may be.

Another problem that has been caused by the charismatic renewal, and been very divisive, is its insistence that one *has to* be able to "speak in tongues" if one truly is a Christian, (to prove that one *has* been "baptized by the Spirit"); and I believe that this idea is not even doctrinally correct. It is quite clear, from what St. Paul wrote in the twelfth chapter of his First Epistle to the Corinthians, that "there are *varieties* of gifts",[341] and they are not all the same, and *not everybody has*

---

338   F.L. Cross, editor, and F.L. Cross and E.A. Livingstone, editors of the second edition (revised) of *The Oxford Dictionary of the Christian Church*. Oxford: Oxford University Press, 1958, 1974, 1983, p. 460.

339   Stephen Neill, *Anglicanism*. London & Oxford: Mowbray, c.1958,1960, 1965, 1977. Fourth Edition, p.187.   A footnote there refers to *Wesley's Works*, Vol.xiii (1831), pp.464-6, and gives Wesley's reply: "I pretend to no extraordinary revelations or gifts of the Holy Ghost; none but what every Christian may receive, and ought to expect and pray for".

340   Luke 12:10: "everyone who speaks a word against *the Son of man* will be forgiven; but he who blasphemes against *the Holy Spirit* will *not* be forgiven." This supports my belief that non-Christians may still come to the   One Triune God eventually, even if not until after death ("I have other sheep which are not of this fold"— John 10:16). The statement in Luke 12:10 was in the context of people presuming *to teach others about God* when *incapable of recognizing the Holy Spirit of God them-selves when they met it* in Jesus, so it may be that this long-undefined sin has to do with *misrepresentation of the nature of God to others,* to the point of sacrilege against *the very essence of God Himself* — surely the the ultimate blasphemy.

341   1 Corinthians 12:4

the same gifts. Not only was it *not* expected that everyone would speak in tongues, but St. Paul states emphatically that that was not the most important thing anyway. Love, and building up the Church, were what really mattered. In writing about varieties of spiritual gifts, he used the analogy of the human body having many parts and not all of them having the same function, saying *"the body...has many members.."* [342]

> If the foot should say, 'Because I am not a hand, I do not belong to the body,' that would not make it any less a part of the body. And if the ear should say, 'Because I am not an eye...' If the whole body were an eye, where would be the hearing? If the whole body were an ear, where would be the sense of smell? But as it is....there are many parts, yet one body. [343]

He specifically said that one gift was given to one person and another gift or ability was given to another, as if not everyone had everything:

> *To one* is given through the Spirit the utterance of wisdom, and *to another* the utterance of knowledge according to the same Spirit, *to another* faith by the same Spirit, *to another* gifts of healing...*to another* the working of miracles, *to another* prophecy, *to another* the ability to distinguish between spirits, *to another* various kinds of tongues, *to another* the interpretation of tongues. [344]

Different people had different gifts and abilities. He admonished them later in that chapter, that they should "earnestly desire the higher gifts", as if to imply that that speaking in tongues and interpreting were "at the bottom of his list", (he actually *told* the Corinthians that prophecy, or *the transmission of the Word of God,* is more important than speaking in tongues), [345] and immediately went on to say that, *even if one did speak in tongues,* there was *"a still more excellent way"*:

---

342 1 Corinthians 12:12
343 1 Corinthians 12:15-20
344 1 Corinthians 12:8-10
345 1 Corinthians 14:4

love, without which all the speaking in tongues in the world would count for nothing: "[Even] if I speak in the tongues of men and of angels, but have not love, I am a noisy gong or a clanging cymbal."[346] So, first of all, it is not necessary that everyone should "speak in tongues"; and, even if people do, if they have not love, it is worth nothing, anyway. It appears that some of the problems which face us today were rampant in the Corinthian Church, as St. Paul laboured to explain that not everyone could aspire to everything, and that that did not matter, that was not God's plan for His Church! It is in this context that he goes on to say:

> And God has appointed in the church first apostles, second prophets, third teachers, then..... *Are all apostles?* [Obviously not.] Are all prophets? [Again, obviously not.] Are all teachers? Do all work miracles? Do all possess gifts of healing? Do all speak with tongues? Do all interpret?[347]

He is obviously implying that, no, not everyone does all of these things, so it follows that not *all* the members of the Church spoke in tongues, even then; and the implication of the context of his writing is that that did not *matter* anyway. He goes on, in the famous thirteenth chapter of that Epistle, to say that what *does* matter is whether or not there is love. So it is not true to say, as is sometimes alleged, that everyone in the early Church spoke in tongues. There was, even then, a real problem of unChristian pride and competitiveness, and sometimes worse, even in the days of the early Church, which had to be addressed by the apostles. St. John spoke of "false prophets",[348] and St. Paul had to insist that any public speaking in tongues must be accompanied by interpretation,[349] and the authenticity of that interpretation had to be convincing,[350] hence the calls for discernment, the "weighing of what

---

346   1 Corinthians 13:1

347   1 Corinthians 12:28-30

348   1 John 4:1

349   1 Corinthians 14:27: "If any speak in a tongue....let one interpret." 1 Corinthians 14:28 "if there is no one to interpret, let each of them keep silence."

350   1 Corinthians 14:29 with regard to prophecy, which is virtually the same as interpreted speaking in tongues: "let two or three prophets speak, and *let the others weigh what is said.*"

was said",[351] and "testing of spirits".[352] So it is apparent that there were "false prophets", even in the earliest days of the Church, people who falsely purported to be inspired by God. Jesus Himself spoke of "false prophets", and said *"by their fruits* you shall know them".[353] When Jesus spoke of the vine and the branches, and the vine bearing fruit,[354] He was using that as a metaphor for a life "rooted and grounded *[in Him] in love,"*[355] and the fruit that results from such a life are demonstrated when God's light and love shine out to others, and God is glorified by it. ("By this my Father is glorified, *that you bear much fruit* and *so prove to be my disciples....If you keep my commandments, you will abide in my love....").*[356] Jesus' commandments were that we should live in love for God and for each other. Without that, all the singing or speaking in tongues in the world proves nothing. St. Paul wrote: "the fruit of the Spirit is *love.."*[357] and made it clear that *love* is the most important attribute of all.[358] If St. Paul was clearly teaching that it is *not necessary* that everyone should "speak in tongues" in the first place, and that, even if people do, *if they do not live in God's love,* it is worth *nothing,* anyway, why do people try to divide the Church on this point, as if, as someone has said, there are "first-class Christians" and "second-class Christians", in defiance of both the Biblical evidence quoted above, and Christ's prayer that His Church might be one?[359] St. Paul wrote that what is needed is *building up the*

---

351 1 Corinthians 14:29 again, with regard to weighing what is said; and *The New Oxford Annotated Bible* has a note on 1 Corinthians 12:10 on the *"ability to distinguish between spirits"* which reads: "power to recognize whether a man is a true or a false prophet (1 John 4.1)."

352 1 John 4:1 "Beloved, do not believe every spirit, but *test the spirits to see whether they are of God;* for many false prophets have gone out into the world." 1 Thessalonians 5:19-21: "Do not quench the Spirit, do not despise prophesying, but *test everything;* hold fast *what is good"*

353 Matthew 7:15-16: "Beware of false prophets, who come to you in sheep's clothing *[in other words they appear superfically to be what they are not],* but inwardly they are ravenous wolves" *[i.e. they are dangerous].*

354 John 15:1-9.

355 Ephesians 3:17

356 John 15:8-10

357 Galatians 5:22-24

358 1 Corinthians 13:13

359 John 17:11, 20-23

Church, the Body of Christ, in love. The word "edify" does not just mean to enlighten and inspire, but to *build up:* from it we derive the word "edifice", meaning "a building". Building up the Church is another Biblical imperative that needs to be emphasized, and it is tied in with love. Paul wrote: *"Make love your aim"* [as he himself said, "love" is the essential ingredient without all else is worthless],[360] and he continued:

> and earnestly desire the spiritual gifts, especially that you may prophesy [i.e. speak the Word of God]. For one who speaks in a tongue speaks not to men but to God...On the other hand, he who prophesies speaks to men, for their upbuilding and encouragement and consolation. He who speaks in a tongue edifies himself, but he who prophesies edifies the Church. Now I want you all to speak in tongues, but even more to prophesy [i.e. *speak the truth that comes from God].* He who prophesies is greater than he who speaks in tongues, unless someone interprets [if the speaking in tongues is genuinely of God, the translated message will also be from God], *so that the Church may be edified [built up].*[361] .... So...since you are eager for manifestations of the Spirit, *strive to excel in building up the Church.*[362]

He had a great deal of trouble with new, enthusiastic, excited Christians who, because they had decided to accept the tenets of the Christian faith, saw themselves as *"born again in the Spirit"*[363] without really understanding what this meant in practice. This is why he spent so much of his time preaching to new converts about what "life in the Spirit" really meant, as opposed to *"life in the flesh".* What he wrote to the Corinthians could well apply today:

> ...I..could not address you as spiritual men, but as men of the flesh, as babes in Christ. I fed you with milk, not solid food, for you were not ready for it; and even [now] you are not ready, for *you are still of the flesh. For*

360   1 Corinthians 13.
361   1 Corinthians 14: 1-5
362   1 Corinthians 14:12
363   John 3:3-6

> *while there is jealousy and strife among you, are you*
> *not of the flesh, and behaving like ordinary men?* [364]

If "life in the Spirit" means in fact *living in the love and holiness of God,* then the selfish lusts and temptations of human nature, which are its absolute opposite if indulged in, *("life in the flesh"),* must inevitably preclude it. These two ways of living are completely incompatible: we cannot have both at once. St. Paul wrote: "Do not be conformed to this world but *be transformed by the renewal of your mind".* [365] We need to think more about what God is like, what the Holy Spirit is like, and less about ecstatic instances we may have experienced in our lives in the sense of that being the totality of our understanding of God. The Holy Spirit has long been associated with *Wisdom,* and one way of describing *"being filled with the Spirit"* is to say that if we were really filled with the wisdom and love of God we would have the *understanding* which would help us to deal with our purely human selfish feelings and act as God would wish us to do. I believe the Holy Spirit can best be defined as *"the very essence of God", the Spirit,* the Personality, the Power, of *the God who is Love*—or, it could be, *Love Itself.* The Holy Spirit has traditionally been associated with Wisdom. [366] Jesus referred to Him as "the Counsellor", see the footnote at the end of this chapter, and perhaps this term may be the best for us to use when referring to Him in the context of *a Person of the Trinity.* The Nicene Creed refers to the Holy Spirit as "the Giver of *Life".* [367] The original title of this book, *"Water in the Desert,"* referred metaphorically to the Spirit of God giving *life* to areas, both physical and spiritual, that would otherwise remain barren. It is as if, in ourselves, we were like a dry sponge, but, if we are saturated with God's Spirit, we can blossom marvellously. A particular metaphor used in the Old Testament for the life-giving work of the Holy Spirit among God's people was that of *water* (some examples are

---

364   1 Corinthians 3:1-3

365   Romans 12:2

366   Proverbs 8:27: "when he established the heavens I was there..." Wisdom 7:22-27: "wisdom, the fashioner of all things, taught me... *she is a breath of the power of God, and a pure emanation of the glory of the Almighty...* in every generation she passes into holy souls and makes them friends of God, and prophets";

367   The Nicene Creed   *(The* [Anglican] *Book of Common Prayer, 1962, Canada,* p. 71-772.

set out at the end of the Chapter on Baptism). "Water" is seen as a metaphor for the idea of *"life," "the water of life* that *comes from God* and nourishes the souls of God's people as the rain nourishes the earth. There are many references to the Holy Spirit in the Old Testament. The following are some examples: *Genesis:* the Spirit of God moving over the face of the waters at the beginning of creation;[368] *Isaiah:* "they rebelled and grieved his holy Spirit....where is he who put in the midst of them his holy Spirit";[369] *Ezekiel:* "A new heart I will give you, and a new spirit I will put within you.....I will put my spirit within you");[370] *Joel:* "I will pour out my spirit on all flesh";[371] and *Psalm 51:* "take not thy holy Spirit from me").[372] Isaiah also wrote:

> For thus says the high and lofty One who inhabits eternity, whose name is Holy: [with capital letters as in the Nicene Creed] *'I dwell* in the high and holy place, and *also with him who is of a contrite and humble spirit....from me proceeds the spirit, and I have made the breath of life'*[373] (the Nicene Creed refers to the Holy Spirit as "The Lord, The Giver of Life").

Note *"I dwell...with him who is of a contrite and humble spirit"*, and the constant theme of God dwelling in and with His people, which is not only in the Hebrew Scriptures, our Old Testament, but continued in the New Testament teaching about "abiding in Christ" (see the chapter on the Atonement). I think that a line in Psalm 119 can be taken in *an eternal,* rather than a literal, sense: *"Give me understanding, that I may live."*[374] The words "Spirit-filled" are almost a meaningless cliche through overuse: perhaps we might do better to think of *"having the mind of Christ"*,[375] and *in Him,* through the Holy Spirit, *coming to God,* which I believe was the whole purpose of the Incarnation of the God of Love in human history.

---

368   Genesis 1:2

369   Isaiah 63:10-14

370   Ezekiel 36:26

371   Joel 2:28-29

372   Psalm 51:11

373   Isaiah 57:15-16

374   Psalm 119:144

375   1 Corinthians 2:16

CHAPTER 8

God as Trinity

Many of our problems stem from the fact that the doctrine of the Trinity has not been clearly understood. Non-Christians have alleged either that Jesus of Nazareth was just an ordinary man, perhaps "a prophet", or that "Christians believe in three gods". I think that what I have already written, about both the Old Testament Scriptures themselves, and the very nature of God, as I understand it, calling for an incarnation in human history, makes sense of the idea of there being One God, who is also, somehow, at the same time, a Trinity of Persons.

If one thinks of God as Love, [376] it becomes easier to deal with. I have already referred to St. Augustine's theory that *Love,* by definition, needs to love and be loved, and so it is feasible to believe that *a God of Love would want to have a relationship of love at the very heart of His being,* so that *Love would flow between the Persons of the Trinity,* each Person of the Trinity being, in turn, and at one and the same time, *the Lover, the Beloved, and Love Itself.*

Love flowing at the heart of the Godhead does not equate to "three gods". We are still talking about One God.

But Love needing to flow between the Persons of the Trinity explains why God is both Three and One.

And another reason for believing that God is both Three and One is that, *because* God is Love, and *Love flows between the Persons of the Godhead,* by extension, *that Divine Love would want to reach out to the*

---

376 1 John 4:8: "He who does not love, does not know God; *for God is love"*; 1 John 4:16: *"God is love,* and he who abides in love abides in God, and God abides in him."

human race, to love us, and show us what Love is like, in the hope that we, in our turn, would learn how to love, too. But in order to do that, *part of* God would have to become incarnate, born in human flesh, in order to identify with His creation, and share the human experience with His people, and teach them about love: both then, while He was still on earth, and now, through His Spirit. For that to happen, God would have to *be* Trinity.

That explains why I believe in the Trinity from the point of view of what God must be like, if He is a God of Love; I believe that *Love Itself must make it necessary* for the eternal God *to be both Three and One;* but I explain later my belief that it was necessary (for God to be Trinity) from the *human* point of view as well, if we are ever to attain to *union with God, and eternal life in Him, in the love that flows at the heart of the Trinity,* through abiding in the Incarnate Christ.

I believe that the way Divine Love extended itself to the human race was to take on humanity, (Jesus experiencing what it was to become human), in order that we might come to experience divinity by abiding in Him, *thus finding union with God in Christ.* If God were not Trinity, then God could not have reached out to experience humanity as we believe He did in Jesus, *or bring us to Himself, in Christ,* as we come to experience God by abiding in Christ.

For those who find it difficult to think of Jesus as being both God and Man, I find it helpful to describe it like this: *that God is Love*: and that part of Divine Love could come to earth and be incarnate as a human being *while still being Love.*

I believe that Divine Love came to earth and was incarnate in history for several reasons: one was to teach us what God is like, what Love is like. Another was to give us a way of communicating with the great God of the universe, the great and glorious Trinity, who would otherwise be forever beyond our reach: because, if God is love, then surely Love would love His creation, and want to bring us to Himself, and love us, and hope that we would love Him back: and this could only happen if He made Himself known and visible and tangible among us.

As St. John wrote in his First Epistle: "That which was from the beginning" [you remember the opening line of St. John's Gospel: "in the beginning was the word, and the word was with God, and the word was God"],

That which was from the beginning, which we have heard, which we have seen with our eyes, which we have looked upon and touched with our hands, concerning the word of life— the life was made manifest, [made clear to us], and we saw it, and testify to it, ... the eternal life which was with the Father... —that which we have seen and heard we proclaim also to you, so that you may have fellowship with us [and with God]. [377]

But to have that fellowship, one with another, and with God, we have to have divine Love, the Holy Spirit of God, within us, individually and corporately, and start to share in the life of God as His life flows through us. As we abide in Christ, as we consciously try to live our lives in Him (as St. Paul said, in God "we live and move and have our being"),[378] as we try to ask Him into our hearts, and live all our lives as if He was always with us, *we can come to know something of His divinity, something of His divine Love, something of His Spirit, as He lives in us and we live in Him.*

I believe that the whole point of the Incarnation and the Atonement (the Atonement being the doctrine of *why* God came to earth, and lived among us and died and rose again) was that we might come to God through Christ. As St. Paul put it, *"in Christ, God was reconciling the world to Himself."* [379]

I believe that the way we come to God through Christ is for us to experience *something of His divinity,* while He has taken on Himself the experience of *sharing our humanity:* so that *He knows what it is to suffer and to die* (as well as to experience the joys of life), and can *share with us* all we go through in this life, even to its temptations and its pain. And just as He has come to know the human, we can come to know the divine, as *humanity and divinity meet in Him,* and *humanity and divinity can also meet in us, as we learn to abide in Christ.*

St. Paul called this merging of humanity and divinity *"a new creation":* he said "if anyone is *in Christ,* he (or she) is a new creation", and he referred to Christ as *"the first-fruits* of that *new creation."* [380]

---

377 1 John 1:1-3

378 Acts 17:28

379 2 Corinthians 5:19

380 2 Corinthians 5:17, 1 Corinthians 15:23; Ephesians 2:14-16

Irenaeus was a Bishop of Lyons who lived from about 130 to 200 A.D. Arthur Cushman McGiffert noted that "It is Irenaeus' interpretation of Paul, in fact, which has been received ever since in the Catholic church...To no other Father does Catholic theology owe so much," and wrote of him:

> According to Irenaeus *Christ was true God, but he was also true man, for otherwise he could not have united God and man*

> *Upon the union of God and man brought about by Christ* Irenaeus laid the very greatest stress....*in it...he found the very heart of Christianity.*

> As salvation includes not only man's release from [sin] but also his deification it must have another basis than the mere victory of Christ over Satan [sic], [the major thesis of this book]

> This basis Irenaeus found in *the union in Jesus Christ* of *the mortal nature of man* with *the immortal nature of God...*

> *Becoming incarnate, [Christ] united the nature of God with the nature of man* and thus deified the latter, *giving it the quality of divinity—immortal life —in which it was lacking.....*

> How could we *be joined to incorruptibility and immortality* unless first *incorruptibility and immortality had been made what we were* so that the *corruptible might be absorbed by incorruptibility and the mortal by immortality* and we receive *the adoption of sons;*

> And it is impossible, Irenaeus says, to live without life, and *the substance of life is participation in God.* [381]

But for this to be complete—for us to come to experience something of divinity through Christ, for us to be able now, spiritually, to "abide in

---

381   Arthur Cushman McGiffert. *A History of Christian Thought, Volume 1: Early and Eastern, From Jesus to John of Damascus.* New York, London: Charles Scribner's Sons, 1947, pp. 142-148.

Christ", *God first experienced our humanity,* so that He could identify Himself with us, and we could identify ourselves with Him.

If it is hard for *us* to reach up to divine standards, and try to "abide in Christ" in our living here on earth, we need to reflect that it was hard for *God* to take on humanity, with all its weaknesses and temptations. W.H. Auden wrote a poem about the Virgin Mary contemplating the pain her child would experience in taking on our humanity:[382]

> O shut your bright eyes that mine must endanger
> with their watchfulness
> Protected by their shade, escape from my care
>
> what can you discover from my tender look
> but how to be afraid?
>
> Love can but confirm the more it would deny.
> Close your bright eyes, Sleep.
>
> What have you learned from the womb that bore you
> but an anxiety your Father cannot feel? Sleep.
>
> What will the flesh that I gave do for you,
> All my mother love, but tempt you from His will
>
> Why was I chosen to teach His Son to weep?
> Little One, sleep, dream.
>
> In human dreams earth ascends to heaven
> where no one needs to pray, nor ever feel alone.
>
> In your first few hours of life here, O have you
> chosen already what death must be your own?
>
> How soon will you start on that sorrowful way?
> Dream while you may."

God did not have to do this for us, but in His love for us He took on our flesh, our weakness and our suffering, to experience for Himself, and share with us, our living—and our dying—that in the end *He might take us to Himself: that we might live, and die, and*

---

382   W.H. Auden, "For the Time Being: A Christmas Oratorio—At the Manger: Mary." *English Masterpieces Vol. VII: Modern Poetry, 2nd Edition,* edited by Maynard Mack, Leonard Dean and William Frost. Eaglewood Cliffs, N.J.: Prentice Hall Inc., 1961 p.241

live again, in Him. And all this would not be possible if God were not Trinity: Three Persons in One God.

I will say more in the chapter on the Atonement about the historic misunderstanding of the verse that "God so loved the world that He gave His only begotten Son", [383] which has been understood as if it related to two separate human beings, one victimized by the other. I think we need to think less in human terms about human fathers and human sons, and more in terms of *God* being revealed to us in Christ: there is *One God* who is revealed to us in three ways. Jesus was a very real human being, but, nevertheless, He was, even while on earth, still the fullness of God that came to us to reconcile us with Himself.

I am concerned that there seems to be a tendency for people to concentrate on the *three Persons* of the Trinity, *individually*, rather than on *the Trinity Itself* (which underlines for the Muslim world that we seem to "worship three gods"); some people emphasize devotion to Jesus, others claim to be "Spirit-filled," some treat the "Father" as if "He alone was God" (see discussion following).

Of course too much concentration on the Trinity runs the risk of becoming Unitarian or deist: but I believe that God calls us, as part of our worship and devotion, *to make a deliberate effort to keep this precious balance in our minds and worship "One God in Trinity, and the Trinity in Unity."* [384] In other words, we should treat "God" as "God," understanding *the Persons-of-the-Trinity-between-whom-Love-flows* in terms of *our relationship* with each of those Persons, and not defining *the Godhead Itself* in terms of any one of these Persons.

There is a tendency to identify "God *the Father*" as "God *Almighty*" (which He is), [385] but in doing so we blur the distinction between Father, Son, and Holy Spirit, and thus contribute to the gradual down-

---

383 John 3:16

384 Athanasian Creed - *The* [Anglican] *Book of Common Prayer, 1962, Canada,* pages 695-698. That Creed says that the Son is *"equal to the Father as touching his Godhead;* less than the Father as touching his Manhood. Who although he be God and Man, yet he is not two, but is one Christ; One, however, not by conversion of Godhead into flesh, *but by taking of Manhood into God:"* and "in this Trinity there is no before or after, no greater or less, but *all three Persons are co-eternal together, and co-equal"* (i.e. *one God),* which I believe to be our faith.

385 although what Jesus actually *told* us to say was *"Our Father who art in heaven"* (Matthew 6:9): or see Luke 11:2: *"Father, hallowed be thy name";* see also Matthew

playing, over time, of the significance of *the Son* — and *the Trinity Itself.* As the Athanasian Creed points out: "the Father is almighty, the Son almighty, the Holy Ghost almighty; And yet there are not three almighties, but one almighty," which is why the blessing in the Prayer Book runs (I believe correctly): "The blessing of *God Almighty,* the Father, the Son, and the Holy [Spirit]..." [386]

The Biblical metaphor of *"the Bread of Life"* [387] can be used to illustrate how all three Persons of the Trinity interact with us *at the human level,* while God the Trinity still exists ("in tact, as it were") in eternity. When the Israelites escaped from Egypt and were travelling in the wilderness on their journey to the promised land, they faced real hunger and thirst, and began to think that they might have been better off staying in Egypt. They were tempted to think that God would be of no help to them in this crisis, and in fact challenged Him. In the words of Psalm 78 they cried: "Can God spread a table in the wilderness?.... Can he also give bread or provide meat for His people?" [388] The Book of Exodus [389] describes how God did feed them, with the bread of heaven, the manna that they found in the mornings, and with meat when the quails came in the evening ("Moses... said...'the Lord gives you in the evening flesh to eat and in the morning bread to the full'....").

> 'At evening you shall know that it was the Lord who brought you out of the land of Egypt [the evening when the quails come] and in the morning [when the manna comes] you shall see the glory of the Lord.' [390]

This theme was repeated a few verses later: "At twilight you shall eat flesh [meat], and in the morning you shall be filled with bread; *then you shall know* that I am the Lord your God." [391] Although it is suggested that the manna in the wilderness might well have been the honey-dew excretion of insects which feed on the twigs of the tamarisk tree, "for

---

7:21: "...the will of *my Father who is in heaven*" and "Mark 11:25: "...so that *your Father* also *who is in heaven* may forgive..."

386 e.g., *The* [Anglican] *Book of Common Prayer, 1962, Canada, page 86*

387 John 6:35, 48: "I am the bread of life"

388 Psalm 78:19-20

389 Exodus 16

390 Exodus 16:6-8

391 Exodus 16:12

people of faith the *[real]* answer was that this natural phenomenon [which occurred just when the people were so hungry] was *bread which the Lord had given*". [392] However it may have come about, it has always been the Biblical understanding that *the Lord had given it — "bread from heaven"* [393] for them to eat. This passage makes it clear that it was not *only* about a miraculous feeding of hungry people: it was also about the people coming to *know* that the Lord their God was with them and was to be trusted: "You shall know that it was the Lord..... you shall see the glory of the Lord.....you shall *know* that I AM the Lord your God."

Similarly, the miracle of Jesus' feeding the Five Thousand— incidentally the only miracle to be recorded in all four Gospels[394] —was about *more* than just feeding the people. It was about the people *knowing*, as a *result* of that miracle, that God was active among His people: that *the Lord* had provided for them. When Jesus, in effect, *"prepared a table in the wilderness"* (in the words of Psalm 78), and provided bread and fish for the hungry crowd to eat, it left the people awed, and wondering *"who is this?"* They would have known the story in Exodus, and the wording of Psalm 78—*and* Psalm 105, which also referred to "the bread of heaven" given in the wilderness *("He gave them bread from heaven");* and Jesus' hearers would have seen Messianic significance in His actions. Jesus' actions were indeed deeply symbolic. This was more than a mere meal—more than a miracle—it was a *sign* by which God's people would know that God was there and involved with His people. It was seen as a sign, even then.

St. John's Gospel [395] records that "When the people saw the sign which he had done, they said, 'This is indeed the prophet who is to come into the world!' " (the special prophet foretold by Moses in the Book of Deuteronomy).[396] They did not know what other suggestion to make, but implicit in this was the admission that Jesus was no

---

392 *The New Oxford Anotated Version with the Apocrypha, expanded edition,* Revised Standard Version: notes on Exodus 16 verses 14 and 15.

393 Psalm 105:40-42: Note that this passage continues [after "He gave them bread from heaven in abundance"] *"He opened the rock, and water gushed forth; it flowed through the desert like a river.* For he remembered [his covenant with Abraham]"

394 Matthew 14:13-21; Mark 6:32-44; Luke 9:10-17; John 6:4-14.

395 John 6:14

396 Deuteronomy 18:15

ordinary man, that *God was somehow in all this*: God was there: *God had again provided food for His people.*

Jesus went on to talk about the significance of this, and Who He was, when the crowds returned the next day, to the place where they had eaten the bread, and not finding Him there, came looking for Him, wanting more. He reproached them for the fact that, in effect, they were only interested in more free .meals, and were not seeking Him for Himself because of Who He was. He said:

> 'Truly, truly, I say to you, you seek me, not because you
> saw signs, but because you ate your fill of the loaves.
> Do not labour (strive) for the food which perishes, but
> for the food which endures to eternal life', [397]

and went on to say "I AM the Bread of life - he who comes to me shall not hunger, and he who believes in me shall never thirst..... and him who comes to me I will not cast out." [398]

This is a difficult passage, where Jesus spoke of the manna in the wilderness, which, though God-given, was a purely physical substance which, while it assuaged the people's hunger for the moment, did not prevent them from dying eventually (which was also the case with the feeding of the Five Thousand); and He contrasted this with the life of God that would come to us in the Eucharist (which had yet to be instituted) to nourish our souls, to eternal life—"the true Bread from heaven".

As the note in my Bible puts it "Jesus himself is God's gift of sustenance for time and eternity." [399] The immediate response to what Jesus said at the time was: "Lord, give us this bread always." [400]

However, it was not until after the Last Supper, and the Crucifixion and Resurrection, that His disciples began to have a better understanding of what He was talking about.

When Jesus *first* spoke of this, in the context of the Feeding of the Five Thousand, contrasting the *spiritual* food that nourishes

---

397 John 6:26-27

398 John 6:32-37

399 *The New Oxford Annotated Bible with the Apocrypha, expanded edition, Revised Standard Version,* part of note on John 6:36-40

400 John 6:34

the soul for eternity as opposed to *physical* food which only feeds our mortal bodies while we are on this earth, some of the people who heard Him did not understand the symbolism of what He was saying, and started to draw back in their bewilderment. He then asked His disciples if they, too, wished to go away, to leave Him, and Simon Peter answered Him: "Lord, to whom shall we go? You have the words of eternal life, and we have believed, *and have come to know,* that you are the Holy One of God." [401] Sometimes what keeps us going is faith, as it did with St. Peter, even when he did not understand. *We* may not always understand, but like St. Peter, *we have come to know* (shades of both the story of the manna in the wilderness and the Feeding of the Five Thousand)—we come to know that *God is with us;* that this nourishment and life *comes to us from God.* If God were not Trinity, all this would not be possible.

Jesus, at every Eucharist, is known to us again in the Breaking of Bread. The Breaking of Bread, in the way instituted by Jesus, has always been a hall-mark of Christians' gathering in His Name ever since—from the first Easter Sunday, when the two disciples travelling to Emmaus did not at first recognize the muffled stranger who joined them in their journey and illumined their hearts and minds with new understanding of the Scriptures; but when, at supper, "He took the bread, and blessed, and broke it, and gave it to them," they recognized Him immediately, and returned at once to Jerusalem, and told the other disciples *"how he was known to them in the breaking of the bread."* [402] The Book of the Acts of the Apostles refers to Christians in the earliest days devoting themselves to the apostles' teaching and fellowship, *the Breaking of Bread,* and the prayers.[403] In the Holy Communion service, the Eucharist, we are not just observing an exterior ritual, we are sharing in the spiritual life that comes from God: we are being woven into something much greater than ourselves.

In the same chapter of St. John's Gospel in which the Feeding of the Five Thousand is described [404] Jesus specifically states that [he who

---

401 John 6:67-69

402 Luke 24:13-35

403 The Acts of the Apostles 2:42

404 John 6:4-14

does this] *"abides in me and I in him".* [405] (This is in addition to the passage in the fifteenth chapter about the Vine and the Branches). "Abiding in Christ" is at the heart of the Eucharist, as is the prayer in the Anglican *Book of Common Prayer* that *we may so receive the sacrament "that we may evermore dwell in Him, and He in us".* [406] "To dwell" is to "abide": we pray that we may evermore abide *in Him,* and He *in us.* Forget the hymn "abide *with* me". I am speaking of something deeper. This is why I have given so much emphasis to the concept of "abiding *in* Christ".

Dom Gregory Dix has said: "It is of the deepest meaning of the rite that those who take part are thereby united indissolubly with one another and with all who are Christ's, because *each is thereby united with Him, and through Him with the Father, with Whom He is One;"* [407] and again: *"it is not organisation but the eucharist which is always creating the Church to be the Body of Christ;* to do His will, and work His works, and adore His Father 'in His name', and *in Him* [and this is what I would emphasize] *to be made one,* and *by Him in them* to be made *one with God."* [408]

The Bread of Heaven indeed gives life to the world—*eternal life, in God.* Jesus said *"My Father gives you the true bread from heaven.* For the bread of God is that *which comes down from heaven, and gives life to the world."* [409] That sentence could be rendered: *The Father gives the Son* ("the true bread from heaven....which comes down from heaven"), and thus *life (the Holy Spirit) is given to the world* — spiritual life, eternal life, because God is eternal: thus describing *Father, Son, and Holy Spirit.* One could say: *"the Father sends the Son who sends the Holy Spirit"* (not that this involves any "diluting" of the Holy Spirit,

---

405 John 6:51-56: "I am the living bread which came down from heaven; if any one eats of this bread, he will *live for ever;* and the bread which I shall give for the life of the world is my flesh ... He who eats my flesh and drinks my blood *has eternal life* and *I will raise him up at the last day...* [and] [he] *abides in me and I in him"* — a direct Biblical link between *abiding in Christ* and *eternal life.*

406 *The [Anglican] Book of Common Prayer, 1962, Canada,* pages 83-84

407 Dom Gregory Dix. *The Shape of the Liturgy.* London: Adam & Charles Black, 1945, p.1.

408 Dom Gregory Dix. *The Shape of the Liturgy.* London: Adam and Charles Black, 1945, p.734.

409 John 6:32-33

as it were, but that Jesus was the vehicle through which the Holy Spirit was given to us).[410]   There is One God, but the Father gives, the Son gives, and the Holy Spirit gives, and *this is how God is known to us.*   For me, the symbolism of "the Bread of *Life*" is a powerful description of God *as Trinity.*

Another, and deeply profound, way of thinking of God as Trinity is Jurgen Moltmann's powerful description of *our being caught up into the Trinity through the Spirit through the Son to the Father,* and receiving, in turn, blessing from the Father through the Son through the Spirit (see the chapter on *The Atonement).*   I refer to it here for the sake of consistency while we are on the subject of "God as Trinity", and expand on it later.

I have said that, while we may think in terms of Christ's being both human and divine in order to understand Him better, we must remember that, *in Himself,* He is "a divine unity, and not a split personality."   Similarly with the Trinity. Although God reveals Himself to us in different ways, first, as a loving Father, secondly, as a Son who has lived on earth as a human being, *so that we can identify ourselves with Him,* and share our lives with Him, (which I believe is *the whole point of the Incarnation and the Atonement,* to bring us to God through Him), and, thirdly, as Spirit to strengthen and inspire us (our "Counsellor,") *we are still dealing with one God.*

---

410   John 14:26: "the Counselor, the Holy Spirit, whom the Father will send *in my name";* John 16:7: "if I do not go away, the Counselor will not come to you, but if I go, *I will send him to you";* John 15:26: "when the Counselor comes, *whom I shall send to you* from the Father, even the Spirit of truth, who proceeds from the Father, *he will bear witness to me".*   In these chapters (John 14-16), *in the text itself,* Jesus' words imply *a Trinitarian context,* and therefore the statement that the Holy Spirit "proceeds", or comes, "from *the Father*" needs to be understood *in that Trinitarian context,* and cannot, to my mind, be used to justify the removal of "the Filioque clause" from the Nicene Creed as if the Holy Spirit only related to the Father and not to the Son. If proponents of this change point to John 15:26 ("proceeds from the Father"), they might equally well remember John 14:18: "I will not leave you desolate; *I* will come to you", and John 14: 20: "you will know that *I am in my Father, and you in me, and I in you."*   I am concerned about a growing tendency to imply that the Holy Spirit has nothing to do with *Jesus.* We cannot let a new generation infer that the Holy Spirit is "the spirit" of a *unitarian god who is addressed as "Father,"* and that Jesus does not come into the picture— see discussion immediately following.

It is *because* the Great God of the Universe is so far beyond our comprehension that *we need* to think of Him in these three ways—which are indeed valid and real—but when we are tempted to think *only* of the three Persons of the Trinity as if dealing with three different "gods", or if we are tempted to think of *One God called "Father"*, as if "somehow Jesus does not quite qualify", we must think again of the *totality* of that Great Godhead, the power, the magnificence, the glory: and remember that we *are* dealing with *One God,* who, in relation to our limited experience and understanding, is as the vast ocean is to a pool of water.

As it is poetically expressed in Psalm 29:

> The voice of the Lord is upon the waters; the God of glory thunders...the voice of the Lord breaks the cedars...of Lebanon...The voice of the Lord flashes forth flames of fire. The voice of the Lord shakes the wilderness...The voice of the Lord makes the oaks to whirl, and strips the forest bare; and in his temple all cry, 'Glory!' [411]

Jesus lived on earth as a human being, but it was *God the Trinity* (even if in muted form) that was revealed to us through His Incarnation.

Confusion in distinguishing between the Persons of the Trinity

An example of what I would regard as confused thinking about the Trinity appears in Eucharistic Prayer 6 in the comparatively new *Book of Alternative Services* of the Anglican Church of Canada. In a foreword to it, it is stated that

> this prayer is the work of an unofficial ecumenical committee of Roman Catholic, Episcopal, Presbyterian, Lutheran, and Methodist scholars. Its source is the eucharistic prayer in the liturgy of St. Basil of Caesarea. It is Eucharistic Prayer D in the Episcopal Prayer Book. This prayer brings to our tradition the richness of the Eastern tradition as well as representing an ecumenical achievement. [412]

---

411   Psalm 29:3-9

412   *The Book of Alternative Services of the Anglican Church of Canada.* Toronto, Canada: Anglican Book Centre, c. The General Synod of the Anglican Church of Canada, 1985, p.207.

Because this was an ecumenical achievement—and may there be many more; and because this was already in the American Episcopal Prayer Book; and because its source is an ancient liturgy which is believed to be descended from one of the Fathers of the Church, a saint, Basil the Great, it would follow that it is not easy to change it at this stage, especially as doing so would not help relations with the Eastern Church.

Nevertheless, I have reservations about the English version of it now being incorporated into our worship. I am sure that it was very laudable devotion "to *Almighty God*" that originally inspired such extravagant wording at the beginning of this prayer, as if one were addressing *the Trinity Itself,* "Almighty and Everlasting God"; but the actual English words say that *"the Father alone* is God", as if to discriminate *between the Persons of the Trinity* (in which case you *have* no "Trinity" — which would deny the heart of the Christian faith):

> It is right to glorify you, *Father,* and to give you thanks;
> *for you alone are God, living and true, dwelling in light*
> *inaccessible from before time and for ever. Fountain of*
> *life and source of all goodness, you made all things..* [413]

and the prayer continues in this vein for paragraphs afterwards, only referring later to Jesus as "your only Son to be our Saviour". The word "Christ" is mentioned several times after that, but one could ask "what *is* the Christ", what is our faith, *if the Father alone is God?* I think this is a prime example of confusing the Godhead as a whole ("Almighty and Everlasting God") with the Persons of the Trinity as *Persons.* One could either drop the word *"Father"* in the above Eucharistic Prayer, and thus the implication that *the Father only* existed "before time and for ever": or, if one wanted to maintain what I understand is the traditional invocation of the Trinity in the Prayer of Consecration: "the Father gave the Son who....", and then calling on the Holy Spirit to complete the whole, one would, I believe, need to word differently the part about "you alone *(Father)* are God" which is now couched in such extravagant and exclusive, and, to my mind, potentially dangerous, terms.

I know that part of the problem stems from the fact that Latin and English cannot reflect adequately the original Greek wording. In addition, the Eastern Church has more of a hierarchical understanding

---

413   *The Book of Alternative Services of the Anglican Church of Canada,* p.207.

of the Trinity than the West, where St. Augustine *saw the Persons of the Trinity more as a great circle of love.* [414] So the Liturgy of St. Basil may not pose difficulties for the Eastern Church as much as it may well have done, when translated into another language (first Latin, and, later, English), in the West, in the past; but I do think that *everything* needs to be critiqued and tested by what is *actually in the Bible,* on an ongoing basis from one generation to another, lest our standards start to slip over time.

The Gospel of St. John opens with the following emphatic statement about the Second Person of the Trinity, the Logos, the Word:

> *In the beginning was the Word,* and the Word was with God, *and the Word was God.* He was in the beginning with God; *all things were made through him,* and *without him was not anything made that was made. In him was life, and the life was the light of men.* [415]

How can we therefore, with good conscience, say in our worship that

> "It is right to glorify you *Father......for you alone are God,* living and true, and dwelling in light inaccessible from before time and for ever. *Fountain of life and source of all goodness you made all things..."*

Surely, any reference to *"the Fountain of Life"* must—or should—refer to *God the Trinity,* see examples given (in this chapter, and the footnote below, and the chapter on Baptism) of both Jesus and the Holy Spirit *also* being, in Themselves, sources of God-given *Life.* [416]

---

414   A theme echoed in the writing of Jurgen Moltmann—see the Chapter on the Atonement (and also the quotations from Bishop Wand and Neville Clark following)

415   John 1:1-4: "In the beginning...."   Re. *"life",* see John 14:6, John 11:25-26, John 6:33, and 1 John 1:1, re. *Jesus* being "the way and the truth and *the life",* "the resurrection and *the life;"* "the Bread [of heaven] which ....*gives life* to the world;" and "the word of *life".* The Nicene Creed calls *the Holy Spirit* "the Lord and giver of *life".* We come back to *the Trinity* at every turn.

416   The Nicene Creed refers to *the Holy Spirit* as "the Lord and giver of *Life";* but it is said of *Jesus:* "in him was life" (John 1:4); "I am the bread of life..[which]...gives life to the world" (John 6:35,33); "the resurrection and the life" (John 11:25); "the way and the truth and the life" (John 14:6); "the word of life" (1 John 1:1); Revelation 21:6 says "to the thirsty I will give from the fountain of the water of life"; and Acts 3:15 refers to "the Author of life"

Although Jesus gave us permission to address *God* as "Father", thinking, I believe, in terms of *relationship,* that we could have this relationship with the Father, I do not think that it could ever have been intended that we should use this licence to deny *faith in the Trinity,* by saying that *only one Person of the Trinity* was God.

If that were so, there would *be* no Trinitarian God. If we are to be Christians, in other words believe that the *Christ is part of a Trinitarian God,* then we must be able to distinguish in our minds between *the Godhead* on the one hand, even if we have permission to approach that Godhead *as if* approaching a father, and *the three Persons of that Trinity,* on the other.

There are dangers in "picking and choosing" from documents of the past, just because they are ancient, and have hallowed associations. We need to look at the whole spectrum of how theological thought developed over the years, and ensure that our liturgies reflect the understandings *matured by reflection over the centuries:* and to check, always, that what we do is not in conflict with Biblical teaching. I am not really coming up with anything new.

I believe that, because of the extraordinary parallelism between the wording of this liturgy and that of the Athanasian Creed,[417] the latter may well have been written to correct misunderstandings arising from the former when the Western Church first tried to translate Basil's liturgy into Latin. The origins of the Athanasian Creed are wrapped in mystery, but I cannot help thinking that surely it could not have been a coincidence that some unknown author (who must have known Basil's liturgy) wrote the following:

> So the Father is God, the Son God, the Holy Ghost God; And yet *there are not three Gods, but one God.* So the Father is Lord, the Son Lord, the Holy Ghost Lord; And yet there are not three Lords, but one Lord..
> [And] ... *all three Persons are co-eternal together, and co-equal,* So that in all ways, as is aforesaid, *both the Trinity is to be worshipped in Unity, and the Unity in Trinity.* [418]

---

417   *The [Anglican] Book of Common Prayer, 1962, Canada,* p. 695

418   *The [Anglican] Book of Common Prayer, 1962, Canada,* p. 696.

Surely, it must be more than coincidence that, after St. Basil's liturgy saying that *"the Father alone is God"* was translated into Latin (which it would have been at some stage), someone found it necessary to spell out that *"the Son [is also] God, the Holy Ghost God, And yet there are not three Gods, but one God...."*. The almost exact parallelism of the words in the two documents would surely suggest that they are related in the mind of the author of the Athanasian Creed. I think that it is unfortunate that, at the same time as we include a liturgy in our new *Book of Alternative Services* which states that *"the Father alone is God"*, we drop the Athanasian Creed from the Book entirely, so that the next generation, for the most part, in the course of time, will never have heard of its claim that *"the Son [is also] God, [and] the Holy Ghost [is also] God..."* [419]

The reason why the Athanasian Creed has come to be down-played in modern times may well be that it presents problems to a generation to whom it has not been properly explained, especially because of its exclusive beginning, *"Quicumque Vult.."* — *"Whosoever would be saved* needeth before all things to hold fast the Catholic Faith. Which Faith except a man keep whole and undefiled, *without doubt he will perish eternally.* Now the Catholic Faith is this.." [420] —and the statement near the end (verse 41) that "they that have done good will go into life eternal; *they that have done evil into eternal fire"* (italics mine).

This needs to be explained, which is why I have devoted so much thought to the subject of what it means "to perish eternally" and go into "eternal fire".

As I set out in more detail in the chapter on "not only Christians being saved", I now believe that the Church may well have been wrong in its traditional belief that anyone who does not "hold fast the Catholic Faith" *in this life* "without doubt...will perish eternally" — note my emphasis on *"in this life"* —the form of that "perishing"

---

419 The situation is not helped by prayers such as that after Psalm 100 on page 838 of *The [Anglican] Book of Alternative Services,* which runs: "God *our Father,* you have created us... you sustain us.... Help us always to give you thanks, for *you alone [Father,* not *"Almighty God"] are worthy* of thanksgiving and praise and honour, now and for ever." I do not think that this does justice to our Christian understanding of *God as Trinity.*

420 *The [Anglican] Book of Common Prayer, 1962, Canada.* p. 695.

being, literally *"eternal fire"*; and I explain my belief that references to "eternal fire" *must* be metaphorical in origin, as one cannot both *perish, i.e., cease to exist*, and *at the same time survive for ever to be tormented by eternal fire.*

This apparent exclusivity has done much to damage Christianity, both in the past and today; but, as I try to show in that chapter, while that particular cultural assumption of the past may need to be corrected, I believe that otherwise the Creed is essentially true, and that *its main purpose was to describe God the Trinity.* If we could once agree that perhaps the exclusiveness, and the misunderstandings, of the past were not "eternal truth", we could then keep extant, for present and future generations, much of the rest of the Athanasian Creed, which contains what I do believe to be "eternal truth" with regard to *the nature of the Trinity.*

At the same time as *The Book of Alternative Services* omits the Athanasian Creed, even as a reference document, and has in it a liturgy referring to *"the Father alone being God"*, it also omits the Filioque clause from the Nicene Creed (see below). While there are reasons for the latter, the fact remains that we are leaving for future generations an approved document which, in total, would, to my mind, appear to deny the doctrine of the Trinity, and the divinity of Christ.

"The Filioque clause" in the Nicene Creed, so called from the Latin (that the Holy Spirit "proceeds" from the Father *and the Son)*, was added to the original wording of the Creed because of the same problem of language described above. Although no problem was anticipated when the Creed was first in its original language, it is my belief that the Filioque clause became necessary when, centuries ago, that Creed was translated into Latin (and, later still, into English). I am concerned by the recent deletion of it in new Anglican liturgies, on the technical grounds that it was not in the original (and to please the Eastern Church, even though that now meant differing from Rome), with its implication, in English at least, that the Holy Spirit proceeds from "the Father" only.

While I know of people who have problems with the Creeds because of the fundamental beliefs stated in them, about the Incarnation, the Resurrection, and Our Lord's coming again, and I have problems with none of these, I do have a concern about the *particularizing of the Persons of the Trinity* into which we have been drawn by our modern liturgists, believing, as I do, that the use of the Filioque clause in our language more closely approximates *the intent of the original* than any implication that the Holy Spirit proceeds from the Father *only*.

One should also bear in mind that, for more than a thousand years, since approximately the ninth century, a prominent hymn in the Western Church, originally in Latin, has been *"Come, Holy Ghost, our souls inspire"*, with its prayerful request (to the Holy Spirit): "teach us to know the Father, Son, *and Thee*, [Holy Spirit] *of Both, to be but One"*. [421] Can a millennium of devotion be thus lightly disregarded?

The Bishop who confirmed me wrote that:

> The Holy Spirit is believed *to proceed from the Son as well as from the Father, and the threefold relation is that of the lover, the beloved, and the love that flows between them.* So close is their unity that the entire Trinity acts in the action of each Person, just as an individual acts as a complete person in every operation of memory, intelligence and will. [422]

I have tried to show how Jesus was/is connected with the God of the Old Testament, in order to show His "divinity," that He was/is of the same substance as that great God, but one cannot then say that *He alone* "is God". In the same way I believe that we cannot *limit* "God" to the Person of *"the Father"*, either, if we believe in God *as Trinity*. We cannot appear to limit *"God"* to any *one* Person of the Trinity, or, in the English language at least, it would appear that we do not *have* a Trinitarian faith.

While there are good reasons for the deletion of the Filioque clause in modern liturgies, I still believe that, without explanation or good teaching about the Trinity being given to the ordinary parishioner, it can have dangerous consequences in that it appears to exclude any participation of the Son in that Godhead, and implies

421 The Anglican *Book of Common Praise, 1938,* hymn 480.

422 J.W.C. Wand: *A History of the Early Church to AD 500.* London: Methuen & Co., 1937, p. 228.

that the Holy Spirit has no relation to Christ.[423] My concern is that the ordinary person in the pew, and new generations to come, going purely by the new text in front of them, will get the impression that the Holy Spirit is the Spirit of the Father only, and therefore has nothing to do with the Son. Could we not compromise, for their sake, by saying that the Holy Spirit proceeds from the Father *through the Son?*

"The trinitarian problem" has been referred to by Neville Clark, not in the context of the Filioque clause but in the context of sacramental theology, saying:

> The part played by the Spirit in the transformation of the fallen world poses at once the trinitarian problem, and more particularly the question of the relation between the Spirit and the Son, so far as this is relevant to sacramental theology. Here the fact of the ascension of Christ is crucial; *and failure to maintain the balance of Christian truth at this point has* led to *disastrous theological confusion....* [a result has been] *the transference to the third Person of the Trinity of so large a part of the present activity of the Godhead that the ascended Christ seems to be deprived of his rightful significance"*

—for a fuller quotation see Clark's book itself.[424]

I believe that *the original intention of the Nicene Creed* (as well as that of the Athanasian Creed) was to express belief in God *as Trinity.* I would point out that the same Nicene Creed says, about which, presumably, there is no argument, that *the Holy Spirit* is "the Lord and *giver of life".* How can one reconcile this with either Basil's liturgy (one can't), or the Biblical teaching about *Jesus* being *the giver of life,*

---

423   How would one then explain how it was that the early Christians (including St. Paul) sometimes referred to the new phenomenon of the Spirit of God working in their lives as being the Spirit of *Christ?*   (Romans 8:9-10, Philippians 1:19, Acts 16:7, 1 Peter 1:11).

424   Neville Clark. *Studies in Biblical Theology No. 17: An approach to the Theology of the Sacraments.*   London, SCM Press Ltd., 1956, pages 75-76.

[425] unless that *One God,* to whom the Creed refers at its beginning, is understood *as Trinity?* In which case it cannot be said with any truth, (in English anyway), that the Holy Spirit *"proceeds from the Father only".* When Isaiah wrote of God, in a passage I have already quoted ("Thus says the high and lofty One, who inhabits eternity, whose name is Holy *... from me proceeds the spirit,* and I have made *the breath of life,"*) [426] I believe that that description of God applied to *the Godhead,* and does not relate to the *relationship* of *"Father"* with *His people.*

I believe that the more we particularize about the Persons of the Trinity, and the more we stretch metaphors to make them carry a literal meaning, the more likely we are to run into difficulties, and become confused in our thinking; and that that has contributed largely to the recent tendency to deny—or at least down-play—the concept of the divinity of Christ. While some people today are rejecting the historic Creeds, and I know Anglican churches where they are not said, I am trying to restate that historic faith as indeed being true in its essentials, and worth believing.

On the other hand, there is the viewpoint that thinks that "not a *word* of them could *possibly* be mistaken", and that if what was decided upon many centuries ago was wording that says that "the Spirit proceeds from the Father", and, by implication, (in English anyway), not the Son, that must be "etched in stone" for ever, because of the old illusion that "the Church could not possibly have made a mistake": and that what was done then cannot be changed now without another "ecumenical council" such as there was before the Church split between eastern and western Europe.

However, until all the churches do come together again, can we not at least *think* about what it is that we *do* believe?

Perhaps the mistake would not be corrected even by reinstating "the Filioque clause" (that the Holy Spirit "proceeds from the Father *and the*

---

425   e.g. John 6:35, John 6:48: "the Bread *of Life";* John 1:4: *"In him was life,* and that life was the light of men"; and Jesus' saying "I came that they might have *life,* and have it abundantly" (John 10:10); — not to mention the fact that there are several references in the New Testament to the Spirit of *Christ:* e.g. Romans 8:9-10, Philippians 1:19, Acts 16:7, 1 Peter 1:1-11.

426   Isaiah 57:15-16

Son"). At that time, the Church was more concerned with Christology and the doctrine of the Trinity than with developing a theology of the Holy Spirit, per se; and now, although the difficulty will remain with us, I think we need to remember the limitations of human language, and not try to define too closely *what part of the Godhead* the Spirit comes from.

Perhaps we should be more specifically teaching our people about the problem, so they understand what is involved, and think of the Holy Spirit in two ways: one, as *the Eternal Spirit of the Eternal God,* and the other *in the terms used by Jesus* for *the Third Person of the* Trinity as *experienced by human beings:* "the Counsellor" or "Comforter." [427]

I think our clergy and theologians also need to think more clearly about how they define God the Trinity: the current Canadian Anglican *Book of Alternative Services* reveals confusion on the subject, both on the part of those who compiled the liturgy and those who now use it without seeing any incongruity or confusion in it. The deletion of "the Filioque clause" in the English language implies to the ordinary person that the Spirit of God is of the Father alone, and not the Son; and as well as the statement that *"the Father alone is God"* in Eucharistic Prayer 6, discussed above, there is a prayer

---

427 John 14:16: "another Counsellor...even the Spirit of truth"; John 14:26: "the Counsellor, the Holy Spirit"; John 15:26: "when the Counsellor comes ... even the Spirit of
truth"; John 16:7-13: "if I do not go away, the Counsellor will not come to you, but if I
go, *I will send him to you...* When the Spirit of truth comes, he will guide you into all the
truth." *The Oxford Dictionary of the Christian Church* writes, of the Greek word used,
"Paraclete", meaning "advocate", the "Johannine epithet of the Holy Ghost", that "It is
traditionally translated 'Comforter'. Though used *of Christ* in   1 John 2:1 *[we have
an advocate with the Father, Jesus Christ the righteous],* and, by implication, in Jn.14:16,
it is ordinarily applied to the Holy Spirit (Jn.14:16, 16:7, etc.) Origen interpreted the
word as meaning 'Intercessor' where the reference is to the Lord, as 'Consoler' (for the
loss of Christ) where it is to be the Holy Ghost. This latter meaning, though not found
outside the NT, may be defended by the context, and was indeed that generally accepted
by the Fathers. But it describes the mission of the Holy Ghost, which is *'to strengthen
and guide the Church into all truth'* less fully than the renderings 'Helper', 'Counsellor',
or the Vulgate translation 'Advocate', preferred by many modern commentators. Several
scholars are in favour of simply transcribing the Greek word as was done in several
ancient versions of the NT". (page 1030).

at the end of Psalm 100 in that book which runs as follows: *"God our Father, you* have created us... *you* sustain us...Help us always to give you thanks, for *you alone are worthy* of thanksgiving and praise and honour, now and for ever". [428] What is meant, of course, is *Almighty God,* God *the Trinity,* not just "the Father". While the Son is thus apparently discounted, at the same time the funeral service in that book, the book which says on more than one occasion that "the Father alone is God", also says "Give rest, *O Christ,* to your servants with your saints...*You only are immortal, the creator and maker of all".* (What does that imply about "the Father"?) [429] This is a change from the original in the Prayer Book, which, like the Gloria in the *Book of Common Prayer,* when it says of Christ *"thou only art holy..."* takes care to specify that Christ, *"with the Holy Ghost,* [is] most high *in the glory of God the Father."[430]* However, this caveat, if it may be so called, is becoming less and less known to the present generation, as the Prayer Book falls more and more into disuse, and is replaced by a book that says simultaneously that "the Father alone is God" and *"Christ...only"* is "immortal, the creator and maker of all", and teaching and thinking about God *as Trinity* now seems to be almost non-existent. The Athanasian Creed has fallen into disuse: but I think we need to be reminded that:

> the Catholic faith is this, that *we worship one God in Trinity, and the Trinity in Unity, neither confusing the Persons, nor dividing the Substance.* [431]

I have come to believe that the teaching in the Athanasian Creed on the subject of the Trinity may well have been written in direct response to questions such as the ones raised here, and (although that Creed in its present form may not be suitable for use in public worship), we should always keep in remembrance its teaching about the Trinity.

---

428 The Canadian *Book of Alternative Services,* p.838

429 The Canadian *Book of Alternative Services,* p.595

430 The Anglican *Book of Common Prayer, 1962,* pp.600 & 86.

431 *The Anglican Book of Common Prayer, Canada, 1962,* p.695.

CHAPTER 9

God as the Divine Healer

When I was asked once to talk about *"Healing in Scripture"*, I had occasion to look particularly at how the theme of healing runs through the Bible—in the context, of course, of other themes such as the goodness of God, and His love for His people, and His desire for our redemption, wholeness, and total well-being.

This led me to see, more than ever, how the Bible shows us a God of Love, who forgives and heals, and desires His people's total redemption.

Even more than that, however, that particular exercise led me to see the nature of God, described throughout the Bible, does indeed support our belief in God as Trinity. My work on that project (on *"Healing in Scripture"*) showed how the *One God* was seen as working consistently for healing among His people, whether experienced by them as Father, Son, or Holy Spirit.

I have already set out Scriptures which point to a Messiah who was also the Incarnate God, to the point where, if Jesus of Nazareth were *not* God Incarnate, there would be no understanding of God as Trinity. I thought it might be helpful if I set out here more references to the *One God,* again expressed as Father, Son, and Holy Spirit, on the subject of *healing*.

In particular one sees again how it is not just the writings of St. John that portray Jesus of Nazareth as God Incarnate, in the context of God the Trinity. The references to healing in the three Synoptic Gospels demonstrate that Jesus' power and personality were seen as setting Him apart from all others, quite apart from what was written by St. John or St.

Paul. While, as I have said before, it is possible that some of the accounts that have come down to us may not be entirely accurate, one cannot dismiss them *all* without dismissing the whole of the New Testament and the whole of the Christian faith. One cannot, therefore, conveniently blame St. John for "a later theology of the Church", and pretend that the rest of the New Testament does not see Jesus as God Incarnate.

There are more than 150 specific references to "health" and "healing" in the Old and New Testaments of the Bible (not including the Apocrypha); and there are many more accounts of what could equally well be called "healing," where other words, such as "cleansed", "made whole", and so on, are used.

"God is love", [432] and that love expresses itself in the desire to make us well and put things right. *Healing is thus one of the attributes of God.*

As early as the Book of Exodus, God is written of as saying: *"I AM the Lord your healer",* [433] or, in the old language, *"I am the Lord that healeth thee".* Psalm 147 says *"he heals the broken hearted, and binds up their wounds."* [434] There is a similar reference in Isaiah. [435]

Among the attributes of the Messiah, according to Isaiah, [436] and quoted by Jesus, [437] was the fact that He would proclaim (among other things) "recovering of sight to the blind" (which is in effect "healing"). Malachi says, referring to the day "when the Lord acts," that the "sun of righteousness shall rise, *with healing in its wings,"* [438] (which was picked up, and referred to the Messiah, in that carol "Hark the herald angels sing"). [439]

St. Peter wrote of Christ, the Messiah, quoting Isaiah, *"by His stripes ye are healed".* [440]

---

432 1 John 4: 8, 16

433 Exodus 15:26

434 Psalm 147:3

435 Isaiah 30:26: "...in the day when the Lord binds up the hurt of his people, and heals the wounds inflicted by his blow."

436 Isaiah 61:1-3 "the Spirit of the Lord is upon me..." ("he has sent me to bind up the broken-hearted"); also Isaiah 58: 6, referring to the coming of the Messiah.

437 Luke 4:16-21

438 Malachi 4:2

439 *The [Anglican] Book of Common Praise (Revised 1938),* hymn 77.

440 1 Peter 2:24, echoing Isaiah 53:5: "He was wounded for our transgressions, he was bruised for our iniquities; upon him was the chastisement that made us whole, *and with his stripes we are healed."*

Isaiah also writes "I have seen" [the ways of the covetous, in other words, idolatrous man] "I have seen his ways, *but I will heal him;* I will lead him and requite him with comfort."[441] Jeremiah has something similar "Return, O faithless sons, *I will heal your faithlessness,*"[442] which equates to forgiveness and deep healing of the soul. Healing can be much more than the healing of some physical condition of the body.

The fact that healing is part of *the nature of God* is seen in the writing in the New Testament about healing being one of the gifts of the Holy Spirit,[443] the Spirit of the God who loves and heals.

There are many stories of healing in the Bible, in the Old Testament as well as the New, as for example, the healing of Hezekiah,[444] Namaan, the commander of the army of the King of Syria who was cured of leprosy,[445] the woman whose son was healed by Elijah,[446] and so on.

There is a significant story in the Book of Numbers about the time when the Israelites were in the wilderness, bitten by serpents, and suffering from lack of food and water:

> And the people came to Moses, and said, 'We have sinned, for we have spoken against the Lord and against you; pray to the Lord, that he take away the serpents from us.' So Moses prayed for the people. And the Lord said to Moses, 'Make a fiery serpent, and set it on a pole; and every one who is bitten, when he sees it, shall live.' So Moses made a bronze serpent, and set it on a pole; and if a serpent bit any man, he would look at the bronze serpent and live. [447]

In other words, instead of the serpent's bite proving to be fatal, the

---

441 Isaiah 57:17-18: "Because of his covetousness I was angry...but he went on backsliding... I have seen his ways, but I will heal him; I will lead him and requite him with comfort"

442 Jeremiah 3:22, echoed in Hosea 14:4: "I will heal their faithlessness; I will love them freely"

443 1 Corinthians 12:9, 28, 30

444 2 Kings 20:5

445 2 Kings 5:1-19

446 1 Kings 17:7-24

447 Numbers 21:5-9

people who were bitten did not die, but survived: which is to say that they were healed of the poison of the bite. Thus the image of the coiled serpent on a pole has long symbolised healing, and has come to be used in connection with doctors and medicine. This story was used by Jesus, when He said, referring to the coming Crucifixion:

> As Moses lifted up the serpent in the wilderness, so must the son of Man be lifted up, that whoever believes in him may have eternal life. For God so loved the world that he gave his only Son, that whoever believes in him should not perish but have eternal life. [448]

In other words, through faith in our Crucified Lord, we can survive this life, to have eternal life in God: eternal life which must include eternal healing. As He did with the tradition of the manna in the wilderness, and water from the rock, Jesus took a tradition that had historical limitations (even the people who were bitten by the serpents, and recovered, died eventually), [449] and gave it eternal meaning in Him.

In the New Testament there are many accounts of Jesus' healing people. The following are some examples:

> Blind Bartimaeus who was held back by the crowd; [450] the raising of Lazarus from the dead; [451] Jairus' daughter; [452] the son of the widow of Nain; [453] the healing of the man who was deaf and had an impediment in his speech; [454] the woman who was healed of the issue of blood; [455] the man with the withered hand who was healed on the sabbath day; [456] the man with dropsy who was also healed on the sabbath day; [457] the sick

---

448   John 3:14-16
449   John 6:49: "Your fathers ate the manna in the wilderness, and they died....I am the living bread..."
450   Mark 10:46-52
451   John 11:1-45
452   Mark 5:22-24, 35-43
453   Luke 7:11-17
454   Mark 7:31-37
455   Mark 5:25
456   Matthew 12:9-13
457   Luke 14:1-6

man at the pool of Bethzatha;[458] Peter's wife's mother;[459] the two blind men who followed Him, and then spread His fame through all the district;[460] the mad man by the sea in the country of the Gerasenes who said his name was Legion, but who was later found with Jesus "clothed and in his right mind";[461] the dumb demoniac whose healing led to the charge by the Pharisees that Jesus's power came from "[Beelzebul], the prince of demons";[462] and the leper who, having been healed, so publicized the fact that Jesus could no longer openly enter a town.[463]

St. Matthew's Gospel says, in the fourth chapter:

> He went about all Galilee, teaching in their synagogues and preaching the gospel of the kingdom and healing every disease and every infirmity among the people. So His fame spread throughout all Syria, and they brought Him all the sick, those afflicted with various diseases and pains, demoniacs, epileptics, and paralytics, and He healed them. And great crowds followed Him from Galilee and the Decapolis and Jerusalem and Judea and from beyond the Jordan[464]

and again, in the ninth chapter, a slightly different version, which gives it extra emphasis:

> And Jesus went about all the cities and villages, teaching in their synagogues and preaching the gospel of the kingdom, and healing every disease and every infirmity. When He saw the crowds, He had compassion for them, because they were harassed and helpless, like sheep without a shepherd. Then He said to His disciples,

---

458 John 5:2-9
459 Mark 1:29-31
460 Matthew 9:27-31
461 Matthew 5:1-20
462 Matthew 9:22-28
463 Mark 1:40-45
464 Matthew 4:23-25

'The harvest is plentiful, but the labourers are few; pray therefore the Lord of the harvest to send out labourers into the harvest'. [465]

Jesus made it clear that His followers were to continue this work. Not only did He command them to do so after the Resurrection, just before the Ascension, but He commanded them to do so, while He was still on earth, before the Crucifixion, when He sent out the twelve on one occasion,[466] and seventy on another.[467]

When Jesus sent out the twelve during His earthly ministry, St. Matthew records that He charged them:

'preach as you go, saying "The Kingdom of heaven is at hand". Heal the sick, raise the dead, cleanse lepers, cast out demons' [468]

St. Luke's acount is as follows:

He called the twelve together, and gave them power and authority over all demons and to cure diseases, and He sent them out to preach the Kingdom of God and to heal.....and they departed and went through the villages, preaching the gospel and healing everywhere... On their return the apostles told Him what they had done....When the crowds ....followed Him....He welcomed them and spoke to them of the Kingdom of God and cured those who had need of healing. [469]

After the Resurrection, just before the Ascension, He said to them: "Go...and make disciples of all nations, baptizing them, and teaching them to observe all that I have commanded you" [470] or, as the Gospel of St. Mark has it, He said:

465　Matthew 9:35-38

466　Luke 9:1-11

467　Luke 10:8-9　"Whenever you enter a town...heal the sick in it and say to them 'The kingdom of God has come near you' "

468　Matthew 10:5-8

469　Luke 9:1-11

470　Matthew 28:18-20, and Luke 24:47 "that repentance and forgiveness of sins should be preached in his name to all nations"

'go into all the world and preach the gospel to the whole creation....And these signs will accompany those who believe: in my name they will cast out demons; they will speak in new tongues; they will pick up serpents, and if they drink any deadly thing, it will not hurt them; they will lay their hands on the sick and they will recover' [471]

After the Resurrection, the disciples continued the healing ministry, from St. Peter and the lame man: "silver and gold have I none, but that which I have I give thee, *take up thy bed and walk,*" [472] to the raising from the dead of Dorcas, [473] and St. Paul doing the same with the young man who fell out of a window during a long night session, [474] and healing the crippled man at Lystra. [475]

It is written in the Book of Acts that:

> they even carried out the sick into the streets, and laid them on beds and pallets, that as Peter came by at least his shadow might fall on some of them. The people also gathered from the towns around Jerusalem, bringing the sick and those afflicted with unclean spirits, and they were all healed. [476]

There are prayers for healing in the psalms and prophetic writings which would have been known and used by the early Church: Psalm 6: *"O Lord, heal me";* [477] Psalm 42: "O Lord, be gracious to me; *heal me,* for I have sinned against you;" [478] (implying that healing and forgiveness go together); and Jeremiah 17: *"Heal me, O Lord, and I shall be healed; save me, and I shall be saved."* [479] And it is also written

---

471   Mark 16: 15-18

472   Acts 3:1-7

473   Acts 9:36-42

474   Acts 20:7-12

475   Acts 14:8-11

476   Acts 5:14-16; see also Acts 8:7 "...many who were paralysed or lame were healed. So there was much joy in that city".

477   Psalm 6:2

478   Psalm 42:4

479   Jeremiah 17:14

in the Book of Jeremiah: *"I will restore health to you, and your wounds I will heal,* says the Lord." [480]

The first chapter of the Book of Genesis says that, when God looked at His creation, He saw that it was good. [481] His intention for us was that His creation in us should continue to be good, and that all that goes wrong in our human living, physical and spiritual, is not His will for us. It is in understanding this that we approach Him to ask for healing for all that may have gone wrong in our lives, and for restoration to wholeness in Him.

As we pray for healing, we must also remember that prayer for healing goes hand in hand with doing everything that can be done by medicine and surgery. We can hardly ask God to "heal us" if we are not using the tools that He has given us for that purpose. It is written in Ecclesiasticus (or Sirach), in the Apocrypha, that we should both pray to God for healing and *also* be subject to the doctors who are meant to be God's instruments of healing:

> Honour the physician with the honour due him, according to your need of him, for the Lord created him; for healing comes from the Most High....The Lord created medicines from the earth, and a sensible man will not despise them. Was not water made sweet with a tree in order that his power might be known? And he gave skill to men, that he might be glorified in his marvellous works. By them he heals and takes away pain; the pharmacist makes of them a compound. His works will never be finished; and from him health is upon the face of the earth.

> When you are sick, do not be negligent, but pray to the Lord, and he will heal you. Give up your faults and direct your hands aright, and cleanse your heart from all sin.

> And give the physician his place, for the Lord created him; let him not leave you, for there is need of him.

---

480   Jeremiah 30:17

481   Genesis 1:21,25, and 31: "God saw everything that he had made, and behold, it was very good."

There is a time when success lies in the hands of physicians, for they too will pray to the Lord that he should grant them success in diagnosis and in healing, for the sake of preserving life. [482]

As we seek for wholeness of mind, body and soul, as we seek to enter more deeply into relationship with the Lord our God, we need to remember to be whole-hearted in our approach to living, and never cut ourselves off from all the means of healing that He has put at our disposal. Some people have done that by saying, for example, that we don't need medicine if we have prayer. We must remember that the two go together: the physical means of healing also come from God, as does the wisdom of the doctor and the skill of the surgeon.

God has already put into the creation plants and herbs that are health-giving, and has given the human race abilities to use them.

We often think of "healing" in terms of physical healing, a "cure" for something vexing our bodies, but healing of mind and soul are also equally—if not more—important.

When a man on a stretcher was let down through the roof of the house where Jesus was, because his friends could not get through the crowds to bring him to Jesus, [483] Jesus' first reaction was to tell him that his sins were forgiven: and only *then* did He tell him to pick up his mattress and walk. Similarly, in the story of the healing of the ten lepers: they were all cured of their physical ailment, their leprosy: but it was the one who came back to give thanks and glory to God who Jesus declared was *"made whole"*, [484] in other words, really healed in his total being.

Both of these stories imply that there is more to "healing" than just a physical cure: in both, the person's *relationship with God* was what made that person truly whole. So our aim must always be for the healing *of the whole person* in the love of God, and, though it may be a temptation sometimes, we must never concentrate on what is wrong with us or other people to the exclusion of focusing on the love and mercy and healing power of God.

This could be summed up in Jesus' saying: "Seek ye first the

---

482   Sirach 38:1-14

483   Mark 2:1-12

484   Luke 17:12-19

kingdom of God, and his righteousness, and all these things shall be yours as well." [485] He had just been talking about the lilies in the field, and saying that we should not be anxious, but trust in God.

St. Mark records that:

> [people] began to bring sick people on their pallets to any place where they heard he was. And wherever he came, in villages, cities, or country, they laid the sick in the market places, and besought him that they might touch even the fringe of his garment; and as many as touched it were made well. [486]

In many cases, it is said that Jesus was moved by compassion, in other words, the divine love almost overwhelmed Him at the sight of His people's need, and it was out of that divine love that He acted.

But there was an occasion when He could do few miracles because of the people's unbelief, [487] which I interpret as meaning, *not* that they didn't *"try hard enough to believe"*, in the sense that we sometimes try to force ourselves to "have faith", but that they just did not recognize in Jesus the Divine Healer.

They did not accept Him for who He was, there was no relationship there with the Divine Love He had come to bring. Relationship with God is the whole basis of the healing ministry.

When the Syro-Phoenician woman came to ask Jesus to heal her child, His immediate reaction, perhaps testing Himself as well as her, was that He had been sent to "the lost sheep of the house of Israel", [488] not to everybody else in the world; and she had taken this humbly, without anger at an apparent rejection, and said "yes, Lord, but even the little dogs eat the crumbs at the master's table;" whereupon Jesus told her that her daughter was healed: and established the precedent that the healing of God was not only for the Jews but for the whole world. This was an encounter at a deep level.

---

485 Matthew 6:33

486 Mark 6:54-56

487 Matthew 13:58

488 Matthew 15:21-28: Jesus' words about "the lost sheep" would seem to show that, even then, He was thinking of the divine mission of the Good Shepherd (John 10) to fulfill the prophecy in Ezekiel 34:1-16: *God* saying *"I myself* will search for my sheep...and rescue them.."* Note that this account is in *Matthew's* Gospel but it backs up John's

A problem can arise sometimes when we get our perspective distorted, and think either that we have to pray with many words, the more the better, or that, if healing is not immediately apparent, it must be the fault of the person needing healing.

When Jesus taught His disciples the Lord's Prayer, in other words, covering all the basics but without endless repetition, He said "Do not heap up empty phrases as the Gentiles do; for they think that they will be heard for their many words. Do not be like them, *for your Father knows what you need before you ask him.*" [489] In other words, we are not so much stating our need — which God knows anyway, better than we do — as putting ourselves, deliberately and trustingly, into direct contact with the Father's love and concern for us, in order to receive His healing power in our lives: and— this is important — being willing to continue to love and trust Him, even if, for reasons which we do not always understand at the time, the answer in the short term appears to be "no".

While we are commanded to continue Our Lord's healing ministry in our generation, to pray for others, and receive, with gratitude, blessings for ourselves, and to have faith in God, putting our lives at His disposal in every way, yet our faith must *not be dependent on whether or not our prayers are immediately answered in the way we think they should be.* If our faith is dependent on our getting what we want, when we want it, then something is wrong. In fact, our faith shines out all the more strongly when it survives being tested. St. Paul had his "thorn in the flesh", [490] which was not removed in spite of his prayer, and he was one of the greatest of all the apostles:

> Three times I besought the Lord about this, that it should leave me; but he said to me 'My grace is sufficient for you, for my power is made perfect in weakness.' [St. Paul goes on to say, paradoxically,] For the sake of Christ, then, I am content with weaknesses..... [and so on], for when I am weak, then I am strong.

Because we human beings are always tempted to ask "why", some people have fallen into the trap of *blaming the person who is apparently*

---

489 Matthew 6:7-13. See also Ecclesiasticus (Sirach) 14:7: *"Do not* prattle in the assembly of the elders, nor *repeat yourself in your prayer."*

490 2 Corinthians 12:7-10

not *"healed"*, for allegedly "not having enough faith". (Surely one could not apply that criterion to St. Paul!)

While we cannot expect always to know the answers to our questions immediately, we must resist this particular temptation, by remembering the time that Jesus came down from the mountain to find His disciples having problems because they could not heal the epileptic boy. They asked Jesus: "Why could we not cast it out?" and Jesus replied "Because of *your* little faith". [491] There is an extra verse in some of the older manuscripts, (a verse 21 which you may remember from the King James version of the Bible): "this kind goeth not out *but by prayer and fasting"* —and *Jesus was talking about the disciples, not the worried father or the child.*

When Jesus was asked, of the man who was born blind, whether it was the man's fault or that of his parents (that he was born blind), [492] Jesus said *"it was not that this man sinned, or his parents"* (but it was an opportunity for Jesus to demonstrate now, in healing the man, the works of God).

Sometimes healing can take time. The tenth leper had presumably gone some way before he decided to come back to thank Jesus, because the other nine had completely disappeared by the time he got back.

When Jesus healed a blind man on one occasion it took several stages: at first the man said that he could see men, but they were "like trees, walking." [493] We must not be impatient for immediate results: in fact, we must not be "impatient" at all.

We must trust that we are in the hands of God, that God is loving, God is good; and that, if we are in His hands, all will be well for us in the end, if not right away.

One of the problems that Jesus encountered was with people who idly wanted to see "signs and wonders" (as Herod did the night before the Crucifixion). [494] When the official from Capernaum asked Jesus to come and heal his son, Jesus replied "Unless you see signs and wonders,

---

491   Matthew 17:14-20, and 21

492   John 9:1-3

493   Mark 8:22-26

494   Luke 23:7 when Pilate learned that he belonged to Herod's jurisdiction, he sent him over to Herod ...[who] was very glad, for he had long desired to see [Jesus], because he had heard about him, and he was hoping to see some sign done by him."

you will not believe." [495]The man's need was genuine, and he reached Jesus on that wavelength when he replied, out of his heartbroken need, "Sir, come down before my child dies." Jesus recognized that genuineness, that faith, and replied at once: "Go, *your son will live.*"

Just as Jesus, moved by compassion, healed those in need around Him, we are called to carry on that work in His Name.

St. James's Epistle says [496]

> Is any among you sick? Let him call for the elders of the church, and let them pray over him, anointing him with oil in the name of the Lord; and the prayer of faith will save the sick man, and the Lord will raise him up; and if he has committed sins, he will be forgiven. Therefore, confess your sins to one another, and pray for one another, that you may be healed. The prayer of a righteous man has great power in its effects.

It is clear, however, that this is not to be taken as an individual matter. The elders, whoever they may be, have been chosen and designated to be elders in the local congregation: they are acting for the whole body of the faithful, which is the Body of Christ in the world; they are acting in the Name of the Lord, and under His authority. Jesus said

> 'when two are three are gathered together in my Name there am I in the midst of them.' [497]

While, of course we can pray to God, and pray for people, in the privacy of our own lives, the power given to the Church was given to the corporate body, or at least two or three people, gathered together, in His Name, to do His will. We cannot set ourselves up as individual healers, as *power* lies in *the presence of Jesus in the group.*

We are acting under authority, just as the Centurion said to Jesus, when asking for healing for his servant, [498] "I am a man set under authority, with soldiers under me..." In other words, in himself, he was only one man: but he had the power of the Roman Army vested

---

495   John 4:46-54
496   James 5:14-16
497   Matthew 18:20
498   Luke 7:2-10

in him, the might of Rome behind him; and similarly he recognized authority in Jesus, when he said that all Jesus had to do was to say the word and his servant would be healed.

Similarly, we too, individually, on our own, are just one person: but when we are thus "under authority," acting as an authorized, recognized part of God's worshipping community, the power of God is vested in us to do His work.

And we have the messages of hope in the Book of Revelation: that one day, when this life has ended, God will wipe away every tear from our eyes; [499] and that in the Holy City we shall see "the river of the water of life ... flowing from the throne of God ... ", and "on either side of the river, the tree of life with... leaves ... *for the healing of the nations."* [500] "The healing of the nations" would imply that, at the end of time, there would be healing, on a massive scale, of all the hatreds and resentment that cause quarrels among people, and wars among nations: and the healing and putting right of all the situations where, now, on this earth, there is cruelty and hatred and suffering and injustice.

The final coming of the Kingdom of God would see the end of all evil and wickedness: and, while I believe that "the nations" will be forgiven and healed, I also believe that there will have to be *a willing acceptance* of that forgiveness and healing before people individually and corporately can become altogether new and reformed, in "a new heaven and a new earth". [501] I believe that this will   happen when "the nations" finally come to see God face to face, [502] but it follows that the reverse side of this is that persistent wickedness that is determined to repulse God and His goodness will eventually cease to exist at the time when evil is finally destroyed for ever.

I believe there is more to the Atonement than just the forgiveness of sins. It is about coming to God, and abiding in His divine Love for

---

499   Revelation 7:17

500   Revelation 22:1-2 (an echo of Ezekiel 47:12 "...on both sides of the river, there will grow all kinds of trees ... Their leaves will not wither nor their fruit fail...because the water for them flows from the sanctuary. Their fruit will be for food, *and their leaves for healing."*)

501   Revelation 21:1

502   Isaiah 52:10: "All the nations of the earth shall see the salvation of our God."

ever; and we need to be healed of all that militates against that perfect consummation.

The phrase "Christ died for our sins" [503] has often been interpreted as if somehow the *only* reason He died was that *our sins* might be forgiven (in the sense of His bearing our *punishment);* but He also died that our sins might be *overcome,* and that, *in Him, we might be healed,* because we cannot take wickedness with us into the next life, and *we need spiritual healing as much as we need to be forgiven.*

We need to remember that God is love: [504] and what else would Love want but total restoration, healing and redemption, the very essence of a Love that cares. I believe our deepest prayer should be: *May that Great Love enfold us for ever....which is the ultimate healing.*

---

503   1 Corinthians 15:3 "...Christ *died for our sins* according to the Scriptures..."
504   1 John 4: 8, 16

CHAPTER 10

God as Love

The nature of God is love.

I believe that "love" *has to be* part of the very nature of the God who made us, because we know that love—real love—is the most inspiring of all human experiences, and the *absence* of love, shown in all kinds of cruelty and hate, the most devastating.

We see how children who are damaged in their early years by lack of love—unkindness or actual abuse, emotional, physical, mental, sexual—usually continue to suffer throughout their lives, and all too often turn to crime, and inflict violence on others. At the very least, many of them go on into adulthood hurting others by their inability to show love as a result of their own early suffering. Suffering in dysfunctional families is thus often passed on from generation to generation, and this *could not be* the will of a good God.

So the call "to love" is not merely a religious idea coming from Christians, and, in fact, other great world religions, as well: *we can see the need for it built into life itself.* We have only to look at the devastation in the world to see what happens when there is no love.

It is our tragedy that even Christians, while piously professing their faith, too often fail to love God or their neighbour, or even, too often, their own children. I am constantly amazed by the way in which people who call themselves Christians can treat other people badly, and *at the same time see no incongruity in this,* no need for repentance, even. One only has to look at any parish to see this, and it must have been the same in New Testament times, because the apostles over and over again strove to remind people that *to be a Christian* was absolutely tied in with *loving each other,* as opposed to indulging purely human impulses and desires.

People find it difficult to envisage what *Love* really is. Sometimes evangelists concentrate on people's need to be forgiven, to assuage feelings of guilt; or try to explain the Atonement by saying that Christ's suffering is a measure of His love for us, which does not really make one feel that one has had *an encounter with the Living God* (as if love could be quantitatively measured against suffering or vice-versa) . I believe that we have to make an effort to *look* for God, and ask Him, if He exists, *to show us* what He is like, to help us to know and love and serve Him.

This chapter tries to show how we can find God, if we look for Him, if we ask for His help, and worship Him, and *love Him for Himself* rather than for what "we can get out of Him"; and this whole book tries to answer those questions that have remained a stumbling block for some people, so that they may come to find God, and learn to love Him *because He is Who He is,* and, in expressing that, we come to worship Him, and are inspired to live with Him and do His will, because that is an extension of the Love we find in Him and come to experience in ourselves.

"Being in Christ" in those days was more than just the figure of speech that it has now become: it was to be a *"new creation",* [505] living *a new life*— life in God.

We have so lost this awareness of the divine call—or commandment—for us to love each other, that candidates for political office can publicly claim "Jesus as their Saviour", in a very pious way, *at the same time* as they are demolishing their rivals in ways that are both cruel and untrue. They seem to see nothing wrong in this (and maybe this is an unfortunate fact of political life today), but they do not seem to realize that, by publicly identifying themselves with Christ *at the same time,* they are in fact "taking the Name of the Lord in vain," [506] and not helping the cause of Christianity, or the Lord they profess to serve.

---

505 2 Corinthians 5:17 "Therefore, *if* any one is *in Christ,* he is *a new creation*"

506 Exodus 20:7. "You shall not take the name of the Lord your God in vain". I believe this does not mean only perjury or swearing, but also bringing the name of God into disrepute (if that were possible), by what we say and do.

As has been stated, after centuries of over-emphasis on sin and punishment, on an angry God who had to be appeased, we have come to think more in terms of God as *Love;* but that concept often does not seem to be clearly understood. It is often taken to mean just that *God will forgive us anyway* for whatever we may choose to do, *just because "He loves us":* but "love" is often not understood in terms of *our loving God and deriving love from Him* that can then flow from us into the outside world.

I think this also stems from Protestant misunderstandings of the Atonement, the so-called "doctrine of assurance"; [507] some have believed that one only has to *say* that one "accepts Jesus as one's Saviour", and then all will automatically be forgiven, so *there is no need for us to bother to "love" each other,* nothing more is then required of us, we are "forgiven" anyway. [508]

There is also the problem of the centuries-old over-emphasis on "sin-and-forgiveness-and-redemption" that had more or less come to supersede the other, equally important component of the Atonement, the original idea of "eternal life" being derived from "being in Christ" or *"being in God," for which love is essential, because God is love.* [509] "Redemption" involves repentance and change as well as "being forgiven." Redemption is more than just "being forgiven", because it

---

507   Claude Beaufort Moss, in *The Christian Faith: An Introduction to Dogmatic Theology* (London: S.P.C.K. 1954) refers to "the doctrine of assurance [which] is extremely dangerous, [which] lies at the root of the individualism and subjectivity which are the bane of all the heirs of the Reformation... *If all that were needed for salvation were justification by faith, guaranteed by the assurance of a man's own heart,* the Church... the sacraments would not be necessary... *the observance of the moral law would not be necessary"* (see Glossary)

508   There is also the view that "God is love, God loves me, and God will forgive me, God will forgive us all in the end, so why worry?" While it is true that God will forgive those who truly repent and change, St. Paul's warnings need to be heeded about "the wages of sin *being death"* (Romans 6:23), and his saying of "enemies of the Cross of Christ whose minds are set on earthly things" that *"their end is destruction"* (Philippians 3:18) in view of the fact that both the *Oxford Annotated Version* of the RSV (p.1426) and *Peake's Commentary on the Bible* (p.988) suggest that these were *"professing Christians",* so it would appear that St. Paul was warning that, even for so-called Christians, *life lived only in the flesh* made abiding in Christ impossible. (Therefore the Atonement is about *more than* just "believing" or "being forgiven".)

509   1 John 4:8,16

is not as if one could then continue just as one was: it is about *being healed* of all that is in us that is not love, and being united with God in His eternal Love.

As I will try to show in the Chapter on the Atonement, *"being in Christ"*, obeying the commandment to love, is a fundamental, and vital, part of coming to God. We may repent of our failures: but we need to be *aware* in the first place of the fact that *"union with God through Christ"* is what our faith is all about, and the fact that *that is not possible* if we systematically choose to live our lives *in defiance of His basic teaching*. While people may be forgiven for individual lapses which they then regret, I believe that the continual association of "Christianity," on the one hand, with sustained and public acts of viciousness that (even unintentionally) make a mockery of the faith, on the other, makes it imperative that the divine commandment *to love* be restated at this time, in the context of making people realize that it is a fundamental requirement for *being* "a Christian".

We should think what we are doing before dragging our Saviour's Name into our own questionable practices (if we are going to indulge in questionable practices) except in the context of repentance: otherwise we continue to contribute to the disrepute in which "Christians" have come to be held by many non-Christians. The fact that the way in which politicians treat each other today is not seen to be anything deserving of repentance, even as people publicly claim their allegiance to Christ, makes me believe all the more that the Gospel *of love* needs to be re-emphasized today.

The theme of divine love runs through the Bible: both God's love for His people (and our need to reciprocate that love, if we are to live in relationship with Him); and God's absolute requirement of us that we treat each other kindly. The prophets gave assurances of God's love for His people, as in, for example, the powerful lament in *Hosea*: "When Israel was a child I loved him." [510] *Jeremiah* wrote of God: "I have

---

510 Hosea 11:1-9: "when Israel was a child, *I loved him,* and out of Egypt I called my son....it was I who taught Ephraim to walk, *I took them up in my arms,* but they did not know that *I healed them.* I led them with cords of *compassion, with the bands of love.....*How can I give you up.....My heart recoils within me, *my compassion grows warm and tender.* I will not execute my fierce anger....for I am God and not man, the Holy One in your midst, and I will not come to destroy."

loved you with an everlasting love"; [511] and *Isaiah* wrote: "I will recount the steadfast love of the Lord...For...he became their Saviour. In all their affliction he was afflicted...in his love and in his pity he redeemed them; he lifted them up and carried them all the days of old." [512]

The term term "steadfast love" is often used to describe God's love for His people in the Old Testament, and the theme of love is repeated over and over again in the New Testament (only so often we do not appear to "take it in"), to the point where St. John stated categorically that "God is love". [513].

Because Love, by its very nature, needs someone to love, and be loved by, St. Augustine saw the whole of the Trinity as being, in itself, an eternal, unbroken, circle of Love (a theme powerfully picked up by Jurgen Moltmann, see the Chapter on the Atonement). [514]

While the eastern church has thought of the Trinity as more of a hierarchy (something alone the vertical lines of a "family tree"), the western church has traditionally seen the Trinity as a circle of equals in a circle of love, each Person of the Trinity being, in turn, equally the Lover and the Beloved and Love itself, although:

> *God the Father,* the God who first loved us, who referred to Jesus at His Baptism as His "beloved Son", [515] is more traditionally thought of as *the Lover, the one who does the loving, who generates Love;*
>
> *God the Son* can be seen as *"the Beloved,"* in loving whom both God the Father and we ourselves have a common bond: Jesus, the object of our devotions,

---

511   Jeremiah 31:3

512   Isaiah 63:7-9.

513   1 John 4:8, 1 John 4:16

514   J.W.C. Wand: *A History of the Early Church to AD 500.* London: Methuen & Co.,1937, p.228: "the Holy Spirit is believed to proceed from the Son as well as from the Father, and *the threefold relation is that of the lover, the beloved, and the love that flows between them. So close is their unity that the entire Trinity acts in the action of each Person,* just as *an individual acts as a complete person in every operation of memory, intelligence and will.*"

515   Matthew 3:17 "...a voice from heaven, saying 'This is my beloved Son, with whom I am well pleased."

through whom we come to approach more closely God the Father; and

God the Holy Spirit could well be defined as *Love Itself.*

This makes sense to me. Even if there *are* three Persons to this Trinity, because God is Love, and Love must need to love and be loved, *Love can still be one,* as we believe God the Trinity is One: and it is *into this great circle of Love that exists at the heart of the Trinity* that we human beings can be caught up on an eternal basis as we come to abide in God, as we "abide in Christ", as I will describe later. I make the point here to show why it is so important for us to learn to love—to love both God and each other — because otherwise *this union with the God of love* would not be possible. The corollary of this, of course, must be that all hatred and evil will be destroyed at the end of time, *because wickedness cannot enter, let alone abide in, the heart of God.*

"Love" is a word which is used in so many contexts, and can have so many meanings, (from liking ice-cream to worshipping the Godhead), that we may sometimes have to do some mental translation when the word is used. I would suggest that *"caring"* would be a good substitute for the word *"love"* in the context of "loving one's neighbour": *really caring* in one's heart about the well-being and happiness of that person, as well as outwardly showing compassionate care and concern in our dealings with them. This is slightly different from the idea of "justice" as an political ideal, an ideological cause which people espouse, worthy and necessary though that idea might be. Loving concern for others has to be *part of a larger concept of love of God and service to humanity in His Name because He has called us to show His love to others.* Our efforts for "justice" cannot be divorced from the larger picture of love for God and neighbour, shown to each individual whom we encounter. Who would not be moved, if someone really *cared* about us, and *showed it?*

However, the word "love" is not quite so appropriate when talking about our love for God, because that includes something of worship and adoration and gratitude as well. So, in thinking of "love", let us remember also the deeper connotations of that word.

Over and over again we need to remember *that God is love,* [516] and,

---

516 1 John 4:8, 1 John 4:16

in a life lived out in real love, one is closer to the divine than perhaps one would realize. (I am talking about real love, as opposed to romantic love, self-interest or "good works", or a portrayal of "love" that comes across to others as hypocritical because one knows—to one's cost—that real love is not to be found there.) This is how I would defend my thesis that "not only Christians" "will be saved".

I believe that good people, of all faiths, who have lived loving and caring lives, will recognize the divine love when they actually meet it in person after death, because they have actually been very close to it all their lives. Some, who may have been cruelly victimized on earth, to the point where they have never experienced love, may be welcomed into the arms of God's redeeming love when they come to die, and will accept in gratitude the richness that, in their poverty and spiritual despair, they had never known before, or believed to be possible.

On the other hand, I also believe that some of the professedly "religious", whatever their "religion" may have been, and however "devout" they may have been in the observance of it, may not be prepared for the fact that, if they have cruelly mistreated their fellow human beings during their time on earth, they may find, at the end of time, that they no longer have the capacity to recognize divine love when they meet it, and that that may be "spiritual death"—nothing to do with the profession of a creed, but everything to do with love, or the lack of it, in our human living. Jesus' parable of the sheep and the goats was about God commending, and choosing for His Kingdom, *those who had shown kindness and compassion (i.e. real love) to other people during their lifetimes.* [517] Even Christians, who are supposed to know this, do need to be reminded of this over and over again. Some think that the profession of a creed is enough; that if one says one is a Christian, one "has been saved" no matter what; and it does not matter how unloving, dishonest or unscrupulous one may be in one's dealings with others, one still has "a seat reserved in heaven", as it were. It is true that real repentence will be met by God's forgiveness; but, in order to repent in the first place, we have to be aware of the vital

---

517 Matthew 25:31-46: the criterion, or qualification, being " 'I was hungry and you gave me food, I was thirsty and you gave me drink, I was a stranger and you welcomed me, I was naked and you clothed me, I was sick and you visited me, I was in prison and you came to me.' "

importance of the command to love, the reality of our disobedience to that command in what we have done, and the spiritual danger which it poses for our souls if we do not consciously try to change our ways and live in the love which God expects of us.

Jesus summed up the whole of "the law and the prophets" as being contained in the commandment to love God and one's neighbour:

> You shall love the Lord your God with all your heart, and with all your soul, and with all your mind. This is the great and first commandment. And a second is like it. You shall love your neighbour as yourself. On these two commandments depend all the law and the prophets. [518]

St. Mark's account adds "There is no other commandment greater than these".[519] Jesus' hearers would have recognized that He was quoting passages in Deuteronomy and Leviticus, their own Scriptures,[520] and been reminded that this really was the core of all the prophetic writings.

(Over and over again the prophets called God's people back to the reality that what God required of them was love, as, for example, *Hosea:* "I desire steadfast love and not sacrifice, the knowledge of God, rather than burnt offerings;"[521] *Micah:* "what does the Lord require of you but to do justice, and to love kindness, and to walk humbly with your God?"[522] and other passages, notably in Isaiah and Amos,[523] about righteous dealing with one's neighbour.) We can visualize, if have to, being kind to one's neighbour, as in the parable of the Good Samaritan,[524] but it can be hard to think of God as being *"Love"* [525] in the abstract, or how we ourselves can "love" Him; and even harder to love other people unless God gives us the strength to do it.

---

518   Matthew 22:36-40

519   Mark 12:29-31 (St. Mark's account also adds to "with all your heart..soul...mind"— "and with all your strength")

520   Deuteronomy 6:4, Deuteronomy 10:12, Leviticus 19:18

521   Hosea 6:6

522   Micah 6:8

523   Isaiah 1:11-17; Amos 5:21-24

524   Luke 10:25-37

525   1 John 4:8,16

How do we set about "loving" God?

The Christian answer would be, of course, through coming to a living relationship with Jesus, through whom we come to God in a way unique to the Christian religion, through the indwelling power of the Holy Spirit—coming to know Jesus as one's Lord and Saviour, by prayer, searching the Scriptures and trying to learn more about the faith, sharing the sacrament of the Eucharist in a worshipping community, and opening one's heart to what God will teach us. The psalmist, hearing God's calling him to find Him, replied: "Thou hast said 'seek ye my face.' My heart says to thee, 'Thy face, Lord, do I seek. Hide not thy face from me.' " [526] In my experience, God will always respond to such a prayer. We learn about God to a great extent by thinking about Him, praying to Him, and searching the Scriptures, in the context of the Christian community which is the Church. A parishioner once asked me why we need to keep praising and thanking God, as we don't expect our children to keep telling us how wonderful we are. While I believe that a key aspect of our faith is the love and praise and prayer envisaged by Jurgen Moltmann as being part of the great circle of love which brings us into the life of the Trinity, (of which I will write more in the Chapter on the Atonement), there is also another part of the answer which I would give to that parishioner.

Not only is praise and thanksgiving due to God, as the creation giving honour to its creator, and not only does it join us with "the Angels, Archangels and all the company of heaven", [527] (as Ezra put it, "the host of heaven worships thee", [528] and would we not want to be part of that?) but it also helps us to focus on *what God is like, who He is, and what He has done.*

Focusing our thoughts on Him with gratitude for what He has done in our own lives helps us to come to know Him better. This concentrates our thoughts on the Something or Someone who is real to us in this way, and "God" ceases to be "a completely unknown quantity" but is "Someone Who..." This was the way in which some of the greatest prayers in the Bible begin. In the days when there was still belief in pagan gods, it was helpful to describe The God in

526   Psalm 27:8

527   *The (Anglican) Book of Common Prayer, 1962, Canada,* p. 79.

528   Nehemiah 9:6

whom the Hebrews believed as "the God *Who...*" From the earliest days the Prayer of Consecration in the Eucharist has taken this form, which we have inherited ("Blessing and glory and thanksgiving be unto thee, Almighty God, our heavenly Father, who [gave thine only Son] who....""). *We are describing the God whom we are addressing, who we are thinking about,* and, in so doing, we come closer to Him in our understanding, we can more easily picture Him in our minds, He is closer to us in our souls.

And reading the Bible with a consciousness of this tendency to speak of "the God *who...*" we can come to find it easier to "fill in the gaps in the picture", as it were, so that "God" ceases to be just an abstract idea, but *"Someone Who.."* An early example of this was a recitation of history, that could be compared in importance with our Creeds, as being part of the identification of the Jewish people's faith in their God:

> You shall make response before the Lord your God, 'A wandering Aramean was my father; and he went down into Egypt...And the Egyptians treated us harshly.... Then we cried to the Lord the God of our fathers, and the Lord heard our voice and saw our affliction.... and the Lord brought us out of Egypt with a mighty hand....and he brought us into this place...And now I bring the first of the fruit of the ground, which thou, O Lord, hast given me.' And you shall... worship before the Lord your God; and you shall rejoice in all the good which the Lord your God has given to you and to your house... [529]

The following are some examples of passages in the Bible that speak of God in terms of *"God Who...":*

> [The God] who inhabitest eternity, whose name is Holy [530]

> Bless the Lord, O my soul, and forget not all his benefits, who forgives all your iniquity, who heals all

---

529 Deuteronomy 26:5-10

530 Isaiah 57:15

your diseases, who redeems your life from the Pit, who crowns you with steadfast love and mercy, who satisfies you with good as long as you live... [531]

O Lord my God, thou art very great! Thou art clothed in honour and majesty, who coverest thyself with light as with a garment, who hast stretched out the heavens like a tent [532]

[Solomon] said 'Blessed be the Lord, the God of Israel, who with his hand has fulfilled what he promised... O Lord, God of Israel, there is no God like thee, in heaven above or on earth beneath, keeping covenant and showing steadfast love to thy servants who walk before thee with all their heart; who hast kept with thy servant David...what thou didst speak....' [533]

And Ezra said 'Thou art the Lord, thou alone; thou hast made heaven, the heaven of heavens, with all their host, the earth and all that is on it, the seas and all that is in them... and the host of heaven worships thee. Thou art the Lord, the God who didst choose Abram, and...

[there follows a recitation of the history of the relationship between God and His people]

Now therefore, our God, the great and mighty and terrible God, who keepest covenant and steadfast love...' [534]

Sometimes, when we feel we need inspiration, it can be helpful to read passages like these. And we do not only need to find Him with our minds. Traces of His handiwork are easily visible to our eyes. Sometimes, especially in the springtime, when, for example, I unexpectedly come across small and beautiful flowers almost hidden underfoot, or my gaze is caught by small birds or insects, and I stop

---

531 Psalm 103:2-5

532 Psalm 104:1-2

533 Solomon's prayer, 1 Kings 8, vv 15 and 23-24

534 Ezra's prayer, Nehemiah 9:6-32.

to marvel at their minute and complete perfection, it almost seems as if God, the Creator of all this beauty, has scattered little tokens of love and beauty for us to find, to remind us of Him, to give us clues as to what He must be like. My heart is stirred on such occasions, and spontaneously, without formality, without words, I am lifted up in sending love back, in appreciation of Who He is and What He has done: and is that not "praise"? Is that not loving the Lord our God? How could we learn to love Him, if we did not think about Him, and all that He has done in our lives, all He has given us; and not only the beauty, but also the power and challenge, of the universe. And then, with our minds filled with a tremendous awe and wonder, somehow, we find we *can* "love God".

The psalmist speaks of meditating on God's law day and night, which is something that does not always resonate with us today![535] "Law" sounds like "precepts" and "statutes", words which are also used,[536] and we are not in the habit of thinking about laws for twenty-four hours a day, and would not feel particularly inspired if we did. The psalms ring a bit hollow when we say them. But *'the Law"* in the Biblical sense meant not only, in the narrow sense, "Law" as in "commandments"; the expression could also be used to describe more generally the sacred writings about *God*. When Jesus spoke about *"the law and the prophets"* [537] He meant the main part of the Hebrew Scriptures, the law and the prophetic writings. Psalm 119, having talked of "precepts" and "statutes" then goes on to say *"Thy testimonies are my delight, they are my counselors."* [538] God is speaking to the psalmist, and the psalmist is hearing Him (His "counsel") through the words of the Scriptures in which the psalmist has steeped himself.

Psalm 1, speaking of *meditating on God's law day and night,* says

---

535   Psalm 1:2: "Blessed is the man...[whose] delight is in the law of the Lord, and on his law he meditates day and night." This theme of "day and night" is also found in Psalm 63:6: "when I think of thee upon my bed, and meditate on thee in the watches of the night," and Isaiah 26:9: "My soul yearns for thee in the night, my spirit within me earnestly seeks thee."

536   e.g. Psalm 119:15-16

537   e.g., Matthew 7:12: "So whatever you wish that men would do to you, do so to them; *for this is the law and the prophets";* Matthew 22:40: "On these two commandments depend *all the law and the prophets."*

538   Psalm 119:24

"blessed is" the person who does so, and goes on to say that he (or she) "is like a tree planted by streams of water, that yields its fruit in its season," [539] carrying the metaphor of drawing nourishment from streams of water: just as physically, in the case of the tree, water keeps it alive and enables it to bloom, so, spiritually, in the case of our souls, we are nourished by "the water of life" that comes from God. I am sure that Jesus, knowing the Psalms, would have had this in mind when He used the metaphor of the vine and the branches to describe our union with God through Him, through the Holy Spirit similarly nourishing us with the life of God. (And all the time we come back to the concept of the Trinity: we need not argue about whether it is "God the Father" or "the Son" or "the Spirit" that gives us that life: let us just say that *it comes from God.)* The psalmist is thinking about God and the things of God all the time; [540] in other words, he is steeped in prayer and meditation and Holy Writ.

If we can saturate ourselves more and more in the Bible, it comes to be with us all the time. The Holy Spirit of God nourishes our souls through our assimilation of Scripture as well as in the Holy Eucharist and our daily living. Christians believe that "word and sacrament" work together to nourish our souls as we grow in God. In Psalm 77 the writer was feeling some sense of estrangement from God: "has his steadfast love for ever ceased? Are his promises at an end for all time? Has God forgotten to be gracious?" And his remedy for feeling that way was to say *(as we can too, in similar circumstances):*

> *I will call to mind the deeds of the Lord;* yea, I will remember thy wonders of old. *I will meditate on all thy work, and muse on thy mighty deeds.* Thy way, O God, is holy... Thou art the God who works wonders... [541]

which leads us to thankfulness and praise, which I spoke of earlier. Similarly, Psalm 143:

---

539   Psalm 1:1-2

540   e.g., Isaiah 26:3-9: "Thou dost keep him in perfect peace, *whose mind is stayed on thee...* Trust in the Lord for ever, for the Lord God is an everlasting rock... *O Lord, we wait for thee;* thy memorial name is the desire of our soul. *My soul yearns for thee in the night, my spirit within me earnestly seeks thee."*

541   *Psalm 77*:11-14

> I remember the days of old, *I meditate on all that thou
> hast done;* I muse on what thy hands have wrought. I
> stretch out my hands to thee; *my soul thirsts for thee like
> a parched land.* [542]

We need *to think about God*, remember Him and all that He has
done and reach out to Him, stretch out our hands to Him. When you
are in love with someone they are not far from your thoughts all the
time; if you are not actually *thinking* about them, you are aware of
them as being there, part of your life, like the air you breathe: and this
is how it should be with us and God.

But I think we need to think about what it means to say that God
is love and "God loves us", and consider *what that love is like,* before
we can reciprocate that love. Some Christians assume that the fact that
"God loves them" somehow relieves them of the obligation to live up
to the standards of holiness and selflessness and love-of-others that
God requires of us, because any forgiveness that might be needed
would automatically be forthcoming "because they are Christians."
"Christ died for our sins" [543] doesn't mean we can feel free to sin with
impunity.

Others feel that anyone who has not professed the Christian faith
in this lifetime is automatically denied any chance to come to God after
this life is over, because they have not met the "technical requirements"
that such Christians believe in. They would discard without a care
people that any decent person would care about, and still claim that
"God is love". I have discussed earlier the theory of "universalism"
(that *everyone* "makes it eventually") which is at the other end of the
spectrum, and equally ridiculous. Of course the wicked and the selfish
and the hateful could never "abide in" God, any more than oil can mix
with water. But I believe that a loving God would want to reach out
in love to a strayed child when that child is not intrinsically bad or
selfish, but just "lost" in the sense of not knowing God, or not having
a right understanding of Christianity (perhaps having been brought up
in another faith but still knowing how to love).

I have known the daughter of a man who committed suicide while

---

542   Psalm 143:5-6
543   1 Corinthians 15.3 — see the Chapter on the Atonement,

she was still in the womb, whose mother "left the Church", and whose whole life has been affected by it. I knew a man who was abused by a priest as a youth, and subsequently had only bitter words for the Church, and his own child and grandchild have been affected by this.

If I, as an ordinary person, could care for these people, who are in effect victims of the actions of others, surely God would want, even more than I do, to reach out to them and try to put matters right. I believe we have been given free-will in this lifetime, and that that free-will extends to the time when we meet God the Trinity: I believe that when people such as those I have described come to see God, and He offers healing of their deep wounds, there may well be a mutual reconciliation; and I, at least, cannot just rule this out and talk at the same time about "God being *Love*".

Loving our neighbour

The difficulty is that to *love Love Itself* one has to be willing to love *in all aspects of life,* and that includes our dealings with other people. Jesus equated *loving God with loving other people,* and ministry to them; for example, when He washed His disciples' feet, He said:

> 'If I, then, your Lord and Teacher, have washed your
> feet, you also ought to wash one another's feet. For I
> have given you an example, that you also should do as
> I have done to you......a servant is not greater than his
> master...' [544]

and

> 'He who has my commandments [to love God and one's
> neighbour] and keeps them, he it is that loves me; and
> he who loves me will be loved by my Father, and I
> will love him and manifest myself to him' [545]

He goes on to say that someone who loves Him will keep His word:

> '*If* [some one] loves me, [that person] will keep my
> word, [the commandment to love], and my Father
> will love him, and we will come to him, and make our

544   John 13:14-16
545   John 14:21

home with him.   He who does not love me does not
keep my words..' [546]

In the verse just quoted, the phrase *"he will keep my word"* refers
to the commandment *to love;* and, when that situation is met, *(note
the "if"),* "the Father and I", (in other words, *God the Trinity),* "will
come to" that person; *and make their home* [i.e. dwell, "abide", live]
with him (or her). I could use that verse alone for the thesis that *what
our faith is all about* is *union with God through Christ;* and that *that*
is tied in with the necessity for love in our present living—love of God
and neighbour—without which everything else is irrelevant.

To paraphrase St. Paul: "if I excel in all virtues and have not love,
I gain nothing, I have nothing; in effect, I am nothing". [547]

As St. John said: *"if we love one another, God abides in us and his
love is perfected in us";* [548] and "whoever keeps his word, in him
truly love for God is perfected.   By this we may be sure that we are
in him; he who *says* he abides in him ought to walk *in the same way
in which he walked".* [549]

He is quite adamant about it.   Even in the early Church it must
have been necessary to say such things: *"he who....hates his brother is in
the darkness still,"* and *"he who does not love abides in death".* [550]

> We love, because he first loved us. If any one says 'I love
> God' and hates his brother, he is a liar; for he who does
> not love his brother, whom he has seen, cannot love
> God whom he has not seen. And this commandment
> we have from him, that he who loves God should
> love his brother also. [551]

I used to find this puzzling, because I thought it was much easier

---

546   John 14:23; and see 1 John 3:9-10, *"God's nature* [which is light and love] *abides in
him"* — in the context of *light* as *love,* and *darknesss* as *hate* ("God *is light* and in
Him is no darkness at all," 1 John 1:5, and "He who....hates his brother is in the
darkness still. He who *loves* his brother *abides in the light"* 1 John 2:9-10)

547   1 Corinthians 13:1-3

548   1 John 4:12

549   1 John 2:5-6

550   1 John 2:9, and 1 John 3:14

551   1 John 4:19-21

to dream about a God of perfection than to put up with some tiresome human being who was making my life miserable!

It wasn't until much later that I realized that loving God is not dreaming about perfection, but living in a relationship with Him, which involves doing things for Him to show my love, and that includes putting up with tiresome people for His sake.

The "love" we are talking about does not necessarily mean liking someone or agreeing with them, or approving of what they do. We do not even have to put ourselves in their path if we do not have to, if doing so would be a potential opportunity for sin on our part, in stirring up our resentments unnecessarily—or maybe even upsetting them.

But the whole point of Jesus' story about the Good Samaritan is that, if a fellow human being is in any kind of need, that person becomes "our job", as it were, for the moment, regardless of who they may be, or how we may feel about them.

St. Paul defined love as follows:

> Love is patient and kind; love is not jealous or boastful; it is not arrogant or rude. Love does not insist on its own way; it is not irritable or resentful; it does not rejoice at wrong, but rejoices in the right. Love bears all things, believes all things, hopes all things, endures all things... faith, hope, love abide, these three; but the greatest of these is love [552]

"Loving God" is not just an intellectual exercise of the mind or an emotion of the heart. It often needs our willpower, too, because the part of *loving God* that validates it is our intention to *obey His commandment* to pass on His love to others. We consciously offer our love to Him *through other people.* Jesus said that "whoever receives one....child in my name receives me; and whoever receives me, receives not me but him who sent me." [553] In ministering to other people we find ourselves ministering to Him. And, although this saying conveys to us the mutuality of ministering *to God* in the people we minister to, it is also Trinitarian in its implications ("receives me...*[and] him who*

552   1 Corinthians 13:8-13
553   Mark 9:37

sent me"). This was the Gospel of Mark, based on early oral tradition, and so its Trinitarian implications cannot be blamed on St. John!

We need to remember that God has made it *a condition of our relationship with Him that we "love" other people,* something that we tend not to take seriously enough.

Over and over again, Jesus emphasized that our sins being forgiven was tied in with *our forgiving other people* [554] for the sins they may have committed against us, as, for example, in *The Lord's Prayer,* [555] and His telling St. Peter to forgive "not seven times but seventy-times seven", in the context of the parable of the unforgiving servant. [556] Over and over again, Jesus taught that we should love our neighbour, as in the parable of the Good Samaritan; [557] and His statement that "all the law and the prophets" are summed up in the two commandments to love [558] was echoed by St. Paul, when he wrote:

> he who loves his neighbour has fulfilled the law. [All] the commandments...are summed up in this sentence, 'You shall love your neighbour as yourself'. Love does no wrong to a neighbour; therefore love is the fulfilling of the law. [559]

Jesus commanded us to: "love your enemies, do good to those who hate you, bless those who curse you, pray for those who abuse you" [560] and to

> "love your enemies, and do good, and lend, expecting nothing in return; and your reward will be great, and you will be sons of the Most High; for he is kind to the ungrateful and the selfish. Be merciful,

---

554 I have found it helpful, when trying to forgive people myself, to think of the line from Psalm 119 (v.144) and paraphrase it, to pray *"God give them understanding, that they may live".* It helps to realize that so often people do *not* always really understand what they are doing: as Jesus said on the Cross, "Father, forgive them; for they *know not what they do."* (Luke 23:24).

555 Matthew 6:9-13

556 Matthew 18:31-35

557 Luke 10:29-37

558 Matthew 22:35-40

559 Romans 13:8-10

560 Luke 6:27-28

even as your Father is merciful. Judge not, and you will not be judged; condemn not and you will not be condemned; forgive, and you will be forgiven; give, and it will be given to you." [561]

From the above, it will be seen that "love" is not a sentimental feeling but an act of the will, to do good in God's Name to the people around us, whether we like them or not, and whether they have injured us or not. So often, it is words again that are our undoing. We cannot always "love", in the normally accepted sense of the word, and therefore we ignore the obedience, the act of the will, that God asks of us under that heading of "love".

Sometimes, it does help to think of the meaning of a word by considering its opposite. The opposite of "love" is to hate, to be resentful, begrudging, spiteful, vengeful; or even, perhaps, indifferent, uncaring.

If we are to call ourselves "Christians", we have to realize that *"loving God" is to put one's life at His disposal* (not that we are not already "in His hands", anyway, in the sense of the relationship of the created to the Creator, but *voluntarily,* of our own free will, *aligning our will with His);* and *"loving one's neighbour"* is to make a deliberate, conscious, and continuous effort, by the grace of God, *to deal with other people in the way that God would wish us to do.*

We can see that even the earliest, enthusiastic, "fired-up", "filled with the Spirit", Christians found this difficult to do. St. Paul urged the new converts: "Do not be children in your thinking; be babes in evil, but in thinking *be mature".*[562]

> I could not address you as spiritual men, but as *men of the flesh,* as *babes in Christ.* I fed you with milk, not solid food; for you were not ready for it; and even yet you are not ready, for *you are still of the flesh. For while there is jealousy and strife among you...*[563]

Even in New Testament times, the early Church encountered the problem of keeping in proper balance what I will be describing as "the

561 Luke 6:35-38
562 1 Corinthians 14:20
563 1 Corinthians 3:1-3

two arms" of the Atonement: on the one hand, the belief (correct in itself) that a mere profession of faith in Christ would suffice, that there was no need for us "to earn" our redemption by doing *anything* ("justification by faith alone"), and, on the other, the absolute need *also* to keep *the commandment to love* in our present living. St. Paul taught, rightly, that we are "saved" by faith in Christ's atoning death and resurrection; but, when this came to be seen as a form of licence to be selfish in one's dealings with others, in complete disregard of the commandment to love, other apostolic writers reminded the early Christians of this imperative, and one wrote that St. Paul's teaching had sometimes been misunderstood:

> Therefore, beloved...be zealous to be found by him without spot or blemish, and at peace. And count the forbearance of our Lord as salvation. So also our beloved brother Paul wrote to you according to the wisdom given him, speaking of this as he does in all his letters. *There are some things in them hard to understand, which the ignorant and unstable twist to their own destruction, as they do the other scriptures.* You therefore, beloved... beware *lest you be carried away with the error of lawless men and lose your own stability.* [564]

The author of the Epistle of James tackled the question of so-called "faith" that did not find its expression in daily living:

> *Be doers of the word* and not hearers only, deceiving yourselves.....*If anyone thinks he is religious, and does not bridle his tongue but deceives his heart, this man's religion is vain.* Religion that is pure and undefiled before God is this... [565]

and he goes on to define the pure, unselfish and loving behaviour that *does* constitute "true religion". It is more than a question of pious words,

---

564   2 Peter 3:14-17.   Re. the probable authorship of this Epistle, see the section on Romans 9:5 in the Chapter on the Divinity of Christ

565   James 1:22-27 (and, re. "bridling the tongue", showing again that, even in the early Church, it was necessary for the apostles to preach about such things, see also James 3:2-12)

empty ritual and parade, and it is immediately invalidated by cruelty and spite. He wrote:

> What does it profit, my brethren, if a man *says* he has faith but has not works? Can his faith save him?...So faith by itself, if it has no works, is dead... I by my works will show you my faith.... Do you want to be shown, you shallow man, that faith apart from works is dead? [566]

Much of the trouble facing the Church stems from the fact that people tend to find it difficult to hold opposing truths in balance.

The apparent contradiction in this debate can be understood if "works" in Paul's context is seen to mean mere obedience to rules and regulations, as opposed to "the fruit of the Spirit" (which is *love*); [567] and in the Epistle of James, "works" means the expression of *love in action*, without which "faith" is indeed barren, the point that the author was trying to make.

So while it is true that, as St. Paul preached, our salvation comes by the grace of God, and we can never be good enough to "earn" it on our own, God *has commanded us* to love (we have the two Great Commandments summed up by Jesus as loving both God and one's neighbour), and we need to be reminded of the imperative to obey these two great commandments if we are not to become estranged from God.

Jesus taught us that *"abiding in Him"* was *predicated on our abiding [living] in His love,* and it is often overlooked that St. Paul himself spoke of "faith *working through love".* [568]

In fact, all St. Paul's teaching about "being *in Christ"* (as in "that I may gain Christ and be found *in Him"),* [569] and the fact that those who are inherently immoral will never "get to heaven," [570] seems to be ignored in arguments about "justification *by faith alone."*

---

566 James 2:14-20.

567 Galatians 5:22

568 John 15:9-12: ".... *abide* in my love. *If* you keep my commandments, you *will* abide in my love .. *This* is my commandment, that *you love one another as I have loved you";* and Galatians 5:6.

569 Philippians 3:8-9 (see also other examples given in the chapter on "Abiding in Christ")

570 Galatians 5:19-21 re. "the works of the flesh", that "those who do such things shall not..."

What St. Paul meant by *"faith,"* as is obvious from his writings, was *the believer's relationship with Christ,* the union with God through Him, which is utterly incompatible with the worldly behaviour that constitutes "life in the flesh"; so, while St. Paul did indeed contrast "faith" with "works", "faith" in his thinking meant *more* than "just *believing"* (see the later footnote quoting *the Oxford Annotated Version* of the Bible regarding the change in thinking about what St. Paul meant by *"faith"* that had occurred even by the time of the writing of the Epistles to Timothy and Titus).

This tension arose again in acute form at the time of the Reformation, when Martin Luther reacted against the many requirements of the mediaeval Church to "earn" salvation by obeying rules and regulations; but then subsequent generations of Protestants have fallen into the same misunderstanding as that addressed by the Epistle of St. James, thinking that "justification *by faith alone"* means it is not necessary to "abide in Christ" or live a life sharing the divine love with others: thinking that God will forgive us anyway, just because "we *believe".* As the author of St. James' Epistle would say, such "faith" is dead,[571] and I think the modern Church needs to be reminded of this.

Sometimes we mistake "social action" for "love": it is a start, but not enough, for, as St. Paul would say, "while there is jealousy and strife among you, you are still in the flesh." [572] Social action is well and good, but we need *also* to learn what it is *to love.*

I think that part of the problem is that people tend not to think very deeply about the meaning of the words they use. Even in New Testament times Christians were debating what it meant to be a Christian, what it meant to love.

The very word "love" has been misunderstood, in the sense that it is assumed that if God loves us He will automatically forgive us for anything we may do, even if we never show love to others, even if we never repent and change our ways.

Perhaps the word "repent" is also misunderstood. We may say we repent, but, as St. James would say, that is not enough. If we do not also try to change our ways, and show our repentance and our faith

571   James 2:14-20
572   1 Corinthians 3:1-3

by "love in action," obeying the divine commandment to love, our so-called "repentance" [573] is not genuine, our "faith" is *dead*.

The word "forgive" can be misunderstood too: God may indeed, in His love for us, be always willing to forgive us, but there must also, at some stage, be a turning on our part from evil to good, from self-centeredness to God-centeredness, from "the ways of the world" to the ways of God, *if we are ever to attain the union with the God of Love* that goes beyond mere "forgiveness" and is our eternal life. (And it may take consciously trying to "abide in Christ" for us to be able to make that change, drawing on divine strength for help to meet such a challenge — which is what "abiding in Christ" is all about.)

Something else that I think has been misunderstood is the way in which Jesus tried to warn us, not only about the importance of our obeying the divine command to love, but also about the consequences of not co-operating with God and obeying His commandments.

For example, I believe the parable of "the wedding garment" [574] was about the grave results that will inevitably ensue if we deliberately and continually disobey God's commandments, but I think this parable is one that is often misunderstood, because (as is so often the case) we fasten on the exterior details rather than the inner meaning.

Jesus was saying that "many are called but few are chosen". He had also said "the gate is narrow and the way is hard, that leads to life, and those who find it are few." [575] We have to respond to God's call and *learn to love.*

Jesus' parables were not meant to be an end in themselves, as stories which we take literally, as if they really happened, and then often dismiss because we don't understand them and the settings seem alien to us. They were intended to be a teaching tool, a vehicle by which Jesus could convey to us eternal truths, including the fact that eternal consequences must inevitably follow if we continually, wilfully and systematically, insist on refusing to co-operate with God, and live lives completely opposed to the commandment to love. This has nothing to do with the fact that God loves us and is willing to forgive us, but

---

573 "the Lord ... not wishing that *any* should *perish,* but that *all should reach repentance*" - 2 Peter 3:9

574 Matthew 22:1-14

575 Matthew 22:14 and Matthew 7:14

everything to do with the fact that, if we are *not willing,* at some stage, to repent and change our ways, and learn to love others, we cannot be "let loose" in heaven to continue creating there the hell and havoc that characterize much of life on earth. *We have to respond to God, and co-operate with Him,* and show His love to others, and *this* is what the Epistle of James was trying to say.[576]

I believe it is also what Jesus was trying to teach in the parable of the wedding garment. The parable of "the wedding garment," when it is read in isolation in a Church service, often comes across to the bewildered congregation as if God was capricious and unreasonable, and the wedding guest unfairly victimized. This parable needs to be understood in the context of Jesus' emphasizing the vital need for us *to respond to God's generosity* by co-operating with Him and obeying His commandments, warning us in the strongest terms of our own eternal loss if we continually defy that call and fail to respond. The original setting of the parable was that of a wedding feast. What used to happen on such occasions was that guests were invited ahead of time, and, in effect, asked to "stand by" while the preparations were made; and, when the dinner was ready, a second call was made to say that everything was now ready. On this occasion, the guests who had already been invited suddenly decided at the last minute that they had better things to do, and could not come. The matters they were concerned with may *well* have been pressing, in the normal course of events, but the *point* of the story is that we are to put God first in everything, and not refuse to come when He calls us, not to tell Him we have more important things to do than to respond to *Him!* When the king heard that the original guests would not come, he told his servant to go out into the highways and byways, and bring in ordinary people who would be glad to have a good dinner, but who would not normally have been invited. The early Church saw in this that the Gospel call included the Gentiles: that the original guests had been the Jews, God's own original people, but that, when many of them rejected His call in Christ, the invitation was then extended to the Gentiles.

The second part of the story was that, even when people who would not normally have been privileged to attend the king's banquet were after all included, one of them proved to be completely un-co-

---

576   James 2:14-20

operative and would not wear the customary wedding garment. One has to assume that the *other* people who came to the wedding, in similar circumstances, managed to conform to what was expected of them in appearance and behaviour; the whole point of the story is about *the one who stood out from the others* by not conforming, not complying; and when his host asked him why, the man had no explanation, no reasonable excuse to offer, but just said nothing. The translated word "speechless" implies to us that he was too terrified to speak, but that is not necessarily the case. It is true that he did not say anything, but it could well be that he did not answer because he had no reasonable explanation to offer: there was no attempt at an explanation or apology. When we look beneath the surface details, we see that there was no relationship between the man and his host; the guest was not complying, in the first place, not communicating in the second. How could there be any real relationship in such circumstances? There are two parts to any relationship; both people have to reach out, the one to the other, and make an effort to make the relationship work, if it is going to succeed, as, for example, in friendship or marriage. So it is with us and God. God's grace calls us, but we have to respond to His call and do our part.

It is believed that the Gospel of St. Matthew, which was drawn from earlier sources, including an early oral tradition, was not written in its present form much before the year 80 AD, after the fall of Jerusalem to the Romans, in 70 AD, and that the part of the parable about sending forth armies and burning up the city was a later insertion, based on the belief at the time that the fall of Jerusalem to the Roman army signified God's anger with His people. Again, that is a detail that should not distract us from the point of the story: which is that, just because the Gentiles had now been called, it did not necessarily mean that their calling would be validated if they then refused to co-operate with God.

If we take seriously the commandment to love, which was a main part of Jesus' teaching and of the New Testament writings, we can see how easy it is for us to fail in this, and *the reality of what Jesus was talking about.* We have to respond to God's call to *life in Him* by being willing to obey the commandment to love: most of us fail in this, most of the time, and we really need God's grace, His help and His strength, to enable us to keep this commandment. People should not be overly confident that they had now been privileged to be included in the Kingdom: *it was still expected that they would conform to what God required of them.*

In that context, "the wedding garment" came to be seen as *righteousness.* *Peake's Commentary* states that "the wedding garment symbolizes *the ethical quality expected in the Church,*" and refers to the passage in the Book of Revelation about *the Church* being clothed in righteousness: "...'[Christ's] Bride, [the Church], has made herself ready; it was granted to her to be clothed with fine linen, bright and pure'—for the fine linen is *the righteous deeds of the saints.*" [577]

Which brings us back to the need to "abide in Christ" and *learn to love* and be like Him, if we are to discover the joy that goes *beyond* being forgiven: the joy of entering the new life that God has given us, *in Him:* and we cannot live that life, we cannot live in Him, we cannot be numbered among the saints, if we are not willing to try to learn to love, because *God is love,* and to abide *in Him* means giving up all that is in us that is not love.

"Abiding in Christ" is tied in with love, and is the second part of the Atonement: maturity in the faith is tied in with union with Christ and showing His love to one another in accordance with His wishes.

As I will try to show in the Chapter on the Atonement, this commandment, which applies to us *in our present daily living,* cannot be reconciled with a "faith" that *only* looks to an event in the past (the Crucifixion); and this convinces me that there *is* a second part to the Atonement which exists in the present time. It is not just a question of "being forgiven", through Christ's death on the Cross in the past but *obeying Christ's imperative commandment in our present living,* without which *we cannot know God* ("he who does not love *does not know God*" [578] — a strong statement which we need to remember), or truly be called "Christian".

I believe that the ultimate purpose of the Atonement was the union with God that is clearly spelled out in the New Testament, and for this

---

577 *Peakes Commentary on the Bible,* page 791; Revelation 19:8

578 1 John 4-7-8: "Beloved, let us love one another; for love is of God, and he who loves is born of God and knows God. *He who does not love does not know God;* for God is love." 1 John 3:14: "He *who does not love abides in death*"—presumably *spiritual death,* as opposed to abiding in *life,* the new life *in Christ,* in God's eternal love

we need to read our Bibles more, and think about what all this *really* means.

People today sometimes *talk* about being *"in Christ,"* as in signing a letter, *"Yours in Christ",* but often it is merely a pious-sounding cliche, empty words that make a mockery of the Christian faith. People have been known to write unkind or spiteful letters, and then sign them "yours *in Christ",* without seeing any incongruity in this, as if they had no idea that to *be "in Christ"* was to be in, and reflect, *the love of God* (Jesus' definition of love was "greater love has no man than this, that a man lay down his life for his friend"). [579] So often we do not think of the *meaning* of the expressions we use, and they become for us little more than fossilised shells.

The chapter in St. John's Gospel which tells of Jesus talking about our "abiding in Him" makes it very clear that "abiding in Him" is tied up with *our loving other people:* [580] that *"abiding in Christ"* is *to live in the divine love in the present time,* and let that love flow through us to others, in all our dealings with them. It is the fact that this part of our "at-one-ment" with God has to take place *in the present time* that has led to my belief that the Atonement is not *only* a past event: *the core of our faith is "abiding in Christ"* and "abiding in *the divine love"* ("God is love, and he who abides *in love* abides *in God, and God abides in him").* [581]

St. Paul wrote about being "rooted and grounded" *in love,* [582] the end result of mutual love when it is not being blocked by our sin or carelessness.

I am sure that, when he wrote that, St. Paul remembered Jesus' saying "I am the vine, you are the branches," [583]—which, in itself, had to do *both* with *abiding in Christ,* which Jesus equated with living *in love,* and bringing forth *the fruit of love* in our lives ("the fruit of the Spirit is love..."): [584]

579 John 15:13

580 St. John 15 (vv. 1-17, the metaphor of the vine and the branches: *"Abide in me, and I in you ... He who abides in me, and I in him, he it is that bears much fruit... abide in my love....")*

581 1 John 4:16

582 Ephesians 3:14-19

583 John 15:1-11

584 Galatians 5:22-23

'I am the true vine....*Abide in me, and I in you.* As the branch cannot bear fruit by itself, unless it abides in the vine, neither can you, *unless you abide in me. I am the vine, you are the branches. He who abides in me, and I in him, he it is that bears much fruit, for apart from me you can do nothing....As the Father has loved me, so have I loved you; abide in my love. If you keep my commandments, you will abide in my love,* just as I have kept my Father's commandments, and abide in his love.' [585]

We speak of course in metaphors, but it is divine love that flows through that vine, into us and through us—"rooted and grounded in love"—so that we bring forth the spiritual "fruit" that God intended us to produce, the divine nourishment of love and goodness and power making it possible for us to do what otherwise, in our human frailty, we could not do on our own: love our neighbour, pray for our enemies, and so on! And being in that relationship with God, as closely related as the leaves are to a plant, we learn to love God and be loved ourselves also. This metaphor also shows how inter-related the parts of the vine are to each other, which means "loving one's neighbour" as we should.

We are part of a greater whole, *caught up into that circle of divine love, which, once we have experienced it, we would never want to lose. It is part of our "being in God".* But I will say more of this in the chapter on the Atonement.

Jesus commanded *all* of His followers, which includes ourselves, *to love* in *the present time* (the two great commandments being to love God and our neighbour with every fibre of our being). [586] He specifically said, in the same context in which He was talking about "abiding in Him": *"This is my commandment, that you love one another, as I have loved you",* and again, *"This* I command you, *to love one another".* [587] It is in that context that St. Paul was talking about the fact that Christians, to be mature in the faith, must rise above "jealousy and strife", and that, until they do so, they will not be "ready" for the

---

585   John 15: v.1, 4-5, 9-10

586   Matthew 22:37-40

587   John 15:12 and John 15:l7

"solid food" that they should eventually be able to digest. It is from the mature "new creation," [588] when we come to be really part of it in all its fullness, that God derives increasing joy, and we share that joy with Him, and find our strength in it, and our faith is fulfilled. We feel His pleasure, we share His joy, when He approves of what we are doing, when we can share with Him His delight in the goodness of His Kingdom and the unfolding of His will. That is as near as we can come, I think, to reciprocity of love with God in this world.

A problem tied in with this that has bothered many people is "why God does not always answer prayer", if it is true that "He loves us". I have tried to show that God, for various reasons, does not always answer our prayers in the way that we think, at the time, that He should, but, for the Christian who trusts, the main thing is that *God is still with us.*

What our prayer should be is that we may always be with Him and in Him, that He will bless us "in the long run" and that "it will be all right in the end"—and that we may not lose faith meanwhile. We just have to trust Him, regardless of what happens, and not automatically feel abandoned if we do not get what we think we want, immediately we ask for it. As I said earlier, I believe that sometimes, for reasons which we cannot always understand, God *does* let history, or nature, take its course without divine interference, but that, even then, He suffers *with* us, even though we cannot see Him, or feel His presence at the time.

The problem has been, I think, as so often in the past, that people sometimes make over-extravagant claims, and other people, seeing this over-extravagance and unreasonableness, automatically reject such claims out of hand, with the result that, in the end, they "throw out the baby with the bath-water," and, in this case, deny that God answers prayers — or that there is a God at all.

While it was not right for people to shrug their shoulders in

---

588   2 Corinthians 5:17 "Therefore, if any one is *in Christ,* he is a new creation". Note the connection between being "a new creation" and being *"in Christ".* Colossians 3:9-11: "...you have put off the old nature with its practices and have put on the new nature, which is being renewed...after the image of its creator. Here there cannot be Greek and Jew, circumcised and uncircumcised...slave, free man, but *Christ is all, and in all."* Galatians 3:28: "There is neither Jew nor Greek, there is neither slave nor free, there is neither male nor female; for *you are all one in Christ Jesus."* Galatians 6:15 "For neither circumcision counts for anything, nor uncircumcision, but *a new creation."*

the old days, and say, in a tone of resignation, when something went wrong: "God's will be done", when they should have been praying and working for the situation to be put right, neither is it right for people to claim, in reaction to this, that they can ask God, and get, *"anything they want"* (misquoting John 16:23-24 and 1 John 3:22).

The result has been that a third group has come to say that the latter claim is both unreasonable, (as if people were treating God as *their servant,* to carry out *their wishes*—like putting money in a juke-box), and untrue (because the desired results of prayer are not always achieved): and such people deduce from this that therefore there is no God, or no possibility of partnership with Him in the affairs of this life.

Surely the problem becomes clearer when we think of it in terms of believing that God, who knows the larger picture, can be trusted to be with His people, and eventually bring good out of a situation: not thinking, as some people seem to, that the "answering" or "not answering" of our prayers *necessarily* reflects our "worthiness" in praying, or has anything to do with God's loving or not loving, or being unable to act if He so chose.

What Jesus was saying about *"ask, and you will receive"* [589] was tied in with *asking in God's Name,* which means asking for what *God wants.* I have already written about "bad things happening to us" not being God's will, not what God *wants,* in the basic sense; but that does not alter the fact that God, for whatever reason, may sometimes have other priorities unknown to us at the time, and may, like a sorrowful parent, be in the unenviable position of having to deny His children's requests for the time being. What we have to do is to align ourselves with God's overall thinking, and *be willing to accept,* in love and obedience, whatever may come to us, our basic prayer being that, whatever happens, *He may be with us,* and that, *in life and death, we may abide in Him.*

What we need—and which God will give us if we ask Him—is the faith that tries to relate to God *on His terms,* and seeks *above all else* to be with Him, to love and serve Him, and do His will, whatever that may be. Though this can be hard sometimes, we must accept that the ultimate good that is God's long-term goal for us may not *necessarily*

---

589   John 16:24, see also Matthew 7:7, Luke 11:9

always be what we, with our limited view-point, may *think* we want in the short-term, when we cannot see the total picture as God can.

But even in this we can find union with Christ, remembering Jesus' prayer, the night before He died, "Father....remove this cup from me; *yet not what I will, but what thou wilt."* [590] The overall goal of God the Trinity was *the redemption of the world* through the death and passion and resurrection of the Son of God; but, as a human being facing death, Jesus felt for a moment the natural human desire to be spared pain, and wondered if there could possibly be any other way. However, even in this, in His putting the outcome of His life in God's hands, *He has enabled us to make the same act of willing obedience, in Him.*

And He said to His disciples: "I will see you again and your hearts will rejoice, and no one will take your joy from you.....Hitherto you have asked nothing in my name; ask and you will receive, that your joy may be full." [591]

What the above passage is saying, I think, is two-fold: first, *that our joy comes from "seeing Christ,"* and thus being with Him *("abiding in Christ"),* and that *that* joy is such that no one can take it from us, no evil can break or destroy it; and secondly, that *"our joy being full"* is tied in with *asking "in His Name"*— which does not necessarily mean always getting what we think we want when we ask for it.

"Asking *in His Name"* implies asking for what is in accordance with *His will* (otherwise a request would not qualify as being made "in His Name", a phrase which implies divine authority and approval for what is being asked for). *Receiving it* must mean seeing those prayers *made in His Name* answered. The implication of what is being said, as I understand it, is that one would have, as it were, *a double dose of joy* ("that your joy may be full") *in sharing in God's joy* in seeing *His will being done;* the joy of being reassured that we are working in partnership with Him—a much higher level of existence than just getting our own temporal concerns addressed as and when we want them—the joy of working *in partnership with Him in bringing His love to this broken world.* This is borne out by St. John's First Epistle: "...and we receive

---

590   Mark 14:26: "Abba, Father, all things are possible with thee; remove this cup from me; yet not what I will, but what thou wilt."

591   John 16:22-24

from him *whatever we ask, because* we *keep his commandments* and do *what pleases him.* And this is his commandment, that *we should believe.....*and *love one another,* just as he has commanded us." All who keep his commandments *abide in him, and he in them.* [592]

In summarizing "all the law and the prophets" in two commandments, to love God, and one's neighbour as oneself, Jesus was saying that *nothing* about God, the nature of God, or His dealings with His people revealed in the Bible, was more important than the fact that we are to live *in love with God and with each other.*

But sometimes, it has to be admitted, when our problems seem so close and overwhelming, and God seems to us to be far distant, "loving God" (and our neighbour!) can seem to be very difficult, and it is at times like this that we need to draw on our "back-up" of intelligence and predetermined faith and scriptural resources—for example, to remind ourselves, that *Christ Himself* has felt God-forsaken, and yet the very next verse of the psalm He quoted on the Cross says at once: *"Yet thou art holy, enthroned on the praises of Israel".* We are reminded that God still exists, and God is good: *and we share this experience with Christ Himself.* [593]

I believe that the Bible can be a great source of comfort and strength when we are seeking to draw closer to God. Sometimes just reading some of those great passages that assure us of the love of God—for example: Jeremiah: "I have loved you with an everlasting love," [594] and Isaiah: "Fear not, for I have redeemed you; I have called you by name, you are mine", [595] —can help us to feel that love, and to reciprocate. And for special reassurance as to God's love for us, my own private recipe for this relationship of love, or the best description of it that I can come up with, is taken from a verse of Psalm 63: "My soul clings to you; your right hand holds me fast." [596] There is a wonderful reciprocal relationship there. We cling to Him, but He holds us fast.

We do not earn the love of God; it is unmerited, undeserved, often

592   1 John 3:22-24

593   Psalm 22:1-3, Matthew 27:46

594   Jeremiah 31:3

595   Isaiah 43:1

596   Psalm 63:8 (translation from *The Book of Alternative Services of the Anglican Church of Canada)*

unsought; but it is there, and it can be the greatest glory of life if we are prepared to try to learn how to move more closely into it, and to devote ourselves to reciprocating it, with all our heart and soul and mind and strength [597] all our lives. We need always to be aware of the presence of God, *His* wishes, *His* will, *His* love. We need to remember always that, without love, what we do is worth nothing. [598] It always seems to come back to *"abiding in Christ"* —who is Love.

It can be difficult to "love" at times, and especially when we have been the wronged party. It can take time for wounds to heal, and for us to be able to leave the past behind us and truly forgive; but if we put our will into gear, and ask Jesus to help us, if necessary *to do it for us,* we have at least taken the first step. It is only inasmuch as *we are in Christ, and He in us,* that it is *possible* for us to look at things as He would do; to have the pity and compassion, and understanding, and patience, and forgiveness, that He would have in the situation in which we find ourselves, and to let Him shower His love on us. Really to live in love we have to let ourselves *feel* God's love, to bathe in it, as it were, to let ourselves be saturated in it, so that an aura of God's love can shine from us, because we are at peace with ourselves, in Him.

What we must not do is ever to indulge in actively *hating* anyone, because active hatred is the opposite of love; and, if we are tempted by our resentments to start to hate, we need to turn back to God, and ask Him to renew in us that vision of His love that will help us through whatever the crisis may be—but always we should try to have that vision before us. The development of the love of God within us is the goal for which we strive.

A good example of the need to look beyond actual *words* to the real meaning of a Biblical passage is the occasion where Jesus talked about not letting anything stand in the way of following Him if we are to be His disciples, and said: "If anyone comes to me and does not hate his own father and mother and wife and children and brothers and sisters, yes, and even his own life, he cannot be my disciple. Whoever does not bear his own cross and come after me, cannot be my disciple." [599] It

---

597   Mark 12:30.

598   1 Corinthians 13:2

599   Luke 14:26-27

is clear from the context that what Jesus was talking about was *putting God first in everything.*

The nearest approximation I can see in His own life was the grief that was caused to His mother as she stood at the foot of the Cross: it must have caused Him the greatest anguish to see her suffer, but He could not turn back. He was not talking about "hating", which would have been completely contrary to His nature, all that He stood for, but about *"counting the cost"* involved in discipleship, *putting God first* in *everything.*

It is so easy to misunderstand the Bible, if one takes a word, and a translated word at that, at its surface face-value, rather than looking at the context and the meaning of what was being said. Jesus never meant that we were "to hate" in the sense in which that word is normally understood.

Another example of how something can misleadingly appear to be contradictory, if taken at face value, is the following passage from the Epistle to the Galatians[600] when St. Paul says, in the context of only four verses: *"Bear one another's burdens* and so fulfil the law of Christ" (which belongs appropriately in this chapter on love), and *"...each man will have to bear his own load".*

These statements appear on the surface to be contradictory, but they are not. The first is what it appears to be, about loving and helping one's neighbour, which is what we have been discussing. The second is talking about being *responsible to God* for one's own work and actions, and, in that sense, we *do,* each of us, *have to carry our own responsibility and accountability to God* for what we do—and what we are. No one else can carry *that* "burden" for us. The Bible does make sense if looked at more carefully!

If we are to have the great privilege of being God's children, not just some part of the created order, then it follows that we are called to be *like Him.* We *have to be like Him* if we are to truly *to be His children.* If He is Love, we have to have His love in us, it is as simple as that.

But to do it, we have to keep our eyes on Him, and draw on His love with all our hearts and minds and souls, and strength, to see our neighbour with God's eyes, and, in effect, let God do the loving

---

600   Galatians 6:2-5

for us. We need to let Him love us, too; and passionately love Him back.

The vision that can inspire us to these heights is thinking more and more about what God is like, what He would do, and what He would wish us to do, in any given situation; being in that close relationship of love with Him where He becomes more real to us than any human situation that might try to distract us.

As I have said, one of my favourite quotations is from Psalm 63: *"My soul clings to you; your right hand holds me fast"*.

We rejoice that we have been privileged to be drawn into the love that flows in and through the Persons of the Trinity; caught up, as Jurgen Moltman[601] has put it, *into the eternal life of the Trinity*—the God who is love.

---

601   Jurgen Moltmann. "The Unity of the Triune God: Remarks on the Comprehensibility of the Doctrine of the Trinity and its Foundation in the History of Salvation", in *St. Vladimir's Theological Quarterly,* vol.28/3, 1984, pp.161-162

CHAPTER 11

Passing on the faith to the next generation

When I have seen teenagers, who could themselves have had very little comprehension of things theological, trying to teach young children faith, I have been much concerned. I have long felt that both the children and the teenagers should have been worshipping God in Church, as part of the worshipping community, with formal theological education *for both* being provided at an adult level when they were individually ready for it.

This belief was reinforced by the following article, entitled *"Churches use 'Wrong Approach —Education Can Be Harmful"*, which appeared in the Victoria daily newspaper about thirty years ago: a review by Louis Cassels, UPI Religion Writer, of a book called *Children, Church and God,* now out of print, which I would like to quote in full, because I think it is so important (the emphases are mine):

> Formal religious education of children before the age of adolescence is worse than useless. It may do permanent harm to their spiritual development.

> That startling assertion is made by two Roman Catholic educators, Dr. Robert O'Neil and Fr. Michael Donovan. O'Neil is assistant professor of psychology at the University of Detroit. Donovan is chaplain to Roman Catholic students at the University of Michigan.

> They are authors of a small paperback book which ought to be read and pondered by parents and pastors of all denominations. The title is Children, Church

and God. It can be ordered from the Corpus Books Division of World Publishing Co. (2231 West 110 St.) Cleveland, Ohio.

What O'Neil and Donovan are saying in dead earnest is that virtually every church in America is going about religious education in the wrong way.

With few exceptions, Catholic and Protestant churches concentrate most of their religious education effort on young children between the ages of 5 and 13. Relatively few resources are invested in educational programs for high school and college students, and still less is done about adult education.

This means, say O'Neil and Donovan, that 'a disproportionate amount of religious education is aimed at those who can least benefit from it.'

They cite contemporary studies of learning psychology which show that pre-adolescent children simply are not able to handle the kind of abstract or analogical thought that is necessary to attain any real understanding of religious concepts.

They can learn the right words and definitions, and parrot them back to their pleased teachers and parents. But the only way they can cope with the ideas behind the words is to reduce them to concrete, oversimplified terms. And this often leads to bizarre concepts of God which are 'worse than no understanding at all' because they become roadblocks to mature religious thought at an appropriate age.

O'Neil and Donovan contend this is the real reason why so many young people abandon religion entirely soon after they reach adolescence. Their growing minds recognize the superficiality and untenability of their childhood concepts of God, and they have been encouraged to regard those concepts as the teaching of the church.

So 'they reject a Christianity which they never learned to know at all.'

O'Neil and Donovan are not suggesting children should be [kept] away from church until they're 13. They are speaking solely of formal religious education—the kind that attempts to impart conceptual knowledge. This, they say, should begin only at adolescence.

But younger children can and should go to worship services with their parents and engage in activities that will cause them to think of churchgoing as a pleasant and interesting experience.

If they ask questions about God or prayer or life after death or other religious concepts, parents should answer them as well as they can, bearing in mind that 'in most instances the questions do not demand a factual, content-type of response to be satisfactory to the child.'

'Most parents are capable of providing all the religious formation that their children will need until adolescence', the authors say.

'Parents are not supposed to teach their children religious concepts. Parents need only be parents...... Children's faith is not in God or in a belief system, but in their parents.'

'Children believe what their parents believe—because they are their parents; they reverence what they perceive is revered by their parents. They respect what their parents respect, not because they understand it, but because they have faith in their parents.'

If parents still feel inadequate to the challenge of providing their children's pre-adolescent formation in religion, the solution lies not in sending the children to a classroom for formal instruction, but in providing classes for adults to learn more about their faith.

I found this to be true in the upbringing of my son, who is now a firmly committed Christian, who always finds a church to go to, in whatever city he may find himself; but the children of many people I know, who were dutifully sent to Sunday School in the accepted way, now not only no longer go to church themselves, but their own children and grandchildren are not church-goers either. While parents and teachers and churches take pride in their Sunday School curriculum, as if children really could understand the profundities of the faith, even in watered-down terms, I think that misunderstandings of it, once embedded in their minds, are worse than waiting trustfully to learn about it when they are older, as the article quoted states. My concerns are also shared by the author of the book: *"Will our Children Have Faith?"* [602] It is a fact that the majority of the younger generation today are not interested in the Christian faith, and something must be done about this.

Sometimes young parents, who often do not have much faith or understanding themselves, are assured that they are doing the right thing in sending their children to Sunday School, but the experience does not last. They find that it "doesn't work" on a long-term basis, partly because they do not have the conviction of the truth of the Christian faith in themselves, and their children pick this up from them, and partly because the child has never learned to encounter God in worship for itself. When the child finds that there is no real faith at home, that friends and contemporaries have no involvement with any church, and that the whole of the outside world is geared to doing other things on Sundays, there is nothing to hold it back from dropping out as soon as it can.

On the other hand, it has been my experience, both as a parent and as a priest, that small children who come to the altar and receive the Sacrament have a great sense of awe, and wonder, and mystery; and, if they are "part of" the worshipping congregation all their lives (not just "in and out" of services briefly), the theological explanations can be given to them at a time in their lives when they are able to bring a more mature understanding to bear, and, at that time, they should be asked to confirm for themselves the promises made for them at their baptism.

We have inherited the idea, right in itself, that one must have a

---

602   John H. Westerhoff III. *Will our children have faith?* A Crossroad Book. New York: The Seabury Press Inc. 1976

strong faith and be in "a state of grace" before presuming to take the Sacrament, and that therefore children, *because they do not understand,* cannot partake in the Eucharist. (Do *we* always understand?)

There are three problems with this kind of thinking, as I see it: one is the result it has had of children being excluded from receiving Communion, which I believe has been one of the main causes of young people now leaving the Church as soon as they are able to; a second problem is that many churchgoers who used to attend "Morning Service", i.e., Matins, no longer feel comfortable in church now that the Anglican Church has moved to making the Eucharist the main Sunday morning service, because they have never been properly taught about what is involved, and do not understand it, and do not feel "good enough", and so they stop going; and a third problem has been the assumption that it is possible to know enough and to be good enough, which should not be our attitude at all! We need to admit that we do not always understand, and are not "good enough", and put our trust in God, and come to Him, for Him to heal, forgive, and enlighten us, and enable us to *"abide in Him"*.

People have said to me: "I want to let my children decide for themselves when they are older" (whether or not to accept the Christian faith and go to church). That *sounds* reasonable, but it isn't really. (Do we wait to feed and clothe them?) Someone who has been taken to church, as a child, is free to decide, on becoming adult, that this is something that he or she no longer wishes to do—unless there has been some "brainwashing" going on, as happens in some of the cults, but this is not the case in the mainline churches.

The fact that taking children to church does *not* stop them from having the freedom to choose for themselves when they are older (whether or not to continue the practice of churchgoing), is demonstrated by the fact that the majority of the children who *have* been "taken to church", in the sense of being exposed to the Sunday School type of experience, too often *have* left the church as soon as they are old enough to decide for themselves what they want to do: hence the fact that there are few people under fifty or sixty in our churches today. So I think that should demolish the idea that "taking a child to church" imprisons its future thinking in some way.

On the other hand, someone who has never had the experience

of going to church at all is not likely to decide suddenly, on growing up, that this is something that he or she wants to do. They have not learned enough about the faith to make an informed decision, and why should they suddenly start now? And, not only do they not have the requisite knowledge of the faith on which to make an informed decision, but they have never "met" God in relationship, so they have no idea of what it could be like, no idea of what they are missing.

Sometimes young people are later attracted to more evangelical churches, even to the cults, to assuage a spiritual hunger which they are aware of, but which they cannot diagnose, even to themselves. Surely the same loving parent who is concerned to give his or her offspring "the chance to decide for themselves" would not want to risk the possibility of seeing their child fall prey to a cult, as many have done, just because the parent decided never to expose it to the "safe" orthodoxy of one of the traditional churches.

Some modern theologians try to *"rethink" the faith* because they think *"it doesn't work"* in today's society, basing that supposition on the fact that few people under fifty or sixty go to church any more, and the children and grandchildren of so many of today's Christians have grown up to be unbelievers.

I believe that they are wrong, if their idea of "rethinking the faith" is to question or deny it, or try to change it from its original apostolic roots. I think the problem is that *the faith itself* has become so corroded and corrupted with human philosphical speculation over the centuries that it is often not *understood* any more, because some of it doesn't seem to make sense, and some people today, in rejecting what doesn't appear to make sense, do not seem to be trying to work out and *understand* what the original message really was, (as I am trying to do). In substituting *more* human ideas for it, whether denials of traditional belief or new speculation about it, they are corrupting it still further, not realizing that the original message of salvation *does* make sense if properly understood. (It will be seen that this whole book is an attempt to make sense of it, without changing the fundamentals of apostolic teaching.)

The Church, in all its branches, needs to look beyond the clutter of the centuries and go back to the original apostolic faith, and really come to understand it. Only then will its representatives be really be qualified to teach it.

In addition to "rethinking" or "rediscovering" *the faith itself,* it may well be necessary to look at the way we *teach it.* In particular, we need to think about the church services which should be being made available for children and young people, but which, so far, are not. The faith itself, I believe, can be accepted with integrity, if thought out and explained and appropriated for oneself and understood; and, if we come to know Jesus as our Saviour, in a personal relationship with Him, in the present time, the rest follows.

I believe that we have been mistaken, not only in teaching children when they are too young really to understand "theology", so that they may end up with bizarre images in their minds, but in having them "taught" by volunteers, who, while sincere and willing, may not really be qualified for the task. I think it says something negative about our priorities that we expect to have professional teachers even in elementary schools, but, when it comes to teaching in Sunday School, "anyone will do" who is willing to volunteer. What sincere lay people can do is to help to make churchgoing an enjoyable experience for the children, and, in so doing, literally *"bring them to Christ",* while leaving adult education to those with theological training who can teach them at a more advanced level later on. (For this to happen, we need to make available some church services that are shorter and simpler, and more suited to youthful participation.) We have traditionally taught eleven and twelve-year-olds in "Confirmation classes", with that usually being the end of their Christian education, and I think this has left many people with an immature understanding of the faith, one that is not strong enough to stand up to the subsequent challenges of life. (I think Confirmation should come later.)

I believe that children and young adolescents are not only too young to understand the profundities of the faith, so that they continue throughout their lives with what are basically child-like understandings, which they often reject later in life, but they are also too young at that time to formulate some of the deeper questions that may come to trouble them later in life: at which time they often find it easier to give up and leave the church than to tackle clergy who may not always be able or willing to help them.

Children need to come to have the personal experience of knowing our Lord *first,* and *then* go on to learn about Him in growing maturity all their lives. I believe that, if we do not proceed along these lines, all the theological "fixing" in the world will be useless.

I would like to refer to a passage from Walter Martin's five-hundred page book, *"The Kingdom of the Cults"*. Without necessarily endorsing all of the contents of that book, I would like to quote a passage to the effect that it is *the basic ignorance of the faith* on the part of many *professing Christians* that has enabled the Jehovah's Witnesses to make so many converts. He writes, at the end of an article on Jehovah's Witnesses and the Watchtower Bible:

> ...let us awake to their perversions of Scripture and stand fast in the defense of the faith 'once delivered to the saints'. Author's Note: Nowhere is this point more forcefully demonstrated than in a book written by a former member of the Watchtower Society, W.J. Schnell *(Thirty Years a Watchtower Slave,* Grand Rapids: Baker Book House, 1956). In this particular reference Schnell succinctly stated the Watchtower methodology in the following words:
>
> 'The Watchtower leadership *sensed that within the midst of Christendom were millions of professing Christians who were not well grounded in 'the truths once delivered to the saints,' and who would rather easily be pried loose from the churches* and led into a new and revitalized Watchtower organization. The Society calculated, and that rightly, that *this lack of proper knowledge of God and the widespread acceptance of half-truths in Christendom would yield vast masses of men* and *women....'* (page 19) [603] (italics mine)

It is partly to try to counter some of these half-truths so easily and gullibly misunderstood that this book is being written.

St. Paul talked about the necessity for our attaining maturity in

---

[603] Walter Martin: *The Kingdom of the Cults,* Limited Edition. Minneapolis, Minnesota: Bethany House Publishers, 1996, p. 125.

our faith, in the same context of its being a protection against false doctrine (and it is interesting to note that this was going on even in New Testament times): "until we all attain to the unity of the faith and of the knowledge of the Son of God, to *mature manhood*, to the measure of *the stature of the fullness of Christ; so that we may no longer be* children, *tossed to and fro and carried about with every wind of doctrine, by the cunning of men, by their craftiness in deceitful wiles.*" [604]

Walter Martin writes at the end of his book (italics mine):

> It has been the experience of the author..... *that there has yet to be born a cultist who can confuse, confound or in any way refute a Christian who has made doctrinal theology an integral part of his study of the Scriptures.* Cults thrive upon ignorance and confusion where the doctrines of the Scriptures are concerned, but *are powerless to shake Christians in their faith or effectively proselytize them when the Christian is well grounded in the basic teachings of the Bible and given over to a study of the great doctrinal truths of the Word of God.* These mighty buttresses of Christian theology must no longer be taken for granted by Christian believers nor should pastors and teachers assume that the average Christian has sound knowledge concerning them. The rise of cultism to its present proportions indicates a great dearth in knowledge where doctrine is involved, and is a decided weakness in the battlements of orthodox theology, which the Church ignores, at the risk of innumerable souls. [605]

I believe that many professing Christians, in our churches, are at risk because they are not equipped with the *sword of the Spirit, which is the word of God* [606] in the way that they should have been, and which I believe God intended the Church to provide to them. (That is one of the reasons that I have included so many Biblical quotations in this

604   Ephesians 4:13-14

605   Walter Martin. *The Kingdom of the Cults*, Limited Edition. Minneapolis, Minnesota: Bethany House Publishers, 1996 , p. 398.

606   Ephesians 6:17

book, to familiarize people with some of the great Biblical truths that are the bastion of our faith). I believe that God's judgment may be more on the failure of the churches to preach the Gospel effectively, than on the individuals who may have been led astray by non-Christian cults. I do *not* think that such people are necessarily damned to all eternity, and so it should be clear that I am not particularly endorsing Walter Martin's implication that innumerable souls may be *"lost"*.

I am, however, supporting his belief that much more needs to be done to teach the faith effectively, and that it is *essential* that the churches come to realize this, and that the faith be clearly taught and understood, if we are to hand it on in any substantive way to the next generation, and combat the present crisis of faith.

A problem known to all clergy is the situation where *grandparents* want to have a new grandchild "christened", but the young parents themselves seem to have no understanding of what is involved in baptism. Getting the baby "done", to please the grandparents, is about the extent of their commitment, and, when they are confronted with the expectation that they will bring up the child in the faith, in the worshipping Christian community, they react by saying that *"they do not want to go to church"* (as if that was all there was to it), that they can teach the child about Christianity and about being a loving and decent person (as if *that* was all there was to it!) *without* "having to go to church", and, in fact, can often find God more easily in a quiet place in the country than they can in any church congregation. Some claim to find God more easily on a golf course!

While it is true that individual experiences of God may indeed occur outside a church building, and that attending some parish church services can sometimes be a frustrating and unsatisfying, even annoying, experience, it is obvious that no one has ever explained to them about the need to identify oneself in life with the true, ongoing, invisible Church, the Body of Christ, the Communion of Saints, in the Eucharist. I think that some of this arises from Protestant misunderstandings of the faith, that "religion" is "between me and my God," and "I don't need any church to come between us." I think that, if parents were taught to understand aspects of the faith which I have tried to outline in this book, and if children were *first* taught to "meet God" in the ritual of the Sacrament of the Eucharist at the altar, and *then* taught the faith in a substantive way when they were older, this situation should not so often arise.

The next chapter deals with misunderstandings about the Eucharist, which I believe arise from the fact that people have not been used to meeting Our Lord in the sacrament of the altar from the time they were little. They come to it, if they come to it at all, as adults, almost as an intellectual exercise, with many questions and little faith.

Jesus said "Let the children come *to me*...And he took them in his arms..."[607]

This was an experience of divine love, not a session in a classroom. When Jesus took those children on His knee, I am sure *He was not talking to them about His coming crucifixion,* as He was to the grown-up disciples; *and so it should be with us.* We need to let the little ones come to Jesus, just as they are, without burdening their minds with teaching that they cannot yet fully understand. Only when they are older, and more able to understand, should they be introduced to the deep waters of theology—but when they *are* ready, they should not then be "brushed off" with inadequate answers; and they should be taught about *"abiding in Christ,"* that *living in the divine love* is what our faith is all about, to produce people so obviously Christ-like that the outside world can see something of God in them.

Two Bible passages that speak to us of this, one from the Old Testament and one from the New, are as follows: "Thus says the Lord of hosts: in those days ten men from the nations of every tongue shall take hold of the robe of a Jew, saying, *'Let us go with you, for we have heard that God is with you'* "[608] and "they recognized that [the disciples] *had been with Jesus".*[609]

Do people see in *us* that we have *been with Jesus?*

---

607   Mark 10:14
608   Zechariah 8:23.
609   Acts 4:13

CHAPTER 12

Misunderstandings regarding the Eucharist

I have known several people who claim to feel revulsion at what they perceive as the idea of *literally* "eating and drinking" Christ's "body and blood" in the Eucharist, and think of it as "cannibalism," a problem that apparently, in too many people, has still never been satisfactorily addressed.

I think it may stem in part from the historical arguments of ultra-devout people in the past who, in their excessive devotion, came to think of the bread and the wine of the Eucharist as being *literally* Jesus' *physical* body and blood (but also it arises from the fact that the people now objecting to such a perceived notion are thinking on a purely intellectual level about what they have never experienced spiritually, and what has never been properly explained to them).

I have already set out my arguments about what I believe should be our processes of Christian Education: first, the spiritual experience, and then the mentally satisfying explanation. I believe that it is when these are lacking that such misunderstandings flourish.

The Roman Catholic Jesuit theologian, Tad Guzie, has given a good description in a recent book of how the Church came to concentrate more on the actual elements themselves (the bread and wine) as objects of devotion, rather than on the *action* of the Eucharist itself. He says:

> none of the earliest christian writers described the
> eucharistic elements as sacred objects. It would have
> been difficult to do so, given the origins of the eucharist

in the blessings and ritual actions of an ordinary jewish meal. But by Radbert's time those origins had long since been forgotten... [610]

The Protestants, at the time of the Reformation, strove to counter the belief of their time that the bread and wine were *literally* changed into *physical* flesh and blood, by saying that it was *the recipient receiving the sacrament with faith* that made it effective. The definition of a "sacrament" is that it is "an outward and visible sign of an inward and spiritual grace". [611]

As I see it, there is truth in both of these arguments. While the Protestants were protesting an over-zealous emphasis on a *physical* miracle, the Catholic side at the time of the Reformation was rightly trying to maintain that somehow *the very life of God* comes to us through the sacrament: that the elements are no longer just "bread" and "wine", but something powerfully above and beyond the mere physical elements.

Where I believe they went wrong was in equating that *"life of God"* with *literal,* human, "flesh and blood". I think most would now agree that the Bread and Wine are not *literally* human flesh and blood, but that they *are also,* when consecrated and received with faith, *the vehicle* through which *the life of God* comes to us to nourish our souls; and in *that* sense they *are* the Body and Blood of Christ.

Think of the *reality* which the bread and wine *symbolize* for us, rather than getting "hung up" on *words* and thinking about material things. Tad Guzie has said:

> From time immemorial, the act of sharing food with another has connoted fellowship, life shared, exultation at being alive. From time immemorial, the image of blood has connoted a 'matter of life and death'........the use of blood in the rituals of primitive man signified his search for life and the preservation of life. When Jesus associated his body and blood, his life and death, with the elements of a communal meal, he evoked

---

610   Tad W. Guzie, S.J. *Jesus and the Eucharist.* Ramsey, New Jersey: Paulist Presss, 1974, p.61.

611   *The [Anglican] Book of Common Prayer, 1962, Canada,* p.550.

symbols which reach back into the origins of man's consciousness [612]

and that at the time of the last supper, "bread and wine already had a religious significance, even a messianic significance". [613] He says:

> ...our problem is to refurbish the radical symbols that have all but disappeared, not because the *symbols* are defective but because our ability to *think symbolically,* to let the symbols of our religious heritage speak to us, has been clouded over by ways of thinking that leave little room for questions of human and religious value. (italics are his). [614]

At the time of the Reformation, the Anglican Church placed in the *Book of Common Prayer* a prayer called *"the Prayer of Humble Access,"* because of its attempts to steer a middle way between Roman Catholic and Protestant doctrines, and this may have contributed to the problem of people thinking in terms of "cannibalism" referred to above:

> *Grant us therefore, gracious Lord,* So to eat the Flesh of thy dear Son Jesus Christ, And to drink his Blood, That our sinful bodies may be made clean by his Body, And our souls washed through his most precious Blood, And *that we may evermore dwell in him, And he in us.* [615]

I can only hazard a guess, when I suggest that one of the reasons for the removal of this prayer in the new liturgy may have been people's revulsion against the idea of "eating flesh and drinking blood". I have been told that other reasons for the current omission of this prayer are the fact that we no longer think so much in terms of dichotomy between body and soul, and that we are trying to move away from emphasizing "humility" and "unworthiness" and so on.

However, when that prayer was omitted from the new Anglican

---

612   Tad Guzie, S.J. *Jesus and the Eucharist.* Ramsey, New Jersey: Paulist Press, 1974, p.55

613   Tad Guzie, S.J. *Jesus and the Eucharist.* Ramsey, New Jersey: Paulist Press, 1974, p.87.

614   Tad Guzie, S.J. *Jesus and the Eucharist.* Ramsey, New Jersey: Paulist Press, 1974, p.59.

615   *The [Anglican] Book of Common Prayer, 1962, Canada,* pp.83-84

liturgy, no comparable prayer was substituted for it with regard to "abiding in Christ", except as an option, or something to be said at the Easter season. To me the heart of that prayer is something that should be at the heart of every Eucharist: that we may *so* partake of *[the reality of]* the sacrament that we may *evermore dwell in Christ, and He in us.*

Let us forget the words that the action was historically (and perhaps misguidedly) couched in, in *the Prayer of Humble Access,* and think instead that what it means is *"partaking of the sacrament in such a way* that *we may really* come *to dwell* (live, abide) *in Christ and He in us"*, which in effect comes to the same thing, but avoids the use of distracting language.

What, to my mind, is of crucial importance, is the concept of *dwelling in Christ, and He in us: a concept so important* that it is really the theme of this book. The fact that such an important concept can be dropped from, or diminished in, our new liturgies makes it that much more urgent that I write it.

Dom Gregory Dix, in speaking of the rich variety of meanings in New Testament allusions to the Eucharist that are already found within the single rite of the broken Bread and the blessed Cup, says that:

> [the Eucharist] is [among other things] the solemn proclamation of the Lord's death [1 Corinthians 11:26]; but it is also the familiar intercourse of Jesus abiding in the soul, as a friend who enters in and sups with a friend [Revelation 3:20]. [616]

I think the Church downplays the idea of our dwelling in Christ, and He in us, at its gravest peril, even if it only happens unintentionally.

And yet the Eucharist is *not only* an individual's dwelling in Christ, and He in each of us separately—although it is that, indeed.

Perhaps the excessive individualism in religious worship since the Reformation has led us sometimes to forget that, as Christians in the Eucharist, carrying out together our Lord's commandment to "do this" in remembrance of Him,[617] *we,* as a Church, in a mystical sense, *are*

---

616   Dom Gregory Dix. *The Shape of the Liturgy.* London: Adam and Charles Black (A. & C. Black (Publishers) Ltd., 1945, p.4.

617   Luke 22:19

the Body of Christ in the world,[618] "the continuation and extension of the mystery of his Incarnation"on earth.[619]

God comes into the gathered body to renew and strengthen it for His work in the world, and He is honouring us by incorporating us into His life in this way, and entrusting us with the mission of representing Him to others.[620]

I think there should be much more teaching on the subject of what the Church *is*.

It might help people with an aversion to thinking about "flesh and blood" in the Eucharist, not only to concentrate upon God, and being incorporated into His life by being nourished with *spiritual food*, rather than anything literal, but to remember, too, that we talk about our relatives being "of our flesh and blood" in the sense of *relatedness*.

When we speak of someone in our family, or our child, for example, as being "of our own flesh and blood", we are not thinking about literal flesh on the body and blood in the vein: what we mean is *"we are made of the same stuff"*, in the sense of being *of the same family*—in this case, the family of God.

The Church becomes *Christ's body* in the world today. We share His humanness and somehow come to know Him in His divinity. Our souls are fed by Him, our spiritual growth is sustained by spiritual nourishment that comes from Him for that purpose.

We have no problem with the idea of a baby being fed at its mother's breast with some substance coming from the mother's

---

618   Romans 12:5: "so we, though many, are one body in Christ, and individually members one of another." 1 Corinthians 12:27: *"you are the body of Christ, and individually members of it."* Ephesians 1:22-23: "...the *church, which is his body*..." Ephesians 5:30 "...the church, because *we are members of his body."*

619   Tad W. Guzie, S.J. *Jesus and the Eucharist.* Ramsey, New Jersey: Paulist Press, 1974, p.144, quoting John Eudes, *The Life and the Kingdom of Jesus in Christian Souls.* New York: Kenedy, 1946, p.251: "It is the plan of the son of God that his whole church should participate in and actually *be, as it were, the continuation and extension of the mystery of his incarnation,* birth...passion and...death"

620   Dom Gregory Dix. *The Shape of the Liturgy.* London: A.& C. Black (Publishers) Ltd., 1945, p. 734: "...*it is* not organization but *the eucharist which is always creating the church to be the Body of Christ;* to do His will, and work His works, and adore His Father 'in His Name', and *in Him to be made one, and by Him in them to be made one with God. That is the consummation of human living and the end of man."*

body to keep it alive. I see this as the same kind of thing. Somehow the nourishment of *the life of God* comes to bless us through the sacrament, and Love should enable us not to fret about *how.* We just find by experience that it *does.*

If children were taught to know God in the sense of relatedness, before they started to ask these kinds of questions, I do not think we would have this problem. I believe that some of the questions about "cannibalism" in the Eucharist would never have arisen if the people concerned had become accustomed to meeting God in the sacrament at the altar since the time they were little.

CHAPTER 13

Fear of Death, and Dying

Possibly as a result of the historical threats of hell and damnation, many people seem to panic when it comes to be time to die. I think that we need both to modify this historical understanding and to remind people of the Biblical teaching that *God is Love,* so that they may not be so afraid to die.

I have tried to reassure people both that repentance and God's forgiveness are still available to them, even if only asked for at the last moment, and that, even if people do not come to understand the Christian faith in this lifetime, I believe that God will still come to meet them, even after death, and in His love take them into His arms, if they are then willing. I have tried to tell people not be so afraid for their loved ones, but commit them to God, in the faith that Christ died for them too.

However, a third option, and one which I believe to be the best, is to start to develop a relationship with God while one is still young and well. It was one of my parishioners who gave me a deeper understanding of the passage in Ecclesiastes *"Remember ...your creator in the days of your youth".* [621] I think that we need to "come to terms" early in life, if possible, with what we believe about God, and our understanding of living and dying, so that, when death *does come,* it is not like an after-thought, a sudden "panic station", but something that we have been expecting and preparing for all our lives.

A verse of a hymn ("Sun of my soul, thou Saviour dear") [622] that

---

621 Ecclesiastes 12:1

622 *The (Anglican) Book of Common Praise (Revised 1938)* : Hymn 18 "Sun of my soul, thou Saviour dear", by Rev. John Keble, 1820.

speaks deeply to me runs as follows: "Abide with me, from morn till eve, *for without thee I cannot live,* abide with me when night is nigh, for *without thee I dare not die".* There are prayers on this theme that one can say all one's life, for example "grant us a quiet night, and at the last a perfect end", and "suffer us not, for any pains of death, to fall from thee"; and "grant us in this world knowledge of thy truth, and in the world to come, life, everlasting", and so on. [623]

I have always been saddened when I have come across people, in my pastoral ministry, who are so much into denial, until the last minute, that they never really have time to "prepare" for death.

I am not talking about sudden and tragic accidents and illnesses that cannot be foreseen, that cut off life prematurely and tragically, and leave heartbroken survivors shatteringly bereaved. I knew a woman whose small granddaughter fell into a well and drowned. There is no comfort for such survivors so desperately bereaved, unless it is the hope that the *child* would have experienced something wonderful at the actual moment of death when it passed into the next life, rescued (as I hope it would have appeared to the child) by God Himself. The grief of those left behind to mourn is something quite other than the subject of this discourse, which is that, when one comes to die at an appropriate age, *death itself* comes as a merciful release which should not be feared.

The distress involved in coming to that point, things like illness, pain, hospitalization, deterioration, and the loss of loved ones, are all terrible things, and not what I want to talk about here, except to say, perhaps, that if we have faith in God, we hope He will give us fortitude and strength in such situations.

I am talking about *death itself,* when it comes in the normal course of events. I am talking about people, especially older people, who find themselves facing dangerous operations, or have been diagnosed as terminally ill, or who are obviously dying, who have never really thought much about the deeper things of life until the last minute, and who miss so much in their living of their earthly life, while they still have it, because of that fact.

What I am saying is not to be confused with a *"you must accept Jesus before you die, or else...."* philosophy. I have had to comfort

---

623   to be found in *The [Anglican] Book of Common Prayer, 1962, Canada.*

several Christian friends who gave the impression that they cared more about their loved ones than they could trust God to do. I totally abhor the kind of "Christianity" that told a twelve-year old girl that her mother would not go to heaven—in other words, the child would never see her mother again—"because she had not accepted Jesus before she died," she had left it too late: her fate was irrevocable, and so was the child's loss. Again, I ask *"what kind of a God do we believe in ? "*

I am sure we should concentrate much more on the loving nature of God, and be able to commit our loved ones to Him without fear. After all, it was St. Paul, who, talking about the spouse married to an unbelieving partner, said that the faith and love of the one who believed would cover the other. [624] I believe in a God "who will have mercy where He will have mercy and compassion where He will have compassion", [625] who taught that there *was* a place in His compassion for those who come "at the eleventh hour" [626]—whatever that eleventh hour may be: and who are we to say that that eleventh hour may not take place after death?

I think we need to think much more in terms of a God who cares for those we love, *as much as, and more than, we do,* and Who can be trusted to take them into His care and keeping, especially if we pray for them, rather than thinking in terms of "who is and isn't saved", which, ultimately, is not our decision anyway.

But although I believe that God will deal with compassion with our loved ones who may not really have known Him in this life, so that we need not be so afraid for them, at the same time I do believe that all our lives would be much richer and fuller if we *did* come to know and love God in our lifetimes, long before we had to begin to face the prospect of death. Let us stop thinking in terms of eventual "rewards and punishments" and think instead of living life to the fullest, in the

---

624   1 Corinthians 7:12-14

625   Romans 9: 15 "For [God] says to Moses, 'I will have mercy on whom I have mercy, and I will have compassion on whom I have compassion' ". (Based on Exodus 33:18 "Moses said, 'I pray thee, show me thy glory'. And he said 'I will make all my goodness pass before you, and will proclaim before you my Name 'The LORD'; and I will be gracious to whom I will be gracious, and will show mercy on whom I will show mercy.' "

626   Matthew 20:1-16

love of God, to the point that, when death inevitably comes, we are not afraid to go to Him.

Which brings me back to the passage from Ecclesiastes: "Remember your Creator in the days of your youth, *before...*" As I was saying to the young couple who I went to visit the night before my husband had his fatal stroke, we need, if possible, to decide on what we believe about God while we are still young, while all is well for us: and then be prepared to continue with that decision all our lives, because whether God exists or not cannot depend on how we may feel at any given moment; our faith is a decision that we make for ourselves for our lifetimes. We need to get to know our Creator in the days of our youth, and *then,* when our bodies fail, when we come to die, we are prepared for what lies ahead.

The parishioner who first showed me that passage from Ecclesiastes in a new light told me of a near-death experience she had once had, when she had almost died, having a baby; but she is not the only person I have known who has given me a first-hand account of the glory and the beauty they have seen at the point of dying, before being brought back to life. Another friend who I knew well, in fact the man who "gave me away" at my wedding, told me after a serious illness that he had actually *seen* "the pearly gates", and that they were indescribably beautiful. You may say that this was the delusion of delirium, I don't know: but many other people who have been pulled back to life from a near-death experience have also been said to have had an experience of something incredibly wonderful at that moment. If that is what "dying" is like, why are we so afraid of it?

My parishioner told me that she had had an "out-of-the-body experience", where it seemed to her as if she herself were floating above the inert body on the operating table, but that she was still attached to that human body by what looked like a silver-coloured cord. It was if a balloon was being held down by a string so that it could not float away. This cord that she saw, that connected her real self to her physical body, was never broken, and her soul did not leave her body. She did not die. When she finally recovered, she talked about this to the hospital chaplain sitting by her bed, and he reminded her of that passage from Ecclesiastes, and told her that it was that "silver cord" that had held her spirit to her body. Presumably it breaks when a person actually dies, which would make sense of that Biblical passage, which she now understood from personal experience:

> Remember your Creator in the days of your youth, before the evil days come, and the years draw nigh, when you will say, 'I have no pleasure in them'; ..... and desire fails; because man goes to his eternal home, and the mourners go about the streets; before the silver cord is snapped, or the golden bowl is broken, or the pitcher is broken at the fountain...and the dust returns to the earth as it was, and the spirit returns to God who gave it. [627]

This passage, she says, confirmed the experience she had had of the "silver cord"—which I have never heard anyone else ever explain, and which I would like to share with you for that reason. It does make one think that the writer of what could, on the surface, appear to be merely a striking piece of poetry, may possibly have known more about death and dying than might appear to a casual reader on a first glance. I think there is a lot more to the Bible than we give it credit for!

She, like all the others, spoke of the wonderful experience that seemed to lie ahead of her, and her reluctance to be pulled back from it. From accounts like this, and my own experience with my husband, I have been able to reassure people that I believe that *death itself*—not the events leading up to it, but actually "passing through the gate", as it were—can be a wonderful experience, something not to be afraid of, but rather embraced with joy.

I remember being called to the deathbed of an elderly woman only remotely connected with the Church, who had not bothered about "religion" all her life, but who was badly frightened when she came to die. She was not in any physical pain. Her distress was mental and spiritual. Her daughter—who, with her husband and family did not come to church either—telephoned me when the dying mother was only hours from death, and asked if I would visit her and try to assuage her fears. I did manage to set her mind at rest, and give her peace, and she died very peacefully a few hours later. However, I could not help reflecting how much of her life had been spent "missing"

---

627   Ecclesiastes 12:1-7

something wonderful, which she had never known about, but which she could have experienced much earlier: an assurance of the love and presence of God, in life as well as in death. How much better it would have been if she had "remembered her Creator in the days of her youth": if she had spent her earthly life with God and not just the last few minutes of it.

> Seek ye the Lord while he may be found, call ye upon him while he is near: let the wicked forsake his way and the unrighteous man his thoughts: and let him return unto the Lord, and he will have mercy upon him; and to our God, for he will abundantly pardon. [628]

Even people who are sincere Christians, who long ago "made the decision for Christ", often seem to panic when the time comes to die. I want to say to the person who is, or will one day be, dying, "trust in God, it *will* be *all right*": God will take care of us, and *whether we live or whether we die*, we *will* be all right, *if we are with Him*. But it would help if we "sought the Lord" and got to know Him better while still in good health!

If one really believed in Him, really loved Him, really trusted Him, would it be so terrible to go to Him if He called? Surely, as Christians, we should not be so afraid of the idea of dying. I would be much more concerned, I think, about the manner of one's death. When I come to die I shall be glad if I manage to get through the ordeal with reasonable dignity and comfort and peace: but it is not *death itself* I fear.

If death really is the pathway to a closer experience of God, should we be so afraid of it?

I am talking about *accepting the inevitable when it comes, without fear, and with faith in God*. I am talking about being able to discuss this with people when "their time comes", rather than shuffling one's feet, as it were, because all they want to do is to think about *surviving*, and the other possibility is not to be mentioned.

I believe that, if one *has* to die, if one's time has come, the actual *process* of leaving this world, going to the arms of God, the process of transfer from one state of being to another, for the person who is dying, should not be as terrifying as we sometimes fear it must be.

---

628   Isaiah 55:6-7

I hope that someone who reads this book will think about these issues before a time of crisis comes, so that they can be prepared and comforted, and at peace: unafraid, knowing that God is with them in life *and in death.*

I would like to quote two passages from the Bible that I would like to be read at my funeral. The Gospel was also read at my husband's funeral, and the other reading then was the passage from the Book of Wisdom, "the souls of the righteous are in the hands of God." [629] The Old Testament reading that I would like to have read at my funeral is from the Book of Job:

> *All the days of my service I would wait, till my release should come.* [Then] *Thou wouldest call, and I would answer thee;* thou wouldest long for the work of thy hands [630]

This sums up my own philosophy of life—not to want to hurry the process, but to wait patiently *"all the days of my service"* for God here on earth, *"until my release should come"*; but *when He calls, I would answer* that call; and we would, as it were, run to each other in a mutual embrace. *"Thou wouldest long for the work of thy hands"*: and if God can long for *me,* how much more must I long for God!

The other reading that I would like to have at my funeral is from the Gospel according to St. John: Jesus's great High Priestly Prayer on the night before the Crucifixion:

> 'I do not pray for these only, but also for those who believe in me through their word [that means us] that they may all be one; even as thou, Father, art in me, and I in thee, that they also may be in us, so that the world may believe that thou hast sent me. The glory which thou hast given me I have given to them, that they may be one even as we are one, I in them and thou in me.....Father, I desire that they also, whom thou hast given me, may be with me where I am, to behold my glory which thou hast given me in thy love for me before the foundation of the world.' [631]

629 Wisdom of Solomon (Apocrypha) chapter 3, verses 1-9.

630 Job 14:14-15

631 John 17:20-24

What more could we ask than to be with Jesus, in the place where He is, and to see the glory of God, which has surrounded Him since before the foundation of the world; to see, in other words, the Incarnate God, the Divine Man,[632] in the glory of the Trinity.

I was at the deathbed of a friend a few minutes before she died, one Maundy Thursday evening. I had left, promising to return after the Maundy Thursday evening service, and she died very peacefully a few minutes later, in the knowledge (if she heard and understood me, which I think she did) that I was going to the Maundy Thursday evening Eucharist, where she would be in our prayers, and that I would be coming back to her immediately afterwards. It was a windy night, and, as I returned to the hospital, I found myself wishing that the winds of God would catch her up, so that she did not have to continue the suffering of her illness any longer, and I found, when I got there, that it was so. It was as if she had blown away like a leaf, and I believe that it was as I had told her: the glory of God would have appeared in the darkness of her twilight, like the morning sun lightening the sky, the love of God taking her to his heart, the glory of God making it all seem worthwhile. I went to a performance of Handel's Messiah the following evening, Good Friday; and it seemed, in my thoughts anyway, in the glory of the music, that it was as if some of God's glory was spilling over from heaven to earth, and I was part of it, or at least aware of it (of something more than the fact that the music was beautiful). I reflected that she was now closer to it than I was, but it was there for both of us, and it was as if I heard "the trumpets [sounding] on the other side."[633]

"God is love".[634] Believe in God, and do not be afraid. It is going to be all right.

Maybe I can quote St. Paul in this context of not being afraid of death, and, indeed, embracing it, in God's due time, as a welcome *"going home"*. This is not the same as being suicidal, or not appreciating

---

632   *The [Anglican] Book of Common Praise (Revised 1938):* hymn 354: "All hail the power of Jesus' Name, Let angels prostrate fall; Bring forth the royal diadem And crown him Lord of all": the fourth verse reads: "Hail him, ye heirs of David's line, Whom David Lord did call, *the God Incarnate, Man Divine,* and crown Him Lord of all".

633   John Bunyon. *Pilgrim's Progress*

634   1 John 4:16

the life that God has given us on earth, or "wanting to die": not at all. It is a sense of being ready, with joyful anticipation, for when the time does come.

St. Paul wrote: "For me to live is Christ, and to die is gain. If it is to be life in the flesh, that means fruitful labour for me." [635] The next words are harder to understand correctly, if taken at face value, because it looks as if he is debating whether to commit suicide or not: "yet which I shall choose I cannot tell. I am hard pressed between the two." I would paraphrase the word "choose" by using the word *"prefer"* (in the sense of "what I *would* choose if there was a choice").

St. Paul could have chosen to precipitate his own death, either by just "giving up" in his prison situation and wasting away, or by provoking the authorities so that he would be put to death, seeking the "glory" of "martyrdom", but I do not think that he was thinking in these terms. I think that, while he was facing the very real and ever-present possibility of death, he was debating whether *his own personal preference* would be *to go to God* (to "be with Christ") at this juncture, which, from his writings, one can see he considered to be *"far better"* than any alternative. In the process he was reassuring people that "it would be *all right"* if he did die. If that happened, they were not to let it discourage them in their faith, or break their spirit. They were to remember that he himself had said *"to depart and be with Christ...is far better"*.

On the other hand, he recognized that his people needed him, and that there was still work for him to do, and for that reason he was "convinced" that God would ensure that he was spared for a little longer, in order to do that work: but he was indeed martyred in the end.

St. Paul wrote:

> My desire is to depart and be with Christ, for that is far better. But to remain in the flesh is more necessary on your account. Convinced of this, I know that I shall remain and continue with you all, for your progress and joy in the faith. [636]

---

635 Philippians 1:21
636 Philippians 1:23-25

In St. Paul's thinking, it did not really *matter* whether he lived or died, and we should have the same confidence. Our concern, like his, should be for those who would be affected and bereaved; but as far as *actually dying,* and *going to be with Christ,* is concerned, we need not be afraid. He was not afraid of death. Of dying, perhaps; but not of going to God. (And for those who think that St. Paul did not really think that Jesus was "God": how do they explain that he saw his resurrected self after death as being *"with Christ"*? If Christ were *not* somehow *part of "God"*, would he not prefer to be with *God?*)

Having dealt with the subject of actually dying, perhaps I can turn for a moment to the subject of the desolation of those who are bereaved, and describe how I personally found help and comfort from God when my husband died.

When he died, the situation could hardly have been "worse", in the sense that he suffered a great deal, both physically and mentally, I think. He could not speak, but I believe he knew, not only that he was dying, but that he was leaving me, in a new job, in a new career, in a new place, among comparative strangers, in a new life where I would really have needed his help. Our financial situation was desperate, in that I had all my student loans to repay, and his forthcoming funeral expenses to pay, on top of the loss of his pension: not to mention, possibly a crisis of faith for us both: where was God in all this, when we had both tried so hard, and sacrificed so much, to serve Him? My husband and I could not even speak to each other. Our only communication was that he could squeeze my hand with one of his (the other was paralysed), in response to what I said to him; and even this precious means of communication was soon lost to us, in the interests of the hospital deciding to keep inserting the intravenous needles into that wrist, although I thought that surely they could have found some other part of the body that did not take away from him his last way of communicating with the world around him. And yet, somehow, in a situation where all was so desperate, so hopeless, so filled with pain, there came through, in the last hours, almost like a trumpet call, a note of hope and reassurance, as if he were trying to tell me that "it was all right".

The night before he died, I was so tired that I could not even move the chair round to the other side of the bed, in order to face him as he lay, unconscious, on his left side facing the door; but I think that he must have been "out of the body" even then, because it seemed to me, as I sat there, looking at his back, that actually he was not on the bed at all. I felt as if he had his arms around me, and he was trying to reassure *me,* that it was *all right!* It was as if God had given him permission to reassure me and say "from where I stand, at the gate of the next world, I can tell you, from what I can see from here, that *it is going to be all right."*

The extraordinary thing that I can't prove, explain, or defend, is that, when, later, I walked, alone, into the room where his dead body lay, I had the sense that Jesus had just walked in through that doorway before me. It was as if I could still feel the rustle of His clothes in the breeze, as if I could still feel the draft of His moving through it, before me. I could feel that He had just been there a minute or two earlier.

A day or two after my husband died, I drove alone along the highway to a funeral home in another town, to make the necessary arrangements, and, as I drove, I felt an extraordinary sense of love all round me. My immediate and unthinking reaction was "how does he know where I am, when I am in a moving car on the highway? How did he find me?" It was the same extraordinary sense of love and comfort and reassurance that I had experienced the night before he died.

And throughout it all, in spite of the grief, the numbness, the desolation, and the very real financial, pastoral, and career crisis, there was this very real sense that, in spite of everything, *"it was all right".*

I cannot explain it. All I know is that he died, as it were, between a Eucharist and a Eucharist. He had his stroke at a Harvest Festival Service, after having received Communion at the early service that morning, and the last words I ever heard him say were to ask the visiting clergyman (I was still a deacon) if it was all right with him if he received Communion again at the second service. For one's last words to be a request to receive Communion, I think is very blessed. And I was kneeling to receive it, for us both, at another church, while we were still bound together in our earthly marriage, in the minutes before he died.

There was a sense of glory and hope, just when one would not have expected it, against all human reason and likelihood. I cannot explain it. I can only say that I believe that God was there, and that, in the end, it will be "all right".

I must have told this to my elderly aunt on my visit to England in 1990, and, apparently, she was much comforted by it. She was at that time in a nursing home, but her daughter (my cousin), and my son and I, had taken her out for the day, to have a picnic on Wimbledon Common. I cannot remember what I said to her, but my cousin told me, years later, that, every time she passed the tree we had sat under on Wimbledon Common, she thought of me, and what I had said to my aunt on that occasion, and how much I had comforted her. My natural reaction was to reply: "I can't remember, now, what I said under that tree all those years ago (let alone remember the tree!) What did I say that was so special?" And my cousin replied "you told her that 'it would be all right' ".

When my husband died, it was as if I had been cut in half, I had lost half of myself; he had gone, and so, apparently, had God. I still believed in my husband's love and continuing existence, just as I still believed in God's love and continuing existence; but that did not seem to make up for the fact that I felt that both of them had gone.

And it came to me, in the words of Psalm 22, that Jesus had said "My God, My God, why hast thou forsaken me?"—that He, too, had experienced what I was feeling now, the feeling that God was not there. Not only had He been through the same sense of abandonment and God-forsakenness that I was going through, but also, in some profound way which is hard to explain, I came to realize that He was *still there, in that place of darkness, even now,* and that therefore He *was* with me, in it, at that very moment, even though I could not feel His presence.

Because the Trinity is One God, and I was sharing the darkness with Jesus, it followed that God had *not* forsaken me. *I was not alone.*

As I have never read this anywhere, I think this understanding of sharing the darkness had to have come to me from God.

It is hard to explain, as it is more an awareness, an intuition, than a rational argument, but I could try to put it this way: If you visualize "time" as being like a short ribbon in the vastness of eternity, which can be looked at like a video-tape, and "frozen", as it were, in a moment of time, rather like pressing the "pause" button on a V.C.R., there is a sense in which, *outside time,* Jesus is still on the Cross (as well as being risen and ascended).

This sense, of going outside "time", in God, is found in the Eucharist, where past, present and future come together in our worship. We also know that we can come spiritually to the foot of the Cross, in our prayers, as our spirits move out of historical time into eternity. We are, after all, dealing with a God who lives, and is at home, in eternity.

If we can think of time, and beyond time, in these terms, it does not seem so hard to understand how we can be aware that our present darkness is shared, outside time, and, therefore, *in* time, by the God *who is not absent after all, because somehow He is there too, in the person of Jesus.* To me *so much* hinges on the doctrine of the Trinity: the belief in the incarnate and crucified God. If Jesus were not somehow part of God, we could not come to God through Him in the way that Christians have learned to do.

It says in the Book of Daniel that God "knows what is in the darkness"[637] and it is my belief that this is not just academic, theoretical, "knowledge of a fact" on His part, but that He knows what is in the darkness *from His own personal experience.*

Is that not a God more "worth-worshipping" than someone who only gathered His information from afar? To me the doctrine of the Trinity is the only understanding of God that really makes sense, and I believe it to be the most compelling of all the religions that the world has ever known.

I was learning to feel inspired, even in my place of darkness, by the realization that my feeling that God was not there was only an illusion arising from my grief: that, even though we may *feel* forsaken by God, we are not; He is still there, suffering silently beside us. That helped me to feel less forsaken, and gradually to feel that I was, as it were, being knitted back together with Him again. There is a line in one of the Psalms: "O knit my heart unto thee, that I may fear thy Name."[638]

Another passage that I have found helpful is in the Book of the Prophet Micah: (and I believe that the word "enemy" does not

---

637 Daniel 2:22 "he knows what is in the darkness and [yet] the light dwells with him."

638 Psalm 86:11, *The [Anglican] Book of Common Prayer* version. *The Book of Alternative Services* also says *"knit my heart to you* that I may fear your name". However, the RSV version of the Bible reads: *"unite my heart* to fear thy name," which, though probably technically correct from the point of view of the actual words being translated, and which could be understood as *"make me wholehearted* in pursuit of my discipleship," does not have the sense of *union with God* or the devotional effect of the version in the two Prayer Books.

necessarily refer to a physical enemy, but to the temptations of the darkness—lack of faith, lack of hope, and the temptation to despair, in a sense of God-forsakenness): "Rejoice not over me, O my enemy; when I fall, I shall rise; *when I sit in darkness, the Lord will be a light to me*" [639] and it continues with hope for the future, in spite of present darkness: *"He will bring me forth to the light out of the darkness: I shall behold his deliverance."*

Another psalm that helped me very much at this time was Psalm 63: *"My soul clings to you, your right hand holds me fast".* [640] The same theme is found in Isaiah: "For I, the Lord your God, hold your right hand; it is I who say to you 'Fear not, I will help you'." [641] Psalm 139 says "Even there your hand will lead me, and *your right hand hold me fast".* [642] Psalm 71, verse 21, runs "You strengthen me more and more, you enfold and comfort me." [643]

Out of the inspiration provided by passages like these, I wrote, or my mind composed, a sort of mantra which I could say over and over again, when I felt almost beyond putting my pain and prayer into words:

"O Great Love, enfold me, help me, and uphold me;
In your mercy hold me in your love."

In fact, I developed it over time, as something I could keep repeating almost automatically to hold myself together:

"O Great Love, enfold me, Help me and uphold me,
In your mercy hold me—in your love.
Keep me in the life of Jesus, Hold me in the heart of God.

O Great Love, befriend me, Help me and defend me,
In your mercy send me —all your love.

---

639   Micah 7:8-9

640   Psalm 63:8 (translation in *The Book of Alternative Services* of the Anglican Church of Canada)th

641   Isaiah 41:13

642   Psalm 139:9 (translation in *The Book of Alternative Services* of the Anglican Church of Canada)

643   Psalm 71:21 (also from the translation in *The Book of Alternative Services* of the Anglican Church of Canada)

Keep me in the life of Jesus, Hold me in the heart of God.

The Bible can be a great source of inspiration and comfort at such times, as I hope the above will demonstrate. Jesus said "[The Holy Spirit] will...bring to your remembrance" [644] [what you need to be reminded of, when you need it]—but one needs to have a basic familiarity with the Scriptures in the first place for this source of divine communication to get through to us. I would recommend that people familiarize themselves, in particular, with some of the more devotional passages of the Bible, as a matter of Christian training and education; and then, when we really need it, these passages will come to mind, and God will speak to us through them.

Another passage that has always had great meaning for me is from the Book of Isaiah:

> But now thus says the Lord, he who created you, O Jacob, he who formed you, O Israel [and we should remember that, through the Christian inheritance from the Jewish faith, this applies to all God's people, including ourselves, not just the Jews]:

> Fear not, for I have redeemed you; I have called you by name, you are mine. When you pass through the waters I will be with you; and through the rivers, they shall not overwhelm you; when you walk through fire you shall not be burned, and the flame shall not consume you. For I am the Lord your God, the Holy One of Israel, your Saviour...Fear not, for I am with you...every one who is called by my name [and are we not called "Christians"?] whom I created for my glory, whom I formed and made. [645]

This particular passage was the basis for the hymn:

> How firm a foundation, ye saints of the Lord, Is laid for your faith in his excellent Word! What more can he

---

644   John 14:26
645   Isaiah 43:5-7

say than to you he hath said, You who unto Jesus for refuge have fled? [646]

This hymn was sung at the service when I was ordained to the priesthood a few weeks after my husband's death:

Fear not, he is with thee; O be not dismayed! For he is thy God, and will still give thee aid; He'll strengthen thee, help thee, and cause thee to stand, Upheld by his righteous, omnipotent hand.

When through the deep waters he calls thee to go, The rivers of woe shall not thee overflow; For he will be with thee, thy troubles to bless, And sanctify to thee thy deepest distress.

I hope that thinking along these lines will make people aware of the presence of God even in the deepest darkness.

I would like to add, because people have asked me, and obviously there are still questions "out there" about the form our resurrected life will take, that the Christian Church does *not* believe in reincarnation. *We are who we are,* each of us a unique creation, known and loved by the God who made us, who has "called us by name," [647] and who would care as much (or more) than we would if our loved ones ceased for ever to exist in recognizable form. We won't wake up and find we are somebody else! That is the point of the sentence in the Creed "I believe in the resurrection of the body." [648]

We will each be, not just some disembodied spirit, but an actual, recognizable, familiar, body, in which we can be recognized and known for who we are, the unique person who we have been in our time on earth. The idea of reincarnation flies in the face of this.

There has been speculation again recently about what form this resurrected body will take, just as in St. Paul's time he was saying that *"some will ask 'How are the dead raised? With what kind of body do they come?' "*. [649]

---

646   *The [Anglican] Book of Common Praise (Revised 1938),* hymn 499.

647   Isaiah 43:1 "I have called you by name, you are mine"

648   Apostles' Creed. *The [Anglican] Book of Common Prayer, 1962, Canada.* p.22.

649   1 Corinthians 15:35

I think some modern writers appear to think that a "spiritual body" [650] must imply something formless and invisible that bears no relation to the person we have known and loved on earth. St. Paul's whole argument contradicts such an assumption: "the spiritual body" is the recognizable, familiar, human being taking on incorruptibility and immortality, with the limitations of "the flesh" being transcended and overcome. Comparing our human life and death to a seed sown in the ground, he wrote:

> What is sown is perishable, what is raised is imperishable. It is sown in dishonour, it is raised in glory. It is sown in weakness, it is raised in power. It is sown a physical body, it is raised a spiritual body ... this perishable nature must put on the imperishable, and this mortal nature must put on immortality. [651]

He is implying that it is still "a body", not just formless spirit, but he is saying that it will no longer be subject to the weaknesses and vulnerability of "the flesh", which will then have been transcended. Presumably we will no longer be in danger of feeling pain, bleeding to death, or starving or drowning: our bodies will be immortal, incorruptible, "raised in glory". [652] He also said: "the Lord Jesus Christ... will *change our lowly body to be like His glorious body.*" [653]

One couple confided in me that their marriage was the second one for both of them, and they asked me what I thought would happen when they met their former partners in the next life. Who would be married to who? I gave them Jesus' answer to a similar question, that we shall not be physical beings in the way that we are on earth, and there will not be marrying and giving in marriage in the way that we have known it in this life. [654] (They were greatly relieved.) However, although there will not be "marriage" as we have known it, presumably, love between people transcends even the love that we may have been blessed enough to know on earth, and love, as love, will still exist. I told them not to worry about it—my old theme: trust in God, and it will be all right!

---

650   1 Corinthians 15:44

651   1 Corinthians 15:42-53

652   1 Corinthians 15:43

653   Philippians 3:20-21

654   Matthew 22:23-30

The people who seem to worry about the form the resurrected body will take seem to imply that such a resurrected body would be entirely separate from God: and it is, in the sense that we are still ourselves, and God is still God. However, if we think in terms of "abiding in Christ" for eternity, if we think of St. Paul referring to the vastness, the love, the holiness, of God the Trinity as something *"in which we live and move and have our being",* [655] and describing our resurrected bodies as quoted above, and St. John saying that we shall see Him as He is, and *we shall be like Him,* [656] there is still an at-one-ment with God which I believe is what gives us our immortality. We only become immortal, I believe, inasmuch as we are *in Him.*

I believe that we can trust the mercy of God to enlighten and forgive us, even if we only discover Him at the last minute, but I think it really helps to work out what we do believe while we are still comparatively young and strong, as it takes time to grow in a relationship with God; times of crisis would not then catch us totally unprepared, whether it is grief and bereavement, or any other kind of crisis: or the time coming for us to die.

While we can encourage people to hope for the eventual mercy of God, even if we only come "at the last minute", if we have learned to *"abide in Christ",* during our lifetimes, before we ever come to die, if the Holy Spirit is dwelling *with us* and being *in us,* (the great teaching in the fourteenth and fifteenth chapters of the Gospel of St. John), we can be "in God," and with God, *in both our living and our dying.*

I think that all our lives, even when things are going well, we should be praying for a good death when the time comes, ("Suffer us not, at our last hour, for any pains of death, to fall from thee" [657]), not only for the sake of our own not suffering, but that we may be among those who *even in death* "have glorified [God]." [658]

---

655   Acts 17:28

656   1 John 3:2: *"..it does not yet appear what we shall be,* but we know that when he appears *we shall be like him, for we shall see him as he is"* (and Philippians 3:20 quoted above: Christ will change our bodies to be like His)

657   The [English, 1662] Book of Common Prayer, Service for The Burial of the Dead.

658   *The [Anglican Book of Common Prayer, 1962, Canada,* p.76 "we bless thy holy Name for all who in life and death have glorified thee", which should be our ambition in living and in dying.

We need to remember, even in the distress of the moment, when the time *does* come for us to die, that "to depart and be with Christ... is far better" [659] than anything we have ever known.

God is love. Do not be afraid.

---

659 Philippians 1:23-25

CHAPTER 14

Historical deviations from the original faith

I believe that the process of deviating from the early apostolic faith started as early as New Testament times, as I will go on to explain in later chapters.

The concept that it was *union with Christ* that gave humanity *"the quality of divinity—immortal life—in which it was lacking"*[660] became obscured early on, because of the popular notion in the culture of the time that everyone survived for ever anyway. "Eternal life" as being *only* to be found in *"union with God"* came to be superseded by the notion that *"eternal life"* was not limited to *abiding for ever* in the eternal God: *eternity could equally well be spent in hell,* in torment, as *punishment for sin.* [661]This arose, as I explain later, from what I believe to be a basic misunderstanding of Biblical texts. [662]

However, this process of deviating from this early faith was exacerbated by several subsequent historical developments: the developing (through what I believe to be a misunderstanding of St. Paul)[663] of the idea of "original sin" which again I describe later; the philosophy of the Middle Ages, and the unfinished business arising from the Reformation, both of which radically affected Christianity's understanding of the Atonement; problems arising from the Reformation itself, which have sometimes led to unfortunate results;

---

660   Arthur Cushman McGiffert. *A History of Christian Thought, Volume 1: Early and Eastern, from Jesus to John of Damascus.* New York, London: Charles Scribner's Sons, 1947, pp.142-148, re. Irenaeus.

661   I think Matthew 25-46 in particular has been misunderstood in this context

662   e.g., Matthew 25:46 amd 1 Corinthians 15:21-22

663   in particular, 1 Corinthians 15:21-22

then the Enlightenment; and then the more recent preoccupation with *"the historical Jesus"* [664] which has tended to detract from belief in the divinity of Christ and the doctrine of the Trinity, and which has not only affected understanding of the doctrine of the Atonement but has also had a radical impact on the traditional understanding of the faith itself.

We need to find some synthesis that deals with these problems, and makes the faith both understandable and reasonable: and I hope that this book, in its totality, will make a solid contribution to a greater understanding of what I believe to be the original faith.

I believe we need, in every generation, to ensure that possibly mistaken assumptions from the historical past do not pass us by unchallenged. If the truth is indeed from God, it will stand up to the test of our thinking!

One of the problems in the history of the earthly branches of the Church has been, I think, its sense of its own infallibility, especially seen in the Papacy, but also seen in most religious institutions. This stems from the belief, correct in itself, that God will guard His people from grievous error, and His Church from destruction. Therefore, it is argued,"the Church" (or Christians) cannot ever be wrong "because God would not allow that to happen": a misunderstanding, I believe, of the authority given by God to the real, "invisible," *eternal* Church. The result of this has been an unwillingness to admit to historical mistakes.

That authority, I believe, was the assurance that when the Church acts according to His will, as His representative, He will support it; but when *human beings in it* are not in conformity with the will of God, it cannot be assumed that "the Church" in that case will automatically receive God's support and endorsement, if what is being done is not in accordance with His will.

I do believe that God will protect His Church, the real, eternal, Church, from *fatal* error, and that *nothing* will be able to separate it from the love of God, nothing will ever be able to destroy it. However, I *also* believe that God's Holy Spirit allows the human element in the Church on earth which is *not* always synonymous with the ideal of the true, the "invisible" Church, to make its mistakes, in the same way

---

664   e.g., the Jesus Seminar: and see my earlier response to Bishop Spong's Theses

that God has given the human race free-will, in order that we may think and choose, and learn and grow. He provides the prophetic element, as He has always done, to call His people back to the truth, if they will only listen; but they have the freedom not to listen, if they so choose.

It is important to remember that what may apply to the invisible, *eternal,* Church does not *necessarily* apply to the human institutions which represent the Church on earth, and *to distinguish between the two,* because they do not always necessarily coincide.

A problem arises when people confuse "the Church itself" with "faith in God", and, when sometimes it seems that "the Church" cannot possibly be right, they lose faith *in God.* Someone told me once about a trial for sexual abuse, where two members of the clergy swore on oath to conflicting stories, so that obviously one of them had to be lying: and, as a result, the person telling me this story had decided never to trust either of those men again, whether they were talking about the Gospel or anything else. I pointed out that the truth of the Gospel was predicated on *much more* than the testimony of any one fallible human being, and did not fall into the same category at all.

While believers may be assured that in the sacraments they can meet God, even if "the Church" itself is composed of sinful people, it cannot be argued that God will automatically protect the Church from all error: this belief, taken at its face value, is altogether too sanguine a philosophy; one that helps us to evade responsibility for our actions. We deduce from it the fallible theory that *whatever we choose to do must be right.* It is an argument on the same level as *"God must approve of suffering, otherwise He would stop it."*

From that follows the idea that the Church can never change, or grow under the direction of the Holy Spirit, because that would be to admit that it was "mistaken" in the past, and "God would never have allowed that to happen".

This, incidentally, was an argument used against the ordination of women as priests, regardless of the fact that not having them earlier could be seen to be not so much a question of divine will versus human "mistake", but rather a logical outcome, a practical consequence, of the historical setting of earlier times. The people who oppose it ignore the fact that slavery was accepted in the early Church and in New

Testament writings.[665]   We certainly judge this to be wrong today, and yet it was acceptable by the standards of the time, and preaching the Gospel and establishing the Church in its earliest years had to take precedence over social reform. In due course of time, Christians came to realize that slavery was not the will of God, and that something had to be done to stop it. The integrity of the Church was not called into question by the abolition of slavery. In fact, we see now that, in fact, it *would have been* if it had *continued* to espouse the cause of slavery. The Church survived "the mistake" of the past.

I think we may now have to admit to another possible "mistake" of the past (about our interpretation of the Athanasian Creed and *only Christians being "saved"),* in order to salvage and affirm what is eternal and true about our beliefs.

I believe that the Church has always held truth in itself, and preserved it, in its documents, for those in future generations who are willing to study and think about what has been handed down, but human beings have sometimes not only misinterpreted the records handed down from one generation to another, but have perpetuated the mistakes that have been made. It is when people do not think critically about such things, that, over time, the faith itself becomes distorted.

One example is the historical fact that more emphasis was put on interpreting literally the background of parable stories in the Synoptic Gospels with regard to hell and so on, as this conveniently coincided with the assumptions of the popular culture of the time, and less emphasis was put on the fact that the alternative to eternal life in God was seen by St. Paul and St. John as being eventual, spiritual, *death.*

The Church taught people about sinners existing eternally in hell *even while it still proclaimed that Jesus said "I am* the Resurrection and the life",[666] (in other words, that *apart from God* there *is* no eternal life), apparently never seeing any incongruity in this; and the apostolic teaching of St. Paul and St. John, which is at least as significant as that of the Synoptic Gospels on any subject, was somehow overlooked.

---

665   e.g., Colossians 3:22: "Slaves, obey...your earthly masters. .."

666   John 11:25-26: "I am the Resurrection and the life, saith the Lord: he that believeth in me, though he were dead, yet shall he live: and whosoever liveth and believeth in me *shall never die."*   What does that mean if everyone survives for ever anyway? Surely it implies that some do die eternally, because we *all* die physically.

We have to remember that in the Synoptic Gospels, (Matthew, Mark, and Luke), we only have reported *memories* of what Jesus *actually said,* put into writing some considerable time later, (and then translated into another language), and human memory can often put its own slant on what it thinks it heard, especially if that human memory is also coloured by the "cultural mindset" of the time; and the popular cultural mindset at the time when Christ lived was belief in hell and everlasting punishment. In fact, inconsistencies in the text itself have long been overlooked and misunderstood, e.g., Matthew 10:28: "rather fear him who can *destroy both soul and body in hell,*" [667] where I argue that the reference to hell is superfluous, unless metaphorical in nature, perhaps a later embellishment, because, *if* the soul is *destroyed,* it *cannot at the same time* last for ever in hell.

I think, in particular, that it is quite possible that, in the passage in St. Matthew's Gospel about "[the unrighteous going] away *into eternal punishment,* but the righteous into eternal life," [668] the words "eternal punishment" were used because that was the impression gained, in the context of this cultural mindset of the time, and *it was not the main point of the parable anyway,* it was just used as a contrast to the benefits of "eternal life".

My reason for this supposition is the fact that *earlier* material, and in fact the larger part of New Testament teaching, shows the apostolic understanding of the opposite of eternal life to be eternal death, destruction, *"perishing",* (the word is also used in the Athanasian Creed). I think it is important to note that St. Paul wrote in one of his earliest epistles of "the *punishment* of eternal *destruction,*" [669] which would seem to contradict the passage in Matthew being discussed.

And, quite apart from anything else, logically speaking, the opposite of "eternal *life*" is "eternal *death*" (not *"punishment"*); but, even if one were to take these words literally, it could be argued that *being condemned to cease to exist would in itself be punishment,* and "eternal" in this context could well mean that *"that sentence stands*

---

667 Matthew 10:28: "do not fear those who kill the body but cannot kill the soul; rather fear him who can destroy both soul and body in hell."

668 Matthew 25:46

669 2 Thesssalonians 1:9

for ever, this is final", [670] as in St. Paul's reference to *"the punishment of eternal destruction"* mentioned above.

It does not *necessarily follow, therefore,* even in that text in Matthew's Gospel, that punishment and suffering *would continue* to be inflicted, *in the present tense, for all eternity.* It is, in fact, completely illogical to take the words "eternal punishment" literally, in the sense of torture being inflicted non-stop for ever, because *it flies in the face of the basic theme of the very parable in which that verse appears,* which is that *God cares about love.* [671]

And does *"eternal damnation"* necessarily mean *being tortured* for ever? It could equally well mean being permanently *condemned.* The *main point* that Jesus was making in this parable was that the people who would be accepted and invited into God's Kingdom at the end of time would be those who had shown care and kindness to others while on this earth: those who knew what it was to *love* (the point I have been trying to make throughout this book).

The rest of the story was just a throw-away line to the effect that *"the others would not make it".* His basic message in that parable was about the need to love and care for others. Would God ask more of us than He would do Himself?

Surely, if His nature is Love, would He not allow the irreparably, irredeemably wicked just to fade away into oblivion, death itself being their punishment, rather than inflict suffering that goes on for ever?

This is another example of undue emphasis being given to the secondary details of a parable, to the point of creating a whole theology out of it, rather than concentrating on the core of the spiritual message that Jesus was trying to teach. In fact, I think it is an example of "the later Church" putting more emphasis on *"eternal punishment"* than on

---

670 There is a reference in the Book of Daniel (12:2) to "everlasting *contempt*" ("And many of those who sleep in the dust of the earth shall awake, some to *everlasting life,* and some to shame and *everlasting contempt"):* and John 5:24 says: "he who hears my word and believes...has eternal life; he does not come into *judgment* [in other versions, *'condemnation'],* but has passed *from death* to life". Everlasting "contempt" or "condemnation" does not *necessarily* equal eternal *punishment* in the physical sense: one has to be alive to suffer physical punishment (which would also be "eternal life"). But *condemnation that lasts for ever* could well be "eternal punishment".

671 Mattthew 25:31-46, re. "the sheep and the goats"

the need to show love to others if one hopes to join the God of Love in His Kingdom.

I do not believe that one can give more credence to parables like this in the Synoptic Gospels than to the writings of St. Paul and St. John, whose teaching was long-term, emphatic, and repeated, with the implications of what they wrote well thought out, and which appeared, respectively, both *before and after* the time when the Synoptic Gospels came into existence in their present form.

The latter were basically an account of stories and actions in Jesus' life, and were not intended to be theological treatises. St. Paul was writing to his contemporaries long before the Synoptic Gospels appeared in the form in which we have them now, and I believe he more accurately portrayed the deeper understanding of the faith that he shared with the original disciples than could have been expected of any chronicler setting out "remembered" parable stories later on.

He taught the same theology as St. John (or the school of thought associated with him) about *"abiding in Christ"* and being *"rooted and grounded in love."*[672]

It is thought that the latter, who gave much thought to the implications of life and death, and love and hate, and the nature of God, specifically sought to elaborate and explain what might not have been so generally well understood in other contemporary teaching and practice.

As the writings attributed to him almost certainly appeared *after* the Synoptic Gospels were circulating in the form in which we have them now, is it possible to speculate that St. John wanted to correct the talk of "eternal punishment" circulating in these Synoptic Gospels, and *insist* on the fact that God is primarily a God of love, and that "eternal life" is *only* "in His Son",[673] the alternative being *"eternal death"*, (which means *not* living for ever, in hell, apart from God).

Certainly the minor details of such remembered parable stories cannot be the arbiter of our theology when apostles of the stature of St. John and St. Paul argue consistently and persuasively to the contrary.

Similarly, the Athanasian Creed, which I believe was basically

---

672   John 5:1-11 and Ephesians 3:14-19. See also discussion re. similarities between the teaching of St. Paul and that of St. John

673   1 John 5:11 ("God gave us *eternal* life, and *this life* is *in his Son*")

intended to be a Christian statement about the nature of God, has been taken not only literally, but mistakenly so. The mistake mentioned above has led later generations to interpret *"perishing eternally"* as meaning that human beings exist for ever in hell, tormented by "eternal fire": and the modern world now rejects this idea, and so it is coming to reject the Creed itself (and in doing so comes dangerously close to rejecting the idea of God as Trinity that that Creed describes).

I am pointing out, not only that St. Paul and St. John spoke about eternal *death* for those who come to be for ever separated from God, but that "perishing eternally" does *not, cannot,* mean surviving and suffering for ever, because *to perish is to die, to cease to exist.* A truer rendition of this phrase would surely be "to perish FOR EVER".

I think the reference to "perishing eternally" in this Creed means that the perishing, the *second,* [674] spiritual, death, is irrevocable, irreversible, *final and for ever,* finished, over, and done with. Therefore, "eternal fire" *must* be a metaphorical description of the eternal holiness and righteousness of God, which is incompatible with evil, and eventually destroys it (as described, for example, in the Epistle to the Hebrews), [675] rather than a literal and factual description of physical flames inflicting permanent torture, but the latter has been the simplistic assumption that has now led people to reject both the historical idea of eternity in hell and the Athanasian Creed.

Distinguishing the historical Jesus from the Risen Lord

I have already suggested that Jesus' referring to dead wood being put on the bonfire was to make a point about *dead wood being discarded* so that it ceased to exist, rather than about *fire and burning.* [676]

It is quite possible that His words were taken so literally that the basic meaning behind them was obscured.

---

674   Revelation 2:11, 20:6, 20:14, 21:8

675   Hebrews 12:29, Hebrews 10:27, Hebrews 10:39 re. *being destroyed* or *keeping [one's] soul*

676   e.g., John 15:5: "I am the vine, you are the branches. *He who abides in me, and I in him,* he it is that bears much fruit, for apart from me you can do nothing. *If a man does not abide in me,* he is cast forth *as a branch* and withers; and the branches are gathered, thrown into the fire and burned." Jesus is speaking *metaphorically* about *consequences,* not hellfire, in effect saying "If a man chooses *not to* abide in me, he [will eventually *perish].*" Note the word *"as",* meaning *"like,"* a branch

At other times, in order to make a point, I think He may simply have been using the language and imagery of His time: and, as I have said, we may have to make allowances for the fact that the Synoptic Gospels, the main source of these ideas, recorded later from earlier accounts, could well have been influenced in their lesser details, albeit unconsciously, by the assumptions generated by the wide-spread popular culture of the time in which these people lived.

I think the current tendency of the modern world to reject the Christian faith is based, not on Christianity itself, but on mistaken understandings of it, of which the contradictory idea of people being consigned to the flames of hell by an allegedly loving God is but one example; and that the idea of "hell", which we have inherited and which the modern world now largely rejects, is not really a Christian idea at all, but one that was adopted by Christianity almost by mistake, in spite of important early apostolic teaching to the contrary.

This illustrates what I said at the beginning of this book: that much of what purports to be the Christian faith that the world is now rejecting is not the Christian faith at all!

CHAPTER 15

Understanding—or misunderstanding— the Bible

The Authority of the Bible

A major problem facing the Church today is the fact that the Bible no longer seems to have the authority and credibility it once did. The Anglican Church's reliance on reason, tradition, and the Scriptures, has been likened to a three-legged stool, and suddenly it seems that one of these supports has collapsed.

Part of the problem has inadvertently resulted from our difficulty in adjusting to the legitimate and good work of Biblical scholarship. People used to think that every word of the Bible was literally dictated by God, and that each part of it was equally inspired. It is good that Biblical scholarship has shown us that this was not so. Our faith ought to be strong enough to survive facing that truth!

The Bible was put together by many different human beings, at different times and places, often drawing from earlier oral traditions: a great anthology of sacred writings. While divine inspiration must have illuminated the thought of many of the prophets, for example, so that what they have left us we can, indeed, say is "the Word of God", at other times more of a purely human element has crept into the writings that eventually came to be put together under the Canon of Holy Scripture (St. Paul wanting his cloak, for example [677]). Sometimes the Bible only reflects a historical situation that, like slavery, for example, may not have been the will of God at all. Sometimes it is just the historical, or even legendary, record of a primitive tribal

---

677   2 Timothy 4:13

people who made many mistakes. We need to be able to distinguish what is what.

The Bible, *taken as a whole,* basically shows us two things: it gives us the story of how the Jews, first coming to understand that there was One God, came to see themselves as His people, in a special relationship with Him, growing in that relationship over the years; and it tells us about the nature of God, gradually revealed to His people over time.

The Bible, in its totality, describes how that originally primitive people struggled to develop their consciousness of being God's people, and to discover what kind of God it was Who they worshipped (that He did not want human sacrifice, for example);[678] how they struggled with their human temptation to sin and stray from God's ways.

It describes the whole theological range of creation, sin, judgment and redemption. It tells how God's love still reached out to His people, to give them forgiveness and redemption, and bring them to Himself. In that sense it is a theological story of the relationship between the people of God and their Maker. Just because there are some unsavoury bits in that story, as there are in many novels and films we come across today, that should not obscure for us the essential themes of the story.

However, even though we should not make the mistake of saying that everything in the Bible is the literal, divinely-inspired Word of God, we should not dismiss the main themes in it, the spirit of it, as it were, either. We have to keep a sense of balance.

It is when this fine sense of balance has been lost, that abuses have occurred, in both directions: both in the liberal camp, of too much questioning and often denying, on the one hand, and in the fundamentalist camp, of taking everything too literally, on the other. In some ways the latter has been the more dangerous, as it has tended to discredit the Bible as a whole.

Just as I believe that Christianity itself has been misrepresented and misunderstood, so I believe that the Bible itself has been similarly misunderstood and gravely misused.

---

678   e.g. Genesis 22 re Abraham and Isaac; Micah 6:7-8: " 'Shall I give...*the fruit of my body for the sin of my soul?'* [What the Lord requires of you is] *to do justice, and to love kindness, and to walk humbly with your God"*

It has been used as the foundation for new "religions" that are not in the true spirit of the Judeo-Christian faith that the Bible portrays. It has been treated as a source of "proof texts," as if it were "a rule book," often taken out of context, often not in the spirit of the Bible as a whole, and often without any understanding of the historical context in which it was written, or any regard to changes in time and culture.

Some texts in the Bible have been dangerously misapplied: for example, the proberb "spare the rod and spoil the child" [679] has been used as a justification for child abuse. Passages about "forgiveness" have been used in some situations to send battered women back to murderous husbands. We realize now that this was wrong. The passage in the Epistle to the Ephesians about wives being subject to their husbands [680] has been used to excuse all kinds of human sin, from spousal abuse to the subordination of women. Similarly, passages about "the Jews," and against homosexual behaviour, have been used in a self-righteous way to inflict incredible cruelties on other people, in a way that is absolutely contrary to Christ's command to love.

It is because of legitimate rejection of this kind of misuse of the Bible, as we try to become more civilised in our behaviour, that the whole of the Bible is tending to become more and more disregarded today, not only by the world at large, but by a great part of the Church itself. The Bible is increasingly being "written off" as no longer applicable in this modern age, when, if used with understanding, for the purpose for which it was intended, it should be a most valuable resource for us, through which God can communicate with us, through the Holy Spirit.

Jesus Himself used the Word of God, the then-existing Scriptures, as "the Sword of the Spirit," [681] when facing the temptations in the wilderness; [682] and we can draw on the Bible in our own lives in the same kind of way. Jesus used Scripture to explain to His disciples "the

---

679   e.g. Proverbs 13:24: "He who spares the rod hates his son, but he who loves him is diligent to discipline him" "

680   Ephesians 5:21-25 "Be subject to one another out of reverence for Christ. Wives, be subject to your husbands..."

681   Ephesians 6:17: "The sword of the Spirit, which is the word of God"

682   Matthew 4:1-11; Mark 1:12-13; Luke 4:1-13.

things concerning Himself," [683] and I believe the Bible can still be a vehicle through which God, through the Holy Spirit, can, and does, speak to His people about "the things concerning Himself."

In fact, it was through my studying and thinking about the Bible that I came to realize that the Synoptic Gospels, with their portrayal of "hell fire" in their reports of Jesus' parables, may have carried more weight in the subsequent thinking of the Church (on the subject of everyone living for ever and some suffering eternally in hell), than the teaching of St. Paul and St. John. The latter flatly contradict them on this subject, in speaking of the eventual *destruction of wickedness,* and the spiritual *death* of those who cannot, or will not, eventually become reconciled to God.

As the writings of St. Paul *predate,* by at least twenty years, the version of the Synoptic Gospels we have now, and those of St. John or his followers almost certainly appeared ten, twenty or thirty years *after* the Synoptic Gospels appeared in their present form, perhaps St. Paul and St. John should be given more weight in our thinking now, and the whole subject of "hell" re-thought.

The present inconsistency speaks against a God of *love,* and mediaeval ideas of hell have done much to put people off what they perceive the Christian faith to be. We need to think again about what the Church *really* believes about "eternal life" being *only* "in God", and not apart from Him: which brings me back to my theme of the importance of re-emphasising the long-neglected teaching about abiding in Christ and *identifying oneself in all one's doing with Divine Love* (which has *not* been a strong point in the history of the Church). See the chapter on the Atonement.

St. Paul on the subject of "sin" and "the law," and "flesh" and "spirit"

I think also that St. Paul's arguments about "sin" and "the law," and *"flesh"* and *"spirit",* have often been misunderstood. I believe it is particularly important to understand his arguments about "flesh" and "spirit" in their true context.

---

683   Luke 24:27 [Jesus, on the road to Emmaus after the Resurrection], *"beginning with Moses and all the prophets* ...interpreted to them *in all the scriptures* the things concerning himself." As I said earlier, this has always been the basic Christian understanding of the role of the Scriptures in illuminating the Christian faith.

The Gnostic heresy maintained that anything material, earthly, and human, was far removed from the spiritual and the divine, as if a "divine spark" of spirituality was trapped in an alien environment. This is completely contrary to the Christian belief that God's creation is good, that "the flesh" was created so that, in it, we could know and love each other, do God's work, and enjoy the goodness that God has put in our lives: to the point where we declare in the Apostles' Creed that we believe in "the Resurrection *of the body*". Furthermore, Jesus Himself took on human flesh in order to share it with us, and, in doing so, bring us to God (as I explain more in the Chapter on the Atonement).

However, "the flesh" *also* has its limitations and its temptations, because of the instinct for self-preservation built into the creation for its survival, and we have to rise above them if and when they conflict with spiritual virtues, and *this* is what St. Paul was talking about. ("The flesh" can also include concentrating unduly on the worldly and the temporal as opposed to the spiritual and eternal, forgetting that Jesus said "My [Kingdom] kingship is *not of this world*".[684])

I wrote earlier of ducks drowning each other in a duck-pond, but this was not "sin", because they did not know that what they were doing was unloving and wrong: they were just over-reacting to the natural urge to procreate that is built into all creation. Actions "in the flesh" *become* sin when laws exist against them which human beings can understand and then decide to disobey, *knowing* that what they are doing is wrong.

St. Paul wrote: "sin was in the world before the law was given, but sin is not counted where there is no law".[685] It is in *this* sense that "the written code kills ["the law" condemns the guilty] *but the Spirit gives [eternal] life.*"[686]

St. Paul was writing of how the basic instincts of the flesh, necessarily built into the natural creation for its physical survival, inevitably conflict with the divine mandate for human beings to live in the *spiritual* sphere, in God, *("in the Spirit")*, and bring God's own love into the world in partnership with Him, something which

---

684 John 18:36: *The Oxford Annotated Version* of the RSV says "Jesus is king of *truth, from God's world*"

685 Romans 5:13

686 2 Cor.3:5-6

we cannot do if we merely continue to live "in the flesh" as the animals do.

It is not that there is anything *wrong* with "the flesh", or that it is inherently evil *in itself,* as I have explained above—after all, Our Lord took on our human flesh Himself, so that He can identify Himself with us in experiencing life in this world; and God meant us to use "the flesh" for good, and to experience through it all the blessings He has given us in this life; but there is a fine balance between providing for the daily needs and care of the body, enjoying, in moderation, the good things of this life, on the one hand, and, on the other hand, living as if gratifying its every whim was the supreme goal of our lives.

That was what St. Paul meant in saying "make no provision for the flesh, *to gratify its desires."*[687] He was *not* saying "make no provision for the flesh" in the sense of not providing for adequate food and shelter and daily needs; he was saying *"do not organize your life on the basis of selfishly gratifying the lusts and temptations arising from the flesh".* He was saying that "those who live according to the flesh set their minds on the things of the flesh, but those who live according to the Spirit set their minds on the things of the Spirit": and that *"to set the mind on the flesh is death,* but to set the mind on the Spirit is *life* and peace." [688]

He described explicitly the difference between the spiritual life and the instincts of "the flesh", whether the physical lusts of the animal life, wanting to gratify one's own physical needs at all costs (for example, the lust of the rapist or murderer, or even just selfishly putting our own needs ahead of those of other people), or the more complicated psychological processes of the evolved human being, who has a brain that, with all its great potential benefits, brings also the temptations to power and one-up-manship that we are all prone to: one could call it "humanity at its worst". [689] He wrote:

---

687 Romans 13:14 (see also Ephesians 4:22-23 "Put off your old nature which…is corrupt through deceitful lusts, and be renewed in the spirit of your minds, and *put on the new nature, created after the likeness of God…")*

688 Romans 8:5-6; and (John 6:63) Jesus said "It is *the spirit* that *gives life,* the flesh is of no avail"

689 Jesus said (contrasting the physical with the spiritual) that a person is not defiled by what goes into him but by what *comes out of him*: "evil thoughts, fornication, theft, murder, adultery, coveting, wickedness, deceit, licentiousness, envy, slander, pride, foolishness. All these evil things come from within…" (Mark 7:20-23)

But I say, *walk by the Spirit,* and *do not gratify the desires of the flesh.* For the desires of the flesh are against the Spirit, and the desires of the Spirit are against the flesh; for these are opposed to each other, to prevent you from doing what you would.... Now the works of the flesh are plain: fornication, impurity, licentiousness, idolatry, sorcery, enmity, strife, jealousy, anger, selfishness, dissension, party spirit, envy, drunkenness, carousing, and the like. I warn you, as I warned you before, that those who do such things shall not inherit the kingdom of God. [690]

But the fruit of the Spirit is love, joy, peace, patience, kindness, goodness, faithfulness, gentleness, self-control; against such there is no law. *And those who belong to Christ Jesus have crucified the flesh with its passions and desires.* [691]

(We need to think of this in the context of Jesus saying: "If [anyone would be my disciple], let him *deny himself* and *take up his cross* and follow me,"[692] and, even more strongly, "whoever *does not bear his ...*

---

690 Some people have taken this to mean that St. Paul is unreasonably saying such people will *never be forgiven,* and contradicting the idea that God is merciful to sinners. I think they are wrong to take this passage that way. I believe that God *will* forgive the penitent sinner, but penitence means repentance and *change;* and that what St. Paul is saying is that people who *continue* to "live in the flesh" *in the present tense* and *never* repent and change *become by their very nature incompatible with the goodness, love and unselfishness of God,* and thus, *because of their own inherent nature,* they will not be *able* to become "at one" with Him in heaven.

691 Galatians 5:16-24: Re "crucifying the flesh", see Galatians 2:19-20: " I have been crucified with Christ: *it is no longer I who live, but Christ who lives in me";* Colossians 3:2-5: "Set your minds on things that are above, not on things that are on earth. *For you have died, and your life is hid with Christ in God....Put to death therefore what is earthly in you:* fornication, impurity, passion, evil desire, and covetousness, which is idolatry"; 2 Corinthians 4:6-11: "...we have this treasure [of the light of God] in earthen vessels... *always carrying in the body the death of Jesus,* so that *the life of Jesus may also be manifested in our bodies...in our mortal flesh";* Philippians 3:8-11" "that I may gain Christ and *be found in Him...that I* may *know him* and *the power of his resurrection...becoming like him in his death,* that if possible *I may attain the resurrection from the dead."*

692 Matthew 16:24, Mark 8:34, Luke 9:23

cross...cannot be my disciple". [693] This theme is constantly repeated and explained by St. Paul, see the footnotes given in this chapter, as being *a key part of the Christian faith.)* The above passage continues: "If we live by the Spirit, let us also walk by the Spirit. *Let us have no self-conceit, no provoking of one another, no envy of one another."* [694] And again he said "I...could not address you as spiritual men, but as men *of the flesh,* as babes in Christ. I fed you with milk, not solid food, for you were not ready for it; and even yet you are not ready, *for you are still of the flesh. For while there is jealousy and strife among you, are you not of the flesh, and behaving like ordinary men?"* [695]

This makes it clear that intellectual assent to a set of beliefs is not the only requirement of a Christian: one has to grow in spiritual maturity in Christ, and learn to master the unruly, undisciplined, selfish, desires of "the flesh" (which basically means being able to love God and other people without being mainly concerned with oneself)—and without the power of God we could not do it.

It was in this context that St. Paul wrote about gaining mastery over one's physical self, like an athlete training for a race; [696] not because this was something that necessarily *earned us a reward,* as our salvation comes by the grace of God; but because we cannot *allow* ourselves to be ruled by the desires and impulses of *"the flesh,"* the animal part of us, as *"slaves to sin,"* [697] if we are to live *in Christ,* through the Holy Spirit within us, and let *God* rule our lives instead.

693　Luke 14:27

694　Galatians 5:16-26

695　I Corinthians 3:1-3. St. Paul compared *growing into spiritual maturity* with the journey from childhood to adulthood, e.g., 1 Corinthians 14:20: "Do not be children in your thinking...but in thinking be mature." (KJV: "in *understanding* be men"); 1 Corinthians 13:11: "when I was a child [I behaved like a child but] when I became a man, I gave up childish ways". We have to *grow out* of living in the "childish" sphere of spiritual immaturity, as if *the affairs of this world* were all-important, and put on *a new nature in the image of God* (Ephesians 4:22-23)

696　1 Corinthians 9:24-27

697　Romans 6:16-20; and v. 22: "But now that you have been set free from sin and have become *slaves of God...*"It is clear that St. Paul is not thinking of salvation just in terms of "being forgiven" but of *being changed* as well. For those for whom the idea of being "a slave to sin" doesn't resonate, think of the people who cannot control their "sexual compulsions", i.e., many serial adulterers, child molesters and rapists: are they not

St. Paul well summarized this conflict between "the flesh" and the Spirit, in saying that we reap what we sow, that "he who sows to his own flesh will from the flesh reap corruption; but he who sows to the Spirit *will from the Spirit reap eternal life".*[698]

To the Romans, he expressed his frustration with his constant battle to overcome the inherent temptations common to humanity: "I delight in the law of God, in my inmost self, but I see in my members another law at war with the law of my mind and making me captive to the law of sin which dwells in my members [i.e., in my natural self].... Who will deliver me from this body of death?...[but] Jesus Christ our Lord!")[699]

I am sure that he did not mean that "the flesh" is evil *in itself,* or *literally* "a body of death", but that is how his teaching often came to be understood, and I believe that that kind of thinking, (that "the flesh" was evil in itself)[700] lay behind the Gnostic heresy, and the Pelagian controversy discussed in the chapter on "Abiding in Christ".

It would have been simpler if it had been understood that *"the flesh" as God made it* has the potential for great good, but that, because human beings have been given free-will, sooner or later the basic animal instincts built into creation for its survival will conflict

---

"slaves" to their own physical desires? Paul's argument is: how can they be "slaves of God" if they are slaves of something else?

698 Galatians 6:7-8

699 Romans 7:22-25

700 The later Gnostic heresy saw "the spiritual", and the holiness of God, as being far removed from the material world, instead of the Christian idea of *God being reconciled with the world* through Christ. *(The Oxford Dictionary of the Christian Church* says (p.573): "The principal anti-Gnostic writers...insisted on the identy of the Creator...the reality of the earthly life of Jesus, esp. of the Crucifixion and Resurrection. Man needed redemption from *an evil will* rather than *an evil environment"* (italics mine). Perhaps in their efforts to fight the heresy of gnosticism and the idea of creation being evil, they may have put emphasis on man's *will* being evil, hence "original sin". My point is that the human being *as a creation* is not evil, but that the physical impulses necessarily built into the creation for its survival can come into conflict with the spiritual life *"in God",* where we have to move beyond the appetites and desires of "the flesh" and be more concerned with loving others than with gratifying the self. Thus it is not that man's *will* is inherently evil, per se, but that human beings *are subject to the temptations of the flesh* which can come into conflict with the demands of the spiritual life.)

with the demands of the spiritual life, and human beings succumb to temptation.

As St. Paul said, *how can people be slaves of God if they are, in effect, slaves of something else* (like sex, for example).[701]

I think that it is *in this sense* that St. Paul saw *the human race* as bringing evil into the world—not because *the flesh* is evil, or because we are tainted with original sin, but because the natural demands of the flesh are necessarily in conflict with the aspirations of the Spirit,[702] and it is when we give in to them inappropriately, and start to sin, that we are ourselves bringing sin and evil into our human situation.

In fact, St. Paul saw "the flesh" as being *holy*, when indwelt by the Holy Spirit as God intended it to be. He wrote: *"God's temple is holy, and that temple you are"*.[703] What he was warning against was letting animal lusts take over and defile that holiness: *"Do you not know that your bodies are members of Christ? Shall I therefore take the members of Christ and make them members of a prostitute? Never!"*[704]

When Jesus said "that which is born of the flesh is flesh, and that which is born of the Spirit is spirit",[705] I believe He meant *not* that "flesh" is intrinsically evil or cursed *in itself*, but just that it will not, by itself, transcend and go beyond this mortal life.[706]

Jesus was not contrasting good and evil, as I see it, but speaking factually about the physical and temporary as against the spiritual and eternal.

(Incidentally, although in any argument one cannot rely solely on any one verse in the Bible, it is worth noting, in the context of the Church's current obsession with sexual orientation and marriage, that all the Synoptic Gospels report Jesus as saying that, at the time of the

---

701 Romans 6:16-20

702 Colossians 3:2-3: *"Set your minds on things that are above, not on things that are on earth.* For you have died, [ie., your previous selfish, self-centered, life, *has been crucified with Christ]* and your life is [now] hid with Christ in God.." See Galatians 5:24 quoted earlier, and Romans 8:13: "if you live according to the flesh you will die, but if by the Spirit *you put to death the deeds of the body* you will live"; and Colossians 3:5

703 1 Corinthians 3:17

704 1 Corinthians 6:15

705 John 3:6

706 Romans 8:13: *"if you live according to the flesh you will die"* (see next page); Colossians 3:5: *"put to death* therefore *what is earthly in you:* fornication, impurity, passion, evil desire, and covetousness which is idolatry"

Resurrection, there will be "neither marrying nor giving in marriage":[707] in other words, *sex*—as opposed to love— is *physical, and of this world,* not the next.)

This is what St. Paul meant when he wrote: *"flesh and blood* cannot inherit the kingdom of God, nor does *the perishable inherit the imperishable...this perishable nature must put on the imperishable, and this mortal nature must put on immortality."*[708]

So how can any Christian maintain that the soul is immortal in its own right (the so-called "Christian Doctrine of Man")[709], when St. Paul is so explicit about "the flesh" being *perishable,* and *not immortal in its own right,* but rather needing to put on the immortality which it does not otherwise have, in order to attain the Kingdom of God?

If we are to go on into eternity with God, *we need to develop the spiritual part of us that will, in Christ, transform the purely human part of us and bring us to God.* While we can live out our human lives on this earth, as physical beings, we cannot transcend this human existence on earth, and continue to live on after it is over, without developing the spiritual faculty that enables us, sooner or later (even if only after death) to recognize and relate to God when we do come to see Him, so that we can *live in Him, in His eternal life and love,* after our mortal life is over (*"God gave us eternal life, and this life is in His Son"*[710]). We must be able to escape from *the corruption that is in the world because of passion* if we are to become *partakers of the divine nature.*[711] As St. Paul wrote to the Ephesians: "Put to death therefore what is earthly in you: fornication, impurity, passion, evil desire, and covetousness which is idolatry....put them all away: anger, wrath, malice, slander, and foul talk from your mouth. Do not lie to one another, seeing that *you have put off the old nature* with its practices *and have put on the new nature* which is being renewed *in knowledge after the image of its creator."*[712]

---

707   Matthew 22:30, Mark 12:25. Luke 20:34-35

708   1 Corinthians 15:50-53

709   see Glossary re. Annihilationism

710   1 John 5:11

711   Romans 6:5: *"... if we have been united with him in a death like his* [i.e., if we have "crucified" in ourselves the sinful passions of the flesh] *we shall certainly be united with him in a resurrection like His"* and   2 Peter 1:4: "that...you may escape from the corruption... in the world... and *become partakers of the divine nature".*

712   Ephesians 3:5-10

I think that the early Church, in its preoccupation with sin and punishment, may have been so distracted by the statement that *"by a man came death"*, [713] taking it as a literal curse, as it were, (because we are descended from Adam and Eve, and were thought to have inherited their guilt and sin), [714] that the second part of what St. Paul was saying in that passage was somewhat eclipsed: that *"in Christ* shall all be made alive": which does not mean just *being forgiven,* but being given *"life"*—eternal life—in God, through being *in Christ.*

The statement *"as in Adam all die, so also in Christ shall all be made alive"* [715] could well have been *just a mere statement of fact,* that human beings, "relying on the flesh alone", without God, do not, cannot, continue into eternity. It could well be rendered: *"in the flesh alone, all die;* [716] but *in God* we can *continue* to live, for ever." [717]

St. Paul was stressing the need to align ourselves *with God* through Christ, [718] and let His power and love transform our daily living, "sitting lightly" to the things of this world, [719] not becoming too absorbed by

---

713 1 Corinthians 15:21

714 I think passages like Romans 5:12-21 on the same theme ("one man's trespass led to condemnation for all men, so one man's act of righteousness leads to acquittal and life for all men") have been taken too literally by subsequent generations, who, concentrating on the *words* Paul used to express his message, thought more of the idea of "the inherited sin of Adam" than the message itself, which, I believe, in essence, was that set out above: that, though through *the flesh as typified by Adam,* comes *death* (note the Biblical reference to *"death"* again, rather than "hell"), nevertheless, *through Christ,* who, while also divine, was human too, we can find both forgiveness and *life.*

715 1 Corinthians 15:22

716 as in Romans 8:13: *"...if you live according to the flesh you will die,* but if by the Spirit you put to death the deeds of the body *you will live. "* (This is echoed in 1 John 2:15-17, see next footnote.)

717 1 John 2:15-17: "Do not love the world or the things in the world. If anyone loves the world, love for the Father is not in him. For all that is in the world, the lust of the flesh and the lust of the eyes and the pride of life, is not of the Father but is of the world. *And the world passes away, and the lust of it;* but he who does *the will of God abides for ever."*

718 Romans 12:2: *"Do not be conformed to this world but be transformed by the renewal of your mind..."*

719 I believe this explains such passages as 1 Corinthians 7, regarding sexual behaviour, and verses such as 29-30: "let those who have wives live as though they had none, [this does *not* mean not having conjugal sex, see verses 2-5 of that chapter], and those who

them,[720] so that eventually we become that spiritual and holy *new creation* [721] that God intended us to be; and, transcending this earthly life, can be with God, in His eternal love, for ever.

---

mourn as though they were not mourning, and those who rejoice as though they were not rejoicing, and those who buy as though they had no goods, and *those who deal with the world as though they had no dealings with it. For the form of this world is passing away"* [i.e. is transient and will not last, as opposed to what is eternal and will last for ever].

720 Remember, too, Jesus' warnings that *"where your treasure is, there will your heart be also"* (Matthew 6:21) and that "No one can serve two masters....You cannot serve God and Mammon" (Matthew 6:24)

721 2 Corinthians 5:17: "if anyone is *in Christ,* he [that person] is *a new creation".* The new translation saying that *"there is a new creation"* does not, to my mind, convey the same sense that the *person* is transformed.

CHAPTER 16

Misunderstanding the Athanasian Creed

A lot of our problems today arise from unexamined assumptions from the historical past. The Athanasian Creed reflects an assumption from earlier times about "being saved" which needs to be re-thought today when we are no longer burning "heretics" at the stake, opening as it does with the statement that one must hold "the Catholic faith" if one is not to *"perish eternally"*. This may be why, while it is contained in the *Anglican Book of Common Prayer,* reference to it is omitted from the new *Book of Alternative Services* of the Anglican Church of Canada (but, as a result, the ordinary person loses valuable teaching about *the Trinity).*

I try to show that misunderstandings of this Creed need to be separated from what is (or may be) eternally true, but we find it easier to disregard the difficulty altogether. I think that we *should* be able to qualify what we believe about "being saved", without at the same time discounting the faith in God the Trinity that that document professed. I believe one can both hold a strong faith in the Trinity and yet not to be seen to claim that anyone who differs from us will automatically forfeit "being saved" in the life hereafter.[722]

As *The Oxford Dictionary of the Christian Church* states:

> Since 1867 many efforts have been made in the C of
> E to have it removed from the service, or truncated,

---

722   as I believe some evangelicals do. Urging people to confess the faith *in order to avoid "being left behind"* in the final judgment, in itself an unworthy motive, appealing to self-interest rather than love of God, must involve people contemplating without a qualm the misfortune of those not so favoured, which is hardly a Christian attitude.

especial objection being made to the 'damnatory clauses' (vv. 2 and 42), but conservative opinion has generally held that, even if it may be considered desirable in the abstract that *certain expressions should be explained or retranslated,* in present circumstances any alteration would give the impression that something of the traditional faith was being surrendered; and in fact no alteration has been made. The BCP version, however, is in places inaccurate and misleading, partly because of mistranslation, and partly because the Reformers based their rendering on an inaccurate text. *In the Anglican Churches outside England its use in worship has been considerably restricted, or even abandoned* (italics mine). [723]

I think it is important that we do not lightly disregard documents simply because we may not always understand or agree with them. When the Bible was put together, its many editors did not choose between sometimes contradictory texts, but included them together, rather than risk loosing some truth that might later be found in them. Thus, although the Bible can be confusing, we still have access to truth from God through pondering what is in it. Similarly, the Athanasian Creed is part of the heritage of the western Church, and truth may still be found in it, as I believe my book shows. If it had not been in our traditional prayer book, and one of the foundation documents of our Church, I might never have thought about it so deeply, and the truths that I believe I have discovered might have remained obscure to me. There is no mention of it now, even as a reference document, in the new Anglican liturgy in Canada. This must surely be a warning against discarding statements of faith when possibly the fault may lie not so much in the underlying meaning of such a document as in our contemporary and superficial misunderstandings of it— misunderstandings which could be corrected in the future if the document were still officially available to ordinary people.

As I have said, thinking about the Athanasian Creed has led me to some of the conclusions set out in this book, and to believe that

---

723   *The Oxford Dictionary of the Christian Church,*   page 101.

this Creed, now in danger of becoming discredited, is closer to the truth than I had at first realized. I believe that this book is true to, and justifies, the Athanasian Creed, if one allows for the following two points:

(1) "the Catholic faith" is not the Roman Catholic Church or even Christianity itself, per se, if that is taken to be just *"followers of Jesus"*, but is the faith that the *One Great God who created the universe* is *also* a *Trinity of Persons* (to whom we can come through Christ in the present time). This was the faith which was professed "everywhere, at all times and in all places", the *original meaning of the word "catholic"*. In other words, "the Catholic faith" is basically about *"coming to union with God"* through Christ which is "our salvation", as I have tried to show: *in this life* I believe we come to God through "abiding in Christ", but I have also set out my belief that it may well be that this same One Great God, *the God Who is Love,* will *also,* one day, call others, those whom He chooses to be with Him *in the next,* even if they have not necessarily professed the Christian faith in this life, if He and they, when they finally meet at the end of time, so choose (see the next chapter on this subject, and the passage in Joel about "those whom the Lord calls"). I believe this Creed has more to do with *the nature of God* than *qualifications for salvation,* especially in view of the fact that the motive for writing it may well have been to counter implied teaching that "the Father alone is God." [724] This should deal with the narrow interpretation that the Creed is saying that if one is not a Roman Catholic—or even a Christian—one is automatically damned eternally. *I believe that its main purpose was to define the Trinity.*

(2) With regard to the "anathemas", although the references to "eternal fire" and people "perishing eternally" have become offensive to modern ears, I think this Creed has long been misunderstood, just as the Biblical teaching it is based on has been misunderstood. I see it not as a curse on unbelievers (the mercy of God on whom He will have mercy[725] being a tenet of this book), but rather as stating

---

724   see earlier discussion in the Chapter on the Trinity
725   Exodus 33:19

as a fact what I believe to be true, that eternal life, continuing to live for ever, is *only* to be found *in union with the eternal God,* however that may come about; and that, if we do *not* somehow, at some time, even if only after death, *willingly* come to be in a close relationship of love with that God, we will *not* continue to exist for ever, but *will* "perish" ("perish" in the sense of ceasing to exist rather than "going to hell", because that is what "perish" means): perishing *not as "punishment"* for intellectual beliefs held in this lifetime, but because eternal life can only be found *"in God,"* not apart from Him. (See the many references in this this book to "perishing", and "eternal fire" being *a metaphor* for the blazing fire of God's *eternal righteousness* destroying all evil at the end of time, rather than literal flames tormenting individual people for ever). In fact it should be obvious that it is not *possible* to "perish eternally" in that sense, because, *if one perishes, one ceases to exist,* one cannot keep on perishing on an ongoing basis for ever: the words can only mean "perishing once and for all, *ceasing to exist for all eternity".*

My concern about the modern discarding of this historic Creed has been two-fold. I believe that its basic teaching about the nature of God the Trinity is so important, for present and future generations, that we cannot afford to disregard it; and, hoping to restore the credibility of this document, and help those who have been offended by what they thought it was saying, I wanted to correct the bizarre ideas mistakenly derived from it which have done so much to damage Christianity.

CHAPTER 17

The traditional belief that one must be a Christian "to be saved"

Christianity's historic claim to be "the only true religion" ("without which one cannot be saved"), is increasingly being treated as if it were an embarrassment in dealing with other world religions, and we have almost reached the point where it is seen as "counter-productive" or impolite to talk about the significance of the Christian faith in today's multicultural world. Some people want to take "Christ" out of "Christmas" for that reason.

A way out of this impasse would be my suggestion that we can still continue to make our unique claim as Christians, without at the same time necessarily seeming to deny "eternal salvation" to others.

Jesus' statement that no one comes to God except through Him [726] has contributed much towards Christians' intolerance of non-believers, but I believe that is because it has been understood almost exclusively in the context of *future salvation* rather than *present reality.*

In the same chapter, Jesus was teaching His disciples about our finding union with God *in this life* through *"abiding in Him",* something which, without Him, would indeed not be possible while we were still on earth *("in that day* [when the Holy Spirit is given] *you will know* that *I am in my Father, and you in me, and I in you").* He was talking about the Holy Spirit dwelling *with us* (verse 16), and being *in us,* (verse 17). The account continues: "if a man loves me, he will keep my word, and [my Father and I]....will come to him and make our home with him."

Surely He was talking *in the context of the present time:* if someone

---

726   John 14:6   (and verses 16-17)

keeps the commandments (to love), *while living on this earth,* God the Trinity will be in him and with him. If this is so, that *one verse,* about no one coming to the Father except through Him, should not be stretched to imply that He was necessarily excluding *for eternity* all who do not accept Him *in this life.* For what it is worth, He did not say "no one *will* come", or "no one *can* come", but "no one *comes*", in *the present tense,* and *that* is what I believe Jesus was talking about. I do not think that that one verse should necessarily be taken as referring to *the eternal future of other people*: an idea, incidentally, which conflicts with Jesus' teaching about God being *love.* If that verse is taken, as it so often has been, as only referring to *the future,* forever excluding all those who did not accept Christ in this life, for whatever reason, it results in a downplaying of the Christian religion, because it is seen as embarrassing in our efforts to "get on" with people of other faiths: in fact, the antithesis of the "love" that Jesus has required of us.[727]

I think that the idea of Jesus being *"the only way"* to God has been ill-defined and misunderstood.

I believe that Jesus *is indeed* the only way to God, in the ultimate sense; that *in Him,* Divine Love, incarnate here on earth in history, was reconciling the world to Himself,[728] so that, *in Christ and through Him,* we can eternally come to God. I do not believe, however, that it necessarily has to follow that our salvation has to depend on making "the right commitment" *in this lifetime,* and that "it will be too late" when we meet Him face to face at the end of time.

The latter idea is driving many fundamentalists to urge people not to risk being "left behind" (at the Second Coming of Christ), but, if one's only concern is for one's own self-preservation, without love of God or neighbour, seen almost as a legal contract, or a right that has been bestowed, it would suggest that such a person is ill-equipped to assume that he or she is "saved"[729] while someone else who may be more

---

727 Matthew 22:37-40

728 2 Corinthians 5:18-19: "... *in Christ God was reconciling the world to himself...*"

729 even St. Paul, though he was an early authority in the Church, had the humility to be aware that it was still possible for him to fall from grace if he did not continue to walk the way of the Cross with Christ: referring to athletes exercising self-control in all things, in order to win a race, he prayed that he might similarly be able to "subdue" his body, i.e., the temptations of it, "lest after preaching to others I myself should be disqualified" (or, in the older translations, "a castaway") (1 Corinthians 9:24-27)

intimately acquainted with *Love* is not, *simply because of the timing of that person's recognition of God as Trinity.* The reaction of many people to the controversy about "Jesus being the only way to God" has been either to discount Jesus or the Bible or both.

While we need to profess unashamedly what we believe, about the divinity of Christ, the basic integrity of the Bible, and the love and mercy of God, and come to Him in this life through Christ for ourselves, I believe that we cannot, must not, judge what may or may not happen to other people in the unfolding of eternity. Jesus Himself commanded us not to judge.[730] Do we so lightly disregard His words when it suits us to do so? Judging others and deciding their fate is God's prerogative, and we usurp it at our peril.

It is my belief that, however the other great world religions may fit into God's scheme of things (Jesus said "in My Father's house are many rooms," and "I have other sheep, that are not of this fold"),[731] it may well be that, in the end, many people of other faiths will recognize, in the great Trinitarian God of the Christian tradition, *(the God who is Love),* when they finally meet Him, that same great God of the Universe that they have, in good faith, been worshipping all along, in their own way; and that, eventually, to use His own words again, "there shall be one flock, one shepherd",[732] even—*and this is important —* even if that does not happen until we all reach the world to come.

Just as St. Paul insisted that the Jewish Messiah was not just for the Jews only, but *for the Gentiles also,* drawing on the Jews' own Scriptures for this belief,[733] so "Christianity," *in its turn,* may not have a monopoly on salvation: our Scripture teaches us that Christ died

---

730 Matthew 7:1: "Judge not, that you be not judged"

731 John 14:2 and John 10:16

732 John 10:16

733 e.g. Romans 3:29-30:" is God the God of Jews only? *Is he not the God of Gentiles also?* [could we not substitute 'is God the God of *professing Christians* only?'] *Yes, of Gentiles also, since God is one",* supported by quotations in Romans 15:8-12; Genesis 12:3, the covenant with Abraham "*'by you all the families of the earth shall bless themselves'"* and Psalm 105:41-42; Isaiah 49:6: " 'I will give you as a light to the nations, *that my salvation may reach to the end of the earth' ";* Isaiah 60:3: "nations shall come to your light"; Isaiah 66:18: " 'I am coming to gather all nations and tongues' "; Zechariah 2: 8--11: "For thus said the Lord of hosts...'I come, and I will dwell in the midst of you, says the Lord. *And many nations* shall join themselves to the Lord *in that day,*

"for the sins of the whole world". [734] We cannot ignore one verse of the Bible, and then over-emphasise another.

Although one must not lean too heavily on any one verse of Scripture in support of a particular argument, as it is the import of the whole of it that counts, it does not hurt to remind those people who *do* attribute supreme importance to one verse of their own choosing, (e.g., Jesus' saying "no one comes to the Father, but by me"), [735] that there *are other* verses in the Bible which are equally significant. St. Paul, in his Epistle to the Romans, was quoting the prophet Joel when he wrote that *"every one* who calls upon the name of the Lord *will be saved".* This is the same passage that was also quoted by St. Peter on the Day of Pentecost. [736]

It can be argued, therefore, that a passage from the Old Testament which was quoted by two of the greatest apostles, on two separate occasions, appearing in the New Testament twice, must be important, and that we are therefore entitled to give it credence.

The prophet Joel in that passage was talking about *the end of time,* not the end of any one particular individual's human life, when he wrote:

> *The sun shall be turned to darkness, and the moon to blood,*
> before the great and terrible day of the Lord comes.
> *And it shall come to pass* [presumably, from the context,
> AFTER that day has come] *that ALL who call upon the*
> *Name of the Lord [at that time] shall be delivered....*

and the same verse continues "among the survivors shall be *those whom the Lord calls."* [737] This agrees with what is written in the Book of Exodus: the God of the Old Testament saying to Moses : "I will be

---

and *shall be my people;* and *I will dwell in the midst of you' "* (see Psalm 34:22 & Revelation 7:9)

734   1 John 2:1-2: "we have an advocate with the Father, Jesus Christ the righteous, and he is the expiation for our sins, *and not for ours only, but also for the sins of the whole world"*

735   John 14:6

736   Romans 10:13, and Acts 2:16-21; both based on Joel 2:32

737   Joel 2:31-32. Note also John 5:21-26, Jesus talking about "eternal life" and, in that context, "[passing] from death to life," said "the Son gives life *to whom he will"* and "he who...*believes him who sent me,* has eternal life"

gracious *to whom I will* be gracious, and will show mercy *on whom I will show mercy.*"[738]

Who are Christians to say that it would then (at the end of time) "be too late" for someone "to be saved"? Who would have the presumption to tell God who He should have mercy on (and, by implication, who He should condemn)? The parable of the labourers in the vineyard does need to be remembered in this context.[739]

I believe that these passages support the view that one does not necessarily *have* to convert to Christianity *before* death. What happens *after* death is up to God.

In addition, it could be argued that, because Joel was addressing God's own people, the Jews, and talking about "the Lord", who is their Lord, in their own prophetic writings, the prophecy would also apply to them, even if "the Lord" did turn out to be the Trinitarian God after all—at the very least, in the sense that if, in that final day, long after any given individual's physical death, "after the sun had been turned into darkness, and the moon into blood", i.e., the world as we know it had been dissolved, they then called on His Name at that time, or He called them, they *would* "be delivered".

Similarly, there are passages in the Old Testament like "The Lord redeems the life of his servants; *none of those who take refuge in him will be condemned*".[740] Are those Jewish people who truly are His servants to be denied that refuge because they did not come to understand the Christian faith *in this lifetime,* and because some Christians are of the legalistic opinion that that disqualifies them for ever?

I believe that the Trinitarian God is the same God whom *the whole world* will eventually encounter one day, but it does not *necessarily* follow that it will automatically be too late for those people who only come to recognize that One, Trinitarian, God, when they meet Him at the end of time, to call to Him then — or *for Him to call them, if He so wishes.*[741]

---

738   Exodus 33:19

739   Matthew 20:1-16: the master of the vineyard, after being generous to those who only came at the end of the day, asked the others who begrudged this generosity: "Am I not allowed to do what I choose with what belongs to me?"

740   Psalm 34:22

741   e.g. Revelation 7:9-15: "...behold, *a great multitude* which no man could number, *from every nation, from all tribes and peoples and tongues* [acknowledging and worshipping God]"

It would, I think, be best, in this context, to think of God as *Love,* which we believe He is [742] *(albeit a Trinity of Persons between whom love flows),* so that, in discussions about eternity, we do not put so much emphasis on "being *a Christian",* in the sense of *"the Christians being right after all",* which carries a hurtful and offensive message to non-Christians, and which has historically been a source of much pain and tragedy.

If God is indeed *a Trinity* of *Persons between whom love flows,* it makes sense to think more in terms of Jesus' being *the revelation of that Trinity* in history, which some people may, historically, in all good faith, have been taught from their earliest days, by people they respect, to question or deny—a mistake, perhaps, but not a sin.

We need to remember, too, that Christians bear much of the responsibility for the fact that the world has not seen in them the love of God which they were supposed to radiate (nor has the faith been explained in terms of God's love). Christians have much to answer for!

Let us think, rather, in terms of the call *(whenever we answer it)* as being *the call of the eternal God, to eternal life, in His eternal love:* to live for ever in and with a God who has love *in Himself*—a God who may be a Trinity of Persons, but Who is *also* Love. *Professing* Christianity *in this life* may not be the *only* way to come to God the Trinity *in the end.* Being "in Christ" is a most special way of being with God in this life, which should not be rejected just because some people have not understood that this is what Christianity is all about; but neither should we assume that those who do not take the Christian Way in this life will not "be saved" in the eternal sense when they see God as He really is, and finally understand what the historical Church has so tragically failed to convince them of. I would put it, rather, that they may have missed some special opportunities in this life. But that is not the same as assuming they are condemned for ever.

And people's opinions may change when, finally, they actually come to see God, after death. As St. Paul said, when we see God "face to face", at that time we "shall know as we are known" or, in another translation, "[we] shall understand fully, even as [we] have been fully

---

742   see all the many texts on this, but, particularly, for a blunt statement, 1 John 4:16: *"God is love,* and he who abides in love abides in God, and God abides in him."

understood."[743] We may then all come to see things differently from the way we did before, and I think that, when that happens, God will meet us in generosity and love. It is not up to us to impose *our* time limits or conditions on God as to who will, and who will not, "be saved", or when or how.[744] ("Am I not allowed to do what I choose with what belongs to me? Or do you begrudge my generosity?")[745] Jesus also said that anyone "who speaks a word against *the Son of Man*" may *be forgiven*; it is surely blasphemy against *the Holy Spirit* (the very essence of what *God Is*) that will *not* be forgiven.[746] (This would be, not because God is unforgiving, but because forgiveness cannot be received when the origin of it is denied). This supports my belief that it may well be possible for someone who did not believe in *"the Son of Man" in this lifetime* still to come to God in the end, if that person finally recognizes and accepts *the Holy Spirit of God*, the very essence of the God of Love (the God who is *also* God the Holy Trinity), when they finally encounter Him, and finally come to understand.

The idea of "being saved" runs through the Bible. It is what redemption is all about. The Jewish prophets preached on the issues of sin and judgment and redemption, calling the people to repentance, and a change in their ways, calling them back to God and His goodness. The early Church struggled with the issue of "unless you are circumcised according to the custom of Moses, you cannot be saved",[747] but worked out, after some struggles, that salvation was through faith in Christ and not through taking on all the requirements of the Jewish religion. The Church of the Middle Ages in particular agonized over the question of "being saved", and Indulgences were sold until Martin Luther precipitated the Reformation by his objection to the principle behind them, preaching that we "are saved" by our faith in Christ.

---

743   1 Corinthians 13:12

744   see discussion of Joel 2:32 which says that "among the survivors shall be *those whom the Lord calls*"

745   Parable of the labourers in the vineyard, Matthew 20:15

746   see Glossary for my definition of what I think is probably "the sin against the Holy Spirit" (Luke 12:10)

747   Acts 15:1

Perhaps the historical belief of the Christian Church (that "only Christians will be saved") is a re-run of the controversies of the early Church, where some thought that only Jewish Christians "qualified" for salvation, and St. Paul insisted that salvation was also available for the Gentiles. [748] Similarly, while I believe that Christians are right to maintain that there is only one God, and that it is to that (Trinitarian) God that all must one day come to be judged, nevertheless perhaps we are being presumptuous to assume that that decision about recognizing God as Trinity *must* be made *in this lifetime,* as if God were not eternal, as if after death would be *"too late".* Perhaps Christians of later generations have fallen into the same self-righteous trap as some in the early Church, regarding non-Christians as being as much "beyond the pale" as the Gentiles were thought to be by the Jewish Christians of earlier days. [749]This would explain a lot of the tragedy of our history.

As the major thrust of this book is the subject of union with God through Christ, through the Holy Spirit, in the present time, I wanted to "clear the decks", as it were, by saying that I am not one of those who say "this way or else...", because I do not think that union with God through Christ can be coerced by threats: nor should it be. I think that our apparent obsession about "being saved" (or *not* "being saved") has been counter-productive. I believe that God is greater and more loving and more merciful than we, with our limited minds, can possibly imagine, and we should have more trust in His love, and His care for all His people.

I think that this tendency to think in terms that *"only Christians will be saved"* (implying that one *has to be* "a Christian" *in this lifetime* "for it to count", although I do not see why physical death should arbitrarily impose that deadline if God and the person concerned are able to be reconciled in the end), was, I believe, sustained over the centuries by misunderstandings of the Athanasian Creed, although

---

748 Romans 3:29-30: "Is God the God of Jews only? Is he not the God of Gentiles also? Yes, of Gentiles also, since God is one"

749 I think people need to be reminded that the mere fact of assuming that "one is saved oneself, and other people are not" carries the inherent spiritual danger of the sins of self-righteousness and pride condemned by Jesus in the parables of the Prodigal Son and the two men who went down to the Temple to pray ((Luke 15:11-32 and Luke 18:9-14).

probably, over time, this became more of an inherited *assumption* on people's part than an individually thought-out analysis of that Creed. I believe that this assumption (that "only Christians will be saved") was accentuated and aggravated at the time of the Reformation, when the Puritan element of Christianity which was trying to stream-line Christian belief into a more disciplined form, as it were, began to take on an even more rigid application of this belief.

But Christ died "for the sins of the whole world",[750] not just one select group. As *The Oxford Dictionary of the Christian Church* states (under "Redemption"):

> ...The theologians of the Reformation claimed to return to the teaching of St. Paul. They denied the idea of Redemption as a restoration to Original Righteousness and, consequently, the possibility of human co-operation with grace *other than by faith alone,* [italics mine], and placed the exclusive emphasis on the forgiveness of sin and justification by imputation of the righteousness of Christ.

> Through the teaching of J. Calvin and, later, of C. Jansenius, the view that Redemption extends only to the predestined was advocated by a number of Protestant and Catholic theologians in the 16th and 17th [centuries]. It was pronounced heretical by Innocent X in the constitution 'Cum Occasione' (1653). Later, the proposition that Christ died for all the faithful, *but for the faithful alone* [italics mine], (pro omnibus et solis fidelibus), was also condemned by Alexander VIII (1690).

> The universality of Redemption, taught already in the NT (eg. 1 John 2:2) *["he is the expiation for our sins, and not for ours only but also for the sins of the whole world"]* was thus safe-guarded, without, on the other hand, prejudicing the fact that its actual application

---

750   1 John 2:2: "[Christ] is the expiation for our sins, and not for ours only [i.e., *not just for 'us Christians']* but also for the sins of the whole world."

does not extend to the damned, nor, as Origen believed, to the fallen angels. [751]

In case someone has a problem with the last few words of the above quotation, my interpretation of what is being said is that it is referring to what is *"irrevocably evil"*, as opposed to, for example, honest followers of one of the other great world religions, or people who have been confused and put off Christianity by unfortunate experiences with some of the people in the churches, or through sheer misunderstanding of what the faith is really all about, who I do not think come into that category at all.

We need to distinguish between "raw evil", on the one hand, and what, for want of a better term, might be called "theological mistakenness", if, indeed, it is that, on the other. Even when people may have sinned greatly in their lifetimes, I believe that God may be gracious enough to forgive us, even on the other side of death, if the sinner, on seeing God, truly repents of the past, and genuinely repudiates all evil: and, of course, only God can be the judge of that.

The idea of *having* to accept Christ *before death*, as I have said above, when I was quoting the prophet Joel, is, I think, an unwarranted limiting of the power of God to do as He wills—the God who has more love than we do. I want to challenge the complacency of those who think that *they* are "saved" and that others are not, within definitions that they themselves have determined. We should have more humility than that: and perhaps remember the Biblical prophecies such as: "all the ends of the earth shall...turn to the Lord; and all the families of the nations shall worship before him" [752] and "to [Him] every knee shall bow...." [753]

How this may come about is not our problem but God's. What we do have to do is to think out for ourselves, with God's help, what the truth is as we can attain to it, and live it out in our own lives, striving always for the highest ideals of love and honesty, and being ready, when appropriate, to give a reasonable account of it to others, without forcing

---

751 F.L. Cross, editor, and F.L. Cross and E.A. Livingstone, editors of the revised second edition of *The Oxford Dictionary of the Christian Church*. Oxford: Oxford University Press, 1958, 1974, 1983.

752 Psalm 22:27

753 Isaiah 45:23, quoted in Philippians 2:10

it upon them, or trying to manipulate them in any way, especially with talk of "being saved"; and we do need to think, too, more clearly about what we actually *mean* by "being saved".

Some fundamentalist Christians, especially Pentecostal ones, equate *"being born in the Spirit"* with *"being saved"*, as if to say, when one has a conversion experience and comes to believe in Christ *as a newly-experienced reality*, one is *at that moment* and for ever *"saved."*[754] This is both true and yet, at the same time, *"not the whole story."* Jesus said "one cannot enter the kingdom of God without being born of water and Spirit. *What is born of the flesh is flesh, and what is born of the Spirit is spirit."*[755] This confirms my belief that life lived merely as "flesh" is perishable, as all flesh must be, and that to come to God one must be "born of the Spirit," as a vital first step, and *live* in the Spirit, through abiding in Christ, rooted and grounded in love,[756] in order to transcend this earthly life, *in Him*. As St. Paul tried to teach the early Christians, an enthusiastic conversion experience was only a first step: at first they were "babes in Christ...still of the flesh;" he said *"while there is jealousy and strife among you, are you not of the flesh and behaving like ordinary men?"*[757] He urged them to *grow* in the spiritual life, and be mature in their thinking,[758] and hinted that it *was* possible to fall away from God if one continued to live in the worldly sphere and not in the spiritual one with God: and thus in the end not "be saved" after all.[759]

Some people seem to think of "heaven" as some kind of lovely garden and often seem to forget that God is part of the scene, that without Him it would not *be* heaven. If we can think of God as Our Father, even if we have never known in this life what the ideal of fatherhood or a happy family life could be like, perhaps we can try to imagine what it might be like to be *"going home,"* at the end of this

---

754 what has been described as "the doctrine of assurance", see Glossary: see also the foot-note in this chapter re. people described as "enemies of the cross of Christ", whose "end is destruction", whose "god is the belly", and the fact that it is believed that St. Paul was talking about people who *professed to be Christians* (Philippians 3:18-19)

755 John 3:5-6

756 Ephesians 3:17

757 1 Corinthians 3:1-3

758 1 Corinthians 14:20

759 1 Corinthians 9:27 "...lest after preaching to others, I myself should be disqualified" (or, KJV, "a castaway")

earthly life, in the most wonderful sense, in the way in which we should like it to be: to be part of the family where we really belong, to be at last where we are really loved: to be with God, for all eternity. If we are dealing with a God who created so complex a universe, surely we do not have to worry about the logistics of *where "heaven" is,* because we can trust that He will somehow provide an environment where we can recognize Him and each other, and live in the love we have so often not found in this life. It is not realistic to believe that, just because we do not actually know "where heaven is", it cannot exist. This is a spin-off from the days when people thought heaven was in the sky, and hell in the bowels of the earth, and, now that modern science has enlightened us in our understanding of the physical universe, we pride ourselves in believing there can be no such place as heaven (or hell). With regard to the latter, I do not believe it exists as a permanent state, because of apostolic teaching about eventual spiritual death, but I certainly believe that "heaven" is to be with God, wherever God is, in the next phase of our existence. I may not know at present how or where that may be, but I do know that, just as our family pets do not understand nuclear physics, for example, so it is possible for things to exist that are beyond one person's (or one animal's) comprehension, and that they continue to exist, even if we do not understand them.

One problem that people have confided in me, with regard to the subject of forgiveness, is that "heaven" would not *be* "heaven" if someone they had had trouble with was there too. I think the answer to that is to realize that the person concerned would have changed, as we ourselves may be changed, by the time we all get to "heaven" (or they/we wouldn't be there!), so that the problems we had on earth would no longer apply. Sometimes I think that the only way in which someone with a stubborn problem might change would be for God Himself to explain it to them at the end of time: and that would indeed be "judgment": but it does not necessarily follow, to my mind, that that "judgment" would automatically be followed by either refusal to forgive and dispatch to "hell" on the one hand, if that person was then truly penitent and changed; or, on the other hand, that person being allowed to continue as they were on earth to cause distress to others in "heaven", wherever that may be. In fact, I think one of the joys of "heaven" may be in that final "changing" which we discover in ourselves and others, and the joyful reconciliation that follows. Perhaps that is the Christian advantage: that we can—or could—enjoy a foretaste of it here, without waiting for the next life. Is that not what Jesus meant by saying "the Kingdom of God" has come near to us in the present time? [760]

I hope that my way of stating the faith will be easier to accept, which is that Jesus was, and is, part of God the Trinity, but that *that need not continue to be seen as a barrier* to our relations with other people in God's world, *if* the Christian faith is understood in the way that I am suggesting, and if the emphasis for the moment is not on "Christianity" per se, but on *the nature of the One God Who is Love.* The fact that God is Love, to my mind, *does* necessitate His being *also a Trinity of Persons between whom love flows,* but we need not for the moment stress that *"faith in Jesus" in this lifetime* —with an over-emphasis on the historical man—is the "be-all-and end-all" of knowing God in the infinite future. This is not the same as saying that "there are many roads to God", as if there were many gods, and everyone will eventually "be saved" regardless. [761] I believe that *God is Who He is,* (as in *I AM who I AM),* [762] whatever we may think about Him in this lifetime, and that, although people may have different ideas of that reality while living on this earth, it is up to them whether, at the end of time, they have enough love in them, enough recognition of Love when they see the Source and Origin of it, that they finally recognize and accept Him as He is —I believe *a Trinity of Persons between whom love flows.* This is where the recent over-emphasis on "the historical Jesus" has been counter-productive in our dealings with other people.

In today's modern world, where thought structures have so changed, that most people no longer go to church, or think about God, or are afraid of hell, "being saved" is now, for the most part, the terrain of fundamentalist Christians, and I think that their narrow definition of it (that they are "saved", and other people aren't) has made the situation worse. Such an attitude carries with it the offensive implication, which civilised people are now trying to move away from, that anyone who is of another faith (including the Jews, God's own original people) will automatically be rejected by Him because they are not "Christian". I make

---

760   Luke 10:9: "The Kingdom of God has come near"

761   see Glossary re. "universalism"

762   Exodus 3:14

no such exclusive claim. Who knows how the Creator of the Universe will relate to His own creation when this life is over, and who would dare to tell Him what He must and must not do with His own! Is that not what the parable of the labourers in the vineyard was trying to tell us? [763]

We live in a century where anti-semitism reached such terrible proportions at the time of Nazi Germany that the Christian churches are, rightly, deeply ashamed of their role in perpetuating the idea that "the Jews killed the Son of God"—to the point where it has become easier to say that Jesus was *not* the Son of God, than to continue to preach the Gospel! Blaming others, especially the Jews, is indeed a sin of the historical Church, which does need to be atoned for, but not at the cost of denying the divinity of Christ. We have to stop allocating blame. The point of the Gospel is that Jesus loved enough to forgive and go on loving, and wanted us to do the same. If we were *really* Christians, we would not be blaming "the Jews" for anything, but remembering that "he was wounded for *our* transgressions, bruised for *our* iniquities...*he makes himself an offering* for sin[764] ....he bore the sin of many and made intercession [for us all]." [765]

I think history proves, over and over again, that the Christian faith has often not been properly taught or understood. I think we need to look at, and possibly re-define, what we mean by "being saved", as a major problem has resulted from an over-simplistic understanding of what "being saved" is all about. It has not only embarrassed Christians in their dealings with people of other faiths, but it has been a cause of distress to many who cannot "buy into" what they have mistakenly understood the Christian faith to be, further fuelling their rejection of it by that expression?" Is it just about escaping hell-fire so that we can roam through sweet gardens in heaven, or is it much more than that, being close to, at-one with, God, in a wonderful way? I believe that Jesus was talking about *at-one-ment with God: now,* through Him, for

---

763 Matthew 20:1-16

764 see footnote in the chapter on the Atonement re. the original Hebrew being slightly different: this is based on the RSV and Vulgate

765 Isaiah 53: 5, 10, 12. Re. v.12: "He bore the sin of many, and made intercession *for the transgressors."* I think it is fair to paraphrase this to say that He made intercession *"for us all"*. Verse 5 points out that *we ourselves* are among that number - "He was wounded for *our* transgressions." In the context itself, it can hardly be alleged that "it was all someone else's fault," i.e., *the fault of "the Jews",* as has historically been the case.

those who are fortunate enough to find that Way *in this lifetime,* (and especially so that God can work through them in this world);[766] but *also,* I believe, *forever, for all His people, whoever they may be, who turn to Him at the end of time*—what else did He mean by saying: "I have other sheep, that are not of this fold; *I must bring them also...so there shall be one flock, one shepherd"* ?[767]

If God is *Love,* I believe that He may eventually accept, even if only after death, those *who have lived with Love all their lives* but may not have professed the Christian faith in this lifetime, *if, when they see God, they accept Him as He is,* even if that means accepting God as Trinity as well as Love (a Trinity of which Christ is part), and *seek to be reconciled with Him.*[768] (This is not to be confused with "universalism", which is the belief that *everybody* will *"be saved"* regardless: see glossary). I believe that the statement that "eternal life" is [only] "in His Son" can still be applicable for them, because, if God is Trinity, being reconciled with God must necessarily entail accepting Christ. Our understanding of God may change when we finally come to see God *as He is.*[769]

It should be noted that, when Jesus spoke of "the sin against the Holy Spirit",[770] He specifically said that "everyone who speaks a word against *the Son of Man* [ie. Jesus Himself] *will be forgiven"* so it could well be argued that someone who had not been convinced *in this lifetime* of the truth of the Christian faith would *not necessarily* be condemned for ever *just for that reason, if* reconciliation of that person with God *the Trinity* was possible in the end, and God so willed. What will *not* be able to be overcome and forgiven is the refusal or inability to recognize or be reconciled with the Spirit of the Eternal God (God the Trinity) when that encounter takes place (as it did on the occasion when Jesus said made that statement).

---

766 John 15:5: "I am the vine, you are the branches. He who abides in me, and I in him, he it is that bears much fruit, for apart from me you can do nothing."

767 John 10:16

768 Note that some in the early Church thought salvation was reserved only for the Jews, not the Gentiles, and St. Paul opposed this way of thinking; I think Christianity has sometimes fallen into the same trap of exclusiveness, concentrating more on having "faith in *Jesus" in this life* than on eventual *eternal* reconciliation with *God the Trinity.*

769 1 John 3:2

770 Luke 12:10

I believe that it is *the inability to relate to the essence of God,* and understand *Love* and be loving *(because God is love)* that will pose the insuperable problem, rather than the question of whether one "believed in Jesus" in this lifetime.

In the meantime, Christians need to show the light of Christ to the world, and can proclaim the Gospel in terms of declaring who we believe God is and what we believe He is like, and warn the world of the very real danger of eternally *"perishing"* for those who live lives of selfishness, violence and hatred and do not know what it is to love, regardless of their religious affiliation, without specifically condemning individuals from other religions who may still come, in the end, to the God of love (and Trinity, of which Christ is part). As I have tried to show in this book, this is not "our call", there is Scriptural justification for "leaving it to God", and Jesus told us not to judge.[771]

Regarding the fact that it has traditionally been believed that one *must* "accept Christ" *in this lifetime, before death,* in order to "be saved", even in New Testament times St. Paul was reassuring people that the love of a faithful husband or wife would "cover" the unbelieving partner—the implication being that it was the *love* of the believer that would accomplish this.[772] So, if an exception can be made in such cases, I believe God can make other exceptions based on love *if and when He so wishes:* that judgment is not ours. Salvation remains through Christ. Conversely merely claiming "to be a Christian" is not enough *by itself* to be a "guarantee" of "eternal life": St. Paul warned that people *whose minds were set on earthly things,* "whose god is the belly," were doomed to destruction, even though *it is believed that these were people who professed to be Christians.*[773]

---

771   Matthew 7:1, Luke 6:37

772   1 Corinthians 7:14

773   Philippians 3:18; and note the fact that both *the Oxford Annotated Version* of the RSV (p.1426) and *Peake's Commentary on the Bible* (p.988) suggest that St. Paul was referring to professing Christians; see too   discussion of Protestant misunderstandings of the Atonement and the fact that what is required of us is *love* and *"life in the Spirit"* (see the glossary re. "the doctrine of assurance"). Note, too, Jesus' saying *"Not every one that says to me 'Lord, Lord' shall enter the kingdom of heaven,* but he who does the will of my Father... [and the will of God is that we should *love*]. On that day* [so we are talking about the end of time] many will say to me '..did we not do many mighty works in your name?' And then [I will say] *'I never knew you' "* Matthew 7:21-23

A recent funeral that I was asked to take confirmed to me my belief that life concentrated only on living *"in the flesh"* would surely, in accordance with the Biblical teaching quoted extensively in this book, lead to one's *"perishing" on an eternal basis,* although I *also* believe that God, in His love and mercy, may give someone "a second chance" when that person finally sees God at the point of death.

I am still haunted by the old lady's lament that she did not think that she was good enough for heaven, but *"she was not bad enough for hell".* The funeral I was asked to take (by another woman, without my previous knowledge) was for someone who had spent her life in doing "good works" and loving her family, and yet who had become estranged from the Church, to the point where the grown children arranging the service flinched at the idea of anything "religious". She certainly was not "bad enough for hell", whatever a fundamentalist Christian might think of the situation: *yet surely, if "heaven" means "union with God," it would therefore follow that she could not qualify for it unless she turned to God, at least after death, and repented of her life without Him.* (I believe that originally her intentions were good, in that she had given Bibles to her adolescent grandchildren; I suspect that, somewhere along the line, "the Church", generically speaking, had failed to give her a sufficient grasp of the faith that she could adequately understand it herself, and impart that understanding to others.)

In saying that it is my belief that God, in generosity and love, may possibly give people "a second chance" when they come to see Him at the time of death, I agree that, *if at that time she felt no more desire to be with God than she had felt during her lifetime,* then presumably she *would* be *as perishable, on an eternal basis, as the worldly things that she had so interested herself in while on this earth.* In such a case I see my role as chaplain as commending to God's mercy a soul who did not understand, who had been "let down" by the ineptitude of the several churches which the family had experienced over the years, churches which had never succeeded in convincing them of the importance of knowing and loving God, and bringing up children to do likewise. The rest is "up to God". But she did ask for me to take her funeral service, knowing that I was an Anglican priest; perhaps in doing that it may have been her first, blind and faltering perhaps, turning back to God. I do not see that it is up to me to condemn her because she did not belong to a Christian church or bring up her children to have any understanding of the faith.

Jesus called His disciples to become "fishers of men" [774] and told St. Peter to feed and care for His sheep in the tradition of the Good Shepherd; [775] presumably bringing back to Him the lost and the strayed is "part of the job". And to the eternal God, I imagine that the thin line between this life and the next would not present an insuperable problem, if it was His will to forgive and heal someone in spite of what may have transpired in the past. As I say, I can only commit someone to the mercy of God, and leave the rest to Him. However, I would imagine that serial murderers, and people involved in child pornography and the sexual abuse of children, who see other people just as objects to be tormented for their pleasure, would not be condemned just on the basis of "being awarded bad points for bad behaviour", as a human court might impose corresponding sentences, as much as on the basis that they had no understanding of empathy or compassion, and thus nothing in common with God. This has to do with a state of sin, as opposed to individual sins: and would move traditional thinking from "punishment for individual sins" to thinking more in terms of compatibility—or lack of compatibility—with God; *for without some compatibility with God we could not expect to share eternal life with Him.*

I believe that the Christian faith, when not distorted or misunderstood, is the truest understanding of "God" that the world has ever known: that Divine Love came to earth, to live and die as a human being in the form of Jesus of Nazareth, and that, as a result, *we can now come to God through Him.* This faith *only makes sense* if there is a reasonable and believable understanding of the Atonement, but the Atonement has been misunderstood for centuries now, and that is another reason why we have come to live in a "post-Christian age" where a large majority of people no longer accept the Christian faith. I have tried to show that the faith *does* make sense if properly understood. While the idea of *"abiding in Christ" in this lifetime* is unique to the Christian faith, and a privilege to experience, I do not think it must necessarily follow that good people of all faiths

---

774 Mark 1:17

775 John 21:15-17, John 10:11

who sincerely love and worship God (or even the woman described above) will not be with Him for ever in the end. So I have tried to give a credible explanation of the Christian faith while *at the same time* demolishing a long-standing historical belief that "professing Christianity" *in this life* is the only way to come to be reconciled with the eternal God, if on all sides there is *Love*. But this very assurance, to be convincing, needs an answer to the question of what happens to those who in the end *do* ultimately, deliberately and finally, *reject* God and His goodness and His love, or are so incompatible in themselves with love and goodness that they would not want to seek reconciliation with God or know what Love is: who will not, even at the end of time, recognize and accept Jesus as One of the Persons of the Trinity and our Saviour and Lord; and I see the Biblical answer as being: "they *perish*".

Because people may still be afraid of what may happen to them, and have a problem with the idea of judgment, and I do not want to instill in people who read this book a fear of spiritual death in place of the old fear of hell, and leave them wondering whether they will be "forgiven" or not, I submit my own theory about how the distinction will be made between those who continue to live for ever in God, and those who do not survive. Basically it can be summed up by saying: do we accept the God of Love, and are we prepared to meet Him *on His terms?*

There is a line in one of the Psalms that says *"give me understanding, that I may live."* [776] It may be only after death, but I believe that eventually one comes to have a real understanding (of who one is, and what one has done, and the motives and actions of other people, and so on)—or one does not. If someone truly saw their situation and understood it in the light shed by the God of truth at the end of time, and saw first-hand the radiance of God's love [777] and heard

---

776 Psalm 119:144. See also 1 Corinthians 13:10-12: "when the perfect comes, the imperfect will pass away...now we see in a mirror dimly, but then face to face. Now I know in part, then I shall understand fully, even as I have been fully understood"; and Wisdom 3:1-9 ("The souls of the righteous are in the hands of God.."): "Those *who trust in [God] will understand truth,* and the faithful will abide with him in love."

777 Isaiah 52:10: [the time when] *"all the ends of the earth shall see the salvation of our God"*

His voice,[778] I think that repentance would be instantaneous, swift and genuine; we would be changed for ever,[779] and there would be no barrier between us and God any more.[780]

I do not think myself that there will necessarily be a formal Judgment Day where we are "judged" en masse, in the sense that "we all turn up in court to hear the sentence"—that, too, is taken from ancient thinking. I think it is more a case of "when I awake, I shall be satisfied with beholding thy form".[781] *We would finally have understanding,* and, as a result, *we would live:* for ever, because we would be *at-one with God.*

I see "Judgment Day" more as a dividing line, the final moment when good and evil are defined and separated for ever, and the latter is irrevocably destroyed. It will surely be only those who are so steeped in evil and hatred that they have become inherently incapable of comprehending goodness and love who will be unable to overcome their own inability to meet God on God's terms. (One wonders if Hitler, on meeting Christ eventually, would see in Him *only* the face of *a much-despised and hated Jew?*)

I have dealt with this in some detail, because what is at stake is "union with God in eternity", (which is different from the idea of heaven or paradise as some sort of a "reward"), regardless of which religion we profess in this life: Scripture points to the fact that it is up to God to do what He will with His own (and the fact that God is

---

778 John 5:25: *"the dead will hear* the voice of the Son of God, and *those who hear will live"* (which would seem to confirm that the final outcome is not certain until *after* our physical death has occurred)

779 1 John 3:2 *"when He appears* [when we finally come to see Him at the end of time] *we shall be like Him* [i.e we shall be *changed] for we shall see Him as He is"* — presumably *seeing Him* as He is would make us *want* to change from our old ways and become like Him. 1 Corinthians 15:51-57 *"...we shall all be changed ...we shall be changed.* For this perishable nature must put on the imperishable, and *this mortal nature...put on immortality."*

780 Ezekiel 37:13-14: *"...you shall know* that I am the Lord, when I open your graves, and raise you from your graves, O my people. And I will put my Spirit within you, *and you shall live"* (the Spirit has long been associated with Wisdom and understanding).

781 Psalm 17:15 or in the version in *the Book of Common Prayer,* "when I awake *I shall be satisfied with thy likeness"*

love). We need to think of salvation in terms of being *reconciled to God,* forgiven, healed, loved, and at peace with Him, no longer estranged from Him or working against Him. We need to think of salvation in terms of being *embraced by Love.*

CHAPTER 18

The traditional belief in hell

Because we human beings tend to think simplistically, we have tended to concentrate more on the negativity of wrath and damnation, which is easier to visualise, to try to frighten ourselves into "being good," (a tactic sometimes still unashamedly employed by some fundmentalist Protestant churches), rather than thinking about *union with God for His own sake, because He loves us and we have come to love Him,* a concept which is not so easy fully to comprehend.

In earlier centuries, the fight against heresy became narrowed to the fact that "there was only one way to be saved, and that was through the institutional Church". Threats of damnation were used to ensure that people "toed the line". However this has back-fired in the modern age, and, after the sickening Religious Wars and tortures and persecutions of the fifteenth to eighteenth centuries, people today want no more threats of damnation, or religious exclusiveness. The concept of "hell fire" and damnation has come down to us from much earlier times, and is a concept widely rejected today. I think that the early Church, because of the overwhelming pressure that existed in the culture of the time about everyone automatically living for ever and some ending up in hell, [782] did not continue to pay as much attention as I believe it should have done to the many references in the New Testament to the eventual, permanent, *destruction* of wickedness which contradicts the idea of the eternal suffering of an individual in hell.

Indeed, I am challenging the so-called *"Christian doctrine of man"*

---

782   "the so-called Christian doctrine of man"   see Glossary re. Annihilationism

because I do not believe it is "Christian" (in the true sense of the word) at all. [783] I think that, historically, some passages in the New Testament have been misunderstood, or just overlooked altogether: for example, St. Paul's reference to the "punishment of eternal *destruction*",[784] the many references in the New Testament to "perishing" as opposed to "eternal life" which I set out in the Chapter on the Atonement, and the reference in the Book of Revelation to "the *second death*." [785] I believe the references in the Athanasian Creed about *"perishing eternally"* and going into "eternal fire" *must* be metaphorical in origin, because, if one *perishes,* one *cannot* at the same time survive for ever to be tormented by eternal fire. Similarly the reference in the Epistle to the Hebrews about God being a consuming fire—and "consume" means "destroy", not burn for ever—must also be metaphorical in origin, because that Epistle also says that "we are not of those who... are *destroyed,* but of those who have faith and *keep their souls*". [786] Jesus in His teaching did refer to "hell" sometimes, as described in the Synoptic Gospels, but it was part of the culture of His time, and was used as *the background of a parable to make a point,* or as *a metaphor,* to distinguish, for example, between the living branch on the vine and the dead wood which any gardener would normally burn as rubbish; [787] but the main thrust of His teaching was about *love,* and I do not think it can be used to justify the mediaeval idea of "the saved" for ever watching the torments of "the damned". That would, in itself, be a denial of the love that is God, which is supposed to be *in* "the saved" in the first place. I cannot think that that would be any good person's idea of "heaven", or that God would wish it to be. It sounds more like some ghastly nightmare out of a concentration camp. *"What*

---

783   see the glossary re "Annihilationism," and the fact that Jesus said "I AM the Resurrection and the life...he that believeth in me... *shall never die*" (John 11:25-26) with its implication that eternal death *is* possible, because we all die *physically;* St. Paul's statement that *"this perishable nature must put on the imperishable, and this mortal nature must put on immortality* (1 Corinthians 15:50-53); and the Chapter on the Atonement.

784   2 Thessalonians 1:9

785   Revelation 20:6, Revelation 20:14. I think Revelation 20:10, on torment for ever and ever, is speaking *of evil itself* being *eternally frustrated,* but it is only one verse among many.

786   Hebrews 10:39

787   John 15:5-6

kind of a God do we believe in? [788] To which I would respond: *"God is not like that"*.

Some modern writers like Bishop Spong —and others I could name— seem to assume that we need to change our understanding of the faith in the light of the discoveries of people like Darwin and Copernicus, and I argue that *the faith is still the same,* even if modern science has enlightened us about some of the things that primitive people did not understand; it is just that we realize now that allowances have to be made for that fact when we read the Bible, as it sometimes reflects the thinking of primitive people, the culture of the times in which it was written, with the result that the Bible does need to be read with that understanding in mind.

One area, however, in which I do believe our thinking needs to be modernized is on the subject of "the torments of hell". In earlier centuries, even in so-called "Christian" countries, torture, the infliction of physical pain, was accepted as a normal practice, as it still is, regrettably, in some parts of the world today. However, societal

---

788 I was interested that a Christian Fundamentalist, who sees God as *love,* and understands the importance of forgiving and being forgiven for those who repent and change, at the same time seemed to expect that God would eventually suitably *punish* the wicked, if He is also a God of *Justice.* My suggestion that *annihilation,* the eventual *destruction* of the incurably wicked, would surely be punishment enough, and result in the end of all evil in the coming of the Kingdom of God, did not seem to resonate with this person, who apparently expected God to inflict pain *as punishment* in proportion to the suffering that had been inflicted by the wicked on earth. I think that some atrocities have been so terrible that no punishment could ever be enough; and would it be in the nature of a *God of Love* to be measuring out pain and suffering to *anyone?* "Eternal death" seems to me to be the answer that is both merciful and practical—and Scriptural, and still consonant with the concept of a God of Justice. While we can never condone wickedness, and some sins against others are not ours to forgive, yet I can see danger in a good and sincere Christian anticipating without a qualm the punishment of others, because this, albeit unwittingly, runs the risk of letting *hatred* touch the heart, unforgiveness bordering on an instinct for revenge, or at least a lack of caring, that is incompatible with aspiring at the same time to live in the divine love. This needs thinking about, especially as I believe some Christian fundamentalists, in trying to convert people, encourage in them a selfish fear of *"being left behind",* and use threats of hell and awful punishment for this purpose. (But I should note here my belief that Justice *does* require *acknowledgement* of sin *at some stage,* and repentance for it, for forgiveness to take effect.)

norms have changed in civilized countries, and civilised people have now come to abhor and condemn all forms of torture. I think the question needs to be asked, on the subject of "the torments of hell": do we believe that God is *less civilized than we are?*

Modern theology holds that "hell" is "separation from God," "separation from all possibility of happiness", as opposed to flames of fire:[789] but I think this idea, too, is still unwittingly based on the traditional idea that every human soul survives for ever, with or without God, and so, if one no longer believes in literal flames of fire (and no one yet seems to have had the courage to say that the traditional idea of the soul surviving for ever without God is in itself contrary to the teaching of the Bible, which I believe it is), the result must be that those who are separated from God for ever by the evil that is in them must be *"dumped somewhere"* away from, and apart from, God. *What else would He do with them?* (But of course I am arguing that the Scriptural position is that such people, truly estranged from God for ever, *perish*, and *do not survive for ever* in a state of "separation from God": that the traditional teaching on hell, whether of literal flames of fire or "separation from God", is misconceived, badly mistaken, and needs to be thought about again.)

With regard to the modern theory about "separation from God", I do not think that this argument passes the test of basic logic. Not only do I believe that if someone was so truly grieved at being separated from God that it was, for that person, the equivalent of "hell," God would accept that as repentance and reconciliation would follow, but it seems obvious *that for those who reject God,* separation from Him, and existence without Him, would not *be* "hell" at all. I do not see that separation from God would constitute for the inhabitants of hell "separation from all possibility of happiness," as by their very nature they have alienated themselves from all that God stands for, and, so, to my mind, that particular sentiment does not ring true: I see it as but an echo of the illogical thinking of past centuries. I argue that, for those who reject God anyway, and do not *want* to have anything to do with goodness and love, it would not *be* "hell" to live without

---

789   *The Oxford Dictionary of the Christian Church, Revised Second Edition,* edited by F.L. Cross and E.A. Livingstone. Oxford: Oxford Universit Press, 1958, 1974, 1983, p. 631 re. hell

Him—it would suit them just fine! I can only point to the Biblical teaching that supports my argument that surviving for eternity is only to be found in God, not apart from Him (see more about this in the chapter on the Atonement).

Let us think of it in terms of God one day *destroying all evil,* and get away from thinking in terms of *people "going to hell"*, which one suspects may have been used as a threat to obtain compliance in the historical past, and which is part of the reason why people now reject the idea of believing in a reasonable and loving God, and "the flames of hell", at one and the same time. I think we would all agree that, when the Kingdom of God does come in its entirety at the end of time, there will be an end to all evil, and in that sense one could think *metaphorically* of the blazing fire of God's eternal righteousness destroying *all* that is not holy, good and true.[790] And would we not rejoice in the annihilation of all wickedness, and the end of all suffering?

I think that that is what lies behind the saying, attributed to John the Baptist in St. Luke's Gospel, about the coming of the Messiah, and the judgment of God eventually sorting out, and destroying, as with fire, all that is evil in this world: "His winnowing fork is in his hand, to clear his threshing floor, and to gather the wheat into his granary, but the chaff he will burn with unquenchable fire."[791] I think we get "hung up" on words like *"unquenchable fire"*. I think that, metaphorically speaking, it is the fire of the *holy righteousness of God* which is *eternal and unquenchable,* and will eventually destroy all evil, but I do not think it must necessarily follow that transient inhabitants of this earth will be made to suffer for ever.[792]

---

790 Hebrews 12:28-29 "let us offer to God acceptable worship, with reverence and awe; *for our God is a consuming fire.*" Hebrews 10:31 says: "It is a fearful thing to fall into the hands of the living God" and verse 39 speaks of the wicked *being destroyed* as opposed to those who *"keep their souls."*

791 Luke 3:17

792 Matthew 25:41 Jesus said, in His parable about the sheep and the goats, that the wicked will be told: " 'Depart from me...*into the eternal fire prepared for the devil and his angels; for'...* " This may have been just the hyperbole which He sometimes used for effect in His stories, and may also have reflected the thinking of His time, especially in the understanding of His hearers about the drastic nature of the condemnation pronounced, which may itself possibly have been exaggerated in subsequent reports handed down to others; but I think that, *on a metaphorical level,* it still is true, in the sense that

I cannot see that eternal suffering of an *individual* is the will of a good God, or that such a concept should be simplistically equated with the metaphorical concept of eternal fire eventually destroying all corruption and wickedness.

The Book of Revelation has been much misused and misunderstood, but there are some profound passages in it, which I think is why it was eventually accepted into the Canon of Scripture, in spite of the fact that there may be passages in it which, making more sense to the people of the time when it was written, are not so helpful for us today. It is one of the problems of our time that some people have fixed their attention on particular passages in that Book which do not relate to its essential themes, and many problems have been caused thereby: but if one sticks to the main themes, of the Lordship of Christ, and the coming of God's Kingdom, and the overcoming of evil, and the perfection of the future in the love of God ("God will wipe away every tear from their eyes" [793]), one should not get side-tracked by details of lesser importance addressed to the Church of the time.

A passage in it that has helped me in my understanding with regard to the destruction of *evil and suffering* at the end of time, which must be a necessary prerequisite for the complete establishment of the Kingdom of God, and surely what most of us would want to see, is the *call to God's people to forsake evil ways.*

The word "Babylon" in the Book of Revelation was used synonymously for corruption and all kinds of evil, and it is the "Babylon" *of evil* that will be destroyed at the end of time. I think we would all agree on that. The passage I am referring to says: "Babylon...has become a dwelling place of demons, a haunt of every foul spirit...*come out of her my people, lest you take part in her sins, lest you share in her plagues*". [794]

God's people are being called to forsake evil, *to come out* of all evil habitations of thought and attitude and practice. If someone should ever be so thoroughly wicked that that person persisted in preferring evil to

---

eventually *evil itself will be destroyed for ever* by the eternal fire of the holiness and righteousness of God.

793   Revelation 7:17

794   Revelation 18:2-4

good, even when facing God at the end of time, then it might well mean perishing along with everything else that is evil at that time.

However, while God's holy, blazing, fire of righteousness is eternal, I do not believe that any *human* sufferings will be. Again, I ask, *what kind of a God do we believe in?* The problem as I see it is that human beings put so much emphasis on mere words and theories, one way or the other, that the vision of God in His love and holiness becomes obscured.

As I have said, the idea of "hell" was in existence before the Christian era, and therefore it is not "Christian" in origin.

According to *The Interpreter's Dictionary of the Bible,*[795] the notion of "the hell of fire"[796] *was in existence before the Christian era.* It says of *"Gehenna"* and *"Hinnom",* the former being the Greek for the Hebrew "Valley of Hinnom", that it was a place where human sacrifice had been so notorious that "the memory of the rituals of cremation gave birth to the notion of *the hell of fire...* (Matt.5:22)...", (Vol.E-J, p.606); and that, *"In the first century B.C.* this name came to be used in a metaphorical sense, to denote the place of fiery torment believed to be reserved for the wicked...." (Vol. E-J, p.361) — italics mine. The latter statement continues (italics mine again):

> The general idea of a punitive conflagration appears, to be sure, in earlier portions of the OT (e.g., Deut.32.22; Isa.33:14), but it is only in the Greco-Roman period of Jewish history that the quite distinct concept of a blazing hell—a lake, or abyss, of fire—begins to emerge (cf. Dan.7:10....). *The concept was doubtless influenced by the infiltration of Iranian ideas, for the articulation of it is clearly patterned on the Avestan doctrine of the ultimate judgment of the wicked in a stream of molten metal...* Nowhere in the Apoc., however (except in the very late passage II Esd. 2:39) is this place actually called Gehenna... [but]... *Gehenna is clearly conceived*

---

795   *The Interpreter's Dictionary of the Bible: An Illustrated Encyclopedia.* Nashville: Abingdon Press, 1962. Vol. E-J, page 606, and pages 361-362.

796   This belief in "hell" *must* involve believing that *all* human souls survive for ever, even if they are alienated from God, and I believe that Jesus disputed this, in saying that *He* (i.e. in Him) was the Resurrection and the Life.

by the NT writers as identical with the "lake of fire" into which Hades (i.e. Sheol, the general abode of the dead) will itself ultimately be cast (Rev.20.14).

Even though *The Interpreter's Dictionary of the Bible* mentions "NT writers" and the Book of Revelation, I have shown (in the chapter on Abiding in Christ), that even the Epistles to Timothy and Titus did not contain "some of [St. Paul's] leading theological ideas...e.g., the union of the believer with Christ," and I have already argued that *"eternal* life" is not to be found apart from God, according to St. John and St. Paul, (and Jesus Himself), [797] and so the Church may have "got it wrong" quite early in its history, in thinking of *eternal suffering in hell.* [798] And although Revelation 20:14 does speak of "the lake of fire", it *also* says "This is the *second death",* which is presumably the spiritual, eternal, death that I have been talking about; even *that* text does not imply that human suffering will be eternal; in fact, *it explicitly states the opposite.*

Obviously I cannot quote the whole article on the page quoted earlier (but the reader can consult it, if desired); but it is interesting to note two things: one is that Philo (c.20 B.C.— A.D.50) speaks of certain punishment being eternal (On Cherubim 1), and the other is the following statement (italics mine):

> The typological use of the name Gehenna reflects a tendency, which developed during the Hellenistic period, to gear visions of the last days to the names of persons and places mentioned in the OT.... This tendency, which helped at the same time to Judaize ideas adopted from foreign sources, *has not yet received the attention which it deserves,* but *it is cardinal for an understanding of Jewish and Christian apocalyptic literature and, in general, of how the Scriptures were popularly interpreted during the crucial intertestamental period.* [799]

---

797 John 11:23-26, Jesus saying to Martha "I AM the Resurrection and the Life"

798 To think of *"eternal life" as "going to heaven"* is *logically incompatible* with thinking of "eternal life" *in hell*

799 *The Interpreter's Dictionary of the Bible: An Illustrated Encyclopedia.* Nashville: Abingdon Press, 1962, Vol. E-J, page 362.

This brings us back to the question of the popular culture in existence at the time of Jesus.[800] It may well be that its use by Jesus, in His parables aimed at local audiences, reflected the historical and cultural "mind-set" of the time, in the context of talking about *good consequences versus bad consequences,* rather than "hell" itself. For example, the parable of the rich man in hell, while the beggar, Lazarus, who had suffered so much in his life-time, was now "in the bosom of Abraham afar off",[801] was not about "hell", as such, but about many other things, and "hell" was used as part of the setting for that story. I do not think that a whole philosophy of "hell" can necessarily be built on this, on a par with some of the eternal truths in the Bible, such as the fact that God *is Love:* and the fact that Jesus said (as just quoted) *"I AM* the Resurrection and the life".

My question is *when,* in the subsequent history of the Church, did the idea of spiritual and eternal death, as spoken of so frequently by St. John and St. Paul, become submerged into the idea of *eternal punishment* current in the popular culture of the time? I think that confusion has arisen between, on the one hand, the apostolic idea of the wicked *being destroyed, perishing,* because they no longer have any affinity with God, and it is not possible for them, as they have come to be, ever to dwell in and with Him; and, on the other hand, the idea that that "perishing" must equal *"punishment",* which is then interpreted to mean having to suffer physical torment for ever; while Biblical texts which might have conveyed a contrary understanding have been ignored.

I think this is another example of Christians taking an idea which has a basis in truth, and then pushing it to an extreme (e.g., the idea that wickedness will be dealt with eventually becomes a relishing of

---

800 John 11:23-26: when Jesus told Martha that her brother Lazarus would rise again, she said *"I know* [in the present tense] that *he will rise again in the resurrection on the last day,"* (which would prove that that was the popular belief of pre-Christian times), and I believe that, when He said, in His reply, *"I AM* the Resurrection and the life," Jesus was *challenging* the currently-held belief that *everyone* automatically rose from the dead and survived for ever, regardless of their relationship with God (which belief in hell must imply) *by specifically tying the concept of eternal life to relationship with Himself:* "he who believes in me, though he die, yet shall he live, and *whoever lives and believes in me shall never die."*

801 Luke 16:19-30

the form of torture with which revenge will be enacted). Logic has not pointed out that a God of Love would presumably not *want* to see *anyone* suffering eternally, if He is *Love Itself;* or the fact that, if the wicked *did* survive, albeit in hell, *evil would still exist—for ever:* and thus the coming of God's Kingdom would not be complete *because evil would not have been destroyed.*

It is my belief that, not only has the historical Church sometimes made mistakes, but that God has allowed it to do so, so that it may think and grow under the guidance of the Holy Spirit, in the freedom which He has given to the human race and to His creation; and I believe that we are also meant to *think* about these things, and correct mistakes if they have been made, in the firm belief that God will always protect the eternal, invisible Church (not necessarily the institutional Church) from fatal error.

Incidents such as I described earlier about people asking about "hell" have led me to ponder the idea of "hell" and *"eternal punishment"* as being the will of a good and loving God. I think that, in particular, Matthew 25:46 (about "eternal punishment") has been misunderstood for many, many centuries. As stated, I believe the early church succumbed to the pre-Christian theories current in the culture of the time, about the soul automatically surviving for ever, in spite of the fact that there is massive Biblical evidence to contradict this. I believe the references to "hell" in the Synoptic Gospels were only the background setting of some of the parables in order for Jesus to make a point about something else, and may have been meant or understood in the context of the culture of the time. I also believe, as argued earlier, that the Synoptic Gospels should not be the sole arbiter of our theology (but even *they* refer to Jesus talking about *"forfeiting one's life,"*[802] or *"losing one's soul"* as the King James version puts it, as I describe later).

I repeat, because I believe it is so important, that, as I quote later, there are many examples of apostolic teaching about *"perishing"* in the New Testament, in the context of *that* being the *opposite* of *"eternal life"* rather than hell; [803] and, as I have said, I believe that the references to "eternal fire" in the Athanasian Creed and

---

802   Matthew 16:26 and Mark 8:36; see also Luke 9:24-25

803   not only St. Paul and St. John refer to "perishing", but Peter, James and Luke also

the Epistle to the Hebrews must have been metaphorical in origin, a metaphor for *the holiness and righteousness of God,* which are eternal, not physical flames burning people for ever, because one cannot both *perish,* i.e. *cease to exist,* and *at the same time* survive for ever to be tormented by eternal fire: but the Church has never faced the logic of this discrepancy. The Epistle to the Hebrews, though it associates God with fire, *also* refers to the eventual *destruction of wickedness,* not its continuing for ever [804] and the Book of Revelation, for all its talk about the fires of hell, then speaks of the final destruction which is "the second death".[805]

So, as a result of years of thinking about these problems, I have come to believe that evil will not last for ever, in any form, anywhere, and there is not a hell of *perpetual punishment,* because, as I demonstrate from the Bible itself, and, indeed the Athanasian Creed as well, the opposite of "eternal life" is not hell but *perishing: "the punishment* of *eternal destruction"*[806] which contradicts the idea of *"eternal punishment" going on for ever.* It is *other religions, non-Christian religions,* who believe, and have believed since pre-Christian times, in human beings surviving for ever, with or without God (with or without Christ), the soul or spirit being seen as immortal in itself. It is not specifically a Christian idea, even though the Christian Church has conveyed that impression.

There was a controversy in the nineteenth century[807]which led to F.D Maurice being deprived from office at King's College, London, "for alleged disbelief in hell." I am using my own arguments on this subject, but references are given for those who want to follow it up.[808]

---

804 Hebrews 10:27-39: "a fury of fire which will consume the adversaries [note "consume" means "destroy", not burn for ever: if something burns for ever, it is not consumed].... But we are not of those who...*are destroyed* , but of those who have faith and *keep their souls".*

805 Revelation 20:9,14.

806 2 Thessalonians 1:9

807 See A.M. Ramsey. *F.D. Maurice and the Conflicts of Modern Theology* . Cambridge: Cambridge University Press, 1951, and Maurice's own writings.

808 Arthur Michael Ramsey. *The Gospel and the Catholic Church.* London: Longmans, Green and Co., 1936, p.210; Michael Ramsey, in *The Anglican Spirit* edited by Dale Coleman (Cambridge, Massachusetts: Cowley Publications, 1991, pp.70-76, referring to the controversy, says F.D. Maurice wrote of *"eternal life, as distinct from everlasting*

There has been argument over whether the resurrection of the body applies not only to Christian resurrection in Christ but to the inhabitants of hell as well. The latter idea is postulated by some Christian fundamentalists today, because it is felt that some kind of body is necessary for the inhabitants of hell, in order that they can *feel* the *pain* of their torments, an idea implied in early, pre-Christian, thought, as in, for example, *"the Avestan doctrine of the ultimate judgment of the wicked in a stream of molten metal,"* quoted earlier, which surely implies pain and suffering (see the footnote regarding the view of some Christian fundamentalists that God would *require* pain and suffering, as punishment, if He is a God of *Justice.)*

There has also been some thinking in Church history that pain is purgative,[809] and theories about purgatory, for example, have been based on the idea that pain can purify. While it is true that suffering can produce good character in this lifetime,[810] the opposite can, and often does, apply; and I believe that historical thinking along these lines has omitted the whole dimension of love from its reasoning. *I cannot see that "punishment" creates "love."* This kind of reasoning resulted in the impasse at the time of the Reformation between Roman Catholicism and Protestantism on the subject of Purgatory. This is an issue that has never been resolved, and it is one where I believe that both sides were wrong. I believe that my emphasis on the hope of *union with God, through "abiding in Christ,"* might well provide an answer that could satisfy both sides, and resolve this centuries-old disagreement. *The Oxford Dictionary of the Christian Church* states, regarding Purgatory, that it is "according to Roman Catholic teaching, the place or state of temporal punishment where those who have died in the grace of God expiate their unforgiven venial sins and undergo such punishment as is still due to forgiven sin, [punishment being thought of as purging

---

life and everlasting punishment," Maurice seeing "eternal life" as "another dimension [than time]. I am using the words *eternal or everlasting life* in the primary, literal, sense of "surviving for ever", which is what I believe the apostles were doing. It will be noted that I am questioning the whole notion of *"everlasting punishment."*

809 See the Glossary re. "apocatastasis", *"The doctrine that hell is in essence purgative and therefore temporary*

810 See Romans 5:3-5 re. "suffering produces endurance...and character...and hope" (but I think that passage refers to the experiences of this life, and does not imply that punishment in hell will change anything)

or expiating sin to make one 'fit for heaven'].[811] This idea was rejected by the Reformers, who taught that souls are freed from sin by faith in Christ alone without any works, and therefore, if saved, go straight to heaven."

It will be noted that neither Roman Catholics nor Protestants saw "salvation" in terms of eternity being dependent on *union with God;* and the resulting stalemate, which has never been resolved, became a question of either punishment or no punishment (and no preparation for union with God either), rather than the alternatives of spending eternity in and with God or perishing altogether, which I believe is the original teaching of the Bible. I believe that the necessary prerequisite for spending eternity in and with God is *neither* punishment or no punishment, and is *more than* either expiating sin, on the one hand, or "being forgiven (and going to heaven)" because of "correct belief" on the other when it may be quite obvious that the person concerned is not *at present* suitable for heaven—which is why the doctrine of Purgatory must have been developed in the first place. *It is whether or not one is sufficiently compatible in oneself with the love and goodness that is God that such union is possible.* For this, "abiding in Christ" helps to prepare us in this lifetime, living "in the Spirit" as opposed to "life in the flesh", and I believe this has to be the answer to the unresolved question left over from the Reformation.

I believe that some rare souls may come to this kind of purity and love in spite of not having been professing Christians *in this lifetime,* and that they may be reconciled to God at the last *because they are already compatible with what God is like: or enough so, that when they meet God their natures are such* that they *can* be reconciled with Him. This is *not* "universalism" as I am at pains to I explain, this is not saying that "everybody will be saved in the end, regardless."

Therefore, can we not just go back to thinking in Biblical terms about the *destruction of wickedness* in the coming of God's Kingdom at the end of time, which presumably is what "perishing" means in the first place, and realize that the opposite, the only alternative, would be eventual, eternal, *union with God through Christ.*

---

811   *The Oxford Dictionary of the Christian Church,* Revised Second Edition edited by F.L. Cross and E.A. Livingstone. Oxford: Oxford University Press, 1958, 1974, 1983, p. 1144 re Purgatory

CHAPTER 19

Misunderstandings around the doctrine of the Atonement, and a re-statement of it that answers these questions

Even the word "Atonement" is ambiguous, and can be understood in two ways. It can mean both *"Atonement"* in the traditional sense of the once-for-all-time death of Christ on the Cross, in the past, which won the forgiveness of our sins, *and* the "at-one-ment" with God that has been made possible for us as a result of that historic event, as we learn to *"abide in Christ"* [812] through the on-going work of the Holy Spirit in our lives in the present time.

I believe that "forgiveness" was *only part of* God's saving action in Christ: the other part of the equation, the second arm of the Atonement, as it were, is sanctification by the Holy Spirit and our being enabled to come to God for ever through abiding in Christ. The following Biblical texts point to the Atonement as having *both* these aspects: forgiveness of the sin of the past *and* sanctification by the Holy Spirit *in new life* in the present (and in the eternal future): "God our Saviour...*saved us...* by the washing of regeneration *and* renewal in the Holy Spirit"; or, as St. Peter put it, "Repent, and be baptized... *for the forgiveness* of your sins; *and* you shall receive the gift of *the Holy Spirit*"; he also said "God

---

812   see the Chapter on *"Abiding in Christ"*, and John 14-17, especially John 15:1-5 about the vine and the branches: "Abide in me, and I in you...He who abides in me, and I in him, he it is that bears much fruit...", and verses 9-10: "abide in my love. If you keep my commandments, you will abide in my love, just as I have kept my father's commandments and abide in his love".

has granted *repentance* [in the present] *unto life,"* meaning life that is eternal. Similarly, St. Paul spoke of *both* "acquittal *and life".*[813] One could think of it as addressing both *what we have done* and *what we are:* what we have done can be forgiven; but what we *are* is what comes to God. The Atonement could be summed up, then, as being both *forgiveness* for the sin of the past, *and* the offer of *new (and eternal) life* for the future as we come *to live and be* in God.

However, I believe that, early in its history, the Church came to concentrate more on the former *(forgiveness)* at the expense of the latter *("life in the Spirit),* thinking of the Atonement mainly as something done by Jesus in the past so that our sins can be forgiven and we can "go to heaven," which is how "being saved" came to be understood,[814] and less on the idea of our being at-one-with God, sharing in His eternal life, *as a new creation,*[815] through "living and walking in the Spirit",[816] *abiding in Christ,* in this world and the next.[817]

We still pay "lip-service" to the latter idea (being *"in Christ"*), as when, for example, we sign letters "yours sincerely *in Christ",* but I think that this has now come to be little more than a figure of speech.

This undue emphasis on the sin-and-forgiveness component of the Atonement may well have arisen from the popular idea, current at the time, that all human beings will *"live for ever",* the only question

---

813   Titus 3:4-5; Acts 2:38 & 11:18; Romans 5:18: "[Christ's] act of righteousness leads to *acquittal and life.."*

814   e.g. Marcus Borg, *The God we Never Knew: Beyond Dogmatic Religion to a More Authentic Contemporary Faith* (HarperSanFrancisco, a Division of HarperCollins Publishers, New York), 1997, page 2 ("the 'popular-level Christianity' of a previous generation... defined salvation as 'afterlife' —as going to heaven")

815   2 Corinthians 5:17: "if anyone is *in Christ,* he is a new creation". Some question whether the Resurrection literally happened or was necessary. I believe the Risen Christ was *a sign* for us to see, the first-fruits, as it were, of that new creation, where humanity and divinity meet, *in Him; e.g.,* 1 Cor.15:20-23 and Ephesians 2:14-16

816   Galatians 5:25: *"If we live* by the Spirit, let us also walk by the Spirit."

817   It is as if the middle of what St. Paul was saying in Romans 6:22-23 was omitted or forgotten, and we went straight from having been "set free from sin", *in the past,* to "eternal life" (taken as being "heaven"), *in the future,* ignoring the fact that the link between the two was *becoming slaves of God and being sanctified* by the Holy Spirit *in the present,* (i.e. abiding in Christ, living in the divine love), *the "end" of which* was eternal life .

being whether in heaven or in hell, and, now that the modern world is rethinking its ideas about "heaven and hell," it is tending, in the process, to reject Christianity itself, as well.

This is unfortunate, as well as unnecessary, because that idea stemmed from widespread popular culture long predating Christianity,[818] and I believe that the Church should not have subsequently reverted to it, in the face of strong and basic apostolic teaching to the contrary, and Jesus' own words that "[whoever believes] in me *shall never die*",[819] which in themselves imply the opposite reality of *eternal death*.

Equally important is the context in which Jesus said "I AM the Resurrection and the life"[820] which has been said at funeral services for two thousand years, with no one thinking anything special of it (except the assumption that "if you believe in Jesus, you are 'saved' and will go to heaven"). Jesus was speaking in the context of the death of Lazarus, and He asked his sister Martha if she believed that her brother would "rise again"— life after death. Martha replied that she subscribed to the belief current at the time (I have said it was pre-Christian) by replying "I know that he will rise again in the resurrection at the last day". That was when Jesus corrected her by saying that resurrection and life were to be found *in Him*.

I believe *that* is the significance of what He was saying: and I maintain that that implies that resurrection and life (although life in that context means more than mere existence) has to imply that continuing to live for ever after this life is over is not to be found *apart from God*.

I think the parables in the Synoptic Gospels which mention hell

---

818   See the chapter on hell regarding the fact that *"this idea was already in existence before the Christian era".* However, although, later, the Church may have been tempted to revert back to it, this was *not* the original, basic, apostolic, teaching of St. John and St. Paul, which was that resurrection from the dead was only to be found *in Christ:* that spiritual and eternal life is *only* to be found *in God,* the God who is Love. St. John wrote: "We know that we have passed *out of death into life, because we love* the brethren. *He who does not love abides in death. Anyone who hates* his brother is a murderer, and you know that no murderer has *eternal life abiding in him."* (1 John 3:14-15). I believe that the Synoptic Gospels, intended to record what was remembered of Jesus' teaching and actions, should not carry the same theological weight, on this subject, as these two great thinkers.

819   John 11:25-26 "I am the resurrection and the life; he who believes in me, though he die, yet shall he live, and..."

820   John 11:23

may have had an effect on the subsequent thinking of the Church that is out of all proportion to their intrinsic significance, when compared with the teaching of St. Paul and St. John (and others). While there is general agreement as to what Jesus said on important occasions, such as the Last Supper and the Crucifixion, we do not always know for certain, in many cases, in dealing with the parables, what Jesus' actual words really were: nor do we know how much the accounts that have come down to us were influenced, on His part, or on the part of His hearers, and their hearers, by the culture current at the time.

For example, St. Luke's Gospel tells of Jesus' saying of the nobleman in a particular parable that the man said "as for these enemies of mine... bring them here and *slay them before me*". [821] Presumably, if Jesus said that, He would have been reflecting a culture in the present time where that kind of thing could happen, if a despot wished it: or He may have been referring to a future where God would destroy *His* enemies: or both. I have said that I believe that Jesus' main emphasis in all His parables was on *good consequences versus bad consequences.* The literal details of such verses cannot be taken as a norm for *our* behaviour and thinking now.

Nor can theological conclusions be drawn from them that have priority over the teaching of someone like St. Paul, who was living and working among early Christians shortly after the Crucifixion, and whose writing reflected his teaching and their understanding *years before* the Synoptic Gospels were put together in the form in which we have them now.

It is believed that the Synoptic Gospels, derived from earlier oral and written traditions, were probably put together in their present form in about 80 AD, after the fall of Jerusalem in 70 AD, almost certainly after the death of St. Paul in about 65 AD. If so, speaking very roughly, that would be approximately twenty or thirty years *after* St. Paul was writing and teaching; and about twenty years before the writings attributed to St. John "put the record straight" by echoing and reaffirming what St. Paul had been saying forty years earlier. I think therefore that we can give greater credence to material that both *predated* and *followed* the Synoptic Gospels.

An example of this kind of discrepancy is that St. Paul, who, as mentioned earlier, died in about 65 AD, wrote to the Thessalonians, in one of his earliest still-surviving epistles, about "the *punishment* of

---

821 Luke 19:27

eternal *destruction*,"[822] which is consistent with the examples that follow about *"perishing"* commonly appearing in the New Testament as being the opposite of "eternal life" or "being saved,"[823] whereas the Gospel of Matthew, which almost certainly first appeared after St. Paul's death, referred to "eternal *punishment*" in one of the parable stories. [824]

Biblical evidence regarding spiritual death as opposed to eternal existence in hell

This is not only to be found in the New Testament. As far back as the Pentateuch or Torah, the Book of Deuteronomy speaks of God as saying: *"I call heaven and earth to witness* against you this day, that I have set before you life and death, blessing and curse; therefore *choose life, that you...may live".* [825]

This may sometimes have been understood in a purely literal, simplistic, way, as referring to this life only, with wrong-doing being punished by *physical death:* but I think *the words themselves denote an eternal context.* This is borne out by subsequent Biblical thinking, to the effect that taking such passages to mean: "if you do good, you will prosper, but if you do wrong, you won't", is contradicted by the fact that the *righteous* can sometimes suffer on this earth, while the wicked can appear to prosper,[826] culminating in the fact that Jesus Himself, the Righteous One who experienced the ultimate in suffering, said to His disciples: "in this world you *[will]* have tribulation, but be of good cheer, I have overcome the world" [827]—which *only makes sense* in the context of "abiding in Christ," because, unless we were abiding in Him, what difference would it make to our tribulation that He *had* "overcome the world"? But, in fact, Jesus makes this explicit, saying "I have said this to you, that *in me* you may have peace." [828]

---

822 2 Thessalonians 1:9

823 as in 1 Corinthians 1:18: "For the word of the cross is folly *to those who are perishing,* but *to us who are being saved* it is the power of God" : see also Philippians 1:28: "...not frightened in anything by your opponents. This is a clear omen to them *of their destruction,* but of *your salvation,* and that from God."

824 Matthew 25:46

825 Deuteronomy 30:19

826 see, for example, the Book of Job and Psalm 73; and Psalm 34:19: "Many are the afflictions of the righteous.."

827 John 16:33

828 John 16:33

There are other references in the Old Testament to *"life"* as opposed to "death" which confirm that these words in Deuteronomy can be understood in an eternal sense. (See the discussion about the connection between "covenant" and "Spirit" and *"life"*—for example, passages from Isaiah and Ezekiel such as: "come to me; hear, *that your soul may live"*, [829] and "I will put my Spirit within you, and *you shall live,"* [830] which *must* refer to eternal life, because the people addressed are already physically alive.) In Psalm 73, the psalmist contemplates "the end" [831] of the wicked who so often prosper in this life, saying "those who are far from thee *shall perish, thou dost put an end to* those who are false to thee," [832] so it would appear that the concept of the wicked living eternally in hell, rather than just ceasing to exist, came later in Jewish history than earlier Biblical thinking. [833]

The idea that "everyone will live for ever," possibly deriving support from those parables in the Synoptic Gospels which mention hell, or a careless reading of the Bible (see footnote below),[834] is quite clearly contradicted by New Testament passages such as the following, which is

---

829   Isaiah 55:1-3

830   Ezekiel 37:14

831   Psalm 73:17-27: "until I went into the sanctuary of God; *then I perceived their end ....* how they are *destroyed in a moment ....* thou dost *put an end to* those who are false to thee"

832   Psalm 73:27

833   see chapter11 re. "The idea of "hell" being in existence before the Christian era..." (but only *later* in OT times)

834   e.g. Hebrews 10:27-39: "a fearful prospect of judgment, and *a fury of fire which will consume* the adversaries [note "consume" means *destroy,* not burn for ever: if something burns for ever, it is not consumed]...it is a fearful thing to fall into the hands of the living God. .. But we are not of those who shrink back and *are destroyed,* but of those who have faith and *keep their souls."* The passage speaks of *"destruction"* versus *"keeping one's soul",* not the soul's continued existence in a hell of fire; but on a careless reading it could well have been misunderstood to fit in with the notions of the culture of the time. Another passage which could well have been misunderstood is Matthew 10:28 "do not fear those who kill the body but cannot kill the soul; rather fear him who can destroy both soul and body in hell": the point Jesus was making was "do not fear things that can destroy the body but not the soul, but rather fear God who can *destroy* both body *and* soul." The words "in hell" are really superfluous, except in a metaphorical sense, because if the soul is destroyed, it cannot last for ever in hell, as I argue about "perishing eternally" in the Athanasian Creed.

frequently quoted without apparently seeing any anomaly in it: "God so loved the world that he gave his only Son, that whoever believes in him *should not perish* but *have eternal life,*"[835] the implication being that the alternative to eternal life in and with God was to perish (not go on living for ever, in hell or anywhere else).[836] Jesus said, of His being the Bread of Life, that "if any one eats of this bread, *he will live for ever.*"[837] If Jesus is to be taken seriously, what does this mean, if we *also* believe that everyone automatically lives for ever, even if in hell?

St. John states categorically that "God gave us eternal life, *and this life is in His Son*"[838]—not "eternal life" *because of* His Son, or *by* His Son, or *through* His Son, but *in* His Son—coming to God through Christ: being in God, in all our living, now and for eternity: in other words, *abiding in Christ.* Jesus also said, according to St. John, "My sheep hear my voice, and I know them, and they follow me; and *I give them eternal life,* and they *shall never perish,* and no one shall snatch them out of my hand".[839]

Jesus Himself defined "eternal life" as *knowing God the Trinity.* He was not talking about the supposed immortality of the soul in its own right when He said: *"this* is eternal life, that *they know thee* the only true God, and Jesus Christ whom thou hast sent".[840]

Paul and Barnabas spoke of "eternal life" *in the context of salvation,* rather than the context of just existing for ever: "Since you judge yourselves unworthy of eternal life...we turn to the Gentiles"; and the Book of Acts

---

835 John 3:16: note that this was *Jesus Himself* speaking (see also Luke 18:30)

836 echoed in John 5:21-26 (v.24: "he who hears my word...*has eternal life;* he ... has passed *from death to life"*)

837 John 6:51 (also John 6:58). John 6:32-58 talks about *"eternal life"* in three contexts: the Eucharist, as above, *and* "abiding in Christ" (verse 56 "Those who eat.. abide in me, and I in them"), and believing in Him (verse 40)

838 1 John 5:11; and in Arthur Cushman McGiffert's book, *A History of Christian Thought, Volume 1, Early and Eastern, from Jesus to John of Damascus,* (New York, London: Charles Scribner's Sons, 1947), page 142, describing the theology of Irenaeus (c.130-200 AD), he wrote: "Becoming incarnate [Christ] united the nature of God with the nature of man and thus deified the latter, *giving it the quality of divinity—immortal life—in which it was lacking."* John 14:19 *"Because I live* [overcoming physical death] *you will live also" [in me;* the whole context is of "abiding *in* Christ", so it has to be *"in me"]*

839 John 10:27-28

840 John 17:3

continues: *"as many as were ordained to eternal life* believed".[841]   St. Peter said to Jesus: "You have the words of *eternal life.* "[842]

The Synoptic Gospels all record Jesus as saying "what will it profit a man if he gains the whole world *and forfeits his life?*"[843]

It should be noted from the latter, (and from the reference in *Luke's* Gospel to *"perishing"* and in *Mark's* to *eternal life in the age to come*[844]), that *there is an inherent contradiction in the Synoptic Gospels themselves* on the subject of hell, the eternal existence of the soul apart from God.

This contradiction needs to be acknowledged and explained if credence is still to be given, even if unconsciously, to "the Christian doctrine of man" (see Glossary) which specifically *contradicts* St. Paul's assertion that *"by a man [by Christ] has come the resurrection of the dead,"* [845] i.e. he is saying that "eternal life" does not happen automatically to everybody, regardless, but comes through *the eternal union with God* which is made possible for us *through Christ. How else* can one explain, or understand, his statement, in the context of Christ overcoming all his enemies, that *"the last enemy to be destroyed is death"?*[846]

Perhaps we should think of the occasions when Jesus referred in His teaching to the final judgment of the wicked, as in, for example, the parable of the tares and the wheat, [847] not in traditional terms of *being burned* (and for ever at that), but rather in terms of being

---

841   Acts 13:46-48: This needs to be understood in context: in the historical event, Paul and Barnabas were saying "if you want to reject this message, we will go to those who will listen"; in the eternal sense, it is true that "eternal life in God" is not available to those who reject Him; but it cannot be inferred that those people could not change their minds later; nor that hell awaited them if they did not, because the alternatives were between eternal life in God or *perishing*

842   John 6:68

843   Matthew 16:26, see also Mark 8:36 ("what shall it profit a man, if he shall gain the whole world, and *lose his own soul?"*— KJV), and Luke 9:24-25 ("whosoever would save his life *will lose it;* and whoever loses his life for my sake, *he will save it.* For what does it profit a man if he gains the whole world and loses or forfeits himself?")

844   Luke 13:1-5, Jesus warning people to repent ["or else"]: the word *"perish"* appears *twice* in that passage; and Mark 10:29-30: "there is no one who... who will not receive ... *in the age to come eternal life"*

845   1 Corinthians 15:21-22

846   1 Corinthians 15:26

847   Matthew 13:24-30

destroyed permanently—ceasing to exist, *perishing*—which I think was the basic meaning of what He was saying.

The apostolic writers wrote in *spiritual terms* of *"death"* as opposed to *"life"* when they could not have been referring to *physical* death, [848] so it would appear that they did not visualize "living for ever" as occurring *apart from God.* [849] How else can one explain St. Paul's emphatic statement that "as in Adam *all die,* so also in Christ shall all *be made alive"?* [850]

He also spoke of *"perishing"* as being, literally, *the opposite* of *"being saved".* [851] We assume that "being saved" means "going to heaven"—or being saved from hell—but *the connecting link in his thinking* is that we are being *saved from perishing,* i.e., we are being saved from eternal *death,* and given, instead, *eternal life, in God.*

St Paul's argument (and mine) can be summed up in his statement that "if you live according to *the flesh* you will *die,* [not *'go to hell'* but *'perish']* but if by *the Spirit* you *put to death the deeds of the body* you will *live".* [852] What could be clearer than that?

He wrote that *"the wages of sin is death,* but the free gift of God is *eternal life in Christ Jesus our Lord",* [853] again contrasting "eternal life"

---

848 e.g., 1 John 3:14: "We know that we have passed out of death into life, because we love the brethren. *He who does not love abides in death";* Romans 8:2: "For the law of the Spirit *of life* in Christ Jesus has set me free from the law of sin *and death";* Romans 8::6: "To set the mind on the flesh *is death,* but to set the mind on the Spirit *is life* and peace"; Romans 8:11: "If the Spirit of him who raised Jesus from the dead dwells in you, he who raised Christ Jesus from the dead *will give life to your mortal bodies also".* The Book of Revelation speaks of "the book of *life"* (Revelation 20:15) as opposed to *"the second death"* (Revelation 20:6 and Revelation 20:14)

849 see footnotes following re "perishing", destruction, "eternal death"

850 1 Corinthians 15:21-22

851 1 Corinthians 1:18: "For the word of the cross is folly *to those who are perishing,* but to us *who are being saved* it is the power of God" (note *the present tense,* about *the process* of "being saved", as opposed to those who think of "being saved" as *a past event,* an accomplished fact, as in "have you been saved?" or "are you [already] saved?" and 2 Thessalonians 2:10 refers to *'those who are to perish,* because *they refused* to *love* the truth and so *be saved."* Both these passages treat *"perishing"* (not hell) as *the opposite of "being saved";* and both carry the implication that, although Christ's work on the Cross was a final, past, event, our salvation is not.

852 Romans 8:13

853 Romans 16:23

with *"death"*; and he also spoke of *"sin, which leads to death"*[854] saying that *"the end of those things* [sin] *is death"*. [855] It is surely clear that he is *not* saying that "sin is inevitably *punished* by *physical* death", although in some cases it may be; in the context of eternal life in God, he is saying that the *opposite* of eternal life, the *result* of persistent, unforgiven, sin, is *eternal death, i.e. perishing,* not continuing to exist for ever (in hell or anywhere else). [856]

Presumably the implication of this is that if we do not come to be "at-one" with God at some stage, even if, perhaps, not until after our *physical* death has occurred, the result will be the *spiritual* and presumably *eternal* death that the apostolic writers referred to in speaking of *"death"* as opposed to *"life"*.

In addition to the teaching of St. Paul and St. John on the eventual *destruction of wickedness,* [857] with "eternal life" being found *only* in God and not apart from Him,[858] there are references in the Epistle of St. James to the possibility of the *death of a soul,* and the fact that *"sin when it is full-grown brings death";* and one in the Second Epistle of St. Peter to "the Lord...not wishing that any should *perish,* but that all should reach repentance." [859]

---

854   Romans 6:16

855   Romans 6:23; and Galatians 6:7-8: "he who sows to his own flesh will from the flesh reap corruption; but he who sows *to the Spirit* will *from the Spirit reap eternal life"*

856   as in 1 Corinthians 3:16-17: "Do you not know that you are God's temple and that *God's Spirit dwells in you?* If any one destroys *God's temple,* God *will destroy* him" (not send him to hell)

857   e.g., St. Paul wrote [of "enemies of the Cross of Christ"] that "their end is *destruction"* (Philippians 3:18);   2 Thessalonians 1:9 refers to "the punishment of eternal *destruction;* 2 Thessalonians 2:8 says "the Lord Jesus *will destroy* [the lawless one]"; 2 Peter 3:7 refers to the end of the present world, the day of judgment, and the *"destruction* of ungodly men"; and St. John says (1 John 3:15) "no murderer *has eternal life abiding in him"*

858   e.g. John 5:21-26: "..the Son *gives life* to whom he will. ... he who...believes *him who sent me,* has *eternal life* ..has *passed from death to life.* ..the dead will hear the voice of the Son of God, and *those who hear will live";*   and John 1:4, John 6:32-58, John 10:10, 1 John 5:11;

859   James 5:20: "...whoever brings back a sinner from the error of his way [i.e. brings him back to union with God] *will save his soul from death";* James 1:13-15, and 2 Peter 3:9. 1 Peter 1: 23 refers to being "born anew, not of *perishable seed but of imperishable".* *"Eternal death"* is also referred to in *The Book of Alternative Services,* p.562

I believe that the idea, old as it may be, that "the damned" would survive for ever, to suffer eternally in hell, is not only not consistent with the teaching of the apostolic writers, but it is not consistent with our most ancient inherited liturgical tradition either: only no one ever seems to have pointed this out.

Ancient liturgical evidence in support of the belief that there CAN be the DEATH of a SOUL

The priestly absolution in the Anglican Communion service, *which is almost certainly inherited from the earliest Christian tradition,* and thus, being in use from the very beginning, must be older (in the Church) than subsequent philosophical ideas about hell and everlasting torment, says: "Almighty God..have mercy upon you; *pardon and deliver you* from all your sins...*and bring you to everlasting life;* through Jesus Christ our Lord", which would seem to imply that "everlasting life" was not thought of by the earliest Christians as something that automatically happened to *everybody.* (Incidentally, this most ancient prayer contains both the aspects of the Atonement I am writing about: *"pardon...your sins...AND bring you to everlasting life".)* [860] Similarly, the words of administration of the sacrament of Holy Communion must have been in existence long before the compilation of the Anglican *Book of Common Prayer* four hundred years ago: "The [Body and Blood] of our Lord Jesus Christ..preserve thy body and soul *unto everlasting life..."* It doesn't specify *"bring you to heaven";* its meaning is "may Christ cause your body and soul to survive this life *and live for ever",* with the implication that the alternative was *not* surviving *"unto everlasting life".* [861] The Latin equivalent,"Custodiat.. in [into] vitam aeternam", could be rendered: "keep and preserve [me], now, and into eternal life." [862] There are references in the funeral service to "the *death*

---

860   the latter ("eternal life") being not so much *a place* for forgiven sinners, but *a sharing in the eternal life of God (e.g.* 1 John 2:24-25: "...then you will abide *in the Son and in the Father.* And this is what he has promised us, *eternal life"* and 1 John 5:20 "we are *in Him* who is true, *in His Son...* This is *the true God and eternal life").*

861   *The [Anglican] Book of Common Prayer, 1962, Canada,* pages 77 and 84.

862   *The English Missal for the Laity:* London, W. Knott & Son Limited, 1933, p.326. (N.B., pre-Vatican II).

of sin" as opposed to *"the life* of righteousness" [863] which I am sure most people do not understand, but which are consistent with St. Paul's arguments about *perpetual sin leading to perpetual death*, explained earlier. The Catechism in the *Book of Common Prayer* to this day contains the prayer that God will "keep us from all sin and wickedness, *and from everlasting death.* "[864] Similarly, the old prayer quoted below and still used in the current *Book of Common Prayer* also contains the statement that "whosoever... believeth in him, shall not *die eternally,*" based, of course, on John 11: 25-26: ("shall never die"). Incidentally the Anglican *Book of Common Prayer* in its Daily Offices of Morning and Evening Prayer [865] has long used a quotation from the Book of Ezekiel when, in the Absolution, it speaks of God "[desiring] not the *death* of a sinner, but rather that he should turn from his wickedness, *and live.* "[866]

It would appear from the above that teaching in the Christian Church about bad people spending eternity in hell must have come later than words traditionally spoken in the liturgy which *would almost certainly have been inherited from the very earliest times. .* It is necessary to understand this concept (that "eternal life" or surviving for ever is only to be found in union with the eternal God) to

---

863 There is a prayer in the funeral service in the old English (1662) *Book of Common Prayer* that God "deliver us not into the bitter pains of *eternal death";* and the Collect at that service reads "O..God, the Father of our Lord Jesus Christ, who is the resurrection and the life; *in whom* whosoever believeth shall live, though he die; and whosoever liveth and believeth in him, shall not *die eternally...* We..beseech thee, O Father, to raise us from *the death of sin* unto the *life* of righteousness. [We pray] that, at..the last day, we may be found acceptable in thy sight; and receive that blessing which thy well-beloved Son shall then pronounce to all that *love* and fear thee, saying Come ...receive the king-dom prepared for you from the beginning of the world..." This is echoed in the *Book of Alternative Services:* among "Additional Prayers", on page 601, one of them reads: "raise us, we..pray, from *the death of sin* to *the life* of righteousness; that...at the resurrection [we may] receive that blessing which your well-beloved Son shall then pronounce..." *"Eternal death"* has long been in the liturgy, inspite of the concept of hell.

864 *The [Anglican] Book of Common Prayer] 1962 Canada*, p.550.

865 The Absolution at Matins and Evensong in the original *Book of Common Prayer.... according to the use of the Church of England;* and in the [Anglican] *Book of Common Prayer, 1962, Canada,* pages 5 and 20.

866 Ezekiel 33:11: "As I live, says the Lord God, I have no pleasure in the death of the wicked, but that the wicked turn from his way and live"

appreciate the necessity of *abiding in Christ*. I believe that these old, inherited, liturgies reflect much earlier teaching, and that when old liturgies are discarded and new ones created, care must be taken that the original understanding of the faith is preserved for those who in the future might never have been exposed to the originals.

The importance of the above in relation to the doctrine of the Atonement

We need to think of the Atonement as having two aspects to it, the first being the forgiveness of sins, which Christ won for us on the Cross in the past; and the second being *His enabling us to identify ourselves with Him in the present,* in both our living and our dying, *now and into eternity,* which was the ultimate purpose of His incarnation, and death and resurrection, in the first place. Logically speaking, just *"being forgiven"* in itself would not necessarily equate to, or explain, our being given "eternal life" in the way that the concept of "abiding in Christ" would do: our being given the opportunity to abide eternally *in the eternal God.* However, I think that the historical tendency to concentrate mainly on *forgiveness* has led to the tendency to believe that "heaven" is *"a place where one goes when one has been forgiven",* without necessarily any connection with God—or anticipated improvement in ourselves! That is why I so strongly believe that the long-neglected concept of "abiding in Christ," which I see as the second part of the Atonement, is as important as the forgiveness of sins in understanding the doctrine of the Atonement; and it is for that reason that I am putting such emphasis on the theme of *"abiding in Christ,"* and *eternal life* being found *only* in God, the God who is *Eternal Love.* Only the concept of "abiding in Christ" makes sense of St. Paul's saying:

> *if we have been united with [Christ] in a death like his, we shall certainly be united with him in a resurrection like his. We know that our old self* [human nature as represented by Adam] *was crucified with him so that* the sinful body might be destroyed and *we might no longer be enslaved to sin* [867]

---

867 Romans 6:56; and Galatians 5:24-25: "Those who belong to Christ Jesus have [metaphorically speaking] *crucified the flesh with its [selfish] passions and desires...*If we live by the Spirit, let us also walk by the Spirit" One *cannot be united with Christ spiritually unless one is prepared to resist the temptations of the flesh as He did,* which we can only

So you also must consider yourselves dead to sin and alive to God [eternally because God is eternal] *in Christ Jesus* [not just "because of him"]. [868]

Only the concept of "abiding in Christ" makes sense of this, and of the Biblical teaching that Christ "overcame *death*". [869] We know that everyone dies eventually, in the physical sense, so the understanding that we have "eternal life" *in Christ* [870] *must* refer to life after our earthly existence is over, so that we never "die" again, but live for ever. The corollory of this must be that, if one is so steeped in evil that one prefers evil to good, even in the presence of God at the end of time, one does not go on living for ever (in hell, or anywhere else), but ceases to exist, *"perishes"*: not as "punishment", in the "rewards and punishment" sense of the word, especially not as "punishment" for intellectual views held in this lifetime which one may wish to revise on actually meeting God: it has to do with being so absolutely incompatible with the love and goodness that is God that reconciliation is impossible, nor is it wished for on either side (just as oil will never mix with water).

This has to do with the *destruction of wickedness,* [871] because there is no place for evil in God's Kingdom. The idea that *wickedness continues* to exist, eternally, in hell, is *not* the original apostolic teaching of the New Testament, as I have tried to show, and I believe that this deviation from the earliest apostolic teaching (that *living for ever* is *only* to be found in abiding *in God, in love)* helps to explain how the

---

do in His strength as we *abide in Him*. It is easy to assume that when St. Paul spoke of *"enemies of the Cross of Christ"* (Philippians 3:18-21), he was speaking of "enemies of the Christian faith"; but I think he meant this *literally*, that people "whose minds are set on earthly things, whose god is their belly," are *ipso facto* inimical to the self-sacrifice which *the Cross stands for;* Romans 13:14:"put on the Lord Jesus Christ, and make no provision for the flesh, to gratify its desires"; and 1 Peter 2:11 "abstain from the passions of the flesh that wage war against your soul."

868   Romans 6:5-11

869   e.g., Romans 6:9: "death no longer has dominion over him"

870   1 John 5:11 "And this is the testimony [of God], that God gave us eternal life, and *this life is in His Son."*

871   see earlier discussion on this; and see also 2 Thessalonians 2:8: "And then the lawless one will be revealed, and the Lord Jesus will ... *destroy him* by his appearing and his coming", and Philippians 3:18 [of enemies of the Cross of Christ] their end is *destruction"*

Church came to concentrate on the "sin and punishment" aspect of the Atonement, and the idea of *abiding in Christ,* sanctified by the Holy Spirit, *in God's love, for ever,* faded over time. [872]

Only the concept of "abiding in Christ" makes sense of the Christian faith as a whole, and the original understanding of the Atonement, and I believe that it is because this has for so long ceased to be a priority in the teaching of the Church, along with the absolute need to love God and neighbour which is fundamental to it, that the Christian faith has come to be so misunderstood, and in danger of being rejected, today.

If we can accept the idea of the Incarnation, that God entered human history in the person of Jesus of Nazareth, that would surely imply a God more greatly-to-be-worshipped than some remote being who had never encountered human existence for Himself.

What distinguishes Christianity from all other religions is the fact that we believe that God knows, *from His own personal experience,* what it is like to live on earth, and suffer, and die, as one of us. He is not a remote being watching us from some other planet, as it were; it is not possible for us to claim that we know or have suffered anything He has not known and suffered. He knows all that we have been through, and much, much more. The Incarnate God knows exactly what evil and suffering entails, and can still forgive, and has, as it were, "earned" the moral right to insist that we forgive also, in His Name and in His strength—the strength which He provides to us as we "abide in Him".

If, as the New Testament teaches, that God was/is really Love, which I believe the-God-to-be-most-greatly-worshipped would be, surely He would want somehow to share that love with us and bring us to Himself: which brings us to the question of how *does* God bring us to Himself: the Atonement in its fullest sense. Surely "abiding in Christ" *has to be* the answer to this.

I believe that in His passion Christ took on Himself the sin and suffering of the whole world. God still suffers when His people suffer;

---

872   In spite of passages in St. Paul's Epistles such as Romans 6:22-23: "But now that *you have been set free from sin* and have become slaves of God, [i.e. you have repented, changed and *been forgiven]* the return you get is *sanctification, and its end, eternal life.* For the wages of sin is death, but *the free gift of God is eternal life in Christ Jesus Our Lord"* [not just *"forgiveness"*] . I think St. Paul makes it clear that this is a *two-part* process.

and gives them the strength they need when they need it; and we can find *identification with Him* whatever we may be going through in our lives. That is not to say that pain is good, or that God wants us to suffer, quite the reverse; I believe God wants our total well-being. He was revealed to us in the Gospels as a God who heals, and, in a broken, hurting world, God is with us, and can understand what we are going through.

We can identify with Him in His suffering and He can share in ours. He can lighten our burden for us, He can share it with us, and through it bring healing and redemption.

When I was in my early teens and came to be confirmed, I wanted to know why Christ "had to die for my sins": in other words, would someone kindly talk to me about the Atonement! I think I was reacting to the over-emphasis on sin and penitence that existed in the Church of England in those days, which led me to ask: was I really so bad, so "awful", that Christ "had to" die for me, and *why was His death necessary anyway?* From there it was a short progression to "I never asked Him to", and "please don't make me feel guilty about it". (Being made to feel unnecessarily guilty has caused many people to leave the Church, including my own grandmother when her husband committed suicide, and I am glad that the Anglican Church at least has recognized that this heavy penitential emphasis needed to be lightened; however, I hope we do not move too far in the opposite direction, because we do need a realistic repentance in order to receive God's forgiveness.) However, when I was asking these hard questions, in my youth, no one talked to me about a God of Love, let alone a God who wanted to live so closely in us, and with us, that we somehow became "at one" with Him; and that this closeness, this union with God through Christ, in some way occurred through our being baptized into Jesus' death and resurrection. No one explained that the Atonement was not just about sin and judgment and redemption: or, at least, "redemption" was not defined as being any more than "forgiveness of sins". I suppose I must have heard St. John's Gospel, about "abiding in Christ", being read in Church; but I never understood the significance of it, or how it tied in with the Atonement, and could be the answer to all my questions.

I realize now that the Atonement includes *both* aspects. It is about being forgiven and redeemed, yes, but also about *nothing less than being caught up into the love and life which is at the heart of God.* These two complementary aspects—*the forgiveness of sins* coming from Christ's passion in the past, and *our coming to God* in the present and future [873] — can be described as "the two arms" of the Atonement, like the two arms on a cross. I believe now that this is the truest and most complete understanding of this difficult doctrine.

Vincent Taylor has well summarized this understanding, as follows (the italics are mine):

> 'Christ died for our sins' does not, as a confession, mean that His work begins and ends with sin; it is a negative way of declaring what is also expressed positively in New Testament teaching, namely, that *He died to 'bring us to God'* (1 Peter iii.18). The determinative conception is the intention that we should *'know God and enjoy Him for ever'*

and

> For purposes of thought it is most useful to isolate Christ's deed *[in the past]* and man's response *[in the present]*, but in practice *without both* there is no 'at-one-ment' and, in consequence, no satisfactory statement of the doctrine. Many popular objections to the Atonement are due to this fatal separation between the deed and the response. The deed is seen in itself, apart from the response it is intended to sustain, with the result that it is viewed as the work of a substitute *[for us]* and as a 'transaction' accomplished on man's behalf. So powerful in their effect are these objections that, although the theories of the Atonement on which they rest belong to the past, *theological reconstruction is impeded by them to this day.* [874]

So I pondered these questions in my youth, but without being

---

873 Acts 11:18: St. Peter defining "salvation": "God has granted *repentance* (in our present lives) unto *life*" (eternal life in the future — eternal life *in God,* which is the subject of this book.)

874 Vincent Taylor, *The Atonement in New Testament Teaching.* London: The Epworth Press, 1940, p. 179.

able to resolve them. It was not until I went to theological college in my fifties, and had an opportunity really to study the subject in some depth, that I learned that there were at least five classic theories of the Atonement, each supported by references from the Bible, and that the Church had never formally opted for any one of these theories at the expense of the others. While from earliest times, in all genuine Christianity, Jesus has been seen as Redeemer, Saviour and Lord, the Bible has been left to speak for itself, with the richness of all its metaphors taken together expressing a truth that no one of them could adequately convey on its own. I believe that, if we look at all of them together, and truly seek to understand, the Holy Spirit will illuminate the teaching of the Bible for us.

I think a problem has been caused by the human tendency to fix on one particular point, whatever it may be, and put undue weight on it, as opposed to looking at the whole, and letting it speak to us in its totality. This can happen in many ways, whether it is concentrating on one metaphor in the Bible to the exclusion of others, or thinking of one Person of the Godhead as different or separate from "God" as a whole: or even concentrating on the act of redemption on the Cross in the past, to the exclusion of God's ongoing work of sanctification in the present time. Problems also arise from the difficulty which we human beings have in trying to express such profound subjects within the limits of human language, but, nevertheless, we need to remember the dangers of making our focus too limited with regard to any one of these points. I think we need continually to go back to the Bible, and ponder the multiplicity of its images. So often, people have tended either to accept without question, or reject completely, the *non-apostolic, non-Biblical,* thought of later generations without ever measuring it against the standards of the Bible, and this has resulted in many problems. Even if subsequent generations may have "muddied the waters", surely it is the apostolic teaching in the New Testament that should guide us, which is that our total redemption consists *not only* of our being forgiven for our sins but *also* our being offered "at-one-ment", union, with God, through Christ, now and for ever.

So, while we need to recognize that we are "saved" by Christ's action, and not by any effort of our own, we also need to let the Holy Spirit work in our lives in the present time, as we "abide in Christ", and He abides in us—coming to union with God through Him, which is our real salvation. Being "let off punishment" is a very negative way of looking at it, and "forgiveness" and "punishment" are not always necessarily mutually-exclusive, as we sometimes find to our cost. There is more to the Atonement than this: the second part of the equation is much more positive. It is no less than *"life in God", through Christ.*

I believe that the understanding of the Atonement that I have come to is closer to the understanding of the Church in its earlier years than theories which were developed later. The only difference is that I am restating it in my own way, one which makes sense to me, and which might, perhaps, help others. Basically, I could sum it up by saying that I have, in effect, taken what Gustaf Aulen [875] has called the "classic" doctrine of the Atonement, (that Christ in His passion and death on the Cross triumphed over evil, sin and death), but explaining in my own way how I see this coming about —*as one arm of the equation;* and, in line with the thinking of people like Vincent Taylor, and others who I will be quoting here, I have combined it with the concept of *"abiding in Christ"* (as the *second* arm of the Atonement.

I believe that not only are we "forgiven", but that we are somehow brought to God through Christ—the real meaning of "at-one-ment", which was also the understanding of the Church in earlier centuries, which is why I am putting such emphasis on the Biblical idea of union with God through "abiding in Christ". [876]

The historical emphasis has usually been more on "redemption" in the sense of forgiveness and "being saved" (in the sense of averting the anger of God and not going to hell) rather than on the result of that redemption: at-one-ment with God through Christ. It is this one-sided viewpoint that I want to challenge. I cannot see God being only interested in our being "forgiven", in the sense of our not being objects of His anger any more. I think He would also want that dissolution of the barriers to result in a closer union with us in love—if He is a God of Love—which would make sense of all the

---

875   Gustaf Aulen, *Christus Victor A Historical Study of the Three Main Types of the Idea of the Atonement,* translated by A.G. Hebert. London: SPCK, 1931, 1970, 1980, p. 159.

876   This is implicit in 2 Peter 1:4 re. escaping the corruption of the world to *become partakers of the divine nature*

emphasis in the writings of St. John about abiding in Christ and living in love: but the tradition of thinking of "being saved" in terms of sacrificial offerings to avert punishment has been so strong that I think that it has overshadowed the second part of the equation in Christian history.

Redemption, as it is traditionally understood, was indeed brought about by *Christ's one, unrepeatable, act in the past,* as the Protestants maintain, yes; (the Anglican Prayer Book refers to "his one oblation of himself once offered, a full, perfect and sufficient sacrifice, oblation, and satisfaction, for the sins of the whole world" [877]). However, the Protestants of the Reformation, in their efforts to correct the very real abuses of the mediaeval Church, may have put too much emphasis on this *former,* historical event of the past (which has been taken by some of their successors as meaning that we only have to accept it, and then no more effort is required of us), while the Catholic side of the Reformation debate put too much emphasis on the *latter* aspect, (sanctification in the present).

The mediaeval Church had been accustomed to see the Mass *primarily* in terms of *"forgiveness of sins"* (which is what upset the Protestants) rather than as a way of *"abiding in Christ,"* and I think the tendency to think of the Atonement predominantly in terms of "forgiveness of sins" continued on both sides after the Reformation.

I think that part of the problem was that for centuries, as I understand it, the Church had tended to concentrate more heavily on the idea of sin and judgment, and the need to be "saved from hell", than on union with God through Christ, although the latter concept was definitely in the thinking of New Testament writers and some of the early Fathers of the Church. I see now that both sides of this equation need to be held in balance.

Old Testament ideas of atonement along these lines already existed:

> Each of the elements found in the [Old Testament] doctrine of atonement is present in the [New Testament]. Here too are guilty human beings who have sinned and

---

877 *The [Anglican] Book of Common Prayer, 1962, Canada,* p.82. See also Hebrews 10:12-18: "But when Christ had offered *for all time a single sacrifice for sins,* he sat down at the right hand of God....*For by a single offering* he has perfected *for all time* those who are sanctified. And the Holy Spirit also bears witness to us..."

deserve punishment. Here too is a sacrifice provided by God. Here too is forgiveness of sins, won by identifying by faith with the atoning sacrifice. [878]

My emphasis on St. John's writing about "abiding in Christ," (in other words, union with God through Christ), is an "unwrapping", as it were, of those last words *"identifying by faith with the atoning sacrifice";* but I think that, in practice, the Old Testament tradition of sin and punishment and sacrifice and forgiveness (in addition to the idea of eternal punishment in hell existing since pre-Christian times) has outweighed the equally-valid New Testament teaching about coming to God through Christ, and has resulted in some of the problems we see today.

I think, too, that St. Paul's teaching about sin and "the law" has not been sufficiently understood. [879] St. Paul argued that "the law" was given to teach primitive humanity the difference between right and wrong, and that, when Christ came, we were no longer "under the law" in the way we were before. He wrote to the Galatians that:

> before faith came, we were confined under the law, kept under restraint until faith should be revealed. So that the law was our custodian until Christ came, that we might be justified by faith. But now that faith has come, we are no longer under a custodian, for *in Christ Jesus you are all sons of God, through faith. For as many of you as were baptized unto Christ have put on Christ.* There is neither Jew or Greek, there is neither slave nor free, there is neither male nor female; for *you are all one in Christ Jesus.* [880]

It could be argued that the traditional emphasis on *"punishment"* for *"sin"* arose, too, from a basic misunderstanding of the fact that,

---

878 Lawrence O. Richards. *Expository Dictionary of Bible Words.* Grand Rapids, Michigan: Regency Reference Library, Zondervan Publishing House, 1985, p.84.

879 see the section on St. Paul on the subjects of "sin" and "the law", and "flesh" and "spirit",

880 Galatians 3:23-28—see Galatians 4:1 "I mean that the heir, as long as he is a child, is no better than a slave"

as St. Paul would say, we are no longer "under the law". Under the law, punishment is meted out for offences against the law: under the law, sin is punished; but Christians are supposed to have moved on from that elemental fact.

While we acknowledge that we do sin, and we do need God's forgiveness, and in and through Christ we receive God's forgiveness with gratitude, that forgiveness is not the "be-all-and-end-all" of the Atonement, because, if we accept St. Paul's arguments, if we are no longer "under the law," then "the law" and its consequences and punishments are no longer the most important criterion in our lives or what we should be most concerned with.

If the concept of law (and punishment) is temporal and earthly, and thus temporary, and the concept of life in God is eternal; *and the latter has superseded the former;* and if the opposite of eternal life must be eternal death, it is now a question of whether we are *spiritually alive for ever "in Christ",* (as envisaged in the passage quoted above), or whether, if we do not eventually come to be in God, we end up spiritually dead for all eternity, as I have tried to show.

I believe, therefore, that what we have to fear if we choose to become eternally estranged from God is not *punishment,* but *annihilation* (and I have explained why).

Believing that the Atonement is about *both* the forgiveness of sins *and* eternal life being made available to us, in God through Christ, I think we should stop thinking in old-fashioned ways of Christ "winning *forgiveness"* for us in some magical way (and then what, if He did not also give us the strength to overcome our sinfulness *in Him* through the opportunity to "abide in Him" which He has given us), and think more of the great opportunity of being with God forever, *in Him,* which He has given us, *which is our real salvation.*

To summarize briefly the history of thinking about the Atonement:

What Gustaf Aulen described as the "classic" doctrine of the Atonement was that Christ had won a great victory over the powers of evil, sin and death, and this was the main doctrine of the Atonement in the Church for the first thousand years of its history.

Although in the second millenium of the Church's history this theory has been largely disregarded, Aulen believes that *"the classic idea of the Atonement and of Christianity is coming back".* [881] He says *"the classic idea emerged with Christianity itself, and on that ground alone cannot be refused a claim,"* [882] although he admits that, *if the classic idea ever again resumes a leading place in Christian theology, it is not likely that it will revert to precisely the same form of expression.*

As I have said, for the first millenium of the Church's history, the "classic" doctrine was the mainly accepted one (a victory over evil, sin and death, however defined), and many of the early theories had in them, *as well,* some form of the idea of our coming to God through Christ: for example "Deification through Incarnation"—Irenaeus' statement that "The Son of God has become what we are in order that we might receive a share in his perfection"; Gregory of Nazianzus' statement that what has not been assumed has also not been saved, and "Deification Through Assimilation to God." [883] I think it would have been much simpler if they had just restated the teaching in St. John's Gospel about "abiding in Christ", which is what I propose to do!

Then Anselm of Canterbury (c.1033-1109) rejected the idea that had come down to him of the Atonement being a ransom paid to the Devil, because he rejected the idea that Satan had some claim over the human race. He developed a theory of "vicarious satisfaction", heavily influenced by the feudal ideas of his time, in which Christ made reparation to the infinite God for the offences committed by human beings, which had become infinite because they related to the infinite God, and required infinite atonement, which only Christ could give because He was infinite too.

The vicarious atonement theories saw Christ as acting apart from us, as a substitute for us, and so on. There were many variations of these vicarious atonement theories, in which Christ suffered on behalf of human beings: He was paying the penalty on our behalf that divine justice required as the result of our offences; He was bearing human

---

881   Gustaf Aulen, *Christus Victor A Historical Study of the Three Main Types of the Idea of the Atonement,* translated by A.G. Hebert. London: SPCK, 1931, 1970, 1980, p. 159

882   Aulen, p. 158

883   Wolfhart Pannenberg. *Jesus—God And Man.* Second Edition: translated by Lewis L. Wilkins and Duane A. Priebe. Philadelphia, Pennsylvania: The Westminster Press, c. 1968, 1977, p.40.

guilt in Himself and somehow purging us of it by doing so; cancelling the sin of "the first Adam"; offering himself as a sacrifice to God the Father in atonement for all the sins of the world.

At the time of the Reformation, Martin Luther reverted to the earlier, classical doctrine of the Atonement (that Christ, on the Cross, had won a great victory over sin and all evil), and, in protest against the abuses of the mediaeval Church with regard to the Mass, he insisted on Justification by Faith alone. However, in the main, both Protestant and Roman Catholic thought continued basically along mediaeval lines, until the Enlightenment in the eighteenth century shattered such theories for ever as being unworthy of a God worth worshipping.

As theology became more and more liberal over the last two hundred years, the significance of the Atonement became generally more and more muted, until Jesus of Nazareth came to be seen by many people as merely an example of moral perfection, rather along the lines of Peter Abelard's earlier theory that Jesus' actions merely inspired in people a loving response—though an example of moral perfection who inspired in us a loving response would not claim to be One with God the Father [884] if He were not indeed so. Although the mediaeval theories of the Atonement have been rightly rejected, I think that traces of them still linger in people's minds, to the point of making it difficult for them to accept the Christian faith.

There are, too, problems arising from earlier in the Church's history. One is the pre-Christian belief that *everyone* lived for ever, thus obscuring the fact that "salvation" means not just being forgiven, but *living for ever in God* through Christ ("perishing" *cannot* mean eternal life in hell).

There is also the problem of the historical doctrine of "original sin"[885] (that humanity is *born* sinful, because of an inherited guilt that in itself has to be atoned for). This has had its effect on the traditional understanding of the Atonement, in the sense that Christ is seen as *the sinless One suffering for the sinful* (which He *was,* but *not* because He was *incapable* of sin Himself: the whole point of the Incarnation was that He shared our human nature with all its disadvantages and temptations); but this point of view has led to distorted views such

884   John 10:30
885   see Glossary

as those of Maurice Wiles which I go on to discuss. Jesus was not just "the perfect sacrifice" to appease an offended god, but *the means by which we can share in* His victory over sin and death.

Problems arising from earlier theories about the Atonement:

(a) The idea that God the Father somehow victimized His Son

A passage in the Bible that I believe has been much misunderstood is: "God so loved the world that he gave his only Son, that whoever believes in him should not perish, but have eternal life." [886]

People have assumed that this `meant that God *"the Father"* was the kind of person who would just hand over his own son, as an innocent victim, to suffer a cruel and undeserved death, while He, "the Father", was apparently completely untouched and unmoved by it all (the old "changelessness" theory); remote and uncaring and therefore, by implication, callous and cruel. (A God of *Love?*)

As a result, many people have inherited, without ever having thought about it, the idea of a cruel father, an unjust father: certainly not a father worthy of love and respect; and therefore a "God" who is not worthy of worship. No wonder the world has rejected such an idea of "God".

This is an example of a text being taken in the wrong way. It was *Jesus who was talking,* and, far from being an unwilling victim, He was talking about the necessity of what was about to happen, and the purpose of it. He was talking about *Love:* the fact that that *God so loved* the world that God was even willing to die for it, meaning that *He so loved,* and that *He was so willing,* if you accept that Jesus is part of the Trinity. He was not talking about some "transaction" or "payment".

He was making a statement about *love, and eternal life,* and the fact that that sacrifice was somehow the necessary link between the two, which in some way has brought together, *in Him, God's eternal love and our eternal life.*

From the earliest days of the Church, Christians have taken the prophecies of Isaiah as referring to Christ, who, as I have tried to show, was seen by them as God Incarnate, and a passage that is helpful in countering the misunderstanding of the passage I quoted earlier

---

886 John 3:16

(about "God gave his Son") is the following, echoed by St. Paul in the Epistle to the Ephesians, see footnote below: "*...he makes himself* [887] *an offering for sin... [and] he shall see the fruit of the travail of his soul and be satisfied...he poured out his soul to death,* and was numbered with the transgressors; yet *he bore the sin of many, and made intercession* for the transgressors". [888] The fact that "he made intercession for the transgressors" is consistent with the character of the kind of God I have been trying to describe. Jesus Himself was an active participant in what was going on. If He was just "some wandering soothsayer" or otherwise purely human man, or whatever people are trying to make of Him today, how would He be able to "bear the sin of many", or "make himself an offering for sin"?

If, instead of thinking of Christ as having somehow "earned" something for us, we thought instead in terms of Christ *enabling us* to have eternal life in God because we are able to abide in Him through His Holy Spirit, I think it would all start to make much more sense. I believe that the historical Atonement and our "abiding in Christ" are closely linked, and the motive behind both was, and is, *Love—the Love which is God.* These problems arise when we try to separate too definitely in our minds the Persons of the Trinity, or do not remember that *the nature of God is One.* I believe—in spite of the fact that it was long believed that this could not be so—that *the whole of God* was involved in the trauma of the Crucifixion, the whole of God suffered the pain of it all. Suppose for a moment that the old "changelessness" theory was correct, which would mean that the Other Persons of the Trinity were not affected by the Crucifixion: could we then believe (if we think we believe in the Trinity) either that God is *One,* or that God

---

887 Isaiah 53:10: The Hebrew says *"thou makest* his soul...", but the RSV version quoted above is based on the Vulgate (the old Latin translation of the Old Testament), and I think the Vulgate reflects the early Christian understanding of that passage, even though the original Hebrew text was slightly different. Moreover, it fits the context of the rest of the passage: "he shall see the fruit of the travail of his soul...he poured out his soul to death.." This is echoed by St. Paul in Ephesians 5:2: "...Christ loved us *and gave himself up* for us, a fragrant offering and sacrifice to God"; Hebrews 9:14 says "Christ.. through the eternal Spirit *offered Himself* without blemish to God"

888 Isaiah 53:10-12. see also the story of Philip interpreting the prophecies of Isaiah to the Ethiopian, Acts 8:26-38

is love? I need we continually need to ask the question: *"What kind of a God do we believe in?"*

If we believe in the Trinitarian God at all, we must believe that All the Persons of the Trinity *agree* in love, even as we are supposed to among ourselves: Jesus prayed to the Father that we might be one, even as He and the Father are One." [889] Could a loving God watch the Crucifixion and not be moved, or care? But even as we remember that God is one, and not divided in His motives, or really in His actions, we have to be reminded that it was not possible for the whole of the Godhead to be physically nailed to a Cross. There had to be an incarnation, God had to be in human form, to *be* on a Cross.

It is rather on the level of the question a parishioner asked me once: "If the Trinity came to dinner, how many places would you lay at the table?" when I replied that the answer, as I saw it, would be "one". It would be for Jesus, *because in Him the whole of God was represented.* Sometimes I think we have problems because words and images, even ideas, get "fossilised" in our minds, to the point where we no longer think about them. It can sometimes help to paraphrase them, or put them in a new way, using different words and images to try to convey the same meaning, so that we can see the original in a new light.

(b) Difficulties arising from the idea that "a sacrifice" was "needed"

One of the problems has been that people have thought of Jesus as somehow, for some reason which they do not understand, having to become a substitute for an animal sacrifice under the Old Covenant ritual, and be put to death as a "sacrifice for our sin". I counter this by saying that *He gave Himself* willingly, and it was not —and I do need to emphasize this—not just because we have sinned and need redemption, but it was *also* because He wanted to bring us to Himself in love, that we might have *eternal life, in Him.*

When St. John wrote of Jesus as being *"the lamb of God"* [890] he was expressing the symbolic idea that Jesus "was sacrificed" at the same

---

889   John 17:11... "Holy Father, keep them in thy name.... *that they may be one, even as we are one."*

890   John l: 29,36; also the many references to *"The Lamb"* in the Book of Revelation; and 1 Peter 1:19: "you were ransomed...not with perishable things...but with the precious blood of Christ, like that of a lamb without blemish or spot."

time as the Passover lambs were being killed, and thus could be seen as the Passover lamb *par excellence,* the offering of the holy God *of Himself,* as opposed to the kind of sacrifice which consisted of the ordinary offering of an ordinary animal by any ordinary, sinful, human being: and thus a sacrifice and an offering was being made to supersede the rituals of the Old Testament and inaugurate the New Covenant. Unlike the sacrifices of the Old Testament, this would cover God's people for ever, because it was, in itself, of God.

The phrase *"Lamb of God"* can therefore be seen as a form of "shorthand" to cover the deep symbolism that I have just described. Jesus (as both Priest and Victim) [891] offered up Himself, as opposed to being a passive "sacrifice". For example:

> ...it was fitting that we should have such a high priest, holy, blameless, unstained, separated from sinners, exalted above the heavens. He has no need, like those high priests, to offer sacrifices daily....he did this once for all when he offered up himself [892]

and

> "Walk in love, as Christ loved us and gave himself up for us, a fragrant offering and sacrifice to God." [893]

Vincent Taylor has said that "the sacrificial aspect of the Atonement is one of the most widely attested ideas in New Testament teaching". [894]

I find this easier to understand in the mystical sense of Christ's offering to the Father love, and worship, and obedience and self-sacrifice, *an ultimate offering of Himself:* an offering *in which we can be included,* as we identify ourselves with Him. I believe that the idea of *our* being *"in Christ"* in our present living—as opposed to the idea of some "transaction" that occurred in the past in which we were not involved—is the only answer that makes sense of all these problems,

---

891   *The [Anglican] Book of Common Praise [Canada], (Revised 1938);* hymn 397, "Alleluia! Sing to Jesus!" by William Chatterton Dix, 1866.

892   Hebrews 7:27

893   Ephesians 5:2; and see also Isaiah 53:10: *"when he makes himself an offering* for sin... he shall see the fruit of the travail of his soul and be satisfied"

894   Vincent Taylor. *The Atonement in New Testament Teaching.* London: The Epworth Press, 1940, p.177.

and so there must be "a second arm" of the Atonement: it is not just that Christ died, but that *He lives,* and *we live* — *in Him.*

(c) The problem of "evil", if Christianity is not a dualistic faith.

A major objection to the "classic" theory as it has been traditionally understood (the victory over evil, sin and death) has been that Christianity is not a dualistic faith, and that God and "the devil" are not rival powers that have to "fight it out" for control. People have tended to think in terms of Jesus fighting the powers of evil as if they were *an external force* to be defeated in some way by the fact of Jesus' death and resurrection: as if there was some sort of a "duel", and Jesus "won", but we are not quite sure what sort of a battle it was, or how He "won" it.

I am suggesting a way round this objection about Christianity not being a dualistic religion, which still allows the "classic theory" to stand (as Gustaf Aulen believed it eventually would): and then combining it with my understanding of *"abiding in Christ".*

Maurice Wiles has written the following about evil (although I do not agree with him when he says that he does not believe that an act of God in history was required to deal with the situation, nor do I agree with him that "the outcome was never in doubt", because I think it could have been, which is why, to my mind, Jesus' achievement in not succumbing to the temptations He endured was of such significance, so much a key to His "victory", as I will explain in a minute):

> [the classic doctrine of the Atonement] has always required careful qualification in Christian thought, because Christianity is not in the last analysis a dualistic faith. The devil is not an equal adversary; the eventual outcome of the struggle is never in doubt.[895] God is the source and Lord of all; and he will be all in all.

Nevertheless, [Wiles continues], with that qualification

---

895 *You will see that I do not agree with the latter sentence.* Jesus did win the battle, but I think He fought it on human terms, and that is why, when He triumphed, He carries us with Him. If the outcome was *automatically* fore-ordained, I do not think it would have carried the same weight as it does now: God's love and self-sacrifice, and the consequent victory, would not have been so great.

the picture could be allowed to stand. And in the demon-ridden world in which the Christian gospel was first preached, it was not merely a possible but an extremely powerful picture. But the implications of this analogy for doctrine will vary in accordance with one's beliefs about the ontological status of Satan and the demons. That is an area of belief in which some form of demythologizing is widely accepted today.... It is important to recognize that evil is more than a matter of the wrong choices of individuals. It operates through unconscious psychological forces and large-scale sociological pressures. The moral evil that grips us has a supra-personal dimension, surpassing not only our practical control but our theoretical understanding also. Thus the area of experience indicated by scriptural talk of the devil and of evil forces continues to be one that needs to be taken seriously. [896]

I agree that that there is a place for thinking of the cosmic dimensions of evil as well as the forgiveness of the sins of individuals; this century alone has seen such horrors that we need to believe in a God who can triumph over anything, even when handicapped by tortured human flesh.

We do not understand how or why: but surely it is possible that evil can multiply itself just as, for example, germs and infections can. St. Paul wrote to the Ephesians:

....be strong in the Lord and in the strength of his might. Put on the whole armor of God, that you may be able to stand against the wiles of the devil. For we are not contending against flesh and blood, but against the principalities, against the powers, against the world rulers of this present darkness, against the spiritual hosts of wickedness in the heavenly places. [897]

For this we need the power of God, *the God who had the power*

---

896 Maurice Wiles. "The Work of Christ" in *The Remaking of Christian Doctrine: the Hulsean Lectures, 1973.* London: SCM Press Ltd., 1974, pp.62-63

897 Ephesians 6:10-12

to triumph over evil in any situation, even in the vulnerability of dying on a Cross, as demonstrated so vividly at the Crucifixion; the God who could make it possible for His people to come to an *at-one-ness* with Him through His atoning and redeeming Love, through the power of the Holy Spirit working in their lives. In this union with God through Christ, we are lifted above and beyond ourselves, and are enabled to work through and transcend evil, *in Him.*

My explanation of the problems arising from earlier, dualistic ("God and the Devil"), thinking is this: We believe that God is God, and the creator of all that is: but when He made light, that entailed the existence of absence of light whenever light was not present; when He poured forth love, it has to follow that, in the places where that love does not reach, there is no love (unless we consciously reach out to Him and bring that love and light into our darkness); He is goodness, but He also gave human beings the power to reject Him, and, in so doing, to reject goodness and truth and love.

While He could flood everywhere with "light" and "love", if He so chose, (at the cost of our free-will, because we would then have no choice in the matter, and in that case would it really be "love" anyway?), it must surely follow that, because of the fact that He gave human beings free-will, we do have the ability to choose between light and darkness, love and not loving, and so on, the ability to choose to indulge the desires of the flesh even when they clash with the call of the Spirit; and I believe that it is when we use that ability to choose unlove, unkindness, cruelty, in fact anything that follows from *the absence of God,* that evil creeps in.

It is not that God made it. [898] I believe that it is because of *our* misuse of our God-given freewill that, to a great extent, *we ourselves have brought evil into the world.* [899] This would make sense of St. Paul's arguments about Christ being the man who cancelled out human

---

898 James 1:13-15: "Let no one say when he is tempted, 'I am tempted by God'; for God cannot be tempted with evil and he himself tempts no one; but each person is tempted when he is lured and enticed *by his own desire.* Then desire when it has conceived *gives birth to sin;* and sin when it is full-grown *brings death.*"

899 I make a distinction between this statement (that we sin *because of the temptations of the flesh* which we yield to but are supposed to overcome by abiding in Christ in the Spirit), and the traditional belief in "original sin".

sin, (and *in whom* we can transcend human death), [900] by being the human being who chose to be and do *only what was of God,* so that we could be identified with *Him,* and not with the evil that *human beings* had brought into the world.

My understanding of the doctrine of the Atonement

I have taken what Gustaf Aulen has called "the classic doctrine" of the Atonement (the victory over evil, sin and death), and believe that the following re-statement of it answers some of the objections that have been made against it.

I see the Atonement as having two parts: the "victory over *sin and evil"* which helps us in our struggle against sin inasmuch as we are in Him, and leads to our *being forgiven* and purified; and the "victory over *death"* which gives us *life,* because, if we are *in Him,* our humanity is caught up into His eternal divinity; and we come to have eternal life, as we "abide in Him" for ever.

Victory over "death"

I believe that, because Christ was part of God, human death could not destroy Him, [901] and His "rising from the dead" was the divine, eternal, dynamic, life in Him welling up again unquenchably, to continue to exist for ever, long past human physical extinction; and we are able to share in that "victory over death," inasmuch as we are in Him and He is in us.

I believe that, although *physical* death is a natural event built into our lives on earth, we can go on living after our physical lives are over,

---

900   1 Corinthians 15:21-22: "For as *by a man came death, by a man has come also the resur-rection of the dead.* For as in Adam all die, so also *in Christ* shall all be made alive." See too Arthur Cushman McGiffert *A History of Christian Thought, Volume 1, Early and Eastern, From Jesus to John of Damascus.* New York, London: Charles Scribner's Sons, 1947: [p.140] " 'It is impossible,' Irenaeus says, 'to live without life and *the substance of life is participation in God'* "; [p.141] "Upon the union of God and man brought about by Christ Irenaeus laid the very greatest stress...in it...he found the very heart of Christianity"; [p.143] "how could we be joined to incorruptibility and immortality unless first incorruptibility and immortality had been made what we were so that the corruptible might be absorbed by incorruptibility and the mortal by immortality and we receive the adoption of sons"

901   St. Peter (Acts 2:24): "... *it was not possible* for him to be held by [death]"

to all eternity, if we are *in and with* the eternal God; and this is made possible by our union with God through Christ, as we come to *"abide in Him"* through the Holy Spirit, now and for ever.

There are dangers in choosing one particular emphasis in Scripture over another and giving it undue weight. There are references in the New Testament both to Christ rising from the dead, and the Father "raising Him" from the dead,[902] which I interpret as meaning the same thing: but the liturgists behind the Anglican *Book of Alternative Services* seem to stress only the passive form of the verb, as in statements such as "by raising him to life you give us life for evermore"[903]—which leave out of the equation entirely the concept of *our being in Christ,* that *He is the bridge* between eternal life and eternal death.

While it is as correct, technically, to say that *God raised Jesus* from the dead as it is to say that *Christ rose again* from the dead, I believe that emphasizing only the *former* obscures the truth about *Divine Life* not being quenched by human death,[904] as if God raised from the grave an inert body which would otherwise have remained "human and dead"; and one with whom we have no particular connection, or no connection that is explained, anyway, except that it is implied that this miracle *somehow* gives us "life for evermore." We need to explain that the link is Christ: it is in our being in Christ that

---

902   e.g. Acts 10:41: *"after he rose from the dead";*   Romans 14:9: *"Christ died and lived again";* 1 Thessalonians 4:14 "we believe that *Jesus died and rose again".* There are about as many references, in all four Gospels as well as the rest of the New Testament, to Christ rising from the dead as there are to him "being raised", and it seems that these phrases were used almost indiscriminately to denote *the Resurrection,* rather than the lesser detail of whether Jesus "rose" or "was raised". For example, St. Paul wrote: "Christ has been raised from the dead", and went on *almost immediately* to say "as *by a man* came death, *by a man* has come also the resurrection of the dead. For as in Adam all die, so also *in Christ* shall all be made alive" (1 Cor.15:20-22): an explanation of the Atonement not found in the simplistic phrase: "by raising him to life you give us life for evermore". Although obviously the power of God was involved, the main emphasis of the faith has always been on *Christ rising from the dead,* from the traditional greeting *"The Lord has risen indeed"* (Luke 24:34), to the statements to this effect in both the Apostles' and the Nicene Creeds. I think it is dangerous to emphasize the passive in our new liturgies, as in the example above, thus distorting understanding about both the Resurrection and the Atonement.

903   *The* [Anglican] *Book of Alternative Services,* Eucharistic Prayer #1, page 194.

904   St.Peter (Acts 2:24) "... *it was not possible for him to be held* [by death]"

we come to eternal life in God. We simply cannot leave Him out of the equation, and treat the two events as being otherwise unrelated (God did a miracle and so we have eternal life); we need to teach our people about *abiding in Christ* and *sharing in His Resurrection by abiding in His eternal life,* or I believe we risk further misunderstandings about the Resurrection and the Atonement.

I have set out earlier my belief that the teaching of St. Paul and St. John about "eternal life" being *only in God,* and not apart from Him, the alternative being "spiritual death", became obscured or muted early in the Church's history, contributing, in part, to centuries of misunderstanding about the Atonement, because, if there was no such thing as eternal death, if *everyone* was seen as living for ever, anyway, even in hell, where was the significance of Christ's overcoming *"death"*? (or the need for us to "abide in Him"?) This, and the possible over-emphasis on the need to be forgiven, led to the belief that, *as long as one was "forgiven",* one would "go to heaven" and not to hell. The emphasis was *no longer* on becoming partakers of the divine nature [905] in order to experience eternal *life in the eternal God,* with "eternal life" itself being found *only in God:* the thinking of the church became focused on sin and forgiveness and whether one was destined for heaven or hell. Of course the Church taught that, to be forgiven, one needed contrition, in other words a renunciation of the sin that was being forgiven; but this was not then translated into an understanding that *what was then required* was relating to and being reconciled with *Divine Love,* in order to *"abide in" God;* and that, without love, and union with God, one would *not* live for ever, in heaven or anywhere else!

I believe that it was because the Church often tended to forget the significance of the victory over "death", and the concept that it was union with Christ that gave humanity *"the quality of divinity— immortal life—in which it was lacking,"* [906] it came to concentrate

---

905   2 Peter 1:4

906   Arthur Cushman McGiffert. *A History of Christian Thought, Volume 1: Early and Eastern, from Jesus to John of Damascus.* New York, London: Charles Scribner's Sons, 1947, p.142-148 re Irenaeus: "Becoming incarnate [Christ] *united the nature of God with the nature of man* and thus deified the latter, *giving it the quality of divinity— immortal life— in which it was lacking"* (and enabling us to share in the divine nature, 2 Peter 1:4)

more and more on "the-victory-over-sin-and-evil" component of "the classic doctrine of the Atonement" (as opposed to the concept of the "the victory over death").   I think that it was *this* that led to the one-sided understanding of the Atonement mentioned earlier, as fear of eternal punishment and the consequent need for forgiveness came to supersede promises of *"life"* in God: and the fact that this eternal life was *predicated on "abiding in Christ", living in the divine love, (at-one-ment with God),* was somehow overlooked.   Although, of course, the Church still professed that Christ had *"defeated death"* [907] and made eternal life available to us, *literally in Him,* I think the emphasis came to be more on "Christ *died for us", understood in the sense of* "died *for our sins"* [908] (which led in turn to the vicarious-suffering theories of the Atonement).

"Eternal life" came to be seen as *"going to heaven"* and "being saved" *because our sins have been forgiven,* rather than in terms of our *eternal existence* being inescapably *linked to union with eternal Love,* which, while also encompassing the forgiveness of sins, *was the ultimate goal for which Christ died.*

It can be argued that, once the significance of the "victory over death" and with it the necessity of "abiding in Christ" became obscured, because *everyone was thought to live for ever anyway,* [909] "being saved" came to be understood as "being saved from *punishment and hell"* rather than "being saved from the annihilation of *eternal death"* which

---

907   1 Corinthians 15:53-57, often used at funerals:*"For this perishable nature must put on the imperishable, and this mortal nature must put on immortality...*[and] then shall come to pass the saying *'Death is swallowed up in victory.' 'O death, where is thy victory?* O death, where is thy sting?' The sting of death is sin..But..*God...gives us the victory through our Lord Jesus Christ"* (I believe this is not about "sin-which-leads-to-death" *being forgiven;* it is about sin and death *being overcome);* and John 11:25-26 *"I am the resurrection and the life;* he who believes in me, *though he die* [physically],*yet shall he live* [eternally], and whoever lives and believes in me *shall never die"* [which *must* mean *"in the eternal sense"];* and Isaiah 25:8 *"He will swallow up death for ever,* and the Lord God will wipe away tears from all faces" (cf. Rev.7.16-17: "they shall hunger no more, neither thirst any more..and *God will wipe away every tear from their eyes.")*

908   as in "Christ died for our sins in accordance with the Scriptures", 1 Corinthians 15:3

909   The so-called *"Christian Doctrine of Man"* (see Glossary). My question is: *who prom-ulgated this "Doctrine", by what authority, and when?* It is interesting to note that it is not listed as such in *The Oxford Dictionary of The Christian Church.*

inevitably ensues from not finally being "at-one" with God. I believe that misunderstandings about the Atonement have led in turn to serious misunderstandings about the Christian faith itself.

Victory over "sin and evil"

As far as "sin" and "evil" are concerned, I have set out my understanding of evil as *resulting from the misuse of our human free-will, rather than its being a rival power in its own right* (this misuse arising from our giving in to the temptations of our animal nature, "the flesh", which I believe is why it is so important that Jesus, *in Himself, conquered* those temptations, so we can share in that victory and do the same *as we abide in Him).* I don't believe the "guilt" of "original sin" comes into it. I think that *this is how God brings us to Himself.*

I believe that Jesus' supreme battle was with *temptations inherent in human nature that can often lead to sin,* such as, for example, hatred, resentment and unforgiveness, and so on, which could well have been evoked by what He went through; and which, if He had succumbed to them, would have broken His ability to remain loving and forgiving even in these extreme circumstances (and, if He is part of God, such a defeat would have affected the Godhead as well, as I will try to show). However, He managed to remain Himself in spite of them, and demonstrated the power of Divine Love to overcome all evil, even in the worst of situations, giving us the opportunity of sharing this with Him; and winning, too, the "moral" right to teach us about forgiveness and love, as I mentioned earlier.

My suggestion that His ordeal was with the weaknesses of "the flesh," as opposed to "evil in the abstract," would be supported by the idea that He laid aside all spiritual advantages to be gained from a sense of the support and presence of God, not to mention His own divine nature, in order to suffer in the flesh, (in the sense of a human being who was being tortured physically, mentally and spiritually), without any overlapping, as it were, of His human flesh and the strength that could have been derived from the divine side of His nature, so that, somehow, in His strength, "the flesh" has been forever sanctified, *"in Him"*—which could be another description of "the Atonement".

I think we have become so accustomed to think that Jesus was "without sin" (which He was) that one assumes that He *could not* have sinned if He had wished to: in other words, that He could never really have been "tempted" because He was somehow born "different" from the rest of us.

He was indeed born to be different from the rest of us, in the sense that He had a divine nature as well as a human one, and in that sense He was unique, but to suggest that He did not also share with us *all that it means to be human* is to deny the deepest truth of the Incarnation.

This, I think, is another example of where later human enthusiasm to particularize and over-emphasize has over-ridden what is actually in the Scriptures. [910] Not only does St. Paul speak of Jesus' emptying Himself of all the advantages of Godhead to be born "in the likeness of men", [911] with all the disadvantages and vulnerabilities of being human, but the author of the Epistle to the Hebrews writes:

> We have not a high priest who is unable to sympathize with our weaknesses, but *one who in every respect has been tempted as we are, yet without sin.* [912]

Contrast this with the later teaching that even the Virgin Mary was born without "original sin," so where is the merit in Jesus' being born "*of the substance of the Virgin Mary His mother*", if she herself was created from the beginning to be somehow different from the rest of humanity?

The whole point of the Incarnation is that He took our nature upon Him [913] and lived and died as one of us; but even our *Book of Common Prayer* has in its Proper Preface for Christmas a statement which, presumably, has come down to us from earlier centuries, and reflects the thinking of those earlier times: "....Jesus Christ....who... was made very man [i.e. truly human] of the substance of the Virgin Mary his mother; *and that without spot of sin, to make us clean from all sin.*" [914] It could be inferred from this that Jesus was made sinless from the beginning, as if He Himself had nothing to do with His lack of sin.

---

910   See Glossary re. "original sin"

911   Philippians 2:6-8

912   Hebrews 4:15

913   e.g. Prayer of Consecration in *The Book of Common Prayer* of the Anglican Church

914   *The [Anglican] Book of Common Prayer, 1962, Canada,* p.79.

I think we need to give Him the credit for being "tempted as we are" and resisting it:

> he had to be made like his brethren in every respect, so that he might become a merciful and faithful high priest in the service of God, to make expiation for the sins of the people. *For because he himself has suffered and been tempted, he is able to help those who are tempted.* [915]

We are told that He resisted temptation in the wilderness.[916] It must therefore have been *possible* for Him to sin, He was not made to be *incapable* of it, and we need to think of what would have happened to the integrity of God if Jesus *had* succumbed to temptation, and what a risk God was willing to take for us in coming to earth and becoming so vulnerable for us. If we can grasp some of the dimensions of the *spiritual* struggle in which Jesus engaged on our behalf, and be assured that *in Him* we can draw on His great spiritual strength to do likewise in our own lives, I think "the Atonement" begins to be much more understandable.

I have spoken of the significance of Jesus' quoting on the Cross the opening words of Psalm 22 ("My God, My God, why hast thou forsaken me?") as being something that assures us that, whatever our place of darkness, whatever our sense of God-forsakenness, Jesus is still there with us in our suffering, even though we may not realize it, and this knowledge can enable us to identify ourselves with God, even then. This was an advantage that Jesus Himself did not have, when He Himself was on the Cross: our strength comes from His. I have also spoken of evil as being *the direct opposite* of all the good attributes of God—the result of the *real*, as opposed to the perceived, *absence of God*. Possibly there is *also* significance in Jesus' quotation from Psalm 22, in that He no longer felt even the comfort and strength to be derived from the presence of God the Father: far from drawing on His own divine attributes, He was declaring Himself open to attack from *all the evil that derives from the absence of God*.

This is not to suggest that He ceased to be divine as well as human, or that "God did not care", but that Jesus fought the battle *as if* there

---

915 Hebrews 2:17-18
916 Matthew 4:1-11, Mark 1:12-13, Luke 4:1-13

was nothing left of help from God to protect Him from all that crawls out of the darkness when God is not there. Far from having divine advantage, as could be inferred from the above quotation from Maurice Wiles, He took on this ultimate handicap of "the absence of God", and still "won". We need to think *not* that "His divinity" left Him, when He was on the Cross, as some have claimed, but that He suffered as a human being, "emptying Himself" as St. Paul would say, of all divine "advantages",[917] so that He could plumb the depth of the human experience, and, having done so, emerge in tact to carry us with Him.

I believe that Jesus, in His integrity, fought the battle *on human terms,* (the whole point of the Incarnation), and that *that is why,* when He triumphed, not only was it such a victory, but *it was one in which He can carry us with Him.* If He had drawn on divine strength, if He had been made to be incapable of sin, if He was not vulnerable to temptation, if the outcome was never in doubt, as Maurice Wiles implies, then we could not relate to Him in His humanity, because He would not have suffered the ravages of temptation as we do: He would have had "special advantages" which we do not. *This way we can fully identify with Him in His human vulnerability and suffering, and He with us: and in identifying ourselves with Him we come to God.*

Athough Jesus, in His integrity, suffered as a man[918] on purely human terms, it was *not just a man* who managed to remain sinless in this situation, but *also God,* if we believe in the doctrine of the Trinity. If Jesus *was* part of God the Trinity, and if He *had* broken under the pressures of the Crucifixion and ceased to be sinless, evil *would* have triumphed over the goodness of God, and I think that *that* was what the battle was all about, the magnitude of which I do not think we have ever thought about in this way. It would have destroyed not only the spiritual integrity of Jesus the man, but the Godhead Itself, if one can put one's mind around such a possibility.

That is why I do not agree with Maurice Wiles' statement that the outcome was never in doubt. If Wiles' belief was correct, that Jesus could not possibly have sinned, I do not think Jesus would really have been suffering as a human being; He would have been "taking

---

917   Philippians 2:7

918   in the *human* side of His nature—not only in His human body, but in His human mind and spirit

advantage" of His divine nature to be super-human in some way, in which case it would not have been such a "victory" or meant so much. And as I have said before, "What kind of a God do we believe in?" He truly won that victory.

If God did indeed take such a risk for love of His people, risking everything for them. even His own identity on an eternal level, we should be more profoundly humbled than we have ever been in thinking of Christ's passion, and more prepared to admit that *there might indeed have been a battle the magnitude of which (or the possible consequences of which)* we have never even thought about: and a Love so great that it would dare to take that risk that we have never even imagined. Our immediate reaction to such a suggestion—as I said above—would be to say that it could not be possible for "God" to be anything other than sinless, and, in fact, the power of goodness and love was so strong that it did triumph: but surely the whole point of the Incarnation was that Jesus took on all the liabilities—and all the risks and temptations—of being human. I believe that Jesus "played fair" by not automatically being protected from sin, because He willingly shared all the vulnerability of our humanity with us, which entailed the fearful possibility that He *could* have succumbed, and brought with it the concommitant risk of breaking the integrity of the Trinity Itself in the process.

Looking at that possibility, we could surely see it as the most fearful battle against sin and all its consequent evil, fought, with terrible potential eternal consequences, *in the very person of Jesus Himself.*

Surely that is a re-statement of the "classic" doctrine set forth in a way that does not clash, as earlier ones did, with the belief that ours is not a dualistic religion. If God, in the person of Jesus, could so demonstrate that, in spite of the handicap of a human body, vulnerable to all the temptations with which we are faced, and tortured to death, *God could still love, and forgive, and remain Himself,* there is now no situation in which we can be overcome by evil *if we are in Christ.*

It has helped me personally to think of the Atonement in terms of *Love—eternal Love—* conquering all that is "un-love," summed up as follows: I believe that the powers of evil can destroy us spiritually, as they *tried to destroy God, by trying to undermine and break Love's power to love,* when Jesus was on the Cross. *Love Itself was on the Cross, the*

Love that is eternal, Love that could not be broken by all that evil in the form of human sin could hurl at it; and *in* that Love—which is eternal, giving *us* eternal life if we are in it—we can similarly triumph over the sin that might otherwise so easily bring us down, and the spiritual death that could then envelop us.

As I see it, not even the Crucifixion could divide God the Trinity in His esssential being, nor break His will to love. The Crucifixion demonstrated that *Eternal Love could not be made to stop loving and forgiving,* even when the worst that the world could do to break it was thrown at it in an attempt to destroy it; and that that Love, having risen above that terrible testing, can now claim our allegiance in loving and forgiving, in His Name and in His strength—which leads us on to "abiding in Christ".

I believe that it is *because* He triumphed, *in His human nature,* over all that tried to destroy Him, physically and spiritually, that He can claim a victory *in which we can be included* as we come to *"abide in Him".*

We have to remember that God—who is One—[919] *gave Himself,* "Love Himself was crucified"; [920] and in the sense that the Trinity *is* divided, in being Three Persons in One God, the Son was offering Himself, willingly and actively, in an act of self-giving and obedience *with which we can now identify ourselves, in Him, in offering ourselves to God.* We become part of *it in Him.*

(The only problem is that, to think this way—that the battle that Jesus fought on the Cross was about not letting hatred, sin and evil defeat and break divine Love, and that in Christ we can share in that victory, and come to God— one has to believe in the divinity of Christ, that Jesus somehow was/is part of God; but on the other hand, if you do not believe in the divinity of Christ, there is no Atonement anyway, no way that we can come to God through Him.)

I believe that this understanding of the "classic" doctrine of the Atonement, when it is then combined with the idea of our being

---

919   Mark 12:29: "Hear, O Israel: The Lord our God, the Lord is one", based on Deuter-
         onomy 6:4: "Hear, O Israel: the LORD our God is one LORD."

920   *The [Anglican] Book of Common Praise (Revised 1938),* hymn 141: "O come and mourn
         with me awhile" by Rev. F.W. Faber, 1849. ("Jesus, our Lord, is crucified...Love himself
         was crucified")

in Christ, does seem to make more sense than any other "theory" of the Atonement that I have ever heard. Perhaps this explanation may shed new light on old words and phrases, and be the different form of expression of the old truth that Aulen referred to.

As H.A. Hodges has tried to show, *our being in Christ is a crucial component of the Atonement itself.* I think this comes close to the understanding of the early Church, both the "classic" doctrine of the victory over evil, sin and death, and our becoming "as He is" [921] through "abiding in Him" [922] (and thus learning to share in His divine nature). [923] I think it was Hodges' writing about the concept of "being in Christ" being an essential component of the Atonement, more than any other, that helped me so much when I was in College. He wrote in his book *The Pattern of Atonement* (the italics are mine):

> We cannot be saved without full repentance [but] we cannot perform this full repentance nor the penance which should go with it. Yet, on the other hand... no one, not even Christ, can do these things for us, if by 'for' is meant 'instead of' us. To this problem there is only one solution. Since we cannot do it alone and He cannot do it instead of us, *it must be both together who do it, He in us and we in Him.* And in saying this we have stepped out of that whole region of substitutions, contracts and external relationships [and] come back at last to that which was missing... *we find our salvation after all in our mystical union with Christ*

and goes on to say:

> Is there then nothing which Christ can be said to do instead of us? Is there nothing to justify the substitutionary language which is so deeply woven into

---

921   1 John 4:17; and Irenaeus' statement that the Son of God has become what we are in order that we might receive a share in his perfection (Wolfhart Pannenberg. *Jesus—God And Man.* Second edition. Translated by Lewis L. Wilkins and Duane A. Priebe. Philadelphia: The Westminster Press, 1968, 1977, p.40.)

922   John 15:1-10

923   2 Peter 1:4 "that...you may escape from the corruption...in the world ...and become partakers of the divine nature"

Christian devotion? Indeed there is, and we see it at two points.

Firstly, in the whole process of our redemption it is He who takes the initiative and retains it throughout. He alone meets the full force of the enemy's power and He alone wins the decisive victory. *None of us could bear the full impact of evil nor the full weight of the suffering which redeems....*

Secondly, to be in Christ *is to be a new creature....* '*Not I, but Christ in me*'. '*Not in myself, but in Christ*'. This is the true substitution, which the theories mishandle and misconceive, but which the Bible and the Church proclaim and on which Christian devotion continually dwells. [924]

I think that is the best description of the Atonement that I have ever seen. The metaphors in the Bible still help to illuminate the totality of our thinking when we take them all together, but I believe that the above description, of how being in Christ is what it is all about, reaches to the heart of the Christian faith. It is "in Christ" that we are both redeemed and brought to a new way of living.

The theme of fellowship with God in and through Christ is also used by C.F.D. Moule, the same theme of the one action in the past leading to communion in the present: "In a word, it is incarnation and resurrection that lends distinctiveness to the Christian phrase 'Christ died for us'. It is the *fait accompli* of the cross, *plus* the constant accessibility of the risen Christ, and the universal scope of God's action in Christ." [925]

The "two arms of the Atonement", which have been referred to as the negative (the forgiveness of sins) and the positive (the bringing of people to God) are referred to again by Moule in another book, where he wrote:

Once limit redemption to Calvary, and you must either repeat or else only remember [the Catholic versus

---

924 H.A. Hodges. *The Pattern of Atonement.* London: S.C.M. Press Ltd., 1955, p. 55.

925 C.F.D. Moule. *The Origin of Christology.* Cambridge: Cambridge University Press, 1977, p. 122.

Protestant controversy of the Reformation which had its effects not only on the doctrine of the Eucharist but also on that of the Atonement]. There is, I think, a resolution of this dilemma only when we give full value to "the mystical union that is betwixt Christ and His Church" as a union of fellowship, distinguishing it at the same time from a union of identity." [926]

.....so great and deep a mystery...the strange paradox which lies at the very heart of our faith, and which arises from the finality and yet constantly repetitive nature of salvation—the finished work of God in Christ, over against his continued work in the Body of Christ which is the Church.....It is the restless question of the relation between the sacrifice on Calvary and (as some would put it) 'the sacrifice of the Mass.' [927]

The Sacrament of the Eucharist must be mentioned in any discussion of the Atonement, for the New Testament clearly states that Jesus instituted that sacrament with the clear command that it was to be repeated often, ("do this, as often as you drink it, in remembrance of me"), [928] and that it *signified* His body and blood given for His people for the forgiveness of sins and the establishing of a new covenant between human beings and God. This was always the understanding of the Church, documented as early as St. Paul's first Epistle to the Corinthians. [929]

It would seem, therefore, that Jesus intended the Eucharist to be an ongoing experience of the redemption once wrought by His passion on earth, and so the Catholic Church has always understood it. The Protestants only reacted against medieval abuses of this understanding, but they tended, as a consequence, to concentrate overmuch on the one act of atonement in the historical past.

We need to avoid the errors made on both sides at the time of the Reformation, and see ourselves in the Church as *offering up in the*

---

926 C.F.D. Moule. *The Sacrifice of Christ.* London: Hodder and Stoughton, 1956, p. 52.

927 C.F.D. Moule. *The Sacrifice of Christ.* London: Hodder and Stoughton, 1956, p. 11.

928 1 Corinthians 11:25

929 1 Corinthians 11:20-29

Eucharist *a self-identification with the offering of love and obedience and worship* offered *by God the Son to God the Father.* Surely, then, we have a fore-taste of the union with God, the reconciliation, the "at-one-ment", which is here now, and yet, at the same time, is still to come.

Karl Rahner has said that "the Christian salvation-reality is essentially sacramental". [930]

Although it was Christ's historical death on the Cross that accomplished our reconciliation with God, I believe, as I have said, that the Trinity as a whole was involved in all of it (and that the nature of God is One). It was God the Father who sent His Son, (as part of Himself); and God the Son who offers Himself to the Father; and it is the power of the Holy Spirit, working mysteriously in our lives as we are "in Christ", that brings us, somehow, *into the love which circulates at the heart of the Trinity.* Human beings are privileged to be caught up in this mystery as a result of their redemption.

Moltmann wrote:

> [the] trinitarian history [of God with Israel, with Christ and with the Church in the power of the Spirit] becomes the history of salvation when poor, sinful, mortal human beings are incorporated into the history of the Son and the Spirit with the Father, in order that they might find divine life in it, until finally the whole creation finds its eternal life in the kingdom of glory.

Which is to say that love flows in the heart of the Trinity anyway, as described by theologians from Augustine to Moltmann; but, *in God's love for us, He has made it possible for us to be caught up into that great circle of love, and be part of it, which is what our salvation is all about.*

Moltmann said that "salvation" means to be assumed, by means of trinitarian history, *into the eternal life of the Trinity,* and went on to say (italics mine):

To include the individual in the circle of divine relations

---

930   Karl Rahner. *Theological Investigations, Volume III, The Theology of the Spiritual Life,* translated by Karl H. and Bonniface Kruger. London: Longman & Todd Ltd., 1967, 1974, p.245.

and draw the soul *into God's most intimate life stream,
this is the essence of revelation and redemption.* [931]

While we will have to wait for the next life to experience the complete fulfillment of our redemption, and experience the wonder of God's love in a much nearer way than is possible for us on this earth, Moltmann, in describing the Trinity as "the circle of divine relations [that draws the individual] into God's most intimate life stream," used the terms "monarchical" and "eucharistic", to describe how God's grace reaching out to us, His blessing coming down to us, and His response to our prayers, *in this life,* is like *one side of a great circle of love,* and the other side of that circle is prayer and praise going back up from us to God, in a great arc, as it were, to complete the circle: and then the process starts again, to continue in an unbroken flow in a great circle of love. [932]

He said of the "monarchical" form, one side of this great circle:

> activity begins with the Father, mediation occurs through the Son, and all action is effected by the Spirit,"

and, of the "eucharistic" side, the other side, of this great circle of love, he said that

> lamentations, prayers, adoration and praise begin with the Holy Spirit and go through and with the Son to the Father.

It is awe-inspiring to think that human beings can have a place in such a tremendous and glorious God, but, in Christ, we can. As Moltmann says, *"the purpose of God's works is not simply that they happen, but that they elicit a response of thanksgiving offered to God."* [933] In other words, as I would put it, God's hope was for a response from us in love.

I have mentioned the parishioner who asked me once why God wanted us—or the Church told us—continually to keep praising and thanking Him, when human parents do not ask their children to keep

---

931 Jurgen Moltmann. The Unity of the Triune God: Remarks on the Comprehensibility of the Doctrine of the Trinity and its Foundation in the History of Salvation, in *St. Vladimir's Theological Quarterly,* vol.28/3, 1984, pp. 161-162

932 Ibid p.163

933 Ibid pp. 163-164

praising and thanking them. This man said that surely God did not need that continual reassurance from us, and asked me to explain this to him.

Part of the answer, I think, is that in worship we verbalize Who God is, and what He has done, and in doing so we come to be more aware of His presence in our lives; but, also, there is a sense in which our praise and love and thanksgiving, in a sacramental sense, *catch us up into the life of God,* in the Eucharist, through each of the Persons of the Trinity participating in it with us, and it is very much more than merely saying politely, as it were, "thank you, you are very kind, I am most grateful."

"Praise and thanksgiving"—prayer—is so much more than spoken words: in the Eucharist we touch the wonderful miracle of the experience of the life of God described by people such as Karl Rahner and Jurgen Moltmann and Walter Kasper. It was Walter Kasper who said:

> "The trinitarian doxology is the soteriology [934] of the world." [935]

This leads us to the subject of "Abiding in Christ".

---

934   see Glossary for definitions of "doxology" and "soteriology"

935   Walter Kasper. *The God of Jesus Christ,* translated by Matthew J. O'Connell. New York, The Crossroad Publishing Company, 1984 (original 1982) p.248.

CHAPTER 20

"Abiding in Christ"

I believe that Jesus' metaphor of the vine and the branches [936] perfectly describes the idea of our being *in God* and yet at the same time still ourselves, so that, while the distinction still remains between us, yet through Christ we become "at one" with Him. God is love, and so the spiritual sustenance—the strength and power of Divine Love—that flows from God into those who "abide in Him" can be compared to the life-giving properties of the parent vine as it nourishes its leaves and branches, so that, while distinct in themselves, both are also one.

Another way of thinking about "abiding in Christ" is to think of it as "practising the presence of God", only in an interior, as well as an exterior, way, remembering that the concept of living IN the eternal God, with the Spirit of God dwelling in, and with, His people, runs through the whole Bible, as does the theme of Divine Love. Love, as I have tried to explain, involves caring for others as *God* would care for them: and loving God *for Himself,* and not just for the benefits we think we can receive from Him, which is not "love" at all.

Why I believe that the concept of "abiding in Christ" has not been fully appreciated in the history of the Church, and needs to be taken more seriously

I believe that my understanding of the Atonement as having two aspects to it, Christ's redeeming obedience and self-giving on the Cross *in the historical past* making it possible for us to come to a continuing

---

936   John15:1-5

"at-one-ness with God" through Him, *now, in the present time, and into the future, for all eternity,* has long been overshadowed in the history of the Church. I think the concept of our *"abiding in Christ"*, as described in the Gospel of St. John, the idea of "at-one-ment" with God, in the sense of *union with God through Christ,* has faded with time. I have come to think that it began to fade as a major component of the teaching of the Church very early in its history: certainly before the time of St. Augustine, who lived from 354-430 A.D. I suggest this because the arguments in the Pelagian heresy in which St. Augustine was involved were mainly concerned with whether human beings are intrinsically sinful, and unable to be "good" without special grace from God (I have to be simplistic here, in order to try to keep to the point), as if the predominant emphasis of the time was on *the sin-and-forgiveness* component of the Atonement, rather than on *"abiding in Christ".*

The preface to the First Epistle to Timothy, in *the New Oxford Annotated Version* of *the Revised Standard Version* of the Bible, [937] would seem to point to an even earlier time, when, as mentioned earlier, in referring to the two letters to Timothy and the one to Titus, it says (italics mine) that "the vocabulary and style of the letters differ widely from the acknowledged letters of Paul; *some of his leading theological ideas are entirely absent (e.g., the union of the believer with Christ...);"* and that *"the faith"* is seen as "a synonym *for the Christian religion rather than the believer's relationship to Christ"* (a summary of future division in the Church!) Although this would not matter in itself, *if taken in conjunction with the rest of the Bible,* it could be that *this marks the beginning of a change in emphasis* in the teaching of the Church.

During the early years there was a great problem with heresies challenging the orthodox faith that Jesus was both God and Man.[938] Among them, the Gnostic heresies claimed that God was far removed from all that was material and human, which was seen to be intrinsically evil.

I believe that the principal anti-Gnostic writers, in their efforts to dispel this idea and insist on the reality of the Incarnation, insisted

937   see also the footnote in the section on Romans 9:5 in the Chapter on the divinity of Christ

938   e.g., Arianism in particular.

that it was *not* the creation itself which was evil, but *human will,* leading to the ideas of original sin as described earlier. (Once this idea was developed, it seemed necessary to say that Jesus—and, in fact, His mother as well—were exempted from this "stain" of "original sin".)

I think this theory of original sin was also deduced from a misunderstanding of St. Paul which led the Church to believe we were all tainted with the *actual* "sin" of Adam, rather than being merely subject to the inherited weaknesses of "the flesh".[939] I believe the idea of "original sin" contradicts *the reality of the Incarnation,* that *Jesus took our nature upon Him* without any special exceptions.

Surely, if the Atonement was understood as the *two* aspects that I have described, the Church would not have become as "bogged down" as it did in debates about sin and justification, in the sense of *"release from punishment for sin".* The *Oxford Dictionary of the Christian Church* states that "the issues raised by Pelagianism....continually reappeared during the Middle Ages, only to break out afresh at the Reformation" [940]—and I believe they are still with us today.

Put very simply, Pelagius claimed that humanity was basically able to "be good" without special grace from God, because God had made His creation good, and we were not *created* as evil or sinful beings.

I have said that I believe that evil does not come from God Himself, but arises from His absence. God has given human beings free-will, but the price of His doing that is that, sooner or later, human beings will make the choice not to align themselves with the goodness of God, and will start to hurt and destroy each other and our world.

It is a price that God has been willing to pay in order that we may learn, and grow, and come to love of our own accord. It is not that God *made* or caused us to be sinful, and to that extent I think Pelagius was right: we are not intrinsically bad; God's creation is good; but we are human, and human beings, without God, can all too easily succumb to temptation and start to sin (see the section on St. Paul and "flesh" and "spirit," and "law" and "sin").

---

939   e.g. 1 Corinthians 15:21-22: "For as *in Adam all die,* so also in Christ shall all be made alive", in the context, I believe, of flesh versus spirit ("as by a man came death, so by a man has come also the resurrection of the dead")

940   F.L. Cross and E.A. Livingstone. *The Oxford Dictionary of the Christian Church,* Second Edition Revised, Oxford: Oxford University Press, 1958, 1974 and 1983, p.1059.

St. Augustine's reply to Pelagius' arguments (putting it very simply) was that we are intrinsically sinful beings, and cannot be good without God, because all goodness comes from God. And I think that St. Augustine was also right. He had inherited the Christian tradition that somehow God and human beings need to come together in Christ, and that without God we are not able to rise to the heights that humanity can achieve "in and with God".

But I do not think he can have understood that inherited tradition in terms of "abiding in Christ", or he would have said so. Instead of thinking clearly in terms of "Christ winning for us forgiveness *first,* and *then* enabling us to to have union with God, through abiding in Him", Augustine concentrated overmuch on human sin and need and hopelessness, and our need for forgiveness, as if dealing with *that* was all that needed to be done; and, in the process, I think the whole *point* of the Atonement, reconciliation with God in His love, and "life", "in Him", came to be somehow overlooked.

Arguments were developed about human beings being born in "original sin", automatically inherited from Adam,[941] rather than being made merely human with potential for both good and evil, and needing to develop the life of the spirit in order to come to God.

The point which Pelagius missed, I think, and so did Augustine, (although the latter was trying to reinforce the idea that human beings

---

941   I am suggesting that it is our misuse of God's gift of free-will that brings evil into the world, *in the context of evil not being "a rival power,"* which makes sense of St. Paul's statement (1 Corinthians 15: 21-22) that *"by man came death* [and through *Christ* comes eternal life]," which I think should be understood in the sense that St. Paul was contrasting, on the one hand, human *physical* death (built into our creation as a safeguard against misuse of our freewill and so inherited by humans from generation to generation), with *eternal resurrection in* Christ, on the other, as our humanity is caught up into His divinity as we abide in Him; but I think this passage came to be interpreted to mean that *the human race is inherently evil, deserving to be punished* by death, and the emphasis came to be on averting punishment, that punishment being understood as being eternal damnation in hell.   I think it was assumed that everyone would survive for ever, anyway, and it became a question of whether it would be in heaven or hell—the word "death" apparently seeming to have lost its meaning in this context! The idea that *eternal life* "is *in His Son"* (not *because of* His Son but *in* His Son—1 John 5:11) became obscured, and with it the concept of *"abiding in Christ",* both in this world and the next: (*"in Christ* shall all be made alive").

do "need God"), is that *"abiding in Christ, living in the love of God,"* is what the Christian faith is all about.

It is not *just* about our sin and our need for God's forgiveness, our weakness and God's power, our sinful nature and God's purity, or our need of God's help from outside, as if it were. It is *also* about *the mystical union of God with His people,* and all that flows from that.

It does sound as if that was not the primary teaching of the Church at that time, any more than it is today. One could deduce, therefore, that an unbalanced understanding of the Atonement (speaking literally in this context), an atmosphere of over-emphasis on human sinfulness and separation from God, may already have been in existence before the time of Augustine and Pelagius, and that it may have been *that* which caused Pelagius to over-react in the opposite direction.

Martin Luther, too, rebelled against this predominant way of thinking hundreds of years later, only *his* definition of the then all-important idea of "justification" ("being saved"), in reaction to the over-emphasis on *sin*—and fear of resulting punishment—was "justification *by faith,*" rather than by good works and the celebration of Masses. However, "faith" then came to be seen mainly as an intellectual belief which would of itself be enough to merit "being saved," without any specific need to keep the commandment to love, without which *"abiding in Christ"* would not be possible. In effect, it was a re-run of arguments of centuries earlier, already resolved in Biblical teaching. [942]

When this teaching is forgotten, and even the commandment to love is disregarded, subsequent distortions of the concept of "justification *by faith alone"* have had an adverse effect on later Protestant thinking, leading to a one-sided idea that if we merely *believe* then we are automatically "forgiven" and "saved" without any serious change on our part. This is based on *only half* the doctrine of the Atonement—and a flawed version at that, based on mediaeval theories about Jesus

---

942　e.g. Romans 3:28: *"A man is justified by faith apart from works of law";*　2 Peter 3:14-
　　　17 (to the effect that St. Paul has sometimes been misunderstood); and James 2:20:
　　　"faith apart from works is barren". All this makes sense if "works" in Paul's context
　　　is seen to mean mere obedience to rules and regulations, as opposed to *'the fruit of the
　　　Spirit,"* (which is *"love"*... Galatians 5:22), and in the Epistle of James "works" means
　　　the expression of love in action, without which "faith" is indeed barren, the point
　　　that the author was trying to make. See the chapter on *"God as Love".*

vicariously winning *"forgiveness"* for us in the past, as opposed to His *also* making it possible for us *to have life* in God the Trinity in the present and in the eternal future, *through identification with Him,* which I believe would still be possible after death if God so chose (see earlier discussion).

The other part of the Atonement, lost in the popular belief that *all* human beings live for ever, even in hell, is about *life (eternal life)* in *the God who is Eternal Love, life and love* being inextricably combined in the Eternal God: it is *only by "abiding in Christ", living in the Divine Love, that we can come to God,* and, sharing His immortality, can *live for ever.* History shows that the commandment to love was often overlooked by *both* sides of the Reformation debate, (e.g.,the burning of "heretics"), and supports my contention that for many centuries the Church has not been teaching that *"abiding in Christ"* is fundamental to our faith, and that "abiding in Christ" *itself is dependent on keeping the commandment to love.*[943]

About a thousand years after the time of Augustine and Pelagius, at the time of the Reformation, a man called Osiander (1498-1552), was involved in controversy which I believe could have been resolved by an understanding of the Biblical tradition along the lines that I have suggested. Justo Gonzalez[944] writes that Osiander had "an understanding of justification [which] was part and parcel of a total theological outlook that differed in many points from that of the other reformers", and says:

> Briefly stated, *Osiander was a mystic, and his theology was,* generally speaking, *one of mystical union with Christ the eternal Word of God.* This most of the other reformers feared, for it tended to obscure the distance between God and us and to focus attention on the eternal Word rather than on the historical revelation of God.

---

943   Matthew 22:37-40, the two great commandments (to love);   John 15:12: *"This is my commandment, that you love one another* as I have loved you;" and 1 John 3:23-24: "And *this is his commandment,*   that we should believe in the name of his Son Jesus Christ *and love one another,* just *as he has commanded us. All who keep his commandments abide in him, and he in them."*

944   Justo L. Gonzalez. *A History of Christian Thought, Volume III, From the Protestant Reformation to the Twentieth Century.*   Nashville: Abingdon Press, 1975, pp. 103-107.

I believe we can focus on *both,* remembering that God is both transcendant and immanent, incarnate in history and yet eternal, and that redemption was both a historical act of the past and a continuing "coming to God through Christ" in the present.

I believe that, again, the two sides in the Reformation debate were focusing narrowly on whether salvation is wrought by the historical death of Christ on the Cross in the past, or by the continuing offering of Masses by the Church in the present (that is to say "salvation" in terms of "being saved", and "forgiven our sins"); and somehow neither side was able to see that there were *"two arms"* to the doctrine of the Atonement (the second one being not the *Mass,* per se, but *"abiding in Christ").*

Because the Protestants were rightly trying to restate the belief that our salvation depends on the historical fact of the Crucifixion, and not on the constant celebration of Masses, [945] or "good works" of any kind, it became easy to think in terms of *anything else* (even union with God through Christ) as being superfluous to the basic fact of Christ's passion and self-giving on the Cross. *Of course,* the celebration of the Mass, and the doing of good works, cannot be a substitute for Christ's redemptive death in history, but the ongoing work of the Holy Spirit in the sanctification of the human soul, and union with God, through Christ, cannot be ignored either, for that is the ultimate goal for which Christ died, and goes beyond the actual forgiving of our sins. [946]

Gonzalez, discussing this in much more detail than I can, refers to a man called Flacius, who opposed the thought of Osiander, because

---

945   The compilers of the Anglican *Book of Alternative Services,* perhaps without conscious thought or intention, have allowed the mediaeval Roman Catholic emphasis on *the Mass* as the perceived instrument of salvation to creep into it, without anyone apparently seeing anything untoward in this, as in, for example, the Prayer after Communion for the Third Sunday of Advent, page 271: *"May this eucharist free us from our sins."* While there may have been a conscious decision to reject the Protestant element in what has been inherited from the Church of England, the result still does not reflect a balanced understanding of the Atonement along the lines expounded here.

946   Titus 3:5-7: "God our Saviour..*saved us,* not because of deeds done by us in righteousness, but in virtue of his own mercy, by the washing of regeneration *and* renewal in the Holy Spirit, which he poured out upon us so richly through Jesus Christ our Saviour, so that we might be *justified* by his grace *and* become heirs in hope of *eternal life".*

his belief was that "God justifies us, not because he sees in us the eternal Word, but *on account of Christ's obedience*" (italics mine).

Again, the emphasis seems to be on "sin" and "justification", as if that was all that the Atonement was about. Flacius was thinking, presumably, of Christ's obedience in the historical suffering of death on the Cross, in the past, and discounting the union of the soul with God in the present, because of the Reformers' obsession with "justification" in terms of *forgiveness of sins,* the forgiveness stemming solely from the historical fact of Christ's death on the Cross, to the exclusion of thinking *as well* of *new life in God,* in the present.

It *was* the offering of Our Lord on the Cross that alone "redeems us," in the sense of "forgiveness of sins," but I do not think that that fact entitled those involved in the drawing up of the *Formula of Concord* (see below) to condemn what I think they had misunderstood of Osiander's teaching about the ultimate aim of the Christian being *"union with God through Christ."*

Indeed, if one does believe that Christ's death on the Cross was the one crucial event that has made all else possible for us, I can still see a solution to the problem of bringing together "the two arms of the Atonement" in that one past event, if I am right in suggesting that Christ not only poured out from His crucified body on the Cross *the blood of the New Covenant for our forgiveness,* but *also the water* symbolising *the outpouring of the Holy Spirit to give new life* to God's people from then on, into all eternity, (which was the description of the New Covenant in the Old Testament) —see section on 1 John 5:8. In such a case, the Cross would be a deeply symbolical demonstration of what the eternal God was doing in a moment of human history, so that the Cross stands for ever as a sign of our total redemption: not just because Christ died on it, but because of what that death meant, *both* in terms of forgiveness, *and* our coming to God through His Spirit, the Spirit of Divine Love. This is not a point of mere academic interest, but one of vital importance: the event in the past must also reach into life in the present, and yet be one. No matter how much some Protestant evangelicals may claim to be "forgiven" and "filled with the Spirit", it has to be recognized that, although the two go together in theory, the criterion for coming to God through the Spirit is *Love in the present time, because God is*

Love, and *without Love* nothing else counts,[947] which brings us back to "abiding in Christ".

Gonzalez describes how the *Formula of Concord* responded to the issues raised at the time of Osiander, saying that "in order to do this, it focused its attention on the question of whether Christ justifies according to his divine nature (Osiander) or according to his humanity (Stancaro)." I would say, over and over again, why could not the Church, in its long history, see that *both* are applicable; Jesus was and is both God and Man! Gonzalez goes on to say: "the Formula affirms that God forgives our sins purely by his grace, without any preceding, present, or subsequent work, merit, or worthiness"— and I subscribe to this, and adds:

> finally *among the views condemned* is that which holds 'that *faith does not look alone to Christ's obedience, but also to his divine nature (in so far as it dwells and works within us), and that by such indwelling our sins are covered up'* (italics mine). [948]

I do not think that the understanding of *"abiding in Christ,"* and the Atonement as I have tried to expound it, should ever be thought of in terms of "our sins *being covered up* by Christ's indwelling" (the constant dwelling on *sin* would seem to prove my point that the understanding of the Atonement had become a one-sided emphasis on sin and forgiveness), nor do I think that we should ignore "the second arm of the Atonement" (any more than we should detract from the first), simply because the Reformers were so concerned that *nothing* should be allowed to detract from Christ's atoning death on the Cross. Gonzalez refers to Osiander's arguments being "in language reminiscent of *the Cappadocians' treatment of the union of God and man in Christ."* [949] The fact that Osiander could be so misunderstood makes me think

---

947   1 Corinthians 13:1-3: "If I speak in the tongues of men and of angels, but have not love....I am nothing."

948   Justo L. Gonzalez: *A History of Christian Thought, Volume III, From the Protestant Reformation to the Twentieth Century:* Nashville: Abingdon Press, 1975, pp.103-107.

949   The Cappadocian Fathers were "the three brilliant leaders of philosophical Christian orthodoxy in the later 4th cent....[who] were the chief influence which led to the final defeat of Arianism...." (which opposed the idea of the divinity of Christ)—*The Oxford Dictionary of the Christian Church.*

that the concept of "abiding in Christ" was not only dimmed by the time of Augustine and Pelagius, but that it had remained dimmed in the millenium that followed—and perhaps it has been ever since. "Justification" has been seen mainly in terms of "being forgiven," or "being saved," and it would seem that an understanding of our *abiding in Christ,"* becoming *"as He is," 950 moving on* from "being forgiven" to *mystical union with God through Christ,* becoming partakers of the divine nature, 951 has been obscured from very early on in the history of the Church, and desperately needs to be restated today.

St. John wrote:

> *God is love, and he who abides in love abides in God, and God abides in him.* In this is love perfected with us, that we may have confidence for the day of judgment, because *as he is so are we in this world.* There is no fear in love, but perfect love casts out fear. For fear has to do with punishment, and he who fears is not perfected in love. *We love, because he first loved us* 952

— in other words, our ability to live in this kind of love is only made possible by God, the God who *is* love, *inasmuch as we abide in God and He in us,* through Christ: the final goal of the Atonement.

I believe that St. John's writings bear out my argument that "fear of punishment" and "wanting to be forgiven" do not comprise *the totality of our faith;* our calling, beyond that, is *to live in and share the divine love through Christ,* something which the Atonement has *also* made possible. Admittedly reaching this goal is not easy, but it *is* possible, if we concentrate on Our Lord, and identify ourselves with Him,

---

950   1 John 4:16-19: and note, with regard to my argument about not thinking exclusively about *"being forgiven",* in the sense which it has often had, of people being more concerned about *"not going to hell"* than with living in a loving relationship with God for its own sake, St. John's statement that *"There is no fear in love, but perfect love casts out fear. For fear has to do with punishment, and he who fears is not perfected in love."* And St. Paul wrote to the Thessalonians: *"For this is the will of God, your sanctification..."* (1 Thessalonians 4:3-8)

951   2 Peter 1:4 "that...you may escape from the corruption...in the world...and become partakers of the divine nature"

952   1 John 4:16-19

drawing on His great strength, and *His love* (which makes it possible for *us* to love) to enable us to do so. This concept should be the core of all our teaching and our greatest endeavours, as we learn to dedicate our lives to the concept of *"abiding in Christ"*— but usually it is not. The fact that the Vatican is still talking about indulgences supports my belief that the *"obtaining forgiveness"* arm of the Atonement is still the one being over-emphasized. Not only does this revive the Reformation controversy about its being only *through Christ* that we obtain redemption, not any efforts of our own, but it substitutes *"our good works"* for the idea of *"abiding in Christ"* which is "the second arm of the Atonement".

It is only *inasmuch as we are in Christ* that the "at-one-ment with God" becomes possible which is what our faith is all about. In fact one could say "the two arms of the Atonement" are covered by Jesus' saying "You are *already* made clean [forgiven] by the word which I have spoken to you. *[Now the next step is] Abide in me, and I in you."* [953]

I think much of our trouble stems from the fact that we seldom articulate precisely what it is that we do believe. Stephen Neill, an eminent Anglican writer, has said:

> More recent pronouncements by some eminent Anglicans have given the impression that the Church of England *no longer knows what it believes, and does not stand for anything particular at all.*
>
> *Confusion in the field of theology* is not helped by *confusion in the area of liturgy...* Every form of liturgical expression has theological implications. Every change in liturgy involves also a change in theology... some... much more serious than others. The wide variety of liturgical forms already existing within the Anglican Communion makes it impossible to refer to any of these liturgies as providing the same kind of theological standard as was provided for four centuries by the Book *of* Common Prayer. *It is not always clear what form of theology these variant liturgies are intended to express.*

953   John 15:3-4

The writer immediately goes on to say (italics mine):

> *Pelagius was the first of English (Welsh) heretics.* Pelagianism is the form of heresy to which Englishmen and their Anglican colleagues of other races have been most inclined. It is possible that our Anglican revisers, *in a perhaps excessive reaction against what was held to be the excessive Augustinianism of the older Anglican tradition,* may have produced what are in fact *characteristic Pelagian liturgies.* While so much as yet remains undecided, no more than a provisional opinion can be expressed. *Note must be taken of the anxiety which is felt in many quarters as to the direction in which the work of liturgical revision seems to be carrying the Anglican world.* [954]

My instinct is also to feel that the Anglican Church has not yet achieved the right balance between, on the one hand, acknowledging human sinfulness to an appropriate degree—we have swerved to a very self-confident stance—and yet, on the other hand, acknowledging that we *are* called "to live in God through Christ." I have expressed concern that our new liturgies almost ignore the concept that *"we may evermore dwell in Him, and He in us."* [955] Mention of the subject of "abiding in Christ" is *"an option"* at the choice of the celebrant! [956] I think our new liturgies use other ways of conveying the idea of "abiding in Christ," such as, for example, the fact that we are "one body, for we all share in the one bread," [957] which, for anyone who knows St. Paul's argument about "participation in the body of

---

954   Stephen Neill. *Anglicanism.* Oxford: A.R. Mowbray & Co. Ltd., c. 1958, 1960, 1965, 1977 (first published in 1958 by Penguin Books Ltd.), p.401.

955   end of "Prayer of Humble Access", Anglican *Book of Common Prayer, 1962, Canada,* pages 83-84

956   even though St. John's Gospel *explicitly links the Eucharist with abiding in Christ* and *eternal life:* John 6:53-58: " 'he who eats my flesh and drinks my blood *abides in me, and I in him ....* he who eats this bread will live for ever'." It is interesting that liturgists who can use a phrase that appears *only once* in the whole Bible, and then out of context (Col. 1:15: "the firstborn of all creation"), appear to disregard *this* passage completely.

957   *The [Anglican] Book of Alternative Services,* page 212, taken from 1 Corinthians 10:16-17

Christ," technically "covers it", ("tasting the Bread of Life", "gathering the Church", "sharing in Christ's resurrection", and so on); but for those who are *not* so familiar with the Bible I do not think the deeper understanding of what we are saying is necessarily conveyed to them, or that the next generation will understand it either.

We are not actually *teaching* our people about *union with God through Christ* in so many words; and I think the passages I have quoted, about *our being drawn into the life and love of the Trinity in the Eucharist,* need a wider publicity and deeper understanding.

The Prayer of Consecration in the old *Book of Common Prayer* that the Anglican Church has used for four hundred years, and which is almost certainly drawn from earlier sources, contains the following double petition that I believe supports my argument that the Atonement has long been seen to have two parts: "[We pray that] we and all thy whole Church *may obtain* remission of our sins, *and all other benefits* of his passion." If *all* that people were interested in was "atonement" in the sense of *forgiveness,* what was the origin of that last phrase?

I think it is time to go back to the Bible and take more seriously the apostolic teaching on the subject, particularly that of St. John and St. Paul; and think more about the idea of "abiding in Christ"—and the divinity of Christ without which this is not possible. We could not be *"in Christ"* if Christ were not eternal and divine. The Christian faith is not just about being forgiven and redeemed, "let off punishment", as it were, but being *"at-one" with God through Christ*—and *living in God's love and sharing it with others.* It is not "either...or", it is "both... and." We worship a God whose greatness cannot be pinned down by our narrow definitions. We need to come to Him in His fullness and trust Him more.

So let us move on to thinking more about "abiding in Christ".

Abiding in Christ

The concepts of our *"abiding in Christ"* and *His abiding in us* are two parts of one whole, and love is a key ingredient of both. To live *in God,* with His Spirit in us, is literally to live in, and pass on to others, God's own love—and we can only do that in His strength, inasmuch as we are in Him, and He in us. As individuals, and as the Church which is the mystical Body of Christ, as we are in Christ and

He is in us, we are to be "knit together in love",[958] so that God and His people may be one.[959] This is what our faith is all about. Remember that we are dealing with One God, who is a Trinity of Persons but One God. We are trying to put into human language divine mystery that is hard for us to express at all, let alone express adequately. For example, if we "ask Jesus into our heart", He comes to us through the operation of the Holy Spirit, who has sometimes been referred to as "the Spirit of Christ,"[960] so let's not get hung up on words! We come to God the Father, in and through Jesus His Son, by the operation of the Holy Spirit in our lives, so let us concentrate on the significance of union with God, which is what "abiding in Christ" is all about, and not worry too much about the words in which the message is cloaked.

Archbishop Hollis has well said that "the very essence of living the Christian life, of being a Christian, is our relationship with Jesus:

> We are to be related to him as integrally as a branch is connected to a tree. *We are part of him in the way that a hand or a foot is part of a body. We are built into him the way one brick is mortared to another, and the whole building held together with the foundation and key stone.* These different metaphors are all in the New Testament. In their own way, Jesus, Paul and Peter insist on the reality of and necessity for our relationship with Christ. This relationship with Christ inevitably involves our relationship with others who are 'in him'. As we cannot be isolated from Jesus, so we cannot be isolated from our brothers and sisters in him. [961]

Hence the insistence of St. John that we "love one another, for love is of God, and he who loves is born of God and knows God. He who does not love does not know God; for God is love."[962] The theme of

---

958 Colossians 2:2

959 e.g. John 17:23

960 e.g. Romans 8:9, 1 Peter 1:11; Acts 16:7 ("the Spirit of Jesus"); Philippians 1:19 ("the Spirit of Jesus Christ")

961 Reginald Hollis. *Abiding in Christ: Meditations on the Lord's Prayer, the Sermon on the Mount, and the Ten Commandments.* Toronto, Ontario: Anglican Book Centre, 1987, p.8.

962 1 John 4:7-8

human beings being reconciled to each other, in love, in God, through Christ, is the profoundest mystery of our faith. Jesus prayed for His disciples (a prayer in which we are included),[963] the night before He died, that "they may all be one; even as thou, Father, art in me, and I in thee, that they also may be *in us,* so that the world may believe.... [and] *the love with which thou hast loved me may be in them, and I in them."* [964]

What Jesus is describing is a form of *union with God,* that the world may know [what love is all about, what God is like]: and we know to our cost that we cannot attain to that kind of love on our own.

I believe that God made His creation a good creation, and I believe He delights in it; but He gave us free-will, and the freedom to make our own choices, and sometimes we make the wrong choices. Without the strength that comes from God, we cannot love, and forgive, and go on loving, in the same way that God can. It is only inasmuch as we are in God, sustained by God, caught up in God, that we can learn to live like God, to the standard that He expects of us. Jesus said "you... must be perfect, as your heavenly Father is perfect" [965] — a tall order, without God's help! And, unless we are part of Him, and He is part of us, the human side of us just cannot reach up to the divine standard. So the call to love, and the call to be "in God", (the God of Love), are deeply connected.

In thinking of "union with God," we need to think more about what God is like, that we may come to Him. I wrote earlier of the old idea that God had no "passions", and, indeed, sinful passions have no part in Him; but I believe He loves, and grieves and suffers, and, provided our motives are not self-serving, we can be united with Him to a certain extent *in* that love and grief and suffering.

The holy asceticism of the past, that saw all feelings and emotion as an indulgence to be suppressed, failed, I believe, to differentiate between those of "the flesh" and those of the "the spirit", and, in so doing, lost a means of "sharing" with God in a vital way. If we were not moved by sorrow, cruelty, or injustice, would we be *like Him,* or

---

963   John 17:20: "I do not pray for these only, but also for those who believe in me through their word."

964   John 17: 21-26

965   Matthew 5:48

able to share our feelings with Him, or able to be *"in Him"*? Jesus was often referred to in the Gospels as being "moved with compassion".[966]

This is also tied up with identifying with Christ in suffering; so that, when we are wronged, we do not react on a purely human level, or we must try not to, because we have the assurance of somehow being upheld in Christ against the onslaught of the evil that might otherwise bring us down.

—Our being in Christ:

Let us look first at the theme of *"being in Christ"*, or "abiding in Christ", (or even *"making the Most High your habitation"*, as it says in Psalm 91— the theme of "being in God" is also found in the Old Testament); and then move on to the complementary idea of our having "Jesus in our hearts", the Spirit of God being *in us.*

There are many verses in the Bible which speak metaphorically of "living *in God"*, or under the shadow of His wings, or in the Rock of the strong refuge that He provides, to the point where *"Rock"* is often used as a metaphor for God—and St. Paul used the term "Rock" *of Christ* (also with a capital "R").[967] Some examples of the use of the metaphor of *"The Rock"* for God are listed in the Appendix.

The theme of *"abiding in Christ"*, that is, *in God*, thus has its counterpart in the Old Testament, of God's people coming to rest in the same Triune God. Our being *in God*, our living our lives *in Him*, can be compared to the way in which a fish in the sea lives its whole life in the ocean. St. Paul said of God *"in Him we live and move and have our being."*[968]

In fact, *Jesus' teaching about our abiding (living) in Him may have been another deliberate, but less obvious, way in which Jesus claimed "divinity".* He knew the Hebrew Scriptures well. He knew the parallels He was making.

And so did St. Paul. As St. Paul said himself, he, Paul, was "brought up at the feet of Gamaliel, educated according to the strict manner of the law of our fathers" [969] and when he spoke of being *"in Christ"* he

---

966   e.g. Matthew 9:36, 14:14, 15:32, 20:34; Mark 1:41, 6:34, 8:2; Luke 7:13
967   1 Corinthians 10:4
968   Acts 17:28
969   Acts 22:3

knew the implication of what he was saying, just as when he spoke of the Rock that was Christ. [970]

But we need to think not only of the divinity implied in that designation, but, as well, of all that is entailed in the idea of *living in God:* being *with God, in* God, protected and helped by God, in order to cope with all that is not of God: "making the most High our habitation," [971] in the sense that we habitually live in Him, like the badgers live in the rocks, [972] spiritually withdrawing from "the strife of tongues" [973] into the quiet place of the presence of God in which we live.

A metaphor closely related to that of *"living in* God" is that of *"hiding* in Him," taking refuge in Him, as in the following:

> *Thou art a hiding place for me* ... thou dost encompass [surround] me with deliverance [974]

> *hide me in the shadow of thy wings;* and *in thee my soul takes refuge; in the shadow of thy wings I will take refuge,* till the storms of destruction pass by [975]

> *in the time of trouble he shall hide me in his tabernacle; yea, in the secret place of his dwelling shall he hide me* [976]

> *Hide me* from the secret plots of the wicked, from the scheming of evildoers [977]

Deliver me, O Lord, from mine enemies; *for I flee unto thee to hide me;* Teach me to do the thing that pleaseth thee... [978]

In metaphors about "hiding and "taking refuge", the key word, to my mind, is *"in",* rather than "hide". The Bible is not talking about

---

970   1 Corinthians 10:4

971   Psalm 91:9

972   Psalm 104:18

973   Psalm 31:20

974   Psalm 32:7

975   Psalms 17:8 and 57:1

976   Psalm 27:5 *The [Anglican] Book of Common Prayer;* or: *"he will hide me in his shelter* in the day of trouble"

977   Psalm 64:2

978   Psalm 143:9-10, *The [Anglican] Book of Common Prayer:* or: *"Deliver me...I have fled to thee for refuge"*

"hiding" in the physical sense, because that would not be possible—
"taking refuge in God" is a *spiritual* exercise, a form of prayer.[979]

The word is not used in the cowardly sense of escaping problems
and difficulties. Jesus said *"in this world you have tribulation;* but be
of good cheer. I have overcome the world". [980] Coming from the man
who was crucified, and yet still spoke of "being *in* God", [981] that is not
running away or hiding from life's difficulties.

We are dealing with the concept of being *with God,* and *in God,*
no matter what else may happen: in effect, being surrounded by the
spiritual protection of God Himself.

In fact, I do not think that *"hiding"* is really the issue at all, when
you look at passages such as the one in Deuteronomy, which is part of
the Torah, the Sacred Law of the Hebrews, one of the earlier writings
in the Bible:

> *The eternal God is your dwelling place* [and
> underneath are the everlasting arms]. [982]

It is about *living.* Your dwelling place is where you live. We are
called, in both the Old and the New Testaments, to spend our lives *"in
God",* to be at home in His presence, surrounded by His power and His
love. It is not about "hiding" from the realities of life: it is about living
our lives to the fullest, spiritually based in God: if we are in God, and
He in us, we are not facing this world's troubles alone. Being "in God"
is not escapism. It is "the other arm" of the Atonement equation I was
talking about earlier, "abiding in Christ", and therefore of much deeper
spiritual significance than might appear to be the case on the surface.

It is about being so "caught up" in God that one can begin to participate
in the divine life, in the sense that, by being in Christ, we can share, not
only in His sufferings, His trials and temptations, but in His victory over
sin and death; and, in Him, can be partakers of His resurrection.

St. Paul was no escapist, and he did not hesitate to face the world

---

979 e.g. Psalm 16: v.1-2:   Preserve me, O God, *for in thee I take refuge...* 'I have no good
   apart from thee' "

980 John 16:33

981 John 17:21 : [Jesus said] "even as *thou, Father, art in me, and I in thee*"

982 Deuteronomy 33:27; and Psalm 90:1 says "Lord, *thou hast been our dwelling place* in all
   generations"

head on, but he spoke of "our life being hid with God in Christ" [983] —and presumably his life was "hid with Christ," if he was an apostle par excellence. He was involved in public preaching, travelling and danger, shipwrecks and beatings and imprisonments and riots. [984] He was not sentimentally "hiding" to get away from "life", but he needed to be *in God* in order to live that life. ("In Him we live and move and have our being.")

St. Patrick was no escapist either, but his "theme-song", as it were, was to invoke the power of the Trinity to help him, and to ask for Christ to be all round him, within, in front, behind, and above and below him. [985] Is that not much the same idea as the metaphor of seeking protection in the walls of a cave in the rocks: being surrounded by God, above, below, and all around: being in God? In effect, he was "putting on the armour of God." [986]

St. Stephen, the first martyr, was active in helping people and active in preaching, but at the same time, when he came to be stoned to death, he had the spiritual resources within him (he was described as "a man full of faith and of the Holy Spirit") [987] to be able to see the heavens opening to greet him before he died, and to forgive those who killed him,[988] a spiritual grace which came, presumably, from the resources of the hidden life of the soul in God, through the power of the Holy Spirit working in him. He drew the strength he needed from his already-existing interior life with God.

Indeed, to come to God through Christ, and lead a Christ-filled life, is the greatest challenge of our lives. There is a sense of quietness, even withdrawnness, spiritually speaking, in the Christian life: *a hiddenness,*

---

983   Colossians 3:3

984   e.g.., see 1 Corinthians 11:23-27

985   *The [Anglican] Book of Common Praise (Revised 1938),* hymn 812: "Invocation of the Trinity, St. Patrick's Breastplate"

986   Wisdom 5:15-19: "The Most High takes care of [the righteous]...with his right hand he will cover them, and with his arm he will shield them. The Lord...will take his zeal as his whole armour....he will put on righteousness as a breastplate, and wear impartial justice as a helmet; he will take holiness as an invincible shield..." Ephesians 6:11-17: *"Put on* the whole armour of God .... that you may be able to withstand in the evil day". Or, to put it in other terms, Colossians 3:12-14: *"Put on then,* as God's chosen ones, holy and beloved, compassion, kindness, lowliness, meekness, and patience .... And above all these *put on love..."*

987   Acts 6:5

988   Acts 7:59-60

if you will, which is not the same as "hiding" in the running-away sense, but which is *a union with God* that is not open to view for every passer-by. What *should* be open to view, as it were, are the *results* of that closeness with God, the fruit of a holy life. It was said of the apostles that people could see that they had been with Jesus.[989]

I think it is true, for example, that we can only forgive deep wrongs inasmuch as our forgiveness is interwoven with Christ's; we cannot do it on our own. It helps me, personally, to think of the metaphor of "hiding" *in the heart of the crucified Christ on the Cross,* when I can say "Lord, you were able to forgive the people who crucified you, please do the same for me: I can't in my own strength, but you can do it for me, while I take refuge in you from the very real and human temptation not to forgive." We sing "Come into my heart, Lord Jesus, there is room in my heart for thee";[990] but the other side of the coin is equally: "let me come into *your* heart, Lord Jesus"—there is room in His heart for us.

However we may phrase it, we are asking to be allowed *to move from our space to God's sphere, and to be held there, so that the forces of evil cannot drag us back to places, spiritual realms, where God's will is not done*—so that *we are in Him* and *He is in us,* and *we are,* in that sense, *one;* and *this* is what our mystical union with God, through Christ, is all about. It is not necessarily physical enemies that we are talking about, when we talk about hiding and refuge, (though physical enemies can cause confusion and temptation for the soul), any more than we are literally talking about physical hiding places. We are asking to come into a safe place where the powers of evil, as it were, cannot get to us, where temptation won't overcome us, where despair will not destroy us. And that is not being childish. In the realm of spiritual warfare, to be in God is the only way to survive. The only way to describe these truths is in metaphor and simile and poetic language. We are not so much running away from conflict as putting on heavenly armour that will enable us to come through it spiritually unscathed.

Corrie Ten Boom wrote a book called *The Hiding Place,*[991]

---

989 Acts 4:13 "They recognized that they had been with Jesus"

990 *The [Anglican] Book of Common Praise (Revised 1938),* hymn 755: "Thou didst leave thy throne and thy kingly crown, when thou camest to earth for me"

991 Corrie Ten Boom (with John & Elizabeth Sherrill): *The Hiding Place* c.1971 Sevenoaks, Kent, U.K.: Hodder & Stoughton Ltd. & Christian Literature Crusade, pp.220-221.

describing how she and her family hid Jews from the Nazis during World War II, her experiences in a concentration camp, and the issue of forgiveness, and I believe the title of her book had a double meaning: that she was not only speaking of the physical hiding place, the secret room where people could hide, but the spiritual hiding place she found in God, which enabled her to come through her terrible ordeal and still be able to forgive and go on loving.

Another way of illustrating the concept of "abiding in Christ," or being *"in God,"* if one can equate Jesus, in one's mind, with the God of the Old Testament, is one that I have derived from a passage in the Book of Hosea.

It can be hard to forgive when the person concerned is completely unrepentant, and when *"forgiveness"* would somehow seem to us to belittle or deny the continuing reality of the wrong that has been done to us: and for *God* to forgive would seem to imply that God does not care about *us,* or how much we have been hurt. But in thinking of the statement that: *"I will heal their faithlessness, I will love them freely,"*[992] I found myself substituting the word "infirmity" for "faithlessness" in my mind: whether sin or sickness, the word "infirmity" covers all that hurts and is wrong in human beings.

When I could think of God saying of those who had wronged me: *"I will heal their infirmities, I will love them freely",* the infirmity was both admitted and released, and love was able to flow freely. I could identify myself both with *prayer for healing of their infirmity* (which I think is what Jesus meant when He said "love your enemies... *pray for those who abuse you"),*[993] and with the Divine Love released to flow without barrier or impediment. I could identify myself with God, as He healed and forgave and loved, and, in a moment of time,

---

992 Hosea 14:4 "I will heal their faithlessness; I will love them freely"; Jeremiah 3:22 "I will heal your faithlessness"

993 Matthew 5:44: "love your enemies and *pray for those who persecute you,* so that you may be *sons of your Father* who is in heaven"; Luke 6:27-36: "love your enemies, do good to those who hate you, bless those who curse you, *pray for those who abuse you"* (or, in the King James Version, "[those who] *despitefully use you")* ".......love your enemies and do good...*and you will be sons of the Most High*; for he is kind to the ungrateful and the selfish. Be merciful, even as your Father is merciful." (I have found, too, that the metaphor of "water in the desert" can be helpful when praying for those who have hurt one: visualizing God's love transforming *their* deserts.)

do the same *in Him.* I was no longer concentrating on *myself,* and *my* "forgiving": I was watching *God,* and combining my action with His: and, *in Him, it was one.*

Jesus' metaphor of the vine and the branches reminds us that, unless leaves and branches are attached to the main stem and roots of the plant, they wither and die, and, deprived of nourishment, do not bring forth fruit. We have to be in Christ, part of the vine, to draw the spiritual nourishment from Him to keep our souls alive and make our lives spiritually fruitful. He said:

> *Abide in me, and I in you.* As the branch cannot bear fruit by itself, unless it abides in the vine, neither can you, unless you abide in me. *I am the vine, you are the branches. He who abides in me, and I in him, he it is that bears much fruit.* [994]

That is a clear example of the two halves of the equation, if I can put it that way. The leaves and branches have to be *in* the vine, that is, part of, the vine, in order to stay alive; and yet the life of the vine flows into them from the root of the plant, and is *"in"* the leaves and branches. St. Paul prayed for the Ephesians that *God* would grant both that *Christ would dwell in their hearts* through faith, and that they might be "rooted and grounded" *in* love:

> *that you being rooted and grounded in love may ... know the love of Christ ... [and be] filled with all the fullness of God.* [995]

St. Paul must have known Jesus' teaching about the vine and the branches, and was expressing the fact that, *because God is love,* to be *rooted and grounded in love* is to be rooted and grounded *in God :*[996] and yet this is through Christ: *Christ* dwelling in our hearts,

---

994 John 15:4-5

995 Ephesians 3:17. In addition to the above, *"being filled with all the fullness of God"* answers the lament of the Psalmist: *"My soul thirsts for thee like a parched land"* (Psalm 143:6). Our knowing the love of Christ, and the full reality of the presence of God in us, is the ultimate answer to the deep human need for love and acceptance.

996 I think it almost certain that both Jesus and St. Paul (and also St. John) would have known and remembered the many references in the Old Testament to the metaphor of people nourished by the Holy Spirit *being like trees putting their roots into the*

and our knowing the love of *Christ,* leads to our being filled with all the fullness of *God* and being rooted and grounded *in the divine Love.*

Similarly, he wrote to the Colossians: "As…you received Christ Jesus the Lord, so *live in him,* rooted and built up *in him* and established in the faith, just as you were taught, abounding in thanksgiving." [997]

We are part of the mystical body of Christ; our religion is not just an individual thing.

St. Paul wrote to the Ephesians:

> you are no longer strangers and sojourners, but…fellow citizens with the saints and members of the household of God, built upon the foundation of the apostles and prophets, Christ Jesus himself being the cornerstone, in whom the whole structure is joined together and grows into a holy temple in the Lord…a dwelling place of God in the Spirit. [998]

And with this kind of thinking he wrote to the Corinthians: "You are….God's building…like a skilled master builder I laid a foundation… Do you not know that you are God's temple and that *God's spirit dwells in you?*" [999]

This brings us to the other part of the equation, Christ being in us, both corporately and individually.

Christ dwelling in us through the power of the Holy Spirit

The theme of God being in His people, through His Holy Spirit, is also one that runs through the Old Testament as well as the New. I am more concerned here to refer to Old Testament passages, because, if you have questions about the truth of the faith, you might find that the Old Testament, subscribed to by the Jews who do not accept Jesus of Nazareth as the Messiah, is more of an "external witness" than the New Testament which subscribes to the Christian faith. There are several references in the Old Testament to the Holy Spirit coming upon

---

water that nourished them and kept them alive – see examples at the end of the chapter on Baptism.

997   Colossians 2:6-7
998   Ephesians 2:19-22
999   1 Corinthians 3:9, 16

people, which need not be listed here, but I would like to quote two from Ezekiel: *"I will put my spirit within you"*; [1000] and "I will put my Spirit within you, *and you shall live"*. [1001]

"Living" in this context cannot mean just our physical existence, as we are physically alive anyway. It *must* refer to the "life in God" that transcends, and lasts beyond, our mortal living and dying.

In the assurance of the Christian faith, we can "ask Jesus into our hearts", as the more evangelical Christians put it, and as the old favourite hymn "O Little Town of Bethlehem" [1002] has it ("O Holy Child of Bethlehem, descend to us we pray: cast out our sin, and *enter in,* be born *in us* today"), without worrying unduly about exactly how this mystery that is our God comes to us. *It is all the same God with whom we have to deal.*

In the Prayer Book confirmation service we ask God that the confirmation candidate will "daily increase in thy Holy Spirit more and more," [1003] but do we stop to think that "being more and more filled with the Holy Spirit" means that Christ is being more and more formed in us?

St. Paul wrote to the Colossians of "the riches of the glory of this mystery, which is *Christ in you"*; [1004] and said to the Romans: "Anyone who does not have *the Spirit of Christ* does not belong to him. But *if Christ is in you..."* [1005] He said to the Galatians: "My little children, with whom I am again in travail until *Christ be formed in you"*; [1006] and to the Corinthians: "Do you not realize that Jesus Christ is *in you?*—unless indeed you fail..." [1007] He was writing to Christians, who had accepted the faith, and accepted his teaching, which eventually was immortalized in the New Testament canon; but even as he wrote, St.

1000 Ezekiel 36:27

1001 Ezekiel 37:14

1002 *The [Anglican] Book of Common Praise (Revised 1938),* hymn 82

1003 *The [Anglican] Book of Common Prayer, 1962, Canada,* p. 560

1004 Colossians 1:27

1005 Romans 8:9-10: see also 1 Peter 1:11: "the Spirit of Christ within them"; Acts 16:7: "the Spirit of Jesus", and Philippians 1:19: "The Spirit of Jesus Christ", all with a capital "S", all connecting the Spirit with Christ; and this *only makes sense* if God is understood *as Trinity.*

1006 Galatians 4:19

1007 2 Corinthians 13:5

Paul knew they had a long way to go, much growing to do, spiritually speaking, *before Christ was really formed in them.* It is as if a seed planted at baptism has to grow to maturity, until more and more of us is given over to God, and the purely human side of us becomes of only secondary importance.

We believe that God's creation, is good, and we thank him for our "creation, preservation, and all the blessings of this life," [1008] but we know that sometimes the spiritual life can come into conflict with the purely human and materialistic instincts, like self-preservation, which we all have.

It is not that there is anything wrong in being human. God made us to be flesh and blood; but, if we only exist on a flesh-and-blood basis, we are not much more than the animals, apart from our minds and psychological processes.

We have to develop our spiritual potential, and come to know God. This spiritual side of us does not just grow, like our arms and legs, all by itself; it has to be nurtured and encouraged. We need the language of spirituality expressed through metaphor. It is in God that our spirits grow.

St. Paul saw this spiritual growth as being a very real process, from being "babes in Christ" to reaching the stature of maturity in Christ. [1009] St. Paul said of himself that he had *"died* to the law, that [he] might *live* to God", saying "I have been crucified with Christ: it is no longer I who live, but *Christ who lives in me."* [1010]

There are many references in the New Testament to being "filled with the Spirit", from the initial Day of Pentecost described in the Book of Acts, [1011] to St. Stephen's martyrdom (he being *"full of the Holy Spirit..."*), [1012] to St. Paul adjuring Timothy to "guard

---

1008 *The [Anglican] Book of Common Prayer, 1962, Canada,* pp. 14-15

1009 1 Corinthians 3:1; 1 Corinthians 14:20: "In thinking be mature"; Ephesians 4:13-14: "..until we all attain to the unity of the faith, and of the knowledge of the Son of God, to mature manhood, to the measure of the stature of the fullness of Christ; so that we may no longer be children..."

1010 Galatians 2:19-20

1011 Acts 2

1012 Acts 6:8-7:60 (Acts 6:5: "they chose Stephen, a man full of faith and of the Holy Spirit")

the truth entrusted to [him] by the Holy Spirit who *dwells within us*". [1013]

One, in particular, is an important statement in St. Paul's Epistle to the Romans:

> *But if Christ is in you,* although your bodies are [spiritually] dead because of sin, *your [eternal] spirits are [eternally] alive* because of righteousness. *If the Spirit of him who raised Jesus from the dead [i.e. the Spirit of God] dwells in you,* he who raised Christ Jesus from the dead *[i.e . God] will give [spiritual, eternal] life to your mortal bodies also through his Spirit which dwells in you.* [1014]

For anyone who might think that even St. Paul did not really believe in the divinity of Christ, surely the above verse, from one of his major Epistles, can only be understood in the context of belief in God *as Trinity.*

In addition, the chapter from the Epistle to the Romans from which this comes contains *both* of the elements I have been talking about, our being *in* Christ and His being *in us.* St. Paul is not *only* talking about Christ and the Holy Spirit dwelling *in us,* as above; the same chapter begins with the statement: "There is therefore now no condemnation for those who are *in* Christ Jesus." [1015]

How else, except in the context of St. Paul's believing in the divinity of Christ, and the nature of God being Trinity, can one explain such statements as "he who is *united to the Lord* becomes *one spirit with him,*" [1016] as if two drops of water were to merge into one, though at the same time we do not lose our own identity and individuality [1017] that are uniquely loved by God.

This passage goes on to say "Do you not know that your body is a temple of *the Holy Spirit within you,* which you have from God? You

---

1013 2 Timothy 1:14

1014 Romans 8:11.

1015 Romans 8:1

1016 1 Corinthians 6:17

1017 The Apostles' Creed: "[I believe in]... the Resurrection *of the body*" (Anglican *Book of Common Prayer,* p.10)

are not your own; you were bought with a price" (which I do not take literally in the sense of some sort of cash payment, but in the sense that "Christ *paid the price* of obtaining this outcome in what He endured in his own body," as described earlier, just as we sometimes say of our own suffering that *"we paid a heavy price"*). That chapter ends with St. Paul saying *"So glorify God in your body"*, i.e., in your human living, "in the flesh", as well as in the spirit. [1018]

Sometimes, when the idea of "living *in*" or "abiding *in*" God through Christ, and the idea of *God* (through Christ, through the Holy Spirit) *being in us,* can be hard to assimilate, when thinking in terms of *"words"*, it can help to use pictorial images in the mind, as mentioned above.

Somehow, if, in whatever mental images may help us, we can come to have a growing sense of God being not only with us, but *in us,* in the present time, we will find it will assuage our present pain and bitterness, because *He is there.*

It is best to try this, to purge ourselves of what burdens us, while the burdens are comparatively light, so that, when real disaster comes, we are used to turning to Him, and letting Him come into whatever situation we may face, so that *we are in Him, and He in us, as we face it together.*

If we are to be filled with all the fullness of the God who is Love, it follows that we must be full of love—and, as we know to our cost, we can only even approach that ideal inasmuch as we are in Christ, and He is in us.

Jesus was quite specific. He said *"If a man loves me,* he will keep my word, and my Father will love him, and *we will come to him and make our home with him";* [1019] and "if you love me, you will keep my commandments" (His summary of 'all the law and the prophets' being that we should love God and each other).

Jesus went on to say "and I will pray the Father, and he will give you another Counselor" (that is, the Holy Spirit) "to be with you for ever, even the Spirit of truth, whom the world cannot receive, because

---

1018 1 Corinthians 6:15-20: "Do you not know that your bodies are members of Christ?..." [i.e., not in the sense of *"members of a club* or organization", but in the sense of being *part of Him,* part of the *Body of Christ]*

1019 John 14:23

it neither sees him nor knows him; you know him, for he dwells with you, and will be *in you.*" [1020] Jesus was saying that He wanted His disciples, His followers, *us,* to be *one in love, and one in God.*

This "love" is not necessarily to be confused with "liking" or "approving"; it is being willing to try, through the grace of God, to share the compassionate mind of God, to have the mind of Christ, [1021] to be "one spirit with Him", [1022] rather than following our own human instincts to nourish a resentment or advance our own interests at the expense of someone else.

St. John repeatedly calls on us to love one another, even going so far as to say that, if we do not, we cannot attain to that high calling of *abiding in, and with,* the God who is Love. He wrote: "Beloved, *let us love one another;* for love is of God, and *he who loves is born of God and knows God.* He who does *not* love does not know God; for God is love," [1023] and "God is love, and *he who abides in love abides in God and God abides in him.*" [1024]

This is from the writer who recorded so much of Jesus' teaching about *"abiding in Him":* as if *abiding in Christ and abiding in God are synonymous,* which I believe they are—it is by abiding in Christ that we come to abide in God—but a key component of both is *love.*

It is only in Christ that we are able to forgive others, or love them, as we should; only *in Him* that we are redeemed.

He was the one who conquered evil, and it is only *in Him* that we are able to triumph over evil too.

It is only through Christ, and *in* Christ, that we are, in the words of a famous hymn, "ransomed, healed, restored, forgiven." [1025]

It is only *in Him* that we are brought to God; and it is, I believe, only through Him that we can really *live* with God, and thus find in Him our eternal home.

1020 John 14:15-17

1021 1 Corinthians 2:13-16: "[…the gifts of the Spirit …are spiritually discerned]…but we have the mind of Christ"

1022 1 Corinthians 6:17

1023 1 John 4:7-8

1024 1 John 4:16

1025 *The [Anglican] Book of Common Praise (Revised 1938),* hymn 353: "Praise my soul the King of Heaven"

CHAPTER 21

The Covenant of Baptism —Water and the Spirit

Perhaps I should add a note to those who have read this far: if you have been estranged from the Church, of whatever Christian denomination, or have never been a part of it, perhaps this is the time to think about whether or not you might take the next step in "doing something about it". I believe *you cannot lose* if you learn to know and love God, and come to experience His presence and His love.

It might be helpful to discuss what I have written in this book with some trusted Christian friend, preferably one with some knowledge and understanding, preferably a member of the clergy, because that would be a good way to clarify in your mind what you agree, or disagree, with, and why, in order to resolve any outstanding issue in your mind with some degree of satisfaction. Although Aidan Kavanagh has said, *"Faith comes not by education but by the grace of conversion,"*[1026] most people who are not already involved with the Church need some impetus of knowledge or information to make them want to enquire further before they even begin to consider investigating whether they might look for a Church which they might then join. But if they do, if they have never been baptized, there would then follow baptism into the faith, which is the "rite of initiation" which joins all Christian believers to "the body of Christ" which is the Church. (I will explain this more fully a little later.)

1026 Aidan Kavanagh. *The Shape of Baptism: The Rite of Christian Initiation — Studies in the Reformed Rites of the Catholic Church, Volume 1.* New York: Pueblo Publishing Company, 1978, page 188. He said this in the context that "it is this last [conversion] for which the catechumenate [see glossary] exists—to develop and deepen it to a point of ... maturity that can be sacramentally sealed by baptism in its fullness"

If they have already been baptized, or have been for many years "lapsed", and especially if their estrangement from the Church was the result of hurt or abuse (or a bad experience with politics in a particular church at a particular time!), again, I would recommend that they seek out a good minister who would listen to their story and give them comfort and understanding, and encourage them "to return to the fold" regardless. Even if much sin against God has been involved, there is such a thing as private sacramental confession, if someone asks for it, where the priest can help the repentant person to put the past behind them, and truly start *"the new life"* in God. And, in addition, we learn by *doing:* in finding good pastoral care, and surrounding ourselves with the faithful community, we move beyond ourselves to letting God and others help us.

William Willimon has said:

> What is that 'assurance' the assertion 'You are baptized' might bring to our pastoral care of troubled persons?

> To answer that question we must inquire into the meaning of baptism, particularly its meaning as the identifying sacrament of the Christian life. But we must start by reflecting upon sacraments. In my opinion, baptism will not again be significant in the life of the church or the lives of individual Christians until we once again affirm what the church has traditionally proclaimed, that (to paraphrase James White) sacraments are *communal events and sign acts through which God gives himself to us* (italics his). [1027]

The old, standard, definition of a sacrament has long been that it was "an outward and visible sign of an inward and invisible grace [coming from God]." [1028]

Willimon goes on to say:

> For too long we Protestants have been in the grip of what White calls an 'Enlightenment' view of the sacraments

---

[1027] William H. Willimon. *Worship as Pastoral Care* (Chapter VII: *Liturgy and Identity: Baptism).* Nashville, Abingdon Press, 1979, pages 149-151

[1028] The Catechism in the [Anglican] *Book of Common Prayer, 1962, Canada,* page 550

that regards such events as baptism and the Lord's supper as human actions we perform in order to help us remember God's actions in the past....[This] view of the sacraments puts primary stress upon the necessity of our worthiness (stated all too often in terms of our *unworthiness*) to participate in the sacraments, of our cerebral understanding of what is going on... and of certain...commitments and experiences we should have in order to bring sufficient faith to the sacraments. Primary responsibility in most Protestant sacramental worship is thus placed upon *me*—my worthiness, my understanding, my commitments, my experiences..... Such an experience could hardly be labeled a 'means of grace'.

In contrast to this human-centered, human-conditioned, Enlightenment view of the sacraments, Christian theology has traditionally asserted that *God* is the actor, and we are the recipients of what God does through the sacraments. The efficacy of the sacraments does not entirely depend upon us...In his infinite love, God has not left us alone. God continually, graciously, gives himself to us and makes himself available to us through...experienced, visible means. [1029]

This reinforces my point that I believe that the "lost and strayed" should return to the Church (perhaps choosing the right one sensibly!) and let God "take it from there". I have always believed that if one really asked God to show one the truth, praying that He would help us to understand and receive that truth, and experience His love, and grow spiritually in Him, that prayer that will always be answered.

It is interesting that in another book, Willimon has said what I have said about the Church of the early centuries moving towards a rather negative over-emphasis on sin at the expense of the positive vision of *"life in God"*. He writes:

1029 William H. Willimon. *Worship as Pastoral Care* (chapter VII *Liturgy and Identity: Baptism*) Nashville, Abingdon Press, 1979, pages 150-151

The wide variety of older baptismal imagery was overshadowed by the now central image of baptism *as a bath to wash away the taint of original sin.* Baptism was no longer a time for repentance, confession of faith, *the gift of the Holy Spirit,* death and resurrection, and conversion into the community; it was mostly a time for an individual's sin to be removed *so that his or her soul would be fit for eternity.* [1030]

The old-fashioned view described above did not put sufficient emphasis on the Holy Spirit, because the main emphasis was on *sin.* We are now restoring the emphasis on the fact that "...entering the waters of Baptism means letting go of the life you have clung to, in the confidence that God will give you *a new life by his Spirit.*" [1031]

As the Canadian (Anglican) *Book of Alternative Services* states:

> *Baptism is the sign of new life in Christ. Baptism unites Christ with his people. That union is both individual and corporate.* Christians are, it is true, baptized one by one, but to be a Christian is to be part of a new creation which rises from the dark waters of Christ's death into the dawn of his risen life. Christians are not just baptized individuals; they are a new humanity....
>
> Baptism is participation in Christ's death and resurrection...a washing away of sin...a new birth...an enlightenment by Christ...a reclothing in Christ...a renewal by the Spirit...and a liberation into a new humanity in which barriers of division, whether of sex or race or social status, are transcended...The images are many but the reality is one. [1032]

I have written earlier of the Church being the Body of Christ in the world, and it is *into that Body that we are incorporated through*

1030 William H., Willimon. *Word, Water, Wine and Bread: How Worship Has Changed over the Years.* Valley Forge, PA, Judson Press, 1980, page 59

1031 John Hill. *Thinking about Baptism.* Toronto, Canada, Anglican Book Centre, 1982, page 7.

1032 *The Book of Alternative Services* of the Anglican Church of Canada, Toronto, Canada. Anglican Book Centre, 1985, page 146.

baptism: it is much more than just being initiated into membership in a local Church. *We enter into the Covenant between God and His people, the New Covenant instituted in the death and resurrection and ascension of Christ,* as we make our own profession of faith, and commitment to God, in our Baptismal Covenant,[1033] and are baptised into "the blessed company of all faithful people". [1034]

The Israelites believe—and have done so since they began to see themselves in a special role as the people of God—that God made a covenant with them through Abraham:[1035] and they in return made a covenant with God, renewed in each generation. As William Willimon has written,

> Circumcision was the rite of initiation into this covenant. One was not born a Jew, but made a Jew through the incorporating act of circumcision. In the new Israel (the Church) baptism is not described as circumcision until the ...book of Colossians (2:11-12) [and then only in a metaphorical sense]. But the idea that one becomes a member of the new covenant community only by being ritually initiated into that community hark (sic) back to Jewish circumcision." [1036]

(That passage in Colossians reads: "in him...you were circumcised in a circumcision made without hands, by putting off the body of flesh in the circumcision of Christ; and you were buried with him in baptism [the symbolism of drowning in water and dying], in which you were also raised with him through faith.") [1037]

When St. Paul began to make many converts among uncircumcised Gentiles, and the orthodox Jewish faction in the Christian community tried to insist that those new converts had to be physically circumcised, as was the tradition of the Jews, if they were to be accepted into the community of Christians, St. Paul took the position that it was

---

1033 *The Book of Alternative Services of the Anglican Church of Canada.* Toronto, Canada, Anglican Book Centre, 1985, pages 158-159.

1034 *The [Anglican] Book of Common Prayer, 1962, Canada,* page 85.

1035 Genesis 15:5-18, Genesis 17:1-14

1036 William H. Willimon. *Word, Water, Wine and Bread. How Worship Has Changed over the Years.* Valley Forge, PA, Judson Press, 1980, p.26

1037 Colossians 2:11-12

not necessary. In his Epistles he referred to this vexed question on several occasions, saying on one occasion that *"in Christ Jesus* neither circumcision nor uncircumcision is of any avail, but *faith working through love"*;[1038] on another, "neither circumcision counts for anything nor uncircumcision *but keeping the commandments of God,"* [1039]and on another that "neither circumcision counts for anything, nor uncircumcision, but *a new creation."* [1040] He said *"real* circumcision is a matter of the *heart, spiritual and not literal",* [1041] and it was on this basis that Christianity came to understand that physical circumcision was no longer necessary for Christians for initiation into the Covenant with God: and baptism came to be the inaugural rite.

This understanding of *"true circumcision"* being *spiritual, a covenant with God,* as opposed to a physical, literal formality, was supported by Old Testament teaching. As far back as the Book of Deuteronomy it was written that "the Lord God will *circumcise your heart* and the heart of your offspring, *so that you will love the Lord your God* with all your heart and with all your soul, *that you may live."*[1042] An earlier verse bids the Israelites to "circumcise...the foreskin of your heart, and be no longer stubborn," [1043] while Jeremiah refers to the house of Israel as "uncircumcised in heart."[1044] Jeremiah wrote: "Circumcise yourselves to the Lord, remove the foreskin of your *hearts,* O men of Judah and inhabitants of Jerusalem." [1045] And he wrote of the days when the Lord would make a new covenant with His people:

> Behold, the days are coming, says the Lord, when I will make a new covenant with the house of Israel and the house of Judah, not like the covenant which I made with their fathers [the covenant involving physical circumcision].... my covenant which they broke... says the Lord. But this is the covenant which I will make with the house of Israel

---

1038 Galatians 5:6
1039 1 Corinthians 7:19
1040 Galatians 6:15
1041 Romans 2:29
1042 Deuteronomy 30:26
1043 Deuteronomy 10:16
1044 Jeremiah 9:26
1045 Jeremiah 4:4

after those days, says the Lord: I will put my law within them, and *I will write it upon their hearts;* and I will be their God, and they shall be my people [1046]

just as Ezekiel wrote of the Lord saying "I will put my spirit *within you,* and you shall live", and, in the same chapter, "I *will* [in the future] make a covenant of peace with them...an everlasting covenant" [i.e., a *new* covenant]. [1047] Isaiah, too, spoke of an everlasting covenant. [1048]

Christianity saw itself as "the *new* Israel" with a *New* Covenant, into which we are initiated at our baptism. [1049] St. Paul wrote: "if you are Christ's, then you are Abraham's offspring, heirs according to promise". [1050]

Much of the debate between St. Paul and orthodox Judaism on the subject of evangelising the Gentiles was about whether new Christians *also* had to be circumcised. Willimon writes:

> The early Christians eventually dropped the practice of circumcision because it was too nationalistic, excluded women from full membership, and related too closely to the cultic requirements of the old covenant. *Baptism...became the rite of initiation into the Christian community"* [and the New *Covenant*] ...Paul uses the Hellenistic Christian idea of baptism as death—dying to the old person and rising in the new. Jesus himself had referred to baptism as death (Mark 10:39) [1051]

As St. Paul wrote:

Do you not know that all of us who have been baptized

1046 Jeremiah 31:31-33

1047 Ezekiel 37:14 and Ezekiel 37:26-27

1048 Isaiah 61:8, Isaiah 55:1-3

1049 Neville Clark. *Studies in Biblical Theology No.17: An Approach to the Theology of the Sacraments* London, SCM Press Ltd., 1956, page 73: "The Church is the *new Israel,* the people of the New Covenant"

1050 Galatians 3:29

1051 William H. Willimon, *Word, Water, Wine and Bread: How Worship Has Changed over the Years.* Valley Forge, PA, Judson Press, 1980, pages 26-27. (Mark 10:39: Jesus said to them... "Are you able to drink the cup that I drink; or to be baptized with the baptism with which I am baptized?" And they said to him, "We are able." And Jesus said to them, "The cup that I drink you will drink; and with the baptism with which I am baptized, you will be baptized; but to sit at my right hand...")

into Christ Jesus were baptized into his death? We were buried therefore with him by baptism into death, [by the symbolism of metaphorically drowning in water and dying], so that as Christ was raised from the dead by the glory of the Father, we too might walk in newness of life. [1052]

William Willimon writes:

> Conversion into the faith, initiation into God's holy nation, is ...a radical break with the old life and a radical incorporation into new life... Paul says that [as quoted above] through baptism we are linked to Christ's own dying and rising. We are 'buried' in the baptismal waters.. Then we rise to 'walk in newness of life'.

> Elsewhere....Paul speaks of baptism as the basis for Christian unity...for [we] are all one in Christ. [1053]

> The cleansing waters of baptism wash away all racial, social and sexual distinctions which characterized life in the Old Age.

> Above all, baptism was a Christian initiation. It marked the entrance into a new eschatalogical community gathered in the name of Christ. [1054]

So often human beings concentrate on one aspect of something at the expense of another, forgetting that different truths can be held in balance together. In fact, one can sum up a very basic truth about Baptism in the two words *"water and Spirit"*. Baptism is a washing away of sin, but it is much more than that.

> The idea of baptism as a rite of purification and cleansing, and as such closely associated with the forgivenes of sins,

---

1052 Romans 6:34

1053 Galatians 3:26-28 "For as many of you as were baptized into Christ have put on Christ. There is neither Jew nor Greek, there is neither slave nor free, there is neither male or female; for *you are all one in Christ Jesus."*

1054 William H. Willimon. *Word, Water, Wine and Bread. How Worship Has Changed over the Years.* Valley Forge, PA, Judson Press, 1980, pages 27-28.

finds a place in Paul's thinking; but it is set within a wider context and overshadowed by more distinctively Pauline insights. 'You were washed' passes immediately into 'You were sanctified, you were justified in the name of the Lord Jesus and in the Spirit of our God.' [1055] The association of baptism with the Spirit and 'the name of Jesus' is ... pre-Pauline; but Paul's characteristic interest is *the new life* [italics mine] for which cleansing from sin sets a man free, and his method is to subsume forgiveness under more inclusive concepts....

In few ways is Paul's creative genius better displayed than in his thought about baptism as the channel through which the Holy Spirit is given. *Yet here again he is working with traditional materials; for from its inception Christian baptism had been connected with the Spirit's outpouring.* [1056]

But after we have been baptized, and in then partaking of the sacrament of the Eucharist, (and I have stated the importance of being part of the community of faith wherever we may be, as part of the Church which is the Body of Christ), trying to live a holy life, and aspiring to *union with Christ* in all we do, we come to have a living experience of the divine which is what I have been trying to describe in this book, and we come to *know for ourselves* what all the books in the world could not teach us (to paraphrase St. John).[1057]

We come to have (or we should have) a sense of identity "not rooted primarily in [our] ethnic past or even in the religious rhythms of family and school, *but an identity rooted in the living memory of [our] own baptism into Christ in his Church.*" [1058]

1055 1 Corinthians 6:11

1056 Neville Clark. *Studies in Biblical Theology No.17: An Approach to the Theology of the Sacraments.* London, SCM Press Ltd., 1956, page 23.

1057 John 21:25 : "there are also many other things which Jesus did; were every one of them to be written, I suppose that the world itself could not contain the books that would be written."

1058 Aidan Kavanagh. *The Shape of Baptism: The Rite of Christian Initiation — Studies in the Reformed Rites of the Catholic Church, Volume 1.*   New York, Pueblo Publishing Company, Inc.,1978, page 176

But I would like to repeat my emphasis here that we still need to remember that God is Trinity. Neville Clark has written:

> *The part played by the Spirit in the transformation of the*
> *fallen world poses at once the trinitarian problem, and*
> *more particularly the question of the relation between the*
> *Spirit and the Son, so far as this is relevant to sacramental*
> *theology.* Here the fact of the ascension of Christ is
> crucial; and failure to maintain the balance of Christian
> truth at this point has led to disastrous theological
> confusion. On the one hand the ascension has been
> virtually ignored... On the other hand the ascension has
> been interpreted as the withdrawal of the risen Christ
> and his replacement by the Holy Spirit; *and the result*
> *is the transference to the third Person of the Trinity of so*
> *large a part of the present activity of the Godhead that*
> *the ascended Christ seems to be deprived of his rightful*
> *significance* [1059]

and he goes on to say:

> ...no theology can be regarded as satisfactory which
> appropriates the Spirit to baptism whilst attaching
> Christ to the eucharist. [An excessive and one-sided
> interpretation of these sacraments will often be found to
> lead to trouble].... To ignore either the Lord or the Spirit
> in the interpretation of the sacraments is, in the end, to
> deprive them of the fullness either of their personal,
> redemptive significance or their dynamic power. [1060]

It cannot be said too often, that we have to be careful in keeping in balance in our minds the three Persons of the Trinity (neither confusing the Persons nor dividing the substance" [1061]). But that said, *and it cannot be emphasized too much*, that we believe in *One God in Trinity, and the Trinity in Unity,* yet I think it is legitimate to remind

---

1059 Neville Clark. *Studies in Biblical Theology No. 17: An Approach to the Theology of the Sacraments.* London, SCM Press, Ltd., 1956, pages 75-76

1060 Neville Clark. *Studies in Biblical Theology No. 17. An Approach to the Theology of the Sacraments.* London: SCM Press, Ltd., 1956, page 77

1061 Athanasian Creed. *The [Anglican] Book of Common Prayer, Canada, 1962,* page 695

you again, especially in the context of talking about Baptism, of the close association in the Bible between *water and the Spirit.*

Jesus told Nicodemus that "unless one is born of *water and the Spirit,* he cannot enter the kingdom of God." [1062] In Jewish thought there had long been an association between the idea of *water* nourishing the earth as a metaphor for the outpouring of *the Holy Spirit* (see the earlier discussion on how St. Paul could associate Christ with the Rock that gave the Israelites the life-giving water in the wilderness). Other examples of this association between water and the Spirit (the former being used as a metaphor for the latter) are given below. (See the earlier discussion of the Covenant with Abraham, and the New Covenant instituted in the death and resurrection of Jesus, and the outpouring of the Holy Spirit associated with the inauguration of the New Covenant.) [1063]

The work of the Holy Spirit in our lives being as water nourishing dry land

When Jesus received John the Baptist's question as to whether He was the Messiah, He replied by referring to the prophecies of Isaiah. [1064]

The passage that Jesus quoted that says: "Then *the eyes of the blind shall be opened, and the ears of the deaf unstopped*" and continues "then shall the lame man leap like a hart, and the tongue of the dumb sing for joy," *immediately* goes on to say:

> "*For waters shall break forth in the wilderness, and streams in the desert; the burning sand shall become a pool, and* the thirsty ground *springs of water...*" [1065]

1062 John 3:5

1063 noting particularly passages such as Ezekiel 37:14: "*I will put my spirit within you, and you shall live*", and *in the same chapter,* Ezekiel 37:26-27, "*I will make a covenant of peace with them...an everlasting covenant*"

1064 Matthew 11:5, referring to Isaiah 29:18-19, Isaiah 35:5-6, and Isaiah 61:1

1065 Isaiah 35:5-7 (Isaiah 35:1-10 runs: "*The wilderness and the dry land shall be glad.....the eyes of the blind shall be opened....waters shall break forth in the wilderness, and streams in the desert.....And a highway shall be there...the redeemed shall walk there.* And the ransomed of the Lord shall return, and come to Zion with singing; and everlasting joy shall be upon their heads; they shall obtain joy and gladness, and sorrow and sighing shall flee away")

The passage from which I originally chose the title of *Water in the Desert* for this book is similar:

> 'Behold, I am doing a new thing....*I give water in the wilderness, rivers in the desert,* to give drink to my chosen people, the people whom I formed for myself *that they might declare my praise.'* [1066]

> The wilderness and the dry land shall be glad, the desert shall rejoice and blossom: like the crocus, it shall blossom abundantly [1067]

and

> the Lord will comfort Zion; he will...*make her wilderness like Eden, her desert like the garden of the Lord.* [1068]

Other passages also show that the transformation is more than physical:

> *until the Spirit is poured upon us from on high, and the wilderness becomes a fruitful field, and the fruitful field is deemed a forest. Then* justice will dwell in the wilderness, and righteousness abide in the fruitful field. And the effect of righteousness will be peace.... quietness and trust for ever"; [1069]

> '*I will pour water on the thirsty land, and streams on the dry ground; I will pour my Spirit upon your descendants and my blessing on your offspring.* They shall spring up *like grass amid waters, like willows by flowing streams. This one will say "I am the Lord's..."* ' [1070]

> *I will put in the wilderness a pool of water, and the dry land springs of water.* I will put in the cedar, the acacia, the myrtle, and the olive; I will set in the desert the cypress, the plane and the pine together, *that men may*

1066 Isaiah 43:19-21

1067 Isaiah 35:1

1068 Isaiah 51:3

1069 Isaiah 32:15:17

1070 Isaiah 44:3-5

see and know…that the hand of the Lord has done this, the Holy One of Israel has created it; [and] *The Lord will guide you continually…*and *you shall be like a watered garden, like a spring of water, whose waters fail not.* [1071]

Jeremiah 17:7 reads: "Blessed is the man who trusts in the Lord… *He is like a tree planted by water, that sends out its roots by the stream, and does not fear when heat comes, for its leaves remain green,* and is not anxious in the year of drought, *for it does not cease to bear fruit.* [1072]

Similarly Psalm 1:1-3: *"Blessed is the man… [whose] delight is in the law of the Lord… He is like a tree planted by streams of water, that yields its fruit in its season, and its leaf does not wither."*

Psalm 23:1-3: "The Lord is my shepherd, I shall not want …. *He leads me beside still waters; he restores my soul"*

and in the description of the Kingdom of God in *Revelation 7:17* it is written:

…the Lamb in the midst of the throne will be their shepherd, and *he will guide them to springs of living water*

The prophet Jeremiah described the Lord as being *"a fountain of living water",* saying "they have forsaken the Lord, *the fountain of living water"* [1073] *(in the same chapter* that uses the metaphor of trees being physically nourished by water to describe the

---

1071 Isaiah 41:18-20: This passage begins (v.17): "When the poor and needy seek water, and there is none …. I the Lord will answer them, *I the God of Israel will not forsake them. I will open rivers on the bare heights, and fountains* in the midst of the valleys; *I will make the wilderness a pool of water… ";* and Isaiah 58:11: "The Lord will guide you continually…and *you shall be like a watered garden,* like *a spring of water, whose waters fail not."*

1072 This is in contrast to the "one who trusts in man, who depends on flesh for his strength [NIV] and whose heart turns away from the Lord", who is described (Jeremiah 17:5-6) as being like "a shrub *in the desert … in the parched places of the wilderness,* in an uninhabited salt land."

1073 Jeremiah 17:13

spiritual nourishment that comes from God to those who trust in Him); and, again, "My people have committed two evils: they have forsaken me, *the fountain of living waters,* and hewed out cisterns for themselves, broken cisterns, that can hold no water." [1074] It is clear that *water* is used as a metaphor, by Isaiah and Jeremiah, and the writers of several Psalms, as well as the Gospel of John and the Book of Revelation, to describe how human souls who trust in God are spiritually nourished by the Holy Spirit: *"the water of life"* [1075] that comes from God.

Psalm 36 says "with thee is *the fountain of life"*. [1076]

Jesus used the same metaphor of Himself, saying: "whoever drinks of the water that I shall give him will never thirst; [it] will become *in him a spring of water welling up to eternal life".* [1077] He referred to the famous passage in Isaiah:

> Ho, every one who thirsts, come to the waters; and he who has no money, come, buy and eat!....Why do you spend your money for that which is not bread, and your labour for that which does not satisfy? Hearken diligently to me, and eat what is good...Incline your ear and come to me; hear, *that your soul may live* [1078]

saying, centuries later:

> *'If any one thirst, let him come to me and drink.* He who believes in me, *as the scripture has said,* "Out of his heart shall flow rivers of living water" '

—and the Gospel account continues: "Now this he said about the Spirit, which those who believed in him were to receive; for as yet the Spirit had not been given, because Jesus was not yet glorified." [1079]

1074 Jeremiah 2:13

1075 Revelation 21:6: "To the thirsty I will give from *the fountain of the water of life",* Revelation 22:1: "the *water of life*...flowing from the throne of God...", Revelation 22:17; 'let him who is thirsty...take the water of life"

1076 Psalm 36:9

1077 John 4:14

1078 Isaiah 55:1-3

1079 John 7:37-39

Jesus also said: *"I am* the bread of life; he who comes to me shall not hunger, and *he who believes in me shall never thirst".* [1080]

This is echoed in the Book of Revelation, where *"God"* is spoken of as "the Alpha and the Omega", *"the first and the last"* (which is what the Alpha and the Omega are, the first and last letters of the Greek alphabet), and as being both the One " 'who is and who was and who is to come, *the Almighty',* " and also as " *'the living one [who] died, and behold I am alive for evermore,* ' " [1081] which in the latter case *has* to refer to Jesus, because *it was Jesus who died.*

It is Jesus who can be equated with the Alpha and Omega *Who is God* — if God is not a Trinity, none of this makes sense; and it is written:

> *'I am the Alpha and the Omega, the beginning and the end. To the thirsty I will give from the fountain of the water of life* without payment. He who conquers shall have this heritage, *and I will be his God and he shall be my son.'* " [1082]

St. Paul must have been comfortable with using the metaphors of "water", and spiritual thirst being assuaged, in connection with the Holy Spirit. In addition to his remark about Christ being the Rock [1083] of the Old Testament wilderness experience, [1084] he wrote to the Corinthians as follows:

> *For by one Spirit we were all baptized [with water] into one body*—Jews or Greeks, slaves or free—*and all were made to drink of one Spirit."* [1085]

1080 John 6:35

1081 Revelation 1:8; 1:17; 1:18; see also Isaiah 44:6: "Thus says the Lord, the King of Israel and his Redeemer, the Lord of hosts: *'I am the first and I am the last; besides me there is no god'* " and Isaiah 48:12-13: "My glory I will not give to another. Hearken to me, O Jacob, and Israel, whom I called! *I am He, I am the first, and I am the last.* My hand laid the foundation of the earth, and my right hand spread out the heavens...."

1082 Revelation 21:6-7

1083 1 Corinthians 10:4: "For *they drank from* the supernatural Rock which followed them, [which] *was Christ"*

1084 see Exodus 17:2-6, Numbers 20:2-11, Psalm 105:41

1085 1 Corinthians 12:13. See also John 3:3-6, Jesus' saying: "unless one is *born of water and the Spirit,* he cannot enter the Kingdom of God."

The Book of Revelation refers to "the river of the water of life… flowing from the throne of God…" through the eternal city; [1086] and Isaiah says "with joy you will draw water from the wells of salvation." [1087]

It is interesting to note that, while the theme of water remains constant as a metaphor for our being nourished, indeed kept alive spiritually, by the life of God, and, as shown, it is used most often as a metaphor for the Holy Spirit, ("The Lord, The Giver of Life"), [1088] it is also used in connection with the other Persons of the Trinity.

In the Old Testament passages quoted earlier, it is used in the context of God providing "the water of life", [1089] but, as shown, Jesus used this metaphor in connection with Himself, as well; [1090] and the Book of Revelation on this subject makes Almighty God almost indistinguishable from the One who died. [1091]

We come back to God as Trinity at every turn, but we should not let this confuse us.

We need to remember that we worship One God: "one God in Trinity, and the Trinity in Unity, neither confusing the Persons, nor dividing the Substance", [1092] and look to the God who gives us life, both now and for all eternity, gratefully receiving that gift of life, as we come to abide in Him.

1086 Revelation 22:1

1087 Isaiah 12:3

1088 The Nicene Creed - [Anglican] *Book of Common Prayer,* page 71.

1089 Revelation 21:6, Revelation 22:1, Revelation 22:17

1090 John 4:14, John 7:37-39

1091 Revelation 1:17-18

1092 Athanasian Creed - *The* [Anglican] *Book of Common Prayer, 1962, Canada,* page 695.

APPENDIX

Biblical References to God as The Rock

Deuteronomy 32:3-4: "Ascribe greatness to our God! The Rock, his work is perfect; for all his ways are justice. A God of faithfulness and without iniquity, just and right is he."

Deuteronomy 32:15-18: "...then he forsook God who made him, and scoffed at the Rock of his salvation".... "You were unmindful of the Rock that begot you, and you forgot the God who gave you birth";

I Samuel 2:2: "There is none holy like the Lord, there is none besides thee; there is no rock like our God";

2 Samuel 22:1-2: "And David...said, 'The Lord is my rock, and my fortress, and my deliverer, my God, my rock, in whom I take refuge..... my stronghold and my refuge, my savior;' " and verse 47: " 'The Lord lives; and blessed be my rock, and exalted be my God, the rock of my salvation, the God who...' "

2 Samuel 23: 1-3: "...the last words of David....'The Spirit of the Lord speaks by me, his word is upon my tongue. The God of Israel has spoken, the Rock of Israel has said to me....' "

Psalm 18:1-2 (and see 2 Samuel 22:2)—'I love thee, O Lord my strength. The Lord is my rock, and my fortress, and my deliverer, my God, my rock, in whom I take refuge, my shield and...my salvation...." and verse 31: "For who is God, but the Lord? And who is a rock, except our

God?" (Note, for interest, the combination of the words "God", "rock" and "Saviour" or "deliverer" in the psalm just quoted.)

Psalm 27:5 "...in the time of trouble he shall hide me in his tabernacle; yea, in the secret place of his dwelling shall he hide me, and set me up on a rock of stone"[1093]

Psalm 28:1: "To Thee, O Lord, I call; my rock, be not deaf to me"

Psalm 31:3-4, and verse 23: "Be thou my strong rock and house of defence, that thou mayst save me. For thou art my strong rock and my castle...Thou hidest them [that fear thee] in the secret place of thine own presence....thou keepest them secretly in thy tabernacle from the strife of tongues". (In a similar vein: Psalm 32:7: "Thou art a hiding place for me....thou dost encompass [surround] me with deliverance".)

Psalm 42:9: "I say unto God, my rock...."

Psalm 61:2-4: "Lead thou me to the rock that is higher than I; for thou art my refuge, a strong tower against the enemy. Let me dwell in thy tent for ever! Oh to be safe under the shelter of thy wings!"

Psalm 62:5-6: "For God alone my soul waits in silence...He only is my rock and my salvation, my fortress; I shall not be shaken. On God rests my deliverance and my honour; my mighty rock, my refuge is God";

Psalm 71:3: "Be thou to me a rock of refuge, a strong fortress, to save me, for thou art my rock and my fortress"—or, in the Prayer Book Version, "Be thou my stronghold, whereunto I may always resort; thou hast promised to help me, for thou art my rock and my castle."

Psalm 78:35: "They remembered that God was their rock, the Most High God their redeemer";

1093 Psalms 27 and 31 from versions in *The [Anglican] Book of Common Prayer, 1962, Canada*

Psalm 89:26: "He shall cry to me 'Thou art my Father, my God, and the Rock of my salvation.'"

Psalm 91:1-2,9: "He who dwells in the shelter of the Most High, who abides in the shadow of the Almighty, will say to the Lord 'My refuge and my fortress; my God, in whom I trust'." (This is the psalm that says "Because you have made the Lord your refuge, the Most High your habitation".)

Psalm 92:15: "The Lord is upright: he is my rock...."

Psalm 94:22: " the Lord has become my stronghold, and my God the rock of my refuge"

Psalm 95:1: "O come, let us sing to the Lord; let us make a joyful noise to the rock of our salvation!"

Isaiah 17:10: "For you have forgotten the God of your salvation, and have not remembered the Rock of your refuge";

Isaiah 26:4: "Trust in the Lord for ever, for the Lord God is an everlasting rock"

Isaiah 44:8: "Is there a God beside me? There is no Rock; I know not any";

Jeremiah 16:19: "O Lord, my strength and my stronghold, my refuge in the day of trouble"

and then, of the wilderness experience described in the Book of Exodus,[1094] and in *Psalm 105,* "[He] gave them bread from heaven...He opened the rock, and water gushed forth; it flowed through the desert like a river",[1095] St. Paul wrote:, in *1 Corinthians 10:4,* "For they drank from the supernatural Rock which followed them, and *the Rock was Christ.*"

It is interesting to note a verse at the beginning of chapter 32 of the Book of Isaiah, where, although the word "rock" is not used of

1094 Exodus 16
1095 Psalm 105:40-41

God, as it was in the passages I have quoted, and the word "rock" is not written with a capital "R", nor is the metaphor of "streams of water in a dry place" in this case specifically linked to the spiritual result of the outpouring of the Holy Spirit as it was in the passages quoted, although "[the outpouring of the Spirit] from on high" is referred to in verse 15 of that chapter, these metaphors are used together to describe "the coming age of justice", [1096] in other words, the situation in the future where God's will is done, thus reflecting the will and nature of God Himself: and for that reason this verse is worth noting: "Each will be like a hiding place from the wind, a covert from the tempest, like streams of water in a dry place, like the shade of a great rock in a weary land". [1097]

1096 Note in *The New Oxford Annotated Version* of *The Revised Standard Version* of the Bible, page 860

1097 Isaiah 32:2

Glossary of Terms

"Annihilationism"

— also known as "Conditional Immortality": the idea that the human soul is only immortal under certain conditions, an idea which has generally been disregarded, as the human soul has been thought to be immortal in its own right.

The Oxford Dictionary of the Christian Church states that "*the teaching of the mortality of the soul is generally considered to be opposed to the Christian doctrine of man* and to the dignity and responsibility of the human soul" — but this "doctrine" is not listed in the *Dictionary* itself; and I think it is illogical to ascribe belief in the idea of the immortality of the soul *in its own right* to any *Christian* doctrine, since this idea is not only *pre-Christian* but is subscribed to by many non-Christian faiths today who would not think of this belief of theirs as being a "*Christian*" doctrine.

Nevertheless, the entry continues: "Though still used in certain kinds of popular apologetics, *it has nowadays but few defenders among serious Christian theologians*". I think this is why Christianity continues to have problems.

Although various heretical speculations on the subject in the past were condemned at the Fifth Lateran Council (of the Roman Catholic Church) in 1513, which led to the whole idea being discredited, *this was only four years before Martin*

Luther started the Reformation, a time when the Church of the day was already much in need of reform, and at that time hardly qualified to make major theological decisions about the traditions which it had inherited from the past. When Luther protested against Indulgences, which were based on people's fear of hell, he concentrated, rightly, on the fact that we are saved by Christ, not our own merits, *but he did not deal with the underlying problem of the traditional belief in hell,* which actually contradicts New Testament teaching, as I try to show. However, the Reformation did not tackle this problem either, and I believe the whole question needs to be looked at again now.

I am restating St. Paul's insistence (1 Corinthians 15:21-22) that "as by *a man* [the flesh" as typified by Adam] came *death* [not punishment], by *a man* [Christ] has come also *the resurrection of the dead"* and *"in Christ* [in other words, *only with the eternal God]* shall all *be made alive." "Eternal life"* is God's gift to us *through Christ,* the whole point of the Gospel, and I believe that maintaining that *the soul can survive for ever on its own without God* (i.e. in hell) is to challenge basic Biblical teaching, as I try to demonstrate in the many examples given.

It might be worth noting, in this context, that St. Paul specifically referred to "the flesh" as being, of its very nature, in itself, *perishable and mortal, not* immortal in its own right, as the so-called "Christian doctrine of man" mentioned above would have us believe. In the famous passage often read at funerals (1 Corinthians 15), talking about Christ's victory over death, St. Paul wrote: "For *this perishable nature* must put on the imperishable, and *this mortal nature must put on immortality* [and when that happens] then shall come to pass the saying...'Death is swallowed up in victory' ".

Apocatastasis

"The doctrine that *hell is in essence purgative and therefore temporary,* and that all intelligent beings will therefore in the end be saved." See "universalism" below.

Atonement

(or "at-one-ment")—the bringing together of human beings and God, so that they may be "at one". There have been various theories over the centuries about how the death and Resurrection of Jesus Christ accomplished this, and I have tried finally to make sense of this doctrine.

Catechumenate

Those in the early Church who were being given training and instruction preparatory to Christian Baptism. *The Oxford Dictionary of the Christian Church* states that "in 1962 the catechumenate was restored in the RC Church...the revived catechumenate was of special importance in the mission field," and says that in 1972 "the restored catechumenate became a necessary prelude to all adult baptisms" (in the Roman Catholic Church).

"Christian Doctrine of Man" — see "Annihilationism"

Confirmation

The service in the Western Church (the Church of Western Europe after the schism between the East and West) where children who have been baptized as infants make their adult profession of faith, and, by the laying on of hands by the Bishop, receive the Holy Spirit.

However, in the eastern Church (the Christian Church in Eastern Europe), this part of the service of baptism, administered by the priest, not necessarily a bishop, has always been part of the initial rite of baptism. In the Western Church today, baptism is regaining its status as the main rite of Christian initiation, with a greater understanding of the role of the Holy Spirit in that sacrament.

Creeds

Statements of belief in the Christian faith, taken from the Latin word "credo", meaning "I believe".

The two main ones are the Apostles' Creed which is believed to go back to the earliest times, as a baptismal statement of faith, and the Nicene Creed, named for the Council of Nicaea which met to define what was orthodox belief as opposed to what was heretical. (Although actually there was originally more than one Creed drafted at that time, "the Nicene Creed" as it is now found in Eucharistic worship in both East and West, is, in its present form, the main one to which the name is commonly applied.)

There was also the Athanasian Creed which the Eastern Church has not subscribed to, since it originated after the last "ecumenical council" when all the Churches met together, before the schism between East and West, but it has been one of the major documents of the Western Church for many centuries.

Damasus – Faith of

It is stated in *The Christian Faith in the Doctrinal Documents of the Catholic Church,* (edited by J. Neuner, S.J., & J. Dupuis, S.J., Revised Edition, Christian Classics Inc., Westminster, Md., 1975, pages 10-12), that "The Faith of Damasus" has sometime been attributed to Pope Damasus (ob.384) or to St. Jerome, but, "in reality, it belongs to the fifth century and seems to have originated from Southern Gaul rather than from Spain," and it states that "it is our hope *that we shall receive from Him eternal life, the reward of good merit,* or else (we shall) receive the penalty of *eternal punishment for sin.*"

I am making the point that, for at least a millenium and a half, "eternal life" has been seen as *a reward, rather than as union with God in Christ,* wherever or however that may come about; but it is not, in my opinion, logical to call it "eternal life" if those receiving the penalty of "eternal punishment for sin" *also survive for ever* (in hell)..

Diocese

The grouping of local parishes under the governance of a bishop in a Diocese. Several Dioceses (with their several bishops) form a Provincial Synod, whereas a national synod gathers to meet about the affairs of the Church in a country as a whole.

Doctrine of Assurance

Claude Beaufort Moss, in *"The Christian Faith: An Introduction to Dogmatic Theology"* (London: S.P.C.K., 1954, page 198) refers to *"the doctrine of assurance",* which, he says "is extremely dangerous" and "lies at the root of the individualism and subjectivity which are the bane of all the heirs of the Reformation." He goes on to say that *"if all that were needed for salvation were justification by faith, guaranteed by the assurance of a man's own heart,* the Church...the sacraments would not be necessary...*the observance of the moral law would not be necessary".* It should be remembered that even St. Paul, who had obviously "accepted Christ", had the humility to admit that, if he failed to subdue the temptations of the flesh, he might still "be disqualified" (1 Corinthians 9:27). See also Philippians 3:8-14 ("for his sake I have suffered...that I may gain Christ and be found in him...that I may know him and the power of his resurrection, becoming like him in his death, that if possible I may attain the resurrection from the dead. Not that I have already obtained this or am already perfect; but I press on to make it my own, because Christ Jesus has made me his own.") Some effort is required on our part: we can't simply sit back and say "we are saved".

Doxology

"An ascription of glory to the Persons of the Holy Trinity" *(Oxford Dictionary of the Christian Church)*. It is generally used to describe an uplifting of praise or worship to God. In the sense in which Walter Kasper used it, quoted in the book, I understand it to mean a continuing stream of love and glory (into which I believe human beings can be assimilated, as explained in the book), as if it were a love song.

Eucharist Holy Communion or "The Lord's Supper"

Eucharistic Prayer

The prayers said by the celebrant over the bread and wine in the Eucharist, in which the elements of bread and wine are consecrated.

Faith of Damasus – see "Damasus"

"Filioque clause"

The words in the Nicene Creed *"and the Son"* are, in Latin, *"filioque"* (as in the Holy Spirit proceeding from "the Father *and the Son"*). In the original Greek, the Creed stated that the Holy Spirit *"proceeds from the Father"*. As I explain in the book, I believe that it was when the Creed was translated from Greek into Latin, with the problem of *a different language appearing to carry a different meaning,* (a problem perpetuated in subsequent translation into English) that the words *"and the Son"* were added to the statement about the Holy Spirit proceeding from the Father, to ensure that God was still understood as Trinity. The Eastern Church has not felt this to be necessary, and there is continuing disagreement on this subject to this day.

Gnosticism

"It is now generally held that Christian Gnosticism had its origins in trends of thought already present in pagan religious circles *[The Oxford Dictionary of the Christian Church]*...The function of Christ was to come as the emissary of the supreme God, bringing 'gnosis' [knowledge]. .....As a Divine Being He neither assumed a properly human body nor died, but either temporarily inhabited a human being, Jesus, or assumed a merely phantasmal human appearance. The principal anti-Gnostic writers, such as Irenaeus, Tertullian, and Hippolytus, emphasized the pagan features of Gnosticism, and *appealed to the plain sense of the Scriptures as interpreted by the tradition of the church, which had been publicly handed down by a chain of teachers reaching back to the Apostles.* They insisted on the identity of the Creator and the supreme God, *on the goodness of the material creation, and on the reality of the earthly life of Jesus, esp. of the Crucifixion and the Resurrection.* Man needed redemption from *an evil will* rather than an evil evironment...." [italics mine].

With regard to the last sentence, it will be noted that I have argued that it was not human *will* that was evil, in itself: in other words, *"the flesh"* is not intrinsically evil in itself —Jesus was able to take on human flesh—but that evil results from human beings giving in to the temptations that "the flesh" is naturally subject to as part of creation: instincts built into all species to ensure their survival, but which human beings should be able to master, with the help of God through abiding ` in Christ , if they so choose . See "original sin" below.

Logos

The Greek word for "Word" applied to Jesus Christ, the Second Person of the Trinity (St. John's Gospel begins with the statement "in the beginning was the Word and the Word was with God and the Word *was* God.)

Nicene Creed see Creeds, above.

Original Sin

> *The Oxford Dictionary of the Christian Church* says that: "In Christian theology, [it is] the state of sin in which mankind has been held captive since the Fall". The Fall itself is described as "the first act of disobedience of Adam and Eve whereby man lost his primal innocence and happiness and entered upon his actual condition of sin and toil....In modern times the whole concept of the Fall has often been rejected as inconsistent with the facts of man's development known to science, esp. with evolution. The Biblical story itself belongs to the realm of myth and is told with much anthropomorphic and metaphorical deail.

> "Orthodox Christian apologists insist, however, *that man possesses a power of moral choice not shared with the animals; that at some stage in human development this God-given power began to be misused; and that once begun, such wrong use has necessarily affected subsequent generations and given rise to the vast accumulated power of sin in the world.*" (italics mine).

I would agree with the first part of this assessment: that humanity has the power of moral choice not shared with the animals, and that in every generation humanity abuses this God-given power, resulting in the reality of sin; but I argue that it is not so much an accumulated "debt" over the generations as a recurring reality in every generation as human beings use their God-given free-will to give in to the temptations and passions and desires of our "animal nature" and make the wrong moral choices, and start to sin. I argue that Christ came, not just that we might be "forgiven", but that we might learn to *abide in Him,* and through the power of the Holy Spirit resist and overcome wrong temptations, and learn to live in the way God wishes us to live, so that we might become "at one" with Him.

However, the idea of "original sin" is slightly different. It was a variation of what is stated above, a distortion of it, in effect, because it assumed that every human being entering the world, even the newly-born, even a child who never lived long enough to commit an actual sin, *automatically bore guilt just for being human,* a guilt which had to be atoned for.

I believe that this arose from a misunderstanding of what St. Paul meant when he said that "by a man came death," as I describe in detail in the book. It has been taken to mean that, because humanity is descended from Adam and Eve, all human beings have inherited the guilt of their sin, and therefore all are automatically sinful and deserving of *punishment,* "death" in the New Testament being interpreted to mean *punishment,* whereas my belief is that what St. Paul was doing was contrasting the naturally occurring physical *death of the flesh* with the eternal life made possible for humanity in Christ.

The importance of the idea of "original sin," historically, is that *humanity, "the flesh",* came to be seen *as evil in itself,* to the point where it had to be declared that the Virgin Mary was born without the stain of it, so that Jesus could not be "contaminated" with it, which I argue denies the reality of the Incarnation, because it has always been believed—at the same time—that Jesus was *fully human,* ("of the substance of the Virgin Mary His mother"), a fact which the Church has never denied.

I argue that this is an important point, in that it is *because* Jesus fully took on our humanity with all its temptations and liabilities, *and overcame them, and remained sinless,* that we are enabled to overcome the inherent weaknesses of "the flesh" as we "abide in Him". My point is that, being fully human, Jesus was subject to, (but was able to overcome in Himself), all the temptations that humanity is subject to, and that therefore *we can share in that victory as we abide in Him, our humanity being*

- 415 -

caught up into His divinity: that *that* is what the Atonement is all about, rather than the need for forgiveness for "original sin," even for those infants who have never sinned.

The whole point of my book is that the Atonement is about more than just forgiveness, necessary though that may be for people who have lived long enough to have committed sins. I believe that God's intention was that, as we "abide in Christ", we can be enabled to overcome the temptations of our animal nature: "the flesh" can be sanctified and made holy, and we can become "a new creation" in Him. This is all dealt with in the Chapters on the Atonement and Abiding in Christ.

Purgatory

"According to Roman Catholic teaching, the place or state of temporal punishment where those who have died in the grace of God expiate their unforgiven venial sins and undergo such punishment as is still due to forgiven sin" *(The Oxford Dictionary of the Christian Church).* Punishment is thought of as "purging" the sin. "This idea was rejected by the Reformers, who taught that souls are freed from sin by faith in Christ alone without any works, and therefore, if saved, go straight to heaven" *(The Oxford Dictionary* again). It will be noted that neither Roman Catholics nor Protestants saw "salvation" in terms of eternity being dependent on union with God; and the resulting stalemate (which has never been resolved) became a question of either punishment or no punishment, (and no preparation for union with God either), rather than the alternatives of spending eternity *in God* or perishing altogether.

As I explain, I believe the necessary prerequisite for spending eternity in and with God is neither punishment or not being punished. *It is whether or not one is sufficiently compatible in oneself with the love and goodness that is God that such union is possible.* I go on to say that, for this, "abiding in Christ" helps to prepare us in this lifetime, living *"in the Spirit"* as opposed to *"life in the flesh,"* and I believe this has to be the answer to the unresolved question left over from the Reformation. I believe that some rare souls may come to this kind of purity and love in spite of not being professing Christians in this lifetime, and that it may be that they *may* be reconciled with God at the last *because they are already compatible with what God is like.* I maintain that this is *not* "universalism": this is not saying that *everybody* will be "saved in the end" regardless.

Salvation

"Being saved" by the grace of God through His redeeming action in the death and Resurrection of Jesus, though whether it is being saved from hell or being saved from perishing is part of the subject of this book. The whole subject of the Atonement is about the accomplishment of our salvation.

Sacrament

An outward action which is a channel by which God can work with, and be known to, people in His Church, long defined as "an outward and visible, sign of an inward, invisible grace." The two main sacraments are Baptism and the Eucharist, but there are also Confirmation, penance, matrimony, ordination, and Extreme Unction at the time of death, though the ministry of healing, anointing with oil, does not need to wait for death.

Sin against the Holy Spirit

Jesus said (Luke 12:10): "everyone who speaks a word against *the Son of Man* will be forgiven; but he who blasphemes against *the Holy Spirit* will *not* be forgiven". This supports my belief that non-Christians may still come to the One Triune God eventually, even if not until after death ("I have other sheep which are not of this fold", John 10:16). The statement in Luke 12:10 was in the context of people *presuming to teach others about God* when *incapable of recognizing the Holy Spirit of God themselves when they met it in Jesus,* so it may be that this long-undefined sin has to do with *misrepresentation of the nature of God* to others, to the point of sacrilege against *the very essence of God Himself*—surely the ultimate blasphemy.

Soteriology

Another word for "salvation", but which also includes not just "being saved" in itself, but "the saving work of Christ for the world", and many of the doctrines covered in this book such as "the doctrines of the Atonement and of Grace ...[and] of human nature as affected by the fall and by sin...and...the doctrine of man's final destiny as the result of [Christ's] work" *(Oxford Dictionary of the Christian Church)*.

Synoptic Gospels

The three Gospels, of Matthew, Mark and Luke, which are written with a common perspective, often sharing common source documents, to the point where they are known as "synoptic" from a Greek word which could be translated as "one eye", i.e., "seeing with one or the same eye".

Theology

The study of matters pertaining to God, from the Greek word, "theos", God, and "logos", the latter meaning in this case more the study of something, as, for example, "anthropology" is the study of "man".

"Universalism"

The idea that everyone will eventually "go to heaven," regardless of whether or not they are Christian, i.e., that "there are many roads to God".

I am trying to make the point that this is not what I am talking about, but I do see mutual "love" as being a means by which

God (the Trinitarian God) can bring people to Himself in the end *if He so wishes.*

I believe that confusion has arisen because the discredited theory of "universalism" omits *love* from its historical arguments, and I believe that it is *love* that unites us with God, *if we eventually come to accept Him as He is, a Trinity of Persons between whom Love flows,* and *are totally reconciled with Him.*

My argument is not to be confused with "Universalism", which is defined as follows in *The Oxford Dictionary of the Christian Church:*

> "(1) the anti-nationalist teaching of certain of the later Hebrew prophets that God's purposes covered not only the Jewish race but also at least some men of other nations [which St. Paul saw as justifying his mission to the Gentiles]

> "(2) the doctrine, also known as [apocatastasis] that *hell is in essence purgative and therefore temporary* and that *all intelligent beings* will therefore in the end be saved."

"Apocatastasis" itself is defined as "..the doctrine that ultimately all free moral creatures will share in the grace of salvation…".

We need to think about what is meant by *"salvation"* here: is it thought of in this context just as "going to heaven" and *not* going to hell? If salvation is what I believe it is, *union with the Trinitarian God of Love, how could that be possible for people who are unable to love? That* should surely be the key determinant: I believe that the key criterion for acceptance by God is *knowing how to love,* which arguments about "intelligent beings" or "free moral creatures" do not at all address.

I think, too, that the idea of hell being "purgative and temporary" is not logical; being *punished* does not transform an evil person into a good one, or *teach that person how to love;* and *God gave us free-will* so that love could be voluntary, not coerced, or *it would not be love* (and without sharing in the divine love how could there be "salvation"); but it does reinforce my belief that the emphasis throughout history has been on punishment, and hell, and not on *life lived for ever in the divine love* of the eternal God.

It also reinforces my belief that logic has not always been the strong point in the history of Christian thought!

BIBLIOGRAPHY

Auden, W.H. Lullaby of Mary at the Manger from "For the Time Being: A Christmas Oratorio—At the Manger: Mary". *English Masterpieces Vol. V11: Modern Poetry, 2nd edition,* edited by Maynard Mack, Leonard Dean and William Frost. Eaglewood Cliffs, N.J.: Prentice Hall Inc., 1961, p.241

Aulen, Gustaf. *Christus Victor. A Historical Study of the Three Main Types of the Idea of the Atonement* translated by A.G. Hebert. London: SPCK, 1931, 1970, 1980

Bicknell, E.J., D.D. (with additional references by Rev. Canon H.J. Carpenter) *A Theological Introduction to the Thirty-nine Articles of the Church of England.* London. Longmans, Green & Co., 1919, 1929,1939,1946

Borg, Marcus J., "The Historical Study of Jesus and Christian Origins" and "From Galilean Jew to the Face of God: The Pre-Easter and Post-Easter Jesus" *in Jesus at 2000* edited by Marcus J. Borg. Boulder, Colorado. Westview Press, 1997.

Borg, Marcus J., *The God We Never Knew: Beyond Dogmatic Religion to a More Authentic Contemporary Faith.* (HarperSanFrancisco, a Division of HarperCollins Publishers, New York), 1997

Clark, Neville, *Studies in Biblical Theology No 17: An Approach to the Theology of the Sacraments.* London, SCM Press, Ltd., 1956

Cotter, Anthony C., "The Divinity of Jesus Christ in St. Paul" in *The Catholic Biblical Quarterly,* Volume VII, Number 3, July 1945

Dix, Dom Gregory. *The Shape of the Liturgy.* London: Adam and Charles Black — A. & C. Black (Publishers) Ltd., 1945.

Eudes, John. *The Life and the Kingdom of Jesus in Christian Souls* Quoted by Tad Guzie *in Jesus and the Eucharist* (see below)

Fretheim, Terence E. *The Suffering of God: An Old Testament Perspective.* Philadelphia: Fortress Press, 1984

Gonzalez, Justo L. *A History of Christian Thought, Volume III, from the Protestant Reformation to the Twentieth Century.* Nashville: Abingdon Press, 1975

Guzie, Tad W., S.J. *Jesus and the Eucharist.* Ramsey, New Jersey: Paulist Press, 1974

Hill, John. *Thinking about Baptism.* Toronto, Canada: Anglican Book Centre, 1982.

Hodges, H.A. *The Pattern of Atonement.* London: S.C.M. Press Ltd., 1955,

Hollis, Reginald. *Abiding in Christ: Meditations on the Lord's Prayer, the Sermon on the Mount, and the Ten Commandments.* Toronto, Ontario: Anglican Book Centre, 1987

Kasper, Walter. *The God of Jesus Christ,* translated by Matthew J. O'Connell. New York: The Crossroad Publishing Company, 1984.

Kavanagh, Aidan. *The Shape of Baptism: The Rite of Christian Initiation— Studies in the Reformed Rites of the Catholic Church, Volume 1.* New York: Pueblo Publishing Company, Inc., 1978

Martin, Walter. *The Kingdom of the Cults.* Limited Edition. Minneapolis, Minnesota: Bethany House Publishers, 1996

McGiffert, Arthur Cushman. *A History of Christian Thought, Volume 1: Early and Eastern, From Jesus to John of Damascus.* New York, London: Charles Scribner's Sons, 1947.

Metzger, Bruce M., "The Punctuation of Rom. 9:5 " in *Christ and Spirit in the New Testament,* edited by Barnabas Lindars and Stephen S. Smalley "in Honour of Charles Francis Digby Moule", Cambridge: Cambridge University Press, 1973.

Moltmann, Jurgen. *The Crucified God.* Munich: Christian Kaiser Verlag, 2nd edition 1973; translated from the German by R.A. Wilson and John Bowden; c. SCM Press Ltd, London, 1974.

Moltmann, Jurgen. "The Unity of the Triune God: Remarks on the Comprehensibility of the Doctrine of the Trinity and its Foundation in the History of Salvation" in *St. Vladimir's Theological Quarterly,* vol. 28/3, 1984

Moss, Claude Beaufort. *The Christian Faith: An Introduction to Dogmatic Theology.* London. S.P.C.K., 1954.

Moule, C.F.D. *The Origin of Christology.* Cambridge: Cambridge University Press, 1977

Moule, C.F.D. *The Sacrifice of Christ.* London: Hodder and Stoughton, 1956

Neill, Stephen. *Anglicanism.* London & Oxford: Mowbray, c. 1958, 1960, 1965, 1977, Fourth Edition

Neuner J., S.J. & J. Dupuis, S.J. *The Christian Faith in the Doctrinal Documents of the Catholic Church,* Revised Edition, Westminster, Md., Christian Classics Inc., 1975.

O'Neil, Robert, and Donovan, Fr. Michael. *Children, Church and God.* Cleveland, Ohio: Corpus Books Division of World Publishing Co. (now out of print), reviewed by Louis Cassels, UPI Religion Writer, in *The Colonist* newspaper, Victoria, B.C., circa 1970.

Pannenberg, Wolfhart. *Jesus—God And Man.* Second Edition, translated by Lewis L. Wilkins and Duane A. Priebe. Philadelphia, Pennsylvania: The Westminster Press, 1968,1977.

Rahner, Karl. *Theological Investigations, Volume III. The Theology of the Spiritual Life,* translated by Karl-H. and Bonniface Kruger. London: Longman & Todd Ltd., 1967, 1974.

Ramsey, Michael, in *The Anglican Spirit,* edited by Dale Coleman. Cambridge, Mass., Cowley Publications, 1991

Ramsey, A.M. *The Gospels and the Catholic Church.* London. Longmans, Green & Co., 1936.

Spong, John Shelby, (Bishop of Newark), on internet at http://www.dioceseofnewark.org.jsspong/reform.html

Strobel, Lee. *The Case for Christ: A Journalist's Personal Investigation of the Evidence for Jesus.* Grand Rapids, Michigan, Zondervan, 1998.

Taylor, Vincent. *The Atonement In New Testament Teaching.* London: The Epworth Press, 1940

Ten Boom, Corrie. (with John & Elizabeth Sherrill): *The Hiding Place.* Sevenoaks, Kent, U.K.: Hodder & Stoughton Ltd & Christian Literature Crusade, 1971.

Wand, J.W.C. *A History of the Early Church to AD 500.* London: Methuen & Co., 1937.

Ward, Keith. *Re-thinking Christianity.* Oxford: Oneworld, 2007.

Westerhoff, John H., III. *Will Our Children Have Faith?* A Crossroad Book New York: The Seabury Press Inc., 1976.

Wiles, Maurice. *"The Work of Christ" in The Remaking of Christian Doctrine: The Hulsean Lectures, 1973.* London: S.C.M. Press Ltd., 1974

Willimon, William H. *Word, Water, Wine and Bread. How Worship Has Changed over the Years.* Valley Forge, PA, Judson Press, 1980

Willimon, William H. *Worship as Pastoral Care.* Nashville, Abingdon Press, 1979

Dictionaries and Bible Commentaries:

The Daily Study Bible: The Letters of John and Jude, Revised Edition, William Barclay. Burlington, Ontario, Canada: Welch Publishing Company Inc., 1958.

Peakes Commentary on the Bible: Matthew Black, General Editor and New Testament Editor, and H.H. Rowley, Old Testament Editor. Wokingham, England: Van Nostrand Reinhold (UK) Co. Ltd.

(c. Thomas Nelson and Sons Ltd., 1962; Van Nostrand Reinhold (UK) Co. Ltd. 1982.)

Penguin Dictionary of Quotations. J.M. and M.J. Cohen. Harmondsworth, England: Penguin Books, 1960.

Expository Dictionary of Bible Words. Lawrence O. Richards. Grand Rapids, Michigan: Regency Reference Library, Zondervan Publishing House, 1985

A Critical and Exegetical Commentary on the Epistle to the Romans. William Sanday and Arthur C. Headlam; Edinburgh: T. & T. Clark, 1902

The Interpreter's Bible: A Commentary in Twelve Volumes: Volume 8, Luke and John. Nashville: Abingdon Press. c. 1982 by Pierce & Smith in the United States of America; copyright renewed 1980, Abingdon Press. 37th Printing 1988

The Interpreter's Dictionary of the Bible: An Illustrated Encyclopedia. Vol. E-J. Nashville: Abingdon Press, 1962,

The Oxford Dictionary of the Christian Church. edited by F.L. Cross and revised second edition edited by F.L. Cross and E.A. Livingstone Oxford: Oxford University Press, 1958, 1974, 1983

Prayer Books and Hymn Books

The [Anglican] Book of Common Prayer 1962 Canada. Toronto: The Anglican Book Centre, 600 Jarvis Street, Toronto, 1962.

The [English, 1662] Book of Common Prayer. London: printed by Eyre and Spottiswoode, Ltd., Printers to the King's Most Excellent Majesty, for the Society for Promoting Christian Knowledge.

The Book of Alternative Services of the Anglican Church of Canada. Toronto, Canada: Anglican Book Centre. c. The General Synod of the Anglican Church of Canada, 1985.

The English Missal for the Laity. London: W. Knott & Son Limited, 1933

The [Anglican] Book of Common Praise [Canada) , Revised 1938, being the Hymn Book of the Church of England in Canada. Toronto: Geoffrey Cumberlege, Oxford University Press, 1938.

Versions of the Bible used:

Except where otherwise specified, Biblical quotations are from:

The New Oxford Annotated Bible, with the Apocrypha, Expanded Edition, Revised Standard Version, edited by Herbert G. May and Bruce M. Metzger. New York: Oxford University Press, Inc., 1973, 1977.

also quoted:

The Holy Bible New International Version. Grand Rapids, Michigan: Zondervan Bible Publishers c.1973, 1978, 1984, by International Bible Society.

"The King James" Authorized Version of the Bible.

SUBJECT INDEX

A

Abelard, Peter 335

Abiding in Christ/Abiding in God xx, xxvi, xxviii, xxx, xxxii, xxxiv, xxxix, xl, xli, 6, 7, 8, 15, 21, 53, 54, 55, 57, 61, 66, 74, 88, 93, 94, 101, 108, 119, 133, 142, 183, 203, 207, 211, 213, 226, 230, 250, 258, 264, 276, 288, 295, 310, 311, 312, 313, 316, 318, 324, 325, 326, 327, 330, 331, 332, 334, 337, 340, 342, 345, 346, 352, 359, 360, 362, 363, 364, 365, 367, 368, 369, 370, 371, 372, 374, 376, 379, 386, 416

Annihilationism xv, xxxiv, 271, 299, 300, 407, 409

Anselm of Canterbury 334

Apostles' Creed 248, 265, 384, 410

Arianism 360, 367

Articles of Religion of C. of E. 32, 34, 51

Athanasian Creed (so-called) xv, xvi, xvii, xxxvi, xxxvii, xlii, 148, 149, 158, 159, 160, 162, 165, 255, 256, 258, 259, 274, 275, 276, 285, 300, 308, 309, 396, 402, 410

Athanasius, St 12, 107, 108

Atonement xiii, xiv, xvi, xxiii, xxx, xxxi, xxxii, xxxix, xli, 3, 4, 8, 10, 13, 15, 16, 18, 20, 21, 31, 40, 53, 54, 61, 66, 80, 84, 85, 88, 94, 101, 108, 119, 120, 142, 145, 148, 154, 157, 179, 182, 183, 184, 185, 189, 194, 200, 206, 207, 208, 252, 253, 264, 265, 291, 293, 295, 300, 303, 312, 313, 322, 324, 326, 327, 328, 329, 330, 331, 333, 334, 335, 336, 337, 339, 340, 343, 344, 345, 346, 347, 349, 351, 352, 353, 354, 355, 359, 360, 361, 362, 363, 364, 365, 366, 367, 368, 369, 371, 376, 409, 416, 417, 418, 421, 422, 424

Auden, W.H. 147, 421

Augustine,St./Augustinianism 33, 55, 72, 143, 157, 185, 360, 362, 370

definition of Trinity as Love 143
Pelagian controversy 269

Aulen, Gustaf 330, 333, 334, 340, 343, 353, 421

B

Baptism 109, 111, 121, 123, 142, 157, 185, 381, 387, 388, 389, 390, 393, 394, 395, 397, 409, 417, 422

Basil, St. (Liturgy of) 60, 158, 159, 162

"Being saved". *See* "Salvation"

Bible/Scriptures xiii, xiv, xv, xvi, xvii, xviii, xxv, xxvi, xxviii, xxix, xxxi, xxxii, xxxiii, xxxiv, xxxix, 6, 7, 11, 12, 13, 16, 17, 27, 34, 35, 39, 54, 56, 57, 58, 59, 62, 63, 64, 65, 66, 70, 72, 76, 77, 79, 83, 88, 89, 90, 92, 94, 95, 96, 97, 98, 99, 100, 104, 106, 108, 110, 111, 116, 118, 119, 121, 122, 123, 130, 139, 142, 143, 151, 152, 157, 166, 167, 168, 177, 180, 183, 184, 188, 189, 190, 192, 193, 202, 206, 212, 214, 223, 224, 226, 237, 239, 245, 247, 261, 262, 263, 264, 270, 275, 280, 281, 284, 293, 301, 302, 305, 306, 307, 309, 311, 317, 329, 332, 336, 346, 348, 354, 359, 360, 370, 371, 374, 375, 376, 397, 406, 413, 424, 425, 426

Bicknell, E.J. 32, 34, 421
Body of Christ. *See* Church
Book of Alternative Services xxviii, 6,
7, 11, 12, 155, 156, 159, 160,
164, 165, 212, 245, 246, 274,
321, 323, 344, 365, 370, 390,
391
Book of Common Prayer xvi, 5, 6, 8,
33, 40, 108, 141, 148, 149, 153,
158, 159, 165, 189, 228, 229,
234, 245, 248, 250, 274, 297,
322, 323, 331, 348, 369, 370,
371, 375, 382, 383, 384, 388,
391, 396, 402, 404
Borg, Marcus xvii, xx, xxiv, xxviii, xxix,
xxxviii, 10, 313, 421
Bread of heaven / Bread of Life 149,
150, 151

C

Cappadocian Fathers 367
Charismatic renewal 8, 135, 136
Christ. *See also* "divinity of..."
Christian Doctrine of Man 271, 346,
409
Christian Education 13, 227
Christianity xiii, xvii, xx, xxi, xxviii, xxix,
xxxv, xxxvi, xxxvii, xxxviii, 9, 10,
14, 16, 25, 26, 40, 42, 53, 61, 65,
72, 133, 134, 135, 146, 160, 182,
184, 194, 218, 225, 235, 252,
260, 262, 276, 277, 278, 280,
282, 283, 286, 287, 290, 292,
296, 313, 314, 326, 329, 334,
340, 343, 392, 393, 407, 424
Church xv, xvi, xviii, xxvi, xxx, xxxi,
xxxii, xxxiv, xxxvi, xxxvii, xxxviii,
xxxix, xl, 1, 2, 3, 4, 5, 6, 7, 8, 9,
10, 12, 13, 14, 15, 16, 18, 19, 22,
23, 24, 25, 32, 34, 38, 51, 52, 53,
54, 61, 62, 66, 67, 70, 71, 72, 75,
79, 97, 102, 106, 107, 120, 126,
128, 133, 134, 135, 136, 137,
138, 139, 140, 153, 155, 156,
157, 158, 159, 160, 161, 163,
164, 167, 172, 178, 183, 185,
189, 195, 196, 199, 200, 201,
202, 204, 206, 212, 216, 217,
220, 221, 224, 225, 227, 229,
230, 231, 237, 246, 248, 253,
254, 255, 257, 261, 263, 264,
269, 270, 272, 274, 275, 276,
279, 283, 284, 285, 286, 287,
291, 292, 294, 299, 302, 304,
306, 307, 308, 309, 310, 311,
313, 314, 315, 322, 323, 326,
327, 329, 330, 331, 333, 334,
335, 336, 345, 346, 348, 353,
354, 355, 356, 357, 359, 360,
361, 363, 364, 365, 367, 368,
369, 370, 371, 387, 388, 389,
390, 391, 393, 395, 396, 407,
408, 409, 410, 411, 412, 413,
414, 415, 416, 417, 418, 419,
421, 422, 423, 424, 425
  as the "Body of Christ" 387
  historical mistakes 253
  visible/invisible 72, 308
Clark, Neville 125, 128, 157, 162,
393, 395, 396, 421
Cotter, Anthony C. 63, 99, 421
Covenants 96
Crucifixion xxiii, 4, 20, 23, 51, 62, 63,
71, 72, 73, 81, 84, 95, 105, 107,
110, 111, 112, 114, 123, 124,
125, 151, 169, 171, 177, 206,
239, 269, 315, 337, 338, 342,
350, 352, 365, 413
Cults 220, 221, 225

D

Damasus, Faith of 410
Death xiii, xvi, xvii, xxiii, xxx, xxxi, xxxii,
xxxiv, xxxvii, xxxviii, xlii, 6, 15,
16, 17, 18, 19, 20, 23, 24, 32, 42,
47, 48, 49, 50, 67, 68, 78, 84, 88,
90, 103, 106, 110, 112, 115, 116,
117, 120, 121, 122, 124, 125,

G

36, 37, 40, 53, 55, 56, 57, 60, 62, 64, 66, 91, 92, 94, 102, 103, 104, 107, 108, 120, 127, 130, 141, 143, 144, 148, 149, 152, 154, 155, 156, 157, 158, 159, 160, 161, 162, 163, 164, 165, 166, 185, 186, 189, 193, 195, 196, 211, 215, 240, 244, 245, 250, 253, 259, 274, 276, 277, 279, 280, 283, 284, 285, 290, 292, 293, 296, 318, 336, 337, 338, 350, 351, 352, 356, 357, 358, 364, 371, 372, 377, 382, 384, 396, 401, 402, 412, 413, 419, 423

U

Union with God through Christ 10, 38, 53, 66, 184, 285, 327, 331, 332, 342, 344, 360, 365, 366, 371
Universalism xxxv, xli, 194, 290, 292, 311, 409, 417, 419

W

Wand, J.W.C. 161, 185, 424
Ward, Keith xx, xxi
Water of life: "water" often used to symbolize divinity (especially the Holy Spirit), and life 91, 120, 122, 123, 125, 126, 128, 131, 142, 157, 179, 193, 400, 401, 402
Westerhoff, John H., III 219, 424
Wiles, Maurice 336, 340, 341, 350
Willimon, John 388, 389, 390, 391, 393, 394, 424